LEHIGH UNIVERSITY

Asa Packer. Portrait by D. W. C. Boutelle, Esq.

LEHIGH UNIVERSITY

A History of Education in Engineering, Business, and the Human Condition

W. Ross Yates

Bethlehem: Lehigh University Press
London and Toronto: Associated University Presses

Associated University Presses
440 Forsgate Drive
Cranbury, NJ 08512

Associated University Presses
25 Sicilian Avenue
London WC1A 2QH, England

Associated University Presses
P.O. Box 39, Clarkson Pstl. Stn.
Mississauga, Ontario,
L5J 3X9 Canada

The paper used in this publication meets the requirements
of the American National Standard for Permanence of Paper
for Printed Library Materials Z39.48-1984.

Library of Congress Cataloging-in-Publication Data

Yates, W. Ross (Willard Ross)
    Lehigh University: a history of education in engineering, business, and the human condition/W. Ross Yates.
        p.   cm.
    Includes bibliographical references (p.   ) and index.
    ISBN 0-934223-17-3 (alk. paper)
    1. Lehigh University—History.   I. Title.
LD2973.Y38   1992   91-60581
378.748′27—dc20   CIP

Contents

Introduction

Lehigh University's history is closely related to the rise and progress of America as an industrial power. Many themes are interwoven with this, and most have subjects far different from trends in manufactures and services. They are variously concerned with life in all its complexity and have joined with applied science and engineering in making the university distinctive. But it has been the need of America for engineers and other technical people that has been the dynamo for furnishing the energy. This is part of what President Peter Likins meant when he said, shortly after taking office in 1982, that Lehigh was "right for the times." The enriching addition to the statement is a reminder that Lehigh has always been right for the times. The scientific and technological revolution in America has overriden all obstacles and taken Lehigh along with it.

Lehigh was organized at a time when Europeans still looked upon America as backward, a land whose inhabitants crudely improvised on models developed by the European heirs to an ancient Graeco-Roman civilization. Just before Lehigh's founding the Civil War removed rebellious elites from power and opened the way for a national promotion of agriculture and industry through the useful arts and sciences. Lehigh was one of many centers appearing in the postwar years for educating young men in the mechanic arts. It progressed along with the others in the measure that the scientific and technological revolution changed the appearance of the landscape and the manners and morals of the people including their perceptions of themselves. As it moved forward, the country became settled; civilization pushed the frontiers into Alaska; and equality ran a hard race with liberty for the benefits.

The First World War marked the beginning of a new era. The United States emerged from that conflict as a great power. No longer were most of the progressive models of science and technology to be found in Europe; they existed in American industries and universities. The worldwide economic depression of the 1930s temporarily slowed but did not halt scientific and technological progress. The Second World War, which put an end to some business badly botched at the end of the first, spurred it on; and the subsequent cold war, with its fighting phases in Korea and Vietnam, while tarnishing the images of science and technology, quickened the pace still more.

A century and a quarter of growth in science and technology enlarged, shaped, and disciplined higher education. Institutions making applied science

7

and engineering a major subject flourished in spite of the high costs. Those not choosing the way of the useful arts and sciences fared less well.

The scientific and technological revolution in America experienced a turning point about the end of the First World War. Americans then broke sharply with the past in the domains of manners, morals, dress, the arts, recreation, education, and attitudes toward labor, women, children, and much else. In most of these domains the break was cleaner than it was in the progress of science and technology. Innovations in corporate management and inventions improving transportation and communication had occurred earlier. The next great period of invention came during the Second World War.

Some analysts have chosen the second rather than the first war as a turning point. Professor Daniel Bell of Harvard is one of these. In *The Coming of Post-Industrial Society*, Bell described the alliance of government, industry, and the universities, which produced the atomic bomb, radar, jet engines, and computers, as beginning a postindustrial age whose axial principle is "the centrality of theoretical knowledge at the source of innovation and of policy formulation" and whose elite consists of a "professional and technical class."[1] There is no reason to quarrel with Bell's analyses. What he called postindustrial society can as well be regarded as a higher stage of industrialism. As for his partiality for the Second World War as a turning point, one need only note that the managerial revolution began much earlier and that the period between the two wars was in any case transitional. Many practices begun about 1917 had delayed effects, among them the promotion by the national government of research in science and a dependence of almost everyone on private and public bureaucracies. It is as reasonable to locate the turning point at the beginning of this transitional period as at the end. Bell's analyses are nevertheless valuable. He identified many developments bearing directly upon the history of Lehigh, not the least being the emergence of a professional and technical elite educated along lines being pursued at Lehigh.

But no one has to juggle concepts about postindustrial society in order to see the break in Lehigh's history in the years from 1918 to 1920. The break is clear from the facts of that history. If a precise date is wanted, let it be 1919, the first postwar year. Before 1919 lies the "old" Lehigh; in 1919 begins the "new" Lehigh, extending at least to 1980, the year selected for ending this historical survey.

The institutional transition from "old" to "new" at Lehigh is best viewed as conservative, preserving continuity in important things. Lehigh has always been a small private university of high standards having a principal emphasis on applied science and engineering. Most of its students have come from middle-class families in the middle Atlantic states. Its faculty has enjoyed a large amount of decentralized control over courses and programs and been pragmatic in the approach to policy. The key features of the old and the new Lehigh have helped preserve these constants.

The old Lehigh cherished an individualistic disposition, which after the First World War became tempered with an organizational ethos. The old Lehigh was essentially a community of faculty and students with a board of trustees closely watching from nearby. In the new Lehigh almost everything that had previously been allowed a freedom to develop on its own became institutionalized. The old Lehigh had no bureaucracy and little administration; the new Lehigh had much of both. In the old university, life for the professors and the students was little regulated, whereas in the new, regulations increased, and students, faculty, and administrators entertained more or less constant discussions concerning what the regulations should be and who should make and enforce them. Departments dealing with testing, counseling, admission, placement, public relations, publications, personnel, community relations, and fund raising characterized only the new Lehigh. In the old Lehigh research was solely a responsibility of the individual professor; in the new, it became an institutional responsibility as well.

There are also differences in jurisdiction between the old and the new Lehigh. A responsibility for the religious formation of students, characteristic of the original university, disappeared in the early years of the new Lehigh. In the old Lehigh, extracurricular activities, including publications and sports, lay outside of the formal structure; the faculty as a body largely ignored them, although as individuals they often participated. In the new Lehigh these things came under strict administrative control. The alumni, loosely organized under the old Lehigh, paid more attention to improving courses of study than to contributing money, whereas in the new Lehigh they were more effectively organized and put financial support ahead of suggestions for educational improvement.

The principal areas of competition also differed. Before the First World War Lehigh (and other schools emphasizing engineering education) competed on two fronts, one being against the supporters of the classical orthodoxy and the other, against a preference of many employers for empirically trained engineers, meaning those having learned all of their skills on the job. By the end of the First World War, these battles had been won. There remained a competition pitting Lehigh against other private colleges and universities offering similar types of courses. In the depression years of the 1930s, a competition between private and public institutions began to be of importance.

Finally, extending over and conditioning all developments, was the changing attitude in the United States toward higher education. During the nineteenth century most people had little regard for a college education as an aid to success in anything but a few professions; and even in medicine, the ministry, and the law one might become distinguished without having a college degree. The attitude changed, and by the end of the First World War, people were more and more looking on a college diploma as a passport to material success. Youths with little interest in education flocked onto the campuses. The "superkindergartener" appeared, to use a term employed by Lehigh's Dean Charles Maxwell McConn. The superkindergarteners were not much attracted to a study of engineering and other applied science. Still, faculty and administration at Lehigh were under pressure to screen them out and to control those who did get in.

Many people have assisted me in producing this history of education at Lehigh. Foremost has been James D. Mack, who before his retirement was director of libraries at Lehigh and archivist for the Alumni Association. Mr. Mack encouraged me to begin the project and aided it in almost every phase. He read the early drafts, made hundreds of suggestions for improvements, checked information, arranged for other people to read selected parts, compiled and sent to me their critiques, safeguarded a duplicate copy, and helped with the index.

Others who read and criticized parts of the manuscript were Preston Parr, dean emeritus and vice president emeritus for student affairs; his wife, Ruth B. Parr, adjunct assistant professor of education and daughter of Dr. Claude Beardslee, former chaplain of the university; Steven L. Goldman, Andrew W. Mellon Distinguished Professor in the Humanities; Stephen H. Cutcliffe, director of the university's Science, Technology, and Society program and former director of the Lehigh University Press; and Paul J. Franz, Jr., professor and vice-president emeritus of development.

Information from personal interviews came from these and from Albert C. Zettlemoyer, former distinguished professor emeritus of chemistry and provost and vice president emeritus; Glenn J. Christensen, former university distinguished professor and provost and vice president; John J. Karakash, distinguished professor emeritus of electrical and computer engineering and dean emeritus of the College of Engineering and Physical Sciences; Robert D. Stout, dean emeritus and professor emeritus of metallurgy and materials engineering; A. Everett Pitcher, university distinguished professor emeritus of mathematics; Lynn S. Beedle, university distinguished professor emeritus of civil engineering; Raymond J. Emrich, professor of physics; and Carl F. Strauch, former distinguished professor of English Several others who might be considered as having been interviewed by mail include Paul Van R. Miller, former dean emeritus and professor emeritus of education, and Albert E. Hartung, distinguished professor of English. Other contributors included Howard R. Whitcomb, professor of government; Hubert L. Flesher, former university chaplain and professor of religion studies; J. Donald Ryan, professor emeritus of geological sciences; Charles B. Sclar, professor of geological sciences; and Hayden N. Pritchard, professor emeritus of biology.

Berry G. Richards, director of libraries, and Philip A. Metzger, director of the Lehigh University Press and curator of the library's collections, opened the resources of the libraries to me and accorded special privileges in using their services. They and other members of the library staffs provided valuable assistance in locating and recording information.

Several persons generously supplied records and the space to examine them. These were John W. Woltjen, vice president for administration and treasurer, and his staff; Claire C. Biser, former registrar, and her assistants; Samuel H. Missimer, former director of admission; and George L. Beezer, former editor in the Office of Publications.

Librarians in the Bethlehem Public Library and the Moravian Archives, Bethlehem, gave helpful service. To Robert Packer Fritz I am indebted for the loan of the diaries of Robert Heysham Sayre, Jr., now located in the Canal Museum, Easton, Pennsylvania.

Stephen H. Cutcliffe, former director of the Lehigh University Press, and Marie C. Boltz of special collections, Linderman Library, were my eyes, ears, and arms for collecting and identifying illustrations. They received much help from Steven J. Lichak, Jr., and Elia Schoomer of Media Productions, Linderman Library; Marvin Simmons of the Office of Publications; Rita Malone and other members of the Office of Media Relations; Glenn Hoffmann from Sports Information; and Michael J. Caruso ('67).

There are many others, for this history marks the end of a work of long duration. These include students, faculty, staff, administrators, alumni, and trustees. They have taught me about Lehigh not knowing what their teaching might lead to. Yes, I mean you, Frank Rabold, and you, Miss Henry, Dave Friedfeld, Pattie Latz, Kevin Cahill, and Ed Kehoe. And many more. Thank you for the education. I hope you like the result. For what it is, it was fun to do.

LEHIGH UNIVERSITY

Part One
The Old Lehigh

1

Founding

Two forces in American industrial life converged to form Lehigh University. One was the wave of scientific and engineering education spreading westward during the nineteenth century. The other was the energy of Asa Packer.

Of the two, the energy of Packer was the more important. The country would have had scientific and engineering education without Packer, but it would not have had Lehigh University.

Packer was born in the seaport town of Mystic, Connecticut, on 29 December 1805. Poor, physically strong, and adventurous, at the age of seventeen he left Mystic and traveled two hundred miles west on foot to a place called Hop Bottom on the upper reaches of the Susquehanna River. There he became a carpenter and soon moved to nearby Springville, where he married a girl from Vermont named Sarah Blakslee and joined Sarah's church, the Protestant Episcopal.

For five years Packer farmed during the summer and in the winter built canal boats for use in hauling anthracite coal to markets in eastern cities. The coal lay in mountains to the south and had recently been tapped to supplement dwindling supplies of wood and charcoal. Tales of fortunes being made in the coal trade were numerous. In 1833 Packer and a younger brother-in-law, James I. Blakslee, crossed the mountains to Mauch Chunk (now Jim Thorpe), a frontier town on the northern edge of the coal country.

They found Mauch Chunk small and dirty and inhabited by merchant adventurers and transient workers, many of whom were fresh from Europe and spoke little if any English. The Lehigh Coal and Navigation Company had several years earlier completed a canal to the town, thereby making coal from the upper reaches of the Lehigh River available for markets in Philadelphia. The company had also built a gravity railroad to haul the coal down from Summit Hill, about eight miles away. The gravity railroad was considered one of the engineering marvels of the times. Mules hauled the empty cars back to the mines and rode down to the canal in the end cars.

Packer and Blakslee found employment as operators of canal boats. Within a few months Packer's wife, Sarah, joined them in Mauch Chunk. Sarah was nursing Lucy, her eldest daughter. Some other relatives followed Asa Packer and James Blakslee to Mauch Chunk.

Operating canal boats in those days could be profitable. Packer saved enough from this work to buy a boat and within a few years owned several. He thereby obtained a small capital with which to expand the boating business and begin other enterprises.

Diversification was common among entrepreneurs in the coal regions. Most undertakings in mining, merchandising, real estate, lumbering, transportation, and the like were interdependent, so that a person engaging in any one of them might increase his income from it by controlling some part of the others.

Packer saw this, and with the assistance of relatives and friends with whom he entered into partnerships, he took advantage of these opportunities. He proved to be a good judge of human nature, and his enterprises prospered. In 1835 he supplemented the operating of canal boats with the business of building them and, at the same time, bought a store of which Blakslee became manager. The Lehigh Coal and Navigation Company was extending the canal northward to White Haven, which necessitated building high-lift locks. Packer obtained contracts for some of the construction. In 1837 he began expanding his merchandising business to include stores in other towns. He also operated a transportation line in partnership with his brother Robert. Soon Asa and Robert were managing two lines down the Lehigh and another south along the Schuylkill. In 1839 Asa and Robert entered the coal business by leasing the Room Run Mines near Nesquehoning from the Lehigh Coal and Navigation Company.

Within Mauch Chunk, Asa Packer was active in church, civic, and political affairs. He helped to found St. Mark's (Episcopal) Church, became a vestryman and warden, and supplied much of the money for its support. He was one of several citizens to whom the cemetery in Upper Mauch Chunk was deeded; he obtained the charter for the Mauch Chunk Water Company; and became active in the Masonic Order. Voters sent Asa to the legislature in Harrisburg in 1841 and again the following year. There he assisted in establishing Carbon County, in which Mauch Chunk is located. In 1843 he began a term as associate judge of Carbon County and was known for the rest of his life as "the Honorable Asa Packer" and "Judge Packer."

He and Sarah lived simply. Sarah refused many of the conveniences that could accompany prosperity and continued to do most of her housework. In Mauch Chunk she bore three children: Mary Hannah (1839), Robert Asa (1842), and Harry Eldred (1850). In addition to these and Lucy, she and Asa adopted a girl, Marian.

Packer probably began in the early 1840s to think seriously about building a railroad for sending coal from the Lehigh region to Philadelphia and New York. He did not have sufficient capital to begin the project himself. An anonymous account of his life, "An Outline of the Career of the Hon. Asa Packer of Pennsylvania" (Bethlehem, 1867), maintains that for years he urged the Lehigh Coal and Navigation Company to build a railroad as an auxiliary to the canal. The statement implies that at a relatively early date he had computed costs and arrived at a conclusion that overland transportation by rail would be more reasonable than the tried and proven method of transportation by water.

Certainly the technological innovations of the 1830s and 1840s in the anthracite coal regions were such as to inspire farsighted men to think in terms of railroads. Within a few years of completing the gravity railroad, the engineers of the Lehigh Coal and Navigation Company had put the mules out of business by devising a "back track" whereby empty cars could be returned to the mines by means of inclined planes and stationary engines. Small gravity railroads were operating in the mines. The first steam railroad in the anthracite regions, owned by the Beaver Meadow Railroad and Coal Company, began running in 1836–37. Within the next few years several small feeder steam railroads were opened. In the Schuylkill region, the Philadelphia and Reading was built and in 1844 carried almost 442,000 tons of coal to Philadelphia.

The directors of the Lehigh Coal and Navigation Company were reluctant to build a competing line. They considered with some reason the model of the Philadelphia and Reading as inapplicable to the situation in the Lehigh Valley. Failing to interest the Lehigh Coal and Navigation Company in a railroad, Packer joined another group of businessmen and with them in 1846 petitioned the legislature for a charter for a road along the bank of the Lehigh opposite the canal. This company was called the Delaware, Lehigh, Schuylkill, and Susquehanna. Neither Packer nor the others urged the project forward. Five years passed with nothing being done to build the road.

By 1851 Packer was accounted a wealthy man. With the charter of the Delaware, Lehigh, Schuylkill, and Susquehanna Company about to expire, he decided to construct the line himself. He became a member of the board of managers in April and several months later purchased a controlling share of the stock and launched an effort to gain a further interest in the company. He persuaded the directors to award the contract for construction to himself, stipulating that payment be made in additional stock and bonds of the company. The initial grading necessary to save the charter was done. Construction was started in earnest in 1852. The line was renamed the Lehigh Valley Railroad. In the summer of 1855 the first trains began regular service between Mauch Chunk and Easton at the place where the Lehigh joins the Delaware River.

The years of building the main line of the Lehigh Valley road marked the growth of a new image of Asa Packer. A small-town businessman was becoming a railroad monarch with a national reputation. He made friends among the operators of railroads capable of benefiting from the new line. His business took him to Philadelphia, New York, and Washington. People at the Merchant's Hotel, a gathering place of businessmen in Philadelphia, saw more of him than did the bankers of Mauch Chunk.

This period of railroad building roughly coincided with his service as a congressman. He was elected on the democratic ticket and served two terms in the House, 1853−57. Why he wished to be a congressman and what he gained from the experience are puzzles yet to be solved. He could expect little for his railroad from the national government. In those pre−Civil War years a laissez-faire Jacksonian democratic philosophy dominated politics. According to it, internal improvements such as canals and railroads might be a concern of the states, but not of the national government. Possibly Packer's motivation was strictly personal. From the time of his coming to Mauch Chunk he had lived with excitement, and politics was exciting. He had been a member of the state legislature and a county judge; the next step up the political ladder was a seat in the Congress. The duties of a congressman were not full time. One account of his life avers that be served his constituents well. Perhaps so; nothing is cited by way of supporting evidence.

He gathered around him a group of capable assistants whose stature grew with his. A few of these, such as James I. Blakslee, had been with him in earlier ventures. Among others were Robert Heysham Sayre, Jr., and Elisha P. Wilbur.

Sayre had been born in 1824, attended public school at Mauch Chunk, and then studied surveying. His early employment included service for the Lehigh Coal and Navigation Company, whereby he gained experience in railroad building by helping to construct the back track portion of the gravity railroad and another small feeder line. He was not yet twenty-nine years of age when Packer made him chief engineer of the Lehigh Valley road. For fifty-six years thereafter, Sayre kept a diary, which is a valuable source of information concerning Packer, the Lehigh Valley Railroad, Lehigh University, and much besides.

Wilbur became a businessman with considerable experience in working with engineers. He was nine years younger than Sayre and had also been educated in the public schools of Mauch Chunk. He first worked in one of Packer's stores, then served as a rodman in a group surveying for the Lehigh Valley road, and finally moved into the counting house. From about 1856 on, he served as Packer's private secretary and was soon in charge of financial operations for most of Packer's enterprises.

The success of the Lehigh Valley Railroad made little change in Packer's manner of living. Although he built a mansion in Mauch Chunk, he did not load it with architectural frills. He bought another residence in Philadelphia and stayed there about three days of the week conducting business. His friend A. K. McClure wrote of him in *Old Time Notes of Pennsylvania*, "He was a man of excellent presence, with a finely chiseled face that was almost a stranger to visible emotion, and he was severely quiet and unassuming in conversation. ... He had no taste for society; indeed all formal duties were extremely irksome to him. His greatest pleasure was to have three friends join him in the evening at his Philadelphia residence, play euchre until about half past ten, and then join him in a drink of good old rye and adjourn."[1]

The Lehigh Valley Railroad became the central interest of Packer's life. He arranged for the railroad to buy vast acreages of coal lands in order to have a sure source of cargo and had the operations organized as the Lehigh Valley Coal Company. The sites of junctions became important, especially those near the lower Lehigh Valley towns of Easton, Bethlehem, and Allentown.

Across the Lehigh River from Easton, the company founded the town of South Easton. From here a bridge over the Delaware afforded a junction with the Jersey Central and the Belvidere-Delaware railroads, which carried the coal respectfully to tidewater opposite New York City and Trenton, New Jersey.

Ten miles upstream from Easton on the northern bank of the Lehigh lay Bethlehem. Moravians had founded Bethlehem as a missionary outpost in 1741 and for a hundred years had controlled the land and kept the town a closed church-village. In 1841 the Moravians had bowed to pressures coming largely from operations on the Lehigh Canal, which flowed between Bethlehem and the river, and the opening nearby of numerous iron mines and blast furnaces. The Moravians had sold most of their holdings, including large farms on the southern bank of the river. Zinc, discovered in large deposits a few miles further south, led in 1853 to the building of refining furnaces on the southern bank; by the end of the decade the operation was known as the Lehigh Zinc Company. An industrial community began growing up around the zinc works, called by various names, of which the designation South Bethlehem endured.

Near South Bethlehem in 1857, the Lehigh Valley Railroad effected a junction with the North Pennsylvania Railroad whereby coal could be transported to Philadelphia.

Also in 1857 Augustus Wolle, a Moravian businessman, with support from Charles Brodhead, another local entrepreneur and member of a politically influential family, organized the Bethlehem Iron Company and Rolling Mills for the purpose of smelting nearby ores and refining the product. Packer became interested in the iron company as a source of rails. Within a few years he and his lieutenants bought stock in the company, whose charter in 1860 was revised and the name shortened to that of Bethlehem Iron Company. The iron company had a seven-man board of directors of whom a majority represented the interests of the Lehigh Valley Railroad.

Allentown, located near a bend where the Lehigh River changes from a southern to an eastern flow, about five miles upstream from Bethlehem, became in 1859 the site of a somewhat less important junction than those at South Easton and South Bethlehem. Near Allentown the Lehigh Valley road connected with the East Pennsylvania leading to Harrisburg.

Money and expert management came from Packer and the Lehigh Valley Railroad to support the local economies of Allentown, Bethlehem, and Easton. At South Bethlehem the people who had made a success of the railroad worked to do the same for the Bethlehem Iron Company. Sayre, general superintendent of the railroad, looked about for the best available ironmaster and found the person he wanted in John Fritz, the superintendent of the Cambria Iron Works in Johnstown, Pennsylvania. Fritz, like Sayre, was an empirical engineer. At the age of twenty-two, Fritz had gained employment in Norristown at the iron works of Moore and Hooven. There, and in subsequent employments, he had learned the business of iron making and developed a reputation of being an inventive genius. Sayre brought Fritz to Bethlehem and put him to work building a furnace and a mill. A flood on the Lehigh and a shortage of materials occasioned by the Civil War delayed construction. The first furnace went into blast on 4 January, 1863, and the rolling mill began operating later that summer.

The war brought additional profits to Packer and his railroad. He was reputedly one of the richest men in Pennsylvania. He was also, like many another industrial pioneer, a philanthropist. He had subsidized volunteers serving from Carbon County in the Mexican War; he had given generously to St. Mark's Church in Mauch Chunk; and he had amply responded to the call of the Episcopal Bishop of Pennsylvania, Alonzo Potter, for funds to support a divinity school in Philadelphia. During the Civil War, Packer encouraged enlistments to the Union cause by continuing the salaries of volunteers among his workers. The problem of how best to spend his surplus money weighed on his conscience.

Education was, perhaps, an obvious choice for philanthropy. In the past, entrepreneurs had supported colleges and universities; more were doing so now, or thinking of doing so.

In the autumn of 1864, Packer requested an interview with the Right Reverend William Bacon Stevens, assistant to Bishop Potter. As Stevens in 1869 recalled the event:

> He came to my house in Philadelphia, and said that he had long contemplated doing something for the benefit of his State, and especially of the Lehigh Valley. From that valley he said he had derived much of the wealth which GOD had given to him, and to the best interests of that valley he wished to devote a portion of it in the founding of some educational institution, for the intellectual and moral improvement of the young men of that region. After conversing with him a little while, and drawing out his large and liberal views, I asked him how much money he purposed to set aside for this institution, when he quietly answered that he designed to give $500,000.[2]

At this point, the money and aspirations of Asa Packer and his assistants in the Lehigh Valley Railroad began to be enmeshed with some changes taking place in American higher education.

Ever since the founding of Harvard in 1636, church-related colleges teaching the classics had dominated higher education in America. The colleges had received most of their students from the upper social and economic classes. The ministry was the only occupation for which they offered anything resembling occupational training. Graduates not electing the ministry might go into business, law, medicine, or public service of various sorts, but they had to learn the skills for their occupation at other institutions, from tutors, or by apprenticeship. In short, the colleges offered what they called a liberal education for gentlemen. The classical curriculum was utilitarian only in an elevated sense, as expressed by the Yale Report of 1828 in the phrases "the discipline and furniture of the mind; expanding its powers and storing it with knowledge." The knowledge with which the mind was to be stored was not of the useful or "common sense" variety, but helped a student to appreciate a valued part of his cultural antecedents.

Some minorities had from their earliest appearance in America opposed this emphasis on the classics. Quakers and their supporters in Rhode Island and Pennsylvania are the most widely known of these. The founding of the University of Pennyslvania in Philadelphia in the mid-1700s marked a dissent favoring an education in the useful arts and sciences. Three-quarters of a century later, Thomas Jefferson registered another dissent in founding the University of Virginia. These forerunners of occupational education had little immediate success in shaking the dominance of the classics. More telling inroads came with an intellectual interest in science and the spread of industry and democratic ways. College faculties, conservative then as now, reluctantly admitted some part of the new knowledge of science and mathematics into the company of classical studies. They preferred the theoretical aspects. Education in science received a boost from European universities, especially those in Germany. The modernization of German universities in the early nineteenth century was an aspect of governmental policies for making Germany industrially important. Berlin, Giessen, Heidelberg, Paris, and other of the great European centers of learning became havens for Americans wishing advanced training not only in the traditional arts and sciences but also in chemistry and physics. By midcentury the more innovative among American educators began to regard the German university with its professional schools of law, medicine, and theology as a desirable supplement to four-year liberal arts colleges.

Inventions and the growth of mining and manufacturing furthered an interest in science, but with greater emphasis on the applied than on the theoretical aspects. The spread of democratic ways provided a social foundation for increases in the availability of education in applied science. Early in the nineteenth century, teachers stressing applications began appearing in some of the republic's most respected colleges, for example, Jacob Bigelow at Harvard, Thomas Cooper at the University of Pennsylvania, Benjamin Silliman at Yale, and Joseph Henry at Princeton. In the 1830s Alexis de Tocqueville noted in *Democracy in America* the preference of Americans for practical over theoretical science.

The few teachers of applied science who succeeded in penetrating the halls of liberal arts colleges encountered much resistance. For the time being, most education in the practical applications of chemistry, geology, mineralogy, and biology took place outside of these colleges. In Philadelphia, for example, the University of Pennsylvania had partially relapsed into traditional ways and did little to promote science. Yet Philadelphia had become the center of the nation's chemical and chemically related industries. The resident who wished training in applied chemistry had to obtain it through self-study supplemented by readings, lectures, or laboratory work sponsored by the American Philosophical Society, the Franklin Institute, several medical and pharmaceutical establishments, or private chemical laboratories.

In one way or another, the number of persons well versed in theoretical and applied science increased. German universities helped to educate most of the best-known teachers of science in America. In 1847 the scientists organized a professional society, the American Association for the Advancement of Science (AAAS). Shortly thereafter the AAAS had branches in all of the leading fields of science. In 1847 Harvard, with money given by Abbott Lawrence, began the scientific school bearing his name and soon afterward hired European-trained Louis Agassiz as professor of zoology and geology. Agassiz gave the school a direction along the lines of his interests. In 1847 Yale opened what became known as the Sheffield School with major emphasis on chemistry and mineralogy. By the time of the Civil War, four-year courses in science were fairly well defined. In the midst of the war (1863) some members of the AAAS assisted in bringing into existance a National Academy of Sciences, patterned after the Royal Society of London. At the end of the war, chemists and physicists began drifting from private laboratories to newly established chairs in colleges and universities.

Progress in engineering education had not kept pace with that in science.[3] Most persons calling themselves engineers had learned their business on the job and thought of themselves as artisans. Still, formal schooling existed for a few. Systematic instruction was about as old for engineering as it was for science. In Europe engineering had been taught from military necessity, using specialized schools. France had taken the lead in 1747, by establishing the École Nationale des Ponts et Chaussées (bridges and roads). Napoleon had launched what later became the renowned École Polytechnique. Other specialized engineering schools had appeared in France and Britain. Germany had turned formal training in engineering over to the *technische hochschulen*. With the progress of the industrial revolution, separate schools of mining had appeared in France, England, and Germany.

In America as in Europe, military necessity produced the first formal instruction in engineering. West Point, founded at the request of President Washington, gave the country the first systematic training in engineering. To West Point goes the credit for establishing engineering education in America on the basis of a thorough study of mathematics.

During the first half of the nineteenth century, a conviction that science had much to give engineering became more widespread and was sometimes supported by engineers seeking professional status. There were not many of these of a standing sufficient to command an audience. In 1813 Alden Partridge, the first civilian engineering professor in the United States, founded a school for teaching engineering that shortly became known as Norwich University. A more publicized institution was formed in 1824 by Stephen Van Rensselaer at Troy, New York. Rensselaer died several years later, and his sons were freer with advice than with money. The institution barely survived and underwent several reorganizations. That of 1835 resulted in changing the name to Rensselaer Institution and involved the hiring of Eliphalet Nott as president.

Nott had from 1804 been president of nearby Union College. He was in the front ranks among innovators in higher education. In the early 1820s he had established at Union a course in science and modern literature as an alternative to the course in classics. Union had attracted able students, some of whom became leaders elsewhere for promoting education in the useful sciences, notably Francis Wayland (Brown), Alonzo Potter (University of Pennsylvania), and Henry Philip Tappan (Michigan).

Nott kept the presidency at Union during his tenure as president of Rensselaer. In the year of his appointment, Rensselaer organized a Department in Engineering and Technology. Amos Eaton directed the course in engineering until his death in 1842. During the tenures of Eaton and Nott, Rensselaer became the first school of higher education in the country to give a degree in civil engineering. In 1845 Nott resigned from the presidency of Rensselaer and established a Course in Civil Engineering at Union. The school underwent a further reorganization and in 1861 took the name of Rensselaer Polytechnic Institute (RPI).

In most of the other purportedly engineering schools, either a weak offering in engineering was added to existing courses of study or the attempt to begin engineering education went awry. An exception was the Polytechnic College of the State of Pennsylvania, which existed from 1853 until the late 1880s and was the first institution in the country to offer degrees in mining engineering and mechanical engineering. But at Harvard, Yale, and several other places, engineering education was added to newly established scientific departments and was weak. At the University of Pennsylvania, under the prodding of reformers, a School of Mines, Arts, and Manufactures was organized in 1852 and limped along until it was closed near the beginning of the Civil War.

In sum, by contrast with education in science, at the end of the Civil War, education in engineering was primitive. In 1866 the nation possessed only about three hundred persons who had been graduated as engineers during the most recent thirty-one years.[4] A drive for professional standing was lagging. No truly national engineering society existed, although one — the American Society of Civil Engineers (ASCE), founded 1852 — had intentions of being national; and the AAAS had added an engineering section. Few teachers of engineering could be found, and most of these were graduates of West Point or were persons with much experience in science and weak credentials in engineering.

The whole subject of engineering education was obscure. No one knew with certainty how many years a course in engineering should take or even what branches of engineering should be included within a university. The relationship between theory and practice was hazy. Several experiments were under way. RPI had added a theoretical aspect to practical field work. Yale and Harvard had added a practical element to drill in the classroom and the laboratory. A statement made a few years later by the industrialist and Lehigh trustee Eckley B. Coxe sums up the situation: "The problem seems to be: *Not knowing exactly what you want to do or the material you have to do it with, what is the best way of doing it?*"[5]

The Right Reverend William Bacon Stevens, before whom Asa Packer presented the idea of founding a university, was knowledgeable in science and scientific education. A new Englander by birth and breeding, he had attended private schools and as a young man moved to Savannah, Georgia, to study medicine with Dr. Edward Coppée.[6] In due time Stevens received medical degrees from the Medical College of South Carolina and Dartmouth, married Dr. Coppée's daughter Alathea, and began practising medicine, first with Dr. Coppée and later by himself.

Stevens was still at Savannah when he cooperated with others in founding the Historical Society of Georgia. He edited the first two volumes of the society's *Collections* and in time wrote a two-volume history of the colony and state (1847, 1859).

Self-study prepared Stevens for the ministry. He was ordained a deacon in 1843, and the following year he became a priest and went to Athens, Georgia, where he organized a parish and built a church. Athens was the seat of the University of Georgia. Shortly after arriving in the town he became professor of belles lettres, oratory, and moral philosophy at the university. He remained at Athens until 1848, when he answered a call to come to the historic parish of St. Andrews in Philadelphia.

In Philadelphia, Stevens came to the notice of Alonzo Potter, bishop of the Episcopal Diocese of Pennsylvania. Potter may well have been Stevens's principal mentor in matters of educational philosophy. As a youth Potter had a brilliant career at Union College, first as a student, graduating with highest honors at the age of nineteen, and later as a teacher of mathematics and natural philosophy. He was ordained a priest in 1824 and in the same year married Sarah Maria, only daughter of President Nott, by whom he sired six sons and a daughter.

In 1845 Potter moved to Philadelphia to begin his duties as bishop of the diocese. Almost as soon as he arrived he became a trustee of the University of Pennsylvania and soon made a reputation for promoting educational reform. He idealized the German university and also wanted higher education to be put on a democratic basis for the benefit of all talented youth.

In 1861 Bishop Potter opened the Divinity School in Philadelphia. Stevens became professor of liturgics and homiletics at the school and, a few months later, in 1862, assistant bishop to Potter.

Possibly Asa Packer first considered approaching Bishop Potter with the idea of founding a university. However, in the summer of 1864 Potter's health was failing. Stevens was performing most of his duties.

Although knowledgeable in science, Stevens had little understanding of engineering and, apparently, few if any ideas concerning engineering education. But Stevens was zealous for the cause of a useful higher education with a dual emphasis on applied science and the formation of moral character. He was able to articulate ideas that in Packer's mind were cloudy. Stevens continued in his 1869 address (previously cited) with his account of Packer's visit:

> Filled with profound emotions at the mention of such a gift [that is, $500,000] for such an object, I asked the noble donor what specific plans he had framed in his own mind in reference to it. His reply was, "I am not much acquainted with these matters, but you are, and I want you if you will to devise a plan which I can put into effective operation." I told him that I would make the attempt. I did so.

What other subjects might Stevens and Packer have discussed? One could have been the availability of government money. The topic was current and had been controversial when Packer had been in Congress. Later, in 1862, Congress had passed the Morrill Act providing for land-grant colleges teaching agriculture and the mechanic arts. Educators in many places were petitioning state legislatures for a share of the land-grant money. Ezra Cornell, for example, sought and obtained funds accorded the State of New York to supplement his gifts; and the civic and industrial leaders who founded the Massachusetts Institute of Technology (MIT) received 30 percent of the land-grant appropriations for Massachusetts.

Packer and Stevens assuredly knew of the land-grant possibilities. Yet in no place in the surviving records of Lehigh University is the subject mentioned. The conclusion seems obvious that Packer was uninterested in agriculture and did not want government money for his university. If Stevens broached the subject, probably Packer only shook his head. The size of his gift, up to that time one of the largest ever made by an American to higher education, was a way of advertising that government aid was unnecessary.

After the initial meetings in the fall of 1864, neither Packer nor Stevens took further action toward founding a university until after the end of the war the following spring.

The name of Robert Sayre is the next to appear on the record as being informed of the design by Packer. Sayre noted in his diary for 12 May 1865, "Went up as far as Slatington with Judge Packer and returned home to dinner. Judge spoke to me of his design to build a college at Bethlehem South proposing to appropriate $500,000 for that purpose."

Rumors began circulating concerning Packer's aims. One was that in the spring of 1865 the president of Lafayette College at Easton and Ario Pardee, a coal operator and sometime associate of Packer, had visited Packer asking for money for Lafayette, and that Packer had seriously considered giving it until he learned that Lafayette was Presbyterian.[7] The rumor seemed plausible only as long as people remained ignorant of Packer's declared intention nine months earlier of building his own university.

Other rumors, also made plausible because of Packer's disinclination to talk, concerned the location of the new institution. Some said it would be at Mauch Chunk. Others suggested a beautiful wooded slope in Fountain Hill about a mile west of South Bethlehem.

Notices of the proposed new school appeared in mid-July as brief items in the Bethlehem church newspaper, *The Moravian*, and the Philadelphia papers. These were followed by an unsigned article in the *Church Journal*, an official organ of the Episcopal Church, for 19 July 1865.[8] The author wrote that the new institution was "to be a sort of Polytechnic Institute" and remarked in part, "Though mathematics and the natural and applied sciences will be the chief subjects of attention, yet the pupils will pay so much of regard to the classics as may enable them to take hold of almost any profession which they may prefer." The author of the article in the *Church Journal* called the institution "Packer College" and speculated on the fitness of the location in South Bethlehem.

The site that Packer selected for his university was not then within the legal limits of South Bethlehem (although popular usage easily overlooked legal distinctions). In the summer of 1865 South Bethlehem was being separated from Saucon Township and incorporated as a borough. A dirt road called Packer Avenue was located about a quarter of a mile back from the river and became the border dividing the two municipalities. Rising about seven hundred feet on the Saucon Township side of Packer Avenue was a ridge named South Mountain with slopes of from $6\frac{1}{2}°$ to $7°$. Packer had large holdings here, which extended halfway up South Mountain and about a mile eastward. His lands were heavily forested. He had logged off the chestnut trees for use as railroad ties. Packer put aside fifty-seven acres at the extreme western end of this land for his university. The site would allow faculty and students to look across the roofs of South Bethlehem to the old Moravian Borough of Bethlehem on the other side of the river. Plans were underway to build a bridge across the river at New Street, thereby allowing travelers an easy access from Bethlehem through South Bethlehem to the campus.

The location had the advantage of being within walking distance for managers of the Lehigh Valley Railroad. Upstream about half a mile were the home offices of the railroad; and near these was the mansion of Robert Sayre. Convenient, too, was a newly completed Episcopal church, the Church of the Nativity, situated across the road from Sayre's dwelling.

Having determined on the site, Packer selected his trustees. These were himself, his elder son Robert, Stevens, Sayre, and the Honorable John W. Maynard, president judge of the judicial district of Northampton and Lehigh counties.

With the governing body established, Packer left on a trip to Europe. He was absent from the first three sessions of the Board of Trustees.

The trustees held their organizational session 27 July 1865 at the Sun Hotel, a favorite meeting place in Bethlehem for businessmen. The board elected Elisha P. Wilbur as treasurer and the Rev. Eliphalet Nott Potter as secretary. Neither was a trustee. Wilbur had charge of financial matters for the Lehigh Valley Railroad. The Rev. Potter was the youngest son of Bishop Alonzo Potter and a grandson of President Nott of Union and had recently come to town to be rector of the Church of the Nativity. The board recorded "that the institution shall consist of a college proper as usually organized, together with a scientific school embracing the whole class of physical sciences taught in the best institutions of its kind." The trustees decided to advertise for an architect and to construct the main building of stone.

Sometime, at the first meeting or shortly thereafter, the trustees agreed that the institution should be called Lehigh University and that the principal building should be named Packer Hall.

The second meeting was held 4 September at the Church of the Nativity. Stevens had by now devised a seal for the university, which he described at length, and reported that competitive bidding was inappropriate for selecting an architect. He proposed Edward Tuckerman Potter, another son of Bishop Alonzo Potter. E. T. Potter had designed the Church of the Nativity and was well known as an architect in New York City. The board agreed to the appointment.

Also at the meeting of 4 September, Stevens reported that he had visited various colleges and institutions of learning, "especially Yale and Harvard," for the purpose of collecting information in regard to their systems of study and government. He presented the board with circulars and schedules (none of which has survived) and said that he had asked Professor George J. Brush of Yale "to draw up a plan of a Scientific School," a Mr. Thurston R. Jencks of Medford, Massachusetts, to provide a plan for a course of studies, and a Reverend Mr. Perney of Litchfield, Connecticut, "to furnish the outlines of a plan for furnishing a Library."

The third meeting was held two days later, 6 September, and was given over almost entirely to matters of buildings and grounds. Architect E. T. Potter was present. He and the trustees walked from the Church of the Nativity to the site of the new campus and detected two problems. One concerned the ground to the west. Packer Hall was to be built facing the proposed New Street Bridge. Potter wanted to locate the president's and professors' houses on the downhill slope west of Packer Hall, but there was not enough space for this. Could more land be obtained adjoining the western side of Packer's grant of fifty-seven acres?

The second problem involved the awkward presence of a Moravian church. In 1864 Packer had sold a lot on the proposed campus to the Moravians for their south-side congregation. The Moravians had promptly begun construction. By the end of July 1864 they had a building under roof, a three-story brick structure with a square tower on the eastern end. Before the year was out they had dedicated the large lecture room to the worship of God and were holding services there. The lot was naturally an integral part of the campus. Could it be repurchased from the Moravians, along with the nearly completed church?

These problems were for Sayre to solve. A division of labor had been worked out between him and Stevens. Sayre was to be in charge of the physical aspects, whereas Stevens would take initiatives in academic matters.

More than a month elapsed before the fourth meeting of the trustees. In retrospect, the trustees seem to have been awaiting the return of Packer from Europe before making any more key decisions.

It is fitting at this point to speculate concerning matters that might have influenced Stevens's thinking for Lehigh. He had on 4 September mentioned visiting Yale and Harvard and some other schools and asking information from men named Perney, Brush, and Jencks. Extant records include nothing to show that Perney and Brush supplied any written advice. In October 1865, Jencks responded with a lengthy, handwritten manuscript that is presently housed in the Linderman Library. Jencks covered a wide range of subjects, from educational philosophy to detailed requirements for admission and floor plans for buildings, and gave considerable space to a projected school of "Farming and Gardening." No further reference to Jencks's manuscript appears in the university's records. Probably it had no great influence with Stevens, Packer, or anyone else.

What schools besides Yale and Harvard might have influenced Stevens? Union, Bishop Potter's alma mater, is one possibility. Rensselaer is another. Asa Packer's son Robert had enrolled in RPI for the year 1863−64.[9] But lacking a classical course, it could not have served as a good model. The same was true for the Polytechnic College of the State of Pennsylvania, which is nowhere referred to in the early records of Lehigh.

Most of the other prominent courses or schools of science and engineering were, like Lehigh, at the stage of beginning or had not yet been organized. Cornell, MIT, Stevens Institute of Technology (SIT), and Johns Hopkins had not been opened to students. Courses in applied science and engineering at the University of Pennsylvania, Princeton, and Dartmouth were still in the future. The School of Mines at Columbia had been organized for only two years and was too new for anyone to know much about. The University of Michigan, which had successfully implanted the idea of utilitarian education in the Northwest Territory, was probably known to Stevens, but there seems to have been no connecting link between it and him. The same was true of Brown University, at which Francis Wayland was making educational history.

Nor did the colleges of the Lehigh Valley have anything that Stevens could use. Moravian College was a preparatory school for a theological seminary. Muhlenberg was still known as the Allentown Collegiate Institute and Military Academy; the name was changed in 1867 to Muhlenberg, a college that the controlling Lutherans hoped would prepare students for the ministry.

Lafayette was the only college of acceptable academic standing in the valley, and it had nothing that either Stevens or Packer could use. Founded in 1826 as a work-study institution under Presbyterian control, it soon adopted a modified four-year classical course. Financially it was seldom more than a few steps ahead of a sheriff's sale. It survived the Civil War largely because the faculty agreed to teach for little or no pay. William C. Cattell had become president in 1863; with his approval the faculty had instituted a four-year course in the Bible. By the spring of 1865 the college faced a real threat of having to close for lack of funds. In the nick of time Cattell received a promise of twenty thousand dollars from Ario Pardee. Within the next few months other gifts of money came in, mostly for chemistry; and in the winter of 1865−66, Pardee gave again, this time one hundred thousand dollars. The result was the Pardee Scientific School and a major thrust into scientific and engineering education.

While Stevens was working on academic matters, Sayre was addressing himself to the two problems suggested by architect Potter. Sayre quickly solved the one of obtaining more land on the west. The owner, Charles Brodhead, agreed to donate seven acres, thus bringing the border of the campus to a roadway, which was later called Brodhead Avenue. The other problem was not so easily removed. The Moravians resisted Sayre's offers to purchase their church, and for months negotiations dragged on.

Asa Packer met his trustees in an official capacity for the first time on 11 October. Architect Potter presented plans for Packer Hall and the landscaping, which the trustees approved with minor changes. The most important business concerned the selection of a president. Stevens was ready with the name of Henry Coppée, son of Dr. Edward Coppée and Stevens's brother-in-law.

As a young man Coppée had been employed in building the Central of Georgia Railroad from Savannah to Macon, studied engineering at West Point, and served with other members of the class of 1845 in the war with Mexico. Following the war he had briefly taught French at West Point, seen garrison duty at Fort McHenry near Baltimore, and returned to West Point to instruct in geography, history, and ethics. He had remained at West Point until 1855, when he had accepted an appointment at the University of Pennsylvania to succeed W. B. Reed as professor of belles lettres and English literature.

When the Civil War had begun, Coppée had opted for the Union cause and indicated a willingness to serve in the army if a suitable commission were offered, but it was not. His birth and rearing as a southerner were against him. Eventually he was commissioned colonel upon the staff of

Governor Curtin and passed the time editing a new publication, *United States Service Magazine*. Coppée was still engaged in this and was writing a military biography of General Grant, whom he had known as a student at West Point, when Stevens contacted him for the position of president of Lehigh University.

Although Coppée was fairly well known in Philadelphia, Packer had not met him. Accordingly, at the meeting of 11 October the trustees postponed the selection of a president until Packer had talked with Coppée. The two men met, and on 4 November Stevens formally offered the position to his brother-in-law, who accepted.

In the fall, winter, and spring of 1865−66, planning for the university went steadily ahead. A testimonial dinner for Packer, held 23 November at the Sun Hotel and attended by leading political and business figures from Pennsylvania, provided publicity. Maynard set to work drafting a charter to be presented to the legislature when it met early in the year.

Anticipating that the charter would provide for ten trustees, the board, at a meeting on 13 December, co-opted five more. These were Packer's younger son, Harry E., Dr. G. B. Linderman, who had married Packer's daughter Lucy, R. H. Sayre's brother William H., John Fritz, and Joseph Harrison, Jr., of Philadelphia.

Harry E. Packer was fifteen years of age, a fact not at all worrisome to his father nor, presumably, to the other trustees. All understood that Harry would not participate in meetings of the board until his father died or gave permission.

The 13 December 1865 meeting was the last that Stevens attended for several years. He had succeeded Potter as bishop of Pennsylvania and was administering the diocese without help. A promise of relief appeared in the form of a decision to split his jurisdiction by creating a Diocese of Pittsburgh. The relief came too late to save him from a breakdown. While attending ceremonies of the consecration of the bishop of Pittsburgh, Stevens was stricken and was for a time critically ill. When he recovered, travel was prescribed, and on 20 February he sailed for Europe, leaving the task of organizing Lehigh University to Coppée.

On 9 February 1866, Governor Curtin signed the charter giving legal existence to "a polytechnic college" with a power to grant "such degrees in the liberal arts and sciences" as the faculty with the consent of the trustees might decide. The word "engineering" did not appear in the text of the charter; but then, the wording was such as to be of little importance for educational policy.

As late as 13 February the trustees were apparently planning on opening the university in 1867 or 1868, whenever Packer Hall would be ready for occupancy. Sometime in the next two months they changed their minds and decided to begin classes the following September. Why?

One reason was success in negotiating for the Moravian church. The

Moravians agreed to sell provided another suitable plot of land was supplied them; and Augustus Wolle and Company donated to the university land on the north side of Packer Avenue for the purpose. The transaction made a building available for temporarily housing the university.

Another probable reason for the change in opening date was that Packer wanted the advantage of opening first, before students could go to Cornell or Lafayette, both of which were served by the Lehigh Valley Railroad. Ezra Cornell and Andrew White were fast organizing their school at Ithaca; and Lafayette was on the verge of beginning instruction in engineering and applied science with Pardee's money.

A third reason for beginning instruction in September was the success of Coppée in securing a top man for the important post of professor of analytical chemistry. This was Charles Mayer Wetherill, who had studied under Alexander Dallas Bache at the University of Pennsylvania and Justus von Liebig at the University of Giessen. Wetherill had a doctorate from Giessen and had distinguished himself in many fields. "No scientists of his period had experienced as wide a contact with the various applications of chemistry as had Wetherill," wrote his biographer, Edgar Fahs Smith.[10]

The board appointed Wetherill to a chair in chemistry at a two-day meeting, 13–14 April 1866. At the same meeting it named the Rev. Eliphalet Nott Potter as professor of mental and moral philosophy and of Christian Evidences and received from Coppée the outline of a "Scheme of Schools of Study, etc., embracing requisites of admission" and a code of bylaws.

Coppée spent the summer of 1866 with his family at the Sun Hotel finishing his biography of Grant and working on the scheme of studies. When completed, these became part of the first *Register* of the university. The original document, in Coppée's handwriting, is presently housed in the Linderman Library.

Coppée wrote that the design of the founder was to provide

the means for imparting to young men of the Valley, of the State, and of the Country, a complete professional education, which would not only supply their general wants, but also fit them to take an immediate and active part in the practical and professional duties of the times. The system determined upon proposes to discard only what has been proved to be useless in the former systems, and to introduce those important branches which have been heretofore more or less neglected in what purports to be a liberal education.

In subsequent sections Coppée set forth the details of the courses of study. All students, he wrote, would during their first two years study the same subjects, irrespective of the fields in which they intended to specialize. The list included finishing Latin and Greek (first year only), French, German, physics, mathematics (two years), chemistry (two years), English (two years), drawing (including in the second year painting if the student desired), anatomy, and physiology.

Coppée continued: Having successfully completed their first two years the students would enter one of five professional schools: General Literature; Civil Engineering; Mechanical Engineering; Metallurgy and Mining; and Analytical Chemistry. He included a diagram to illustrate this branching out by junior and senior schoolmen and informed the reader that other professional schools might be added at later dates.

Coppée prescribed that Christian Evidences would be compulsory in all five schools. There would be no electives.

For the School of General Literature Coppée wrote that students would study Latin and Greek, continue their work in French and German, and take literature, moral and mental philosophy, international law, civil polity, and political economy. In general, the course promised to give students a broader general education than they might expect from the more traditional classical course but a more shallow understanding of Latin and Greek and nothing of Hebrew.

Coppée anticipated that no students would be enrolled in the professional schools for the first two years. For this reason, only one more professor and two instructors were needed in order to begin the school in September. The professor, apparently secured by Coppée, was Edwin Wright Morgan, who had been graduated third in the West Point class of 1837. Morgan had later worked as a railway engineer and been vice-president of Shelby College in Kentucky and superintendent of the Kentucky Military Institute. He was to teach mathematics and drawing until the opening of the professional schools, when his skills in engineering would be needed. The two instructors were J. B. Lespinasse for French and George Thomas Graham for Latin and Greek.

The only other persons needed were a janitor and a curator of the museum. For this latter (part-time) position the trustees selected a local Moravian, William Theodore Roepper, who was managing financial affairs for the Moravian congregation and was also a metallurgist and geologist of distinction. Roepper joined the faculty with the understanding that in the autumn of 1867 he would have a full-time post as professor of mineralogy and geology.

Also, in the summer of 1866 Coppée filled the position of professor of physics and astronomy with Alfred Marshall Mayer, who had studied physics in Paris under Henri Victor Regnault. Mayer, with assistance from Joseph Henry, head of the Smithsonian Institution, had been teaching at the Pennsylvania College of Gettysburg and had received an honorary Ph.D. degree from it. Although Mayer was not scheduled to begin teaching until the fall of 1867, he was present for the opening exercises.

While Coppée worked on academic matters, Sayre pushed ahead with the construction. A man named James Jenkins was hired as superintendent. By the end of August the foundations of Packer Hall were laid, work had begun on the president's house, and the remodeling of the Moravian church, now called Christmas Hall, was finished. The first floor of Christmas contained the chemical laboratory, a room for a library, and a chapel. Classrooms and the president's office occupied the second floor. The third story had a drawing room on the north side, and across the hall to the south, dormitory rooms; dormers had been added there to aid lighting and the circulation of air. The many springs on the mountainside supplied water, and outdoor privies took care of sewage.

Thirty-nine boys responded to advertisements for students and were admitted. All but one were formally entitled first classmen, the one second classman being Miles Rock, a Civil War veteran from Lancaster, Pennsylvania. Of the other thirty-eight, ten were from the Bethlehems; seven came from Mauch Chunk; seven came from Tamaqua and other places in the anthracite regions; three were from Philadelphia; one, from Barbados; and the remaining ten hailed from other places in the eastern and border states.

Opening exercises were held 1 September and were duly reported in the issue of *The Moravian* for the sixth. "The formal opening of the Lehigh University took place on Saturday afternoon last, at Christmas Hall. Quite a large number of its friends and invited guests from this place and other points in the Lehigh Valley, were present." After an opening prayer by the Reverend Potter, Coppée introduced Asa Packer. "In a few modest, heartfelt words the Judge stated his design in endowing the University and his conviction that in the hands of its faculty that design would be fully met." William Sayre and Judge Woodward of the Supreme Court of Pennsylvania talked briefly. Each member of the teaching staff "spoke upon the subjects to which his professorship relates." Coppée delivered the principal address, outlining the educational philosophy underlying instruction. The reporter wrote, "Probably there will be some dissent from some of his conclusions and positions, but no one will dispute the elegance of the diction and the vigor of the thoughts."

Entry into college life for thirty-nine young men began the next day but one.

2
Settling In: 1866–1880

During Lehigh's first fourteen years, all of the essentials that have persisted to the present time appeared, intermingled with those of less permanent duration. Put together, they add up to a school seeking to find itself in a fast-changing world. The early Lehigh exactly fits a description given by Henry Adams of post–Civil War America, "trying, almost as blindly as an earthworm, to realize and understand itself: to catch up with its own head, and to twist about in search of its tail. ... The generation between 1865 and 1895 was already mortagaged to the railways, and no one knew it better than the generation itself."[1]

Probably the citizens of the Bethlehems felt something of Henry Adams's puzzlement as they watched the construction in progress on South Mountain. Sayre had a branch railroad line called the Mott Street Railroad built to transport sandstone quarried in Potsdam, New York, and other materials up the hillside. On the campus, workers unloaded and stored the materials near improvised carpenters' and blacksmiths' shops and stables. Houses for the president and for two professors were completed long before Packer Hall, which took three years to build.

In the meantime, faculty and students improvised accommodations. Coppée, Wetherill, Mayer, and their families spent time in the Sun Hotel before transferring into temporary quarters rented for them near the campus. A few of the students took quarters in Christmas Hall; the rest found rooms in town. A student dining service, intended eventually to be located in Christmas Hall, was set up in rented quarters on Brodhead Avenue. Roepper taught mineralogy, geology, and blow-pipe analysis in a room on the second story of the Lehigh Valley Railroad telegraph office. A bell purchased for the spire of Packer was temporarily installed in the tower of Christmas; and an organ for the chapel, bought in Boston at a cost of $270, was put in the improvised chapel in Christmas.

Before Packer Hall was completed, Sayre had provided for an observatory, and the faculty had created the nuclei of a museum and a library. Sayre donated five thousand dollars for the Observatory, which was erected in 1868 for Professor Mayer and contained the best equipment available. Roepper began collecting minerals and stuffed animals and birds for a museum, considered essential for a practical education. A library originated from two actions. One was the setting aside of a room in Christmas Hall in 1866 for the storage of books. The other was the formation in the same year by the Reverend E. N. Potter of a literary society called the Junto for the purpose of maintaining a reading room.

In 1869 Packer Hall was fully occupied and the Mott Street Railroad and the temporary structures disappeared. The chemical laboratory, classrooms, chapel, library, and president's office were moved to Packer Hall.[2] Roepper began arranging his museum specimens in a large room in the central portion of the second floor. Christmas Hall became, for a few years, a living and dining place for students.

In the outside world, no one paid much attention to what was happening on the slope of South Mountain opposite Bethlehem. At the national level notices of Lehigh's existence were few and far between. Newspapers accepted paid advertisements for students and from time to time included the name of Lehigh in their stories.

The new university had to prove itself by its own efforts. Given the novelty of its mission and the trustees' inexperience with college life, the comparison of this early proving to the activity of an earthworm catching up with its own head and twisting about in search of its tail appears in order. Maynard had written the charter; the trustees had adopted bylaws; and Coppée had composed a *Register* describing the courses of study and listing rules governing admission, student progress, and conduct. None of these documents accurately described the university as it developed during the first fourteen years. Especially, the rules for student life and the courses of study, elaborately described in the *Register*, represented intentions, many of which were not carried out. The actuality resulted from decisions of Packer and his aides and from choices made by the students and the faculty.

Control over the university presents the most obvious distinction between written provisions and practice. The charter and bylaws specified that ten trustees were to control the university. An Executive Committee was empowered to act between sessions of the board. In practice, Packer, Robert H. Sayre, and Elisha P. Wilbur made the important decisions. Wilbur as treasurer took charge of finances. Sayre was chairman of a Building Committee and the most active member of the Executive Committee. Although Packer, Sayre, and Wilbur usually deferred to the faculty in educational matters, they frequently directed details of physical organization.

Natually, problems developed. It was through these and the solutions offered that Lehigh took on much of its character.

The most perplexing problems arose from the difficulty of attracting and keeping students. Many of the men admitted in the first few years were members of families of which the father was in some way connected with Packer's railroad or his university. William R. Butler and Lentz E. Klotz of Mauch Chunk were sons of suppliers of building materials. Harry A. Packer, Charles W. Roepper, and Harry St. Leger Coppée had fathers on the faculty or the board. Sons of Bethlehem businessmen included Clarence A. Wolle and George A. Jenkins. Edward C. Boutelle's father was a local landscape painter of considerable ability. Names of other students suggesting a relationship to founders, builders, or professors are Richard Brodhead, Richard J. Carter, Asa A. Packer, Charles and William C. Wetherill, and Henry S. Drinker.

When the local supply of students dwindled, and the novelty of being one of the first to attend a new university ended, enrollments declined. Thirty-nine entered in 1866. This figure was not exceeded until 1873. Nineteen new students came in 1867, thirty-four in 1868, twenty-four in 1869, fourteen in 1870, and thirty-four in 1871.

Rates of attrition were alarming. More than half of those admitted as first classmen dropped out within three years. The total enrollment five years from the opening date stood at seventy-two, of which more than half were entering students. Only six were graduated in 1869 at the first commencement exercises. The number was doubled for 1870, but fell back to seven in 1871.

Some reasons for low enrollments and high attrition were obvious. The chances of becoming an engineer by the empirical route were still good, and youths were under great pressure to go to work as soon as possible. Taking time for a four or five-year course in higher education was a luxury that many felt they could not afford.

Some other schools attracted students that Lehigh might have liked to have. In Lehigh's backyard were Lafayette and Cornell. Lafayette had an established reputation in the liberal arts and began in 1867 accepting students for its new scientific and engineering programs. Cornell was organized on a much larger scale than Lehigh and offered a greater variety of practical courses. In the fall of 1868 Cornell began accepting students: 332 freshmen and 80 students with advanced standing.[3]

Secondary schools in the country did not have "college prep" courses as they did later, much less courses of study fitted for sending students to the newly organized scientific and engineering departments. This caused problems of admission that educators met in several ways. Some schools — for example, Cornell — set entrance requirements low. This helped to bring in students but raised other problems for the quality of education. Many colleges (e.g., Columbia School of Mines, Swarthmore) solved the problem by adding a preparatory course designed to produce students capable of meeting high entrance requirements.

Lehigh began by accepting neither option. The faculty insisted on high entrance requirements and made no provision for a preparatory course. The professors prepared, administered, and graded entrance examinations; they accepted "on condition" applicants who failed to meet one or two of the entrance requirements; and they permitted reexaminations. These provisions helped in getting students but were less successful in keeping them. A man accepted on condition had to work harder than normal in order to keep up with his class. Although the faculty dismissed relatively few students for academic reasons, a letter from the president to a parent recommending that a son be withdrawn because of a parlous academic situation had the same effect — and was fairly common.

Costs of attending Lehigh were high. The board in 1866 approved a yearly tuition for the first and second year schoolmen of $90 and for students in the schools of special instruction, $100. Upon discovering the relatively high cost of technical education, in 1869 the board raised the figures. Henceforth the first and second year schoolmen would pay $125 and the junior and senior classmen, $150, except for students in the School of Analytical Chemistry, who would pay $179. In 1870 the trustees lowered tuition to $100 for the first two classes but allowed it to remain as before for students in the special schools.

These figures on tuition at Lehigh were much higher than those for students attending Lafayette, Cornell, and many other schools.[4] Costs of living were also higher for Lehigh students than for those attending Lafayette or Cornell. In organizing Lehigh, Packer had opted against dormitories, saying that it was better for the boys to live in town. Packer made exceptions to this rule only for temporarily housing students in space not needed for other purposes. Most Lehigh students had to rent rooms in private dwellings; and in the expanding industrial area in which Lehigh was located, housing was almost always in short supply. Landlords and landladies charged what the traffic would bear.

The small size of the student body adversely affected the size of the teaching staff, and this possibly also helped to depress enrollments further. The plan for five professional schools carried with it an implication that within a few years of the opening, the faculty would include a professor for each school. The number of students enduring to the third year, when selection of a special school of instruction became necessary, did not immediately permit this.

Most of the students in the first few years chose analytical chemistry or engineering. The number in analytical chemistry was never lower than four. Professor Wetherill had been provided for the chemists. The numbers of students in civil and mechanical engineering, branches as yet poorly distinguished from one another, were until 1871 fairly evenly divided and after 1868 never totaled fewer than eleven. Coppée had provided one professor to head both branches, Edwin Dwight Morgan. For the moment, this seemed sufficient. When Morgan unexpectedly died in 1869, Coppée replaced him with Lt. Hiero B. Herr, West Point class of 1866, who resigned his commission in order to accept the professorship at Lehigh.

Mining and Metallurgy presented Coppée with a problem. Although the Lehigh Valley seemingly offered great opportunity for mining engineers, in 1868 no Lehigh students selected the field; and in 1869 only three chose mining and metallurgy. Coppée added one man, Richard P. Rothwell of Wilkes-Barre, to the teaching staff, with the rank of demonstrator, to take charge of field trips for the miners. The following year, 1870, five students chose mining and metallurgy.

But Coppée had difficulty in finding a suitable professor. Then Rothwell resigned, leaving the university without a teacher of any sort in the field. Coppée's initial reaction was to close out the school, at least for the present. He encouraged the students to switch from mining to civil or mechanical engineering and was successful in this except for one person, Henry S. Drinker, a nephew of one of the men who had gone to Europe with Packer in 1865.

Drinker's account of the matter illustrates the sort of improvising to which Coppée was driven:

> President Coppee sent for me and suggested that it seemed hardly worth while to continue the course for one student, and that I had better transfer to Civil Engineering. To this I objected on the ground that I has come to Lehigh to study Mining Engineering, that the course was advertised in the Register, and that I had given a year to it. Dr. Coppee acknowledged the justice of the claim, and did me the honor to confer with me as to what could be done. After consultation with Mr. Rothwell I purchased three ponderous volumes entitled "Crooke's Metallurgy," from which I proceeded daily to lecture to myself, making copious notes. Dr. Coppee, who while a distinguished Man of Letters, was rather at sea in Metallurgy and Mining, would the next day examine me from my notes and now and then I would run up to Wilkes-Barre to derive fresh inspiration from a day in contact with the practical work in Mr. Rothwell's office, and during the year I trudged out every Saturday with Miles Rock, of '69, to the Friedensville Zinc Mines, of which he was the Surveying Engineer, and spent the day in survey work. We walked out from Bethlehem to Friedensville in the morning [a distance of about four miles], and back in the evening, and it was my duty to carry the transit out and back. In June, 1871, I presented a Thesis on the Mines and Works of the Lehigh Zinc Company, and received my diploma.[5]

Not surprisingly, in the summer of 1871 Coppée presented the trustees and the students with a professor of mining and metallurgy, Benjamin West Frazier, who had degrees from the University of Pennsylvania and had studied at the École des Mines in France and the mining school at Freiburg, Germany.

Classics suffered the most from the small size of the student body. During Lehigh's first five years the School of General Literature, home of the classics, never enrolled more than three students at a time. The number was too small to justify the appointment of a professor. The need for more instruction was greater in other fields. An instructor, who had been hired to take care of Latin and Greek for the first and second year students, was given the task of teaching the upper classmen.

That is, the School of General Literature was not established, even though *Register*s continued to treat it as existing. It is reasonable to suppose that the situation had a depressing effect on the admission of students desiring a classical education, even of the vocational sort being advertised.

The failure of the student body to increase in size led the trustees to experiment with several correctives.

One was the addition of a preparatory course. The trustees advertised for it in the *Register* of 1869−70. The first class began in September 1871 with a gratifying number of forty-nine pupils. The minimum age for admission was set at fifteen. Pupils were organized in sections A, B, and C according to level of proficiency. Examinations for entry into the first class of the university were to be held at the end of every semester. Preparatory students could thus enter the first class whenever they were ready.[6]

The professors and the instructors had to take on the teaching and disciplining of the preppers, and they objected. On 29 October 1871 the faculty formally recommended that the preparatory class be abolished and the regular course be extended from four to five years. The trustees refused this request. Coppée sided with the trustees and, in his report to them of 20 June 1872, wrote that discontinuing the preparatory class "would rob the valley and the country in its vicinity of the means of preparation to enter our first class, what was intended by the founder to be a blessing to this region will partially fail of its purpose."

The regular students in the university agreed with the faculty in opposing a preparatory class. Many students were rooming and boarding in Christmas Hall, which now had to be used for the preppers. Regular students moved out and found rooms in town at considerably higher cost to themselves. Packer and the trustees, already sensitive to the financial burden being born by the students, were sympathetic. They made a further exception to the policy of "no dormitories" and ordered the erection of Saucon Hall near the eastern end of Christmas. Students moved into Saucon at the beginning of the fall semester 1873.

Although the preparatory course helped to increase enrollments, it lacked the lasting effect of another measure. At the board meeting of 3 July 1871, Packer announced the abolition of tuition, effective immediately.

Making Lehigh free for students was not the only innovation that Packer had in mind. Education in science had proved to be more expensive than anyone had guessed. Packer's initial gift of $500,000 was nearly spent. The time had come to put the university on a permanent financial basis. Packer had a plan, which he revealed in three stages:

(1) At a board meeting 21 June 1871, Packer proposed that twelve persons be added to the board (thereby violating the provision in the charter setting the number at ten). The additional twelve included the Reverend Cortlandt Whitehead, rector of the Church of the Nativity; the Reverend Leighton Coleman, rector of St. Mark's in Mauch Chunk; Robert A. Lamberton, general counsel to the Lehigh Valley Railroad; H. Stanley Goodwin, assistant superintendent to Robert H. Sayre; Eckley B. Coxe, Charles C. Skeer, and William L. Conyngham, miners and shippers of anthracite; Franklin B. Gowan, president of the Reading Railroad; Charles Brodhead; Elisha P. Wilbur; George W. Childs; and Henry Ingersoll.

(2) At the next meeting of the board, a special meeting held on 3 July, these appointments were ratified, and Packer announced the abolition of tuition and continued with his plan of financing. The board should raise an endowment of $125,000. If the board succeeded in this, he would add $250,000. In the meantime he would personally support the university to the tune of $20,000 per year. If the board would bring in another $125,000, he would give an additional $250,000. The university would then have the income from an endowment of $750,000, minus $10,000 annually, which would be set aside to be added to the endowment. The board accepted this proposal.

(3) At a special meeting on 21 October 1871, a committee consisting of five of the new trustees was appointed "to operate in the city of Philadelphia in furtherance of the effort to raise money to secure to this University the benefit of the offer made" by Packer. The five were Ingersoll, Gowan, Coxe, Childs, and Harrison. All were wealthy and had many wealthy friends. All but Coxe lived in or near Philadelphia.

The plan was imaginative and bold, but it did not work. At the meeting of 20 June 1872, the committee of five reported without explanation that it was "inexpedient" to raise money in Philadelphia for the purpose intended by the founder. And so the matter of finding money for the university was left in Packer's hands. He accepted the defeat of his proposal and registered no complaint that has been recorded. Tuition remained free. For the remainder of his life Packer gave monthly the sums the university needed to operate along the lines established by 1871. These sums came to considerably more than $20,000 per year, for example, $29,312 for 1872, $46,053 for 1873 (which included the cost of building Saucon Hall), and $34,416 in 1874.

The decision to abolish tuition was fortuitous. After the initial year, the preparatory school did not bring in as many students as expected. Its entering class dropped from forty-nine in the fall of 1871 to forty in 1872 and twenty-five in 1873. Furthermore, in the fall of 1873 America entered upon a severe economic depression, which endured with diminishing intensity for the remainder of the decade. College enrollments almost everywhere fell off. Largely because of free tuition, total enrollments at Lehigh jumped from 73 in the fall of 1872 to 110 the following autumn and remained near that figure for several years. The size of the entering class was by 1874 more than double what it had been in 1869. Even with free tuition many students at Lehigh could not afford to remain in school. In several of the depression years as many as five out of six entering students dropped out before their senior year.[7]

In the spring of 1874 Coppée recommended that the preparatory school be closed out. The trustees agreed, and no more preppers were admitted. Four years later William Ulrich, a German immigrant, opened a private preparatory school near the campus.[8]

In 1871 several other events occurred having no relationship to the great financial decisions of that year. The Episcopal Diocese of Central

Pennsylvania was created with a jurisdiction including the Bethlehems, and Stevens persuaded Lehigh to become formally affiliated with it. In making the recommendation he had the warm support of Packer, Coppée, Goodwin, Robert Sayre, Lamberton, Blakslee, and others. The affiliation did not include clerical control and seems to have been scarcely noticed by the general public.[9]

In 1872 Stevens stepped down as president of the Board of Trustees. The intention of Packer and the charter was that the presidency should be held by the bishop of the diocese in which the university was located. That was now Mark Anthony De Wolfe Howe, the bishop of central Pennsylvania. Howe was a graduate of Brown University and held educational views similar to those of Stevens.

At this point in the narration of events it is fitting to pause in order to appreciate the general position of students, faculty, and courses of study in the opening years of Lehigh University.

From the beginning more than three-quarters of the student body came from the states of Pennsylvania, New Jersey, and New York. The year 1870, in which the students numbered forty-four, provides an example: 65.9 percent came from Pennsylvania; 13.6 percent, from New Jersey; 4.5 percent, from New York; and 6.8 percent, from other parts of the United States. The remaining 9.1 percent—four students—came from Brazil. This Brazilian contingent was unusual. The government was sending students north for a scientific education in order to have cadres qualified to make internal improvements.[10] From 1868 to 1876 Lehigh always had several Brazilians studying science and engineering. A few students came from other foreign countries, mostly located in Central or South America.

The students arrived primarily to study chemistry and engineering. Catherine Drinker Bowen, in her *History of Lehigh University*, characterized them as being of the "flannel shirt variety" as distinguished from the "cigarette brand" at Yale and other places.[11]

A writer in the yearbook, the *Epitome* for 1875, compared Lehigh students to those in liberal arts colleges in these words: "In fairness please remember that Lehigh University is essentially a SCIENTIFIC SCHOOL. That large class from whose ranks are mostly drawn our boating and our ball men, those who having both time and money go to the college as much for culture derived from college life as from the course of study, is wholly wanting at Lehigh. This class rarely finds its way into scientific schools."

When the students arrived on the campus they found their own lodging and reported to the president for registration. Although several fraternities appeared in the 1870s, only one became permanently established, Chi Phi in 1872, and it was not yet a living organization.

The rules governing the students' academic existence were simple and strictly enforced. Six days a week the routine began with fifteen minutes of chapel, conducted by President Coppée. The students then marched to class. Classes were small, rarely having more than twenty students and in most instances, fewer. Three periods of one hour each were used in the morning and two (later, three) in the afternoon.

Recitation was the preferred method of instruction. The professor gave each student a chance to recite and graded him on the performance. This practice of daily grading in each class put a premium on attendance. The rules required that a student who was unprepared to recite must advise his teacher of this before the beginning of the class and provide a satisfactory reason for being unprepared. Teachers kept attendance records and turned them in to the president's office. Unexcused absences were harshly dealt with.

Students faced other sorts of work in addition to recitations. For a time they were required to record all supplemental work in a notebook. Also, first and second schoolmen had to write weekly essays on assigned topics covered by recitations or supplemental lectures. The use of lectures as a principal method of instruction was a German practice whose value was much disputed among American educators. That lectures should supplement recitations was admitted to be good; that they might supplant them was considered questionable.

Saturdays were largely given over to laboratory or field work. Field trips of several days' duration were held several times a year for the technicals. The students traveled by train, making use of free passes supplied by Robert Sayre.

Each student had to write a thesis as a requirement for graduation. The thesis of a technical was generally considered as the beginning of his creative life and usually took the form of a practical problem, which he defined and for which he offered a solution. Some representative titles are found among theses submitted by members of the graduating class of 1872: "Review of the Collective System of the Brooklyn Water Works" (Henry St. Leger Coppée, C.E., son of President Coppée); "Descriptive Paper on Boiler Construction" (the Brazilian R. F. De Miranda, M.E.); "On the Examination of the Water Supply of Bethlehem" (O. M. Lance, A.C.); "Review of the Wrought Iron Deck Bridge of the L. & S.R.R. Co. at Phillipsburg, N.J." (Henry D. Scudder, C.E.).

The school year was divided into two terms, of which the second was for a number of years several weeks longer than the first. Each term ended with a general written and oral examination. That concluding the first term was for the purpose of privately assessing the progress of students and was called the semiannual review. The more important annual review occurred at the end of the school year and was open to the public. It covered the work of the entire year. Clarence Wolle ('69) wrote of the first annual review in Roepper's class, "It took place before quite an audience of interested people from Bethlehem. The examination was almost cruelly rigid, but so thorough were the subjects studied that not a single error was made by the whole class."[12] Seniors at the annual review had to defend their theses. Robert Sayre recorded in his diary for 24 June 1874, "Attended the reading of thesis by the Students of Lehigh University. Heard a very good paper by young Hartshorne on the building of Dams."

The annual review was followed by university week. For the first two years the events of university week were limited to university Sunday, when a noted clergyman delivered a baccalaureate sermon (always printed and circulated), and university day, when commencement exercises were held. Later, social events were added, extending university week to four and five days. On commencement day, more than on any other, the university was on public display, and the trustees spared no expense in making the exercises a gala occasion.

Not all seniors who participated in commencement exercises received a diploma. The rules allowed the faculty to tailor special programs for students unwilling to take a full course of instruction. Such students were referred to as "specials" and, upon finishing their programs, received certificates. For most purposes the specials were considered as having been graduated from Lehigh. A fair number of students in the early years were specials.

Unlike the rules governing academic life, those intended to build good moral character were often indifferently enforced.

The *Register* of 1866 contained prohibitions intended for regulating student life. The men were neither to smoke nor to drink on the campus. They could lodge or board only in houses approved by the president and must open their doors at any time to visits of inspection from the president and the instructors. The students might not leave Bethlehem without permission from the president or the professors. "Every student must obey, without delay, the summons of any Professor or Instructor, or of the Janitor to attend upon any Professor or Instructor." During study hours, lasting from 7:30 to 9:30 in the evening, "No student shall leave his room without permission of one of the instructors. This applies equally to students who occupy rooms in Christmas Hall, and those who live elsewhere in town." All students were to attend chapel and Sunday services at the Church of the Nativity, to which they would march in a body, unless excused in writing by a parent to participate in services elsewhere. They were neither to play cards nor to gamble; and on Sunday, "No games shall be played, nor shall the students go upon the river or ride or drive on that day, except for some necessary purpose."

These and a few more rules of a similar severity strike the modern mind as more suitable for a military academy than a college. Yet rules such as these were common in colleges of the 1860s and 1870s and seem harsh today because values have changed. Occasionally students at Lehigh were disciplined under the rules. All told, the number of disciplinary cases was small. A comparison of the situation at Lehigh and those elsewhere as described, for example, in *Academic Procession* by Ernst Earnest,[13] leaves the reader with a feeling that either the rules at Lehigh were not strictly enforced or that the students voluntarily obeyed them. Probably both situations existed.

By and large, the students were on their own and had to police themselves. Lehigh had a small teaching staff and no deans, and the boys lived scattered over several square miles of the boroughs. Also, the first rules were soon altered to provide less regimentation. The local papers record few complaints against the conduct of students. Town and gown conflicts, which usually involve rowdyness on both sides, were virtually nonexistent. A brawl between toughs of the Bethlehems and the students occurring on Thanksgiving Eve and Day 1868, is notable for its insularity. An editor of the 1875 *Epitome* wrote, "Since that time the students have not been molested."

High jinks of sorts existed, to use a phrase then popular. The faculty regarded several of these as intolerable. One was hazing, which apparently began as soon as the first group of second classmen met the second group of first classmen. Hazing persisted for over a hundred years, in spite of occasional statements by faculty or alumni that it had been banished forever. The faculty punished it whenever a concrete case was brought to their attention, but they did not often go out of their way to find cases.

The faculty rarely took official notice of several other sorts of "tomfoolery," all of which were borrowed from other campuses. One of these was the mock program, a spoof on the real program for commencement exercises that the students drafted and surreptitiously substituted for the real thing. Mock programs appeared for several years. Other activities of longer duration were class suppers, at which faculty looked the other way while students got drunk, the cane rush, in which first and second year classmen beat and clawed one another for possession of a cane, and cremation exercises. The cane rush occurred during the fall, whereas cremation was a spring event, usually scheduled for university week. The students with much ceremony marched to a designated spot and burned a book that they disliked. At first the book was Coppée's *Logic*, a text required of all freshmen. Cremation of *Logic* was said to be disconcerting to the author. Other faculty seem rather to have enjoyed the proceedings.

In the fall of 1880 logic was taken out of the freshman course, and the following spring went by without any ceremony. Then calculus took the place of logic with the sophomore class as sponsor. Throughout the remainder of the old Lehigh, calculus cremation was a notable and sometimes fairly stirring celebration.

A sore point with students during the first seven or eight years was the apparent unconcern of local citizens in allowing their livestock to roam the campus. The mock program for 26 June 1873 sarcastically styled the campus "fine pasture for cows, goats, pigs and other cattle. Children fed on the milk of these cows warranted to imbibe wisdom."[14] About the same time, the students caught an errant white goat and, according to an alumnus, "by a proper use of chloride of iron and yellow prussiate of potash, dyed her a fast blue, and before returning her to her native heath further decorated her with a cast-off telescope hat." In later years a rumor persisted to the effect that once during the early years the boys had taken a cow into the chapel on the third floor of Packer Hall; but in 1921 someone—the editor of the *Alumni Bulletin* suspected Henry R. Price ('70), then president of the Board of Trustees—put the matter right: The cow had been a horse, Price wrote, persuaded by students into the president's office when it was located on the second floor of Christmas Hall to advertise their discontent with animals on the loose.

One nearby establishment was of special interest to many students with some spare time of an evening or a Saturday. This was a brewery located across a creek which bordered the eastern edge of the original campus— "about the only place we ever crossed it in early days," wrote William Griffith, '76. A spring with a large flow of water had motivated George Rennig to locate his brewery there. It was not off limits to students. "The path from Packer Hall to Geo. Rennig's Brewery was more plainly marked than any other on campus," wrote an alumnus.[15]

In general, when students got out of class, they were free to do what they wanted provided they respected the authority of their elders, attended chapel and church, paid their debts, and stayed out of trouble with the local police. Students who behaved themselves were allowed to use university property for some of their activities, provided it was not needed for other purposes.

No written rules governed the students in the domain of extracurricular activities. The word *extracurricular* was not even used until after the First World War. Students could engage in sports, manage publications, and maintain societies of many sorts much as they pleased. That is not to say the university was indifferent to these activities, for it was not. Individual trustees and faculty often encouraged and assisted students in their out-of-class activities. But if money was needed, the students had to provide it and were correspondingly free to govern the spending of it.

An exception to this refusal to provide means for activities was the action of Packer in 1875 of giving an additional fifty-two acres across from the brook leading downhill from the brewery. Although the land became available for various uses, the principal one for which it was intended was as playing fields. This almost immediately became its use.

The university was pledged to contribute a gymnasium, regarded as a means for helping to achieve the educational goal of "a sound mind in a sound body." In keeping with the prevailing opinion, the trustees thought of a gymnasium primarily as a place for gymnastics, secondarily as a place for boxing and wrestling, and hardly at all for team sports.

The *Register* of 1866 contained the promise of a gymnasium, which was not immediately kept. Almost yearly the students petitioned for one, but to no avail. The first facility for physical exercise was a room on the fourth floor of Packer Hall, fitted out in 1874 with rings and Indian clubs and some other equipment.

Originally the students were too few in number to have regularly organized teams. These were ad hoc affairs with captains being chosen by
team members or being self-appointed.

Following the Civil War, an interest in baseball began sweeping the
country, including the Bethlehems. Baseball was Lehigh's first intercollegiate sport. The first game was played with Muhlenberg on Saturday, 13 June
1868. The issue of the *Bethlehem Daily Times* for Monday, 15 June, recorded
it as having taken place "on open lot at the end of Main Street" and noted
that the Lehigh team won "an easy victory."

Track and field also appeared at an early date. Students ran short races on
the towpath of the canal and for a time used a horse-racing track at Ritters-
ville, the site of the present state hospital in East Allentown. Instances of
foot racing and the standing broad jump are recorded as being held near
Saucon Hall. Rugby may have been played about the time that track and
field appeared. Next came football, staged on an informal basis. "At that
time the campus was thickly covered with trees and there was no 'central
avenue' or open space and the matches were carried on in a delightful way
by the rebounding of the ball from the tree trunks."[16]

Sports brought students together as nothing else could. In 1874 they organized the Athletic Association, apparently for the principal purposes of
promoting a gymnasium and other facilities. Earlier, classes had provided
students with some internal organization and social activities. The Athletic
Association cut across class lines. An immediate effect in developing an all-
school spirit appeared in the choosing in 1876 of the university colors of
brown and white. Until 1876 individual classes had colors, but not the university as a whole. Accounts of the choice of brown and white, given much
later by alumni who had participated as students, varied somewhat. One
said the colors were "stolen" from Brown University. Several averred that
the choice was made because brown and white were the colors of the stock-
ings of a young lady whom they admired.[17] Whatever the origin, the use of
brown and white rapidly displaced class colors in popularity.

Sports conspicuous for their absence involved water and horses. The early
*Register*s indicated the presence of a boating club, and several were actually
organized, but none lasted long. The river was unsuitable for boat racing,
and permission could not be obtained to use the canal. As for horses (for
pleasure riding, racing, or polo), students were either too hard-pressed for
money or too occupied with other things to be much interested in "rich
men's pastimes."

In the realm of publications, the sophomore class of 1873 began a monthly
entitled *The Lehigh Journal*, which lasted for one year and four issues into
the fall of 1874. Then the sophomores attempted a yearbook. This proved
more successful. The *Epitome*, patterned after the Yale *Banner*, first appeared for 1875–76. It was from the start a friendly memoir of undergraduate life with a good deal of information about individual students and

a lot of sophomoric humor. In 1884 the juniors took over the editing of the *Epitome* from the sophomores.

The students, then as later, stood in awe of the professors. The professors constituted the faculty, which was only part of the total teaching force. There were no associate or assistant professors. Other members of the teaching force were instructors, lecturers, demonstrators, and assistants. Instructors and assistants were attached to professors, who determined their duties and had, figuratively, a life-and-death control over them. Demonstrators were field men who assisted in shops and mines. Lecturers were professionals who came to the campus to give special instruction, usually in the form of lectures. There were very few demonstrators and lecturers. The instructors and assistants were relatively numerous and did much of the teaching. The assistants, comprising the lowest level of the teaching force, had much the same duties as did graduate assistants at a later date.

The faculty that Coppée assembled in 1866–67 was distinguished, but it did not endure. By 1871 the members of the first faculty were, with the exception of Coppée, gone. Two had died: Morgan in 1869 and Wetherill in 1871. Potter left to become rector of St. Paul's in Troy, New York, and in 1871 assumed the presidency of Union College. Roepper, the eldest of the faculty, resigned in 1869, probably for reasons of health, although until 1871 he retained the less demanding post of curator of the museum. Mayer left in 1871 to become director of the laboratory for physical research at the newly opened Stevens Institute of Technology.

The faculty that Coppée put together beginning in 1871 was also distinguished. In 1871 William E. Chandler took over the duties of Wetherill. Chandler had an A.M. from Columbia and a Ph.D. from Hamilton College. He had served as an instructor in chemistry at the Columbia School of Mines, where his more famous brother, Charles F. Chandler, taught. Lorenzo Lorain occupied Mayer's post in physics for a year and was followed by H. Wilson Harding. Lt. Herr, who had taken over Morgan's duties, resigned in 1874 to go into private practice and was succeeded by Charles L. Doolittle, who had studied engineering and astronomy at the University of Michigan and had a civil engineering (C.E.) degree from Michigan. Charles McMillan filled the spot vacated by Roepper, but with a specialty in civil and mechanical engineering. McMillan resigned in 1875; and after a three-year interval, in which several others successively held the chair in civil and mechanical engineering, Mansfield Merriman arrived. Merriman had studied at Dresden, Berlin, and Yale, which in 1876 had awarded him a Ph.D. degree.

New teaching posts were created in mining and metallurgy (1871) and geology (1873). These were filled respectively by Benjamin West Frazier and by James P. Kimball. Kimball had studied at Harvard, Berlin, Freiburg, and Göttingen and had A.M. and Ph.D. degrees from Göttingen.

No professor filled Potter's empty shoes. Coppée took over the teaching of Christian Evidences. Two instructors assisted him in some other teaching duties. One was William A. Lamberton, who instructed in Latin, Greek, and mathematics. The other was Severin Ringer, a political refugee whom Coppée hired to teach French and German. Ringer's original name was Zygmunt Rodakowski. He had earned a degree in canon and civil law from the University of Krakow in Poland, had practised law in the city of Lemberg, and had then joined a revolutionary plot against Russia, the power occupying his section of Poland. The plot failed and Rodakowski, alias Ringer, fled for his life. Eventually he came to New York, where he was writing articles for a German newspaper when Coppée hired him.

Finally, in 1871 Coppée hired as janitor James Myers, who in time became as much of a fixture at Lehigh as were the senior professors and who was, according to some alumni, more professorial in appearance than they.

Coppée was the only member of the second faculty who was assigned to the School of General Literature. The others were basically applied scientists with varying amounts of practical experience in their fields of specialization. Three (Frazier, Kimball, Merryman) had studied in Europe; three (Kimball, Merryman, Chandler) possessed doctorates. All except Doolittle had studied engineering at schools emphasizing the chemical, physical, and mathematical sciences as the basis of engineering education. As for their extraprofessorial professional lives, Chandler looked to The Chemical Society, a professional organization which his brother and Persifor Frazer of the University of Pennsylvania organized in 1876; most of the others belonged to the AAAS and paid little attention to professional societies such as the ASCE and the American Institute of Mining Engineers (AIME), organized in the coal regions in 1871.

The professors in the technical subjects brought their backgrounds to bear on their teaching at Lehigh. They regarded engineering not so much as an application of science as a form of applied science. The bias in favor of science appeared in the predominance at Lehigh of laboratories over machine shops. Cornell and Stevens Institute maintained shops for instructional purposes, as did departments of engineering in many other schools. Lehigh did not; and whenever students or alumni asked for them, the faculty and the trustees responded by saying that the shops of industries in the Lehigh Valley were sufficient for the educational needs of the students.

The faculty's tendency to regard engineering as an applied science did not save it from pressures (felt everywhere by engineering educators) to increase the number of technical courses at the expense of those intended to provide a broader education. To be sure, Christian Evidences was justifiable on the grounds that it was supposed to promote good moral character. English composition and French and German were thought to correspond to occupational necessities. But what about subjects such as history, literature, physiology, psychology, and political economy? Arguments might be advanced for including these, but still, choices had to be made. The problem of selection, Eckley Coxe is reported to have said, is not so much what should be added as what can be left out with the least loss.[18] Were, in fact, four years enough for an engineering education?

The desires of the professors for more technical courses soon destroyed the original plan of having a common core for first and second classmen. By the fall of 1872 the time set aside for a common core had been reduced from two years to three semesters; by 1873 it was being maintained only for the first year; and by 1878 the common core had been abolished. During the same period various proposals appeared for lengthening the time needed for an engineering degree beyond four years. Thus in 1872 the faculty approved a plan of four and one-half years for obtaining a degree in civil engineering; and the *Register* for 1876−77 specified that "Graduates of the School of Civil Engineering, by remaining one year and pursuing the course of studies elsewhere laid down, may receive the degree of Mechanical Engineer (M.E.)."

The appearance of Lehigh's Chemical Society further illustrates the importance of science. The Chemical Society was the first of Lehigh's course societies, which from time to time absorbed much student and faculty energy during the years before the First World War. A second course society, the Engineering Society, was organized a year following the appearance of the Chemical Society and was at that time much weaker.

William Chandler founded the Chemical Society almost as soon as he arrived on the campus in 1871. He was president most of the time; but faculty and students sometimes held the presidency and other offices. Membership was by invitation and was extended to most of the professors and instructors and to the better students in all of the scientific, engineering, and literary fields of the university. Honorary memberships were offered to, and accepted by, more than one hundred of the world's elite in science and engineering, among them Joseph Henry, Benjamin Silliman, Jr., Persifor Frazer, Baron von Liebig, Charles Eliot, Woolcott Gibbs, Ira Remsen, Joseph Leidy, Fairman Rogers, and Alexander Lyman Holley. Meetings were frequent; faculty and students read papers, which were published in the society's *Journal*. For three years lecture series were organized, bringing to the campus many of the noted names in American science. For four years, 1872−75, an annual address was delivered, being in order of presentation, "Inductive and Deductive Training" (Benjamin Silliman), "The Knight Errantry of Science" (Coppée), "Alchemy and Chemistry" (John C. Draper of the New York University), and "Detailed History of the Anthracite Coal Trade of the Lehigh Region" (Kimball).

Within a few years of its founding the society changed its name to that of the Chemical and Natural History Society. One of Chandler's interests was adding specimens to the university's museum (he had succeeded Roepper as its curator). Making a contribution to the museum was a requirement of membership. And in the summer of 1874 the society sent several people to Texas to collect specimens. The following year an expedition went to Brazil for the same purpose. The specimens sent to Lehigh included large numbers of insects, reptiles, and stuffed birds. Several years later Chandler raised the money necessary to purchase the Werner Collection of stuffed birds.

In the spring of 1874 Coppée submitted his resignation as president. He had guided the faculty and the students through the difficult formative years and desired to relinquish administrative duties in order to devote himself to full-time teaching.

In those years the president was the only administrative officer of the university. He had custody of student records, which he maintained with help from the secretary of the faculty, who was in the beginning an instructor and after 1867, the most junior member of the faculty. The president took the initiative in admissions, assisted by members of the faculty; he prepared the *Register*; he corresponded with parents and tradesmen; he supervised the use of university property (with much help from the janitor and the active trustees); and he represented the university to the public at large.

No one appears to have been surprised at Coppée's desire to devote himself exclusively to teaching. The Executive Committee of the board accepted the resignation and asked that Coppée remain as acting president until a successor could be found. To this he agreed and served for an additional year.

It so happened that a successor stood ready to take over. The Reverend John McDowell Leavitt had delivered the baccalaureate sermon a few weeks before Coppée submitted his resignation. With Packer's approval, Leavitt was appointed, effective 1 September 1875.

Packer and the other trustees quickly found that with Leavitt they had a president who was brilliant, energetic, and tactless. Leavitt had been a child prodigy, graduating from Jefferson College with honors at the age of seventeen. He had studied law with his father and had been admitted to the bar; and after practising law for four years had entered the Episcopal theological seminary connected with Kenyon College in Gambier, Ohio. He was ordained in 1848 and remained for a time as a professor at Kenyon, then moved to Ohio University, which in 1872 conferred on him the degree of Doctor of Divinity.

Leavitt adhered to many of the ideals that had stirred William Bacon Stevens, but he lacked the bishop's orthodoxy and restraint. His tenure of five years was unhappy. A zeal for reform and a lack of tact in proposing it disturbed the professors, who by the time of his appointment were entrenched in control of their several departments. Leavitt also had the disadvantage of serving during a severe economic depression.

In his first year as president Leavitt succeeded in obtaining the addition to the faculty of a professor in Greek and Latin. He forced the issue in his report to the trustees delivered 22 June 1876: "We graduate in Greek & Latin for attainments which would not admit into the Freshman Class of

Yale or Harvard. This seems to me a reproach and a detriment. . . . With a professor of Greek and one of Latin, our Classical Department would be filled. Rather than have it continued in its present condition I would advise its ultimate extinction."

The faculty supported Leavitt. The following year, with enrollment in General Literature standing at three regular and one special students, the faculty deferred recommending the establishing of a classical department until a professor had been appointed to take charge.

The date of the faculty action was 5 February 1877. Packer responded: "Mauch Chunk March 10, 1877 . . . You will please state in the Register that a Classical Professorship has been ordered to be established by us." At a special meeting of the Executive Committee of the board on 30 June 1877, the instructor in classics, William A. Lamberton, was named to fill the chair.

Obtaining the chair in Greek and Latin was one of Leavitt's few successes. The year 1876—77 marked the beginning of several failures. He was determined to increase enrollments and admitted on condition a number of first classmen who did not meet the standards set by the faculty. Sixty students entered, compared with forty-one the preceding autumn.

Immediately Leavitt was in trouble with the faculty. When some of the students did not remove their condition in the time allowed, the professors overrode Leavitt's plea for leniency and voted that the students "be advised to withdraw from the institution until they are properly qualified to enter." Leavitt resisted. He ordered the students to remain in their rooms and threatened to appeal the decision of the faculty to the Executive Committee of the board. The faculty refused to be intimidated and passed a motion stating that they "do not recognize the right of the President to decide upon the legality of their actions or to set aside their decisions in the case of the students retired from the University and hereby call upon him as the Executive to carry out the action of the faculty."

Leavitt gave in to the extent of allowing that the faculty had a right to evaluate the academic progress of students and told the delinquent students to go home; but he carried out his threat of appealing to the Executive Committee. The committee, meeting 3 February 1877, refused to consider the appeal. Three days later Leavitt informed the faculty that the committee "referred the matter to Bishop Howe, that it was the wish of Judge Packer to have the matter settled in the Faculty." Howe mediated an acceptable compromise regarding the issue of the dismissed students; but the faculty had won the battle on the more basic issue of faculty control over educational matters.[19]

For the succeeding two years (1877—79) the entering class numbered thirty-five—slightly more than one-half of what it had been in 1876. Total enrollments in the university dropped to eighty-one in the fall of 1877 and to sixty-six a year later, the lowest figure since before the abolition of tuition.

Virtually every activity suffered. The Chemical and Natural History Society ceased meeting. Its lecture series and the publication of the *Journal* ended.

With the fortunes of the university ebbing, Leavitt prodded the faculty into embarking on a postgraduate program. The faculty had as early as 1873 adopted a modest postgraduate program as an aid to students wishing additional course work. Fewer than half a dozen students had taken advantage of this opportunity. In November 1877, the faculty passed an expanded program leading to the degrees of Master of Arts for students in the liberal arts, Doctor of Philosophy for students in engineering, and Doctor of Science for students in science.

The program remained almost a dead letter. No students signed for postgraduate work in the first two years of its operation. Two entered in the fall of 1879, and five were enrolled in 1880.

Also in 1877 the faculty sought to increase the attractiveness of the university to students by adding a Course in General Science (later renamed Science and Letters). The course was given to the School of General Literature. The *Register* of 1877–78 described the addition as being designed for those who "enter on commercial pursuits, or matters of general industry." The course could for this reason be viewed as a precursor of the Curriculum of Business and Economics; but in the context of the times the Course in General Science was really a slight strengthening of the scientific bent of the university through the school supposedly dedicated to providing a classical education.

During this same period, when enrollments were dropping, Packer decided that the time had come to build a library. The departments then had small, specialized libraries, which provided for many of their immediate needs. Several departments had added reading rooms for the convenience of their students. In his last two reports as president, Coppée had urged that priority be given to an all-university library to house the many gifts to the university of books, periodicals, government documents, stamps, coins, medals, Indian artifacts, and similar items. Leavitt also made the request.

Packer responded by providing a facility far surpassing the expectations of Coppée and Leavitt. The structure was a handsomely designed, semicircular building, reputedly modeled on the plan of a Sicilian castle. It had space for one hundred thousand volumes and alcoves for readers. Packer named it the Lucy Packer Linderman Library after his recently deceased elder daughter, who had married Dr. G. B. Linderman.

Packer stipulated that the Lucy Packer Linderman Library should "be forever a reference library and not in any sense a circulating library" and should serve for "the public as well as for the Faculty and Students of this University."[20] The library was his largest single gift during his lifetime after the original grant of $500,000. He spent $110,213 on it, of which $99,125 was for the building and most of the remainder for books; and he gave in addition many valuable books.

The Lucy Packer Linderman Library was occupied in 1878, and in that year Chandler was named librarian.

About the time that the library opened, a group of alumni appeared requesting that Packer give a radical new direction to his university.

The alumni included Charles E. Ronaldson (M.E. '69), Henry S. Drinker (E.M. '69), Clarence A. Wolle (A.C. '69), William R. Butler (M.E. '70), Henry B. Reed (B.A. '70), Frank L. Clerc (C.E. '71), George P. Bland (C.E. '72), Charles L. Taylor (E.M. '72), Robert B. Claxton (C.E. '73), and Edward H. Williams (A.C. '75, E.M. '76).

They represented an Alumni Association, which had been formally organized in 1876, largely through the efforts of Harry E. Packer. The trustees had officially recognized the Alumni Association by admitting two of its members, Ronaldson and Miles Rock (C.E. '69), to membership for a term of two years. The following year the board increased the number of non-voting alumni members to four. Ronaldson and Rock and other members of the Alumni Association were now using it in an attempt to improve the university along lines that they felt would provide greater service to both students and employers in the Lehigh Valley. They had drafted an address to "The Hon. Asa Packer and the Board of Trustees" on "Technical Education at Lehigh University," which the Alumni Association had adopted.[21]

The address envisaged a complete restructuring of the university. The Course in Classics was to be closed out, and the technical side reorganized to give education to all levels of workers within Lehigh Valley industries:

The University should superintend the education of their working men, should provide courses of instruction that they could avail themselves of, and public lectures upon subjects that especially interest them. ... the higher University course should be in conjunction with the works; it should be arranged with reference to their aims, and illustrated by their practice. The heads of the various departments should be in the confidence of the management of the works; their laboratories, drawing-rooms, workshops, mills, and furnaces, should be open under certain restrictions to the students, there should be certain conditions under which they could enter them, and in return for faithful and equivalent service gain a practical knowledge of their profession. ... In fact, if the schools could be made in all but name a department of the works, their object could best be accomplished.

It is tempting to attribute the address to a reaction against "theory" on the part of university graduates who, upon gaining their first industrial employment, were jolted into thinking that much of what the professors had taught them was useless and that most of what they had to know must be learned by the empirical route. But a reaction of this sort could have been satisfied by less elaborate demands that the courses of study include more shop and field work. The address went much beyond this. It has a technocratic flavor suggestive of reformers about the time of the First World War who emphasized the moral responsibilities of engineers as leaders in society.

While these alumni were pressing for closer unity with industries of the Lehigh Valley, Leavitt was looking in another direction. He wanted a school of law and in the spring of 1878 persuaded the trustees to appoint a committee to work with him on what today might be called a trial balloon to test its feasibility. The committee consisted of Asa Packer, Wilbur, Linderman, and the two lawyers on the board, Charles Brodhead and Robert A. Lamberton.

Several years earlier Lafayette had organized a department of law and begun teaching the subject but had failed to interest many students and had abandoned the project. People at Cornell were discussing the possibility of establishing a school of law. Could Lehigh succeed where Lafayette had failed and perhaps steal a march on Cornell?

In the summer of 1878 Leavitt obtained a promise from Bethlehem's leading attorney, General William E. Doster, to deliver a series of lectures on practice in the courts of Pennsylvania. Coppée agreed to supplement Doster's course with lectures on constitutional law. Leavitt took his proposal to the faculty, which accepted the arrangement and authorized publicity. Shortly thereafter a series of lectures by an Allentown lawyer, Robert E. Wright, and a moot court were added to the experimental package.

Twenty-four students signed for the law lectures, which began and continued through the fall of 1878. Several sessions of moot court were held, chaired by prominent members of the bench.

Neither the alumni nor Lamberton succeeded in their proposals. Packer responded to the disturbing request from the Alumni Association with a polite "no" and an observation that the university seemed to be doing well as it was. Possibly Packer had no need to react to Lamberton's desire for a law school. Near the beginning of the spring 1879 semester, both Doster and Coppée broke off their lecture series and did not resume them. The reasons for this are unclear; but the lack of controversy accompanying the cessation of the lectures suggests that the interest of the students, faculty, trustees, and the community at large was at best lukewarm.

Packer died on 17 May 1879, following nine months of declining health. The Lehigh Valley Railroad was prospering; but enrollments at Lehigh were still down, and its president and alumni seemed to be proposing to direct the university along some novel routes.

Packer's death helped to put a stop to such speculations. It had a unifying and conserving influence, resulting from much more than the money he left behind and the powers he bequeathed to Sayre, Wilbur, and other officers of the Lehigh Valley Railroad. These and others could conceivably have made of Lehigh an arena for contesting money and power. The unifying and conserving influence appears instead to have come from a genuine respect for Packer's genius coupled with a recognition that, after all, what he had wanted for Lehigh had been correctly expressed by Stevens, Coppée, and the faculty, and that this was what the Bethlehems, the Lehigh Valley, the Commonwealth of Pennsylvania, and America really needed.

President Leavitt's time had run out. His report to the trustees in June following Packer's death was characteristically critical and tactless, but it was also a swan song. With Packer gone, there was no one to whom Leavitt could turn. He was also questioning some of the doctrines of his church. He submitted a request for a leave of absence to Bishop Howe on 9 October 1879 and with it included a letter of resignation, to take effect at the pleasure of the board. The letter contains a cryptic sentence, "Let me add I understand the situation & find a sense of relief."

The Executive Committee accepted Leavitt's resignation. The rules provided in such cases for the senior member of the faculty to perform the duties of a president. Accordingly, Coppée again became acting president. On 7 February 1880 the trustees selected one of their own group as the new president, Robert A. Lamberton, solicitor for the Lehigh Valley Railroad (and no relation to Professor William A. Lamberton).

The day on which Leavitt submitted his resignation, 9 October 1879, was also the first Founder's Day. The motion to establish an annual celebration in honor of Packer fittingly came from the faculty, whom Packer had staunchly supported in every major decision except that of beginning a preparatory course. The celebration began at ten o'clock in the morning with the unveiling in the library of a full-length portrait, painted by D. W. C. Boutelle, of Asa Packer. Trustees, faculty, alumni, students, invited guests from a distance, and citizens of the Bethlehems then marched to the chapel in Packer Hall. Bishop Howe delivered a "Memorial Discourse," which was printed, as were subsequent Founder's Day addresses. In the afternoon the students held races and other sporting contests. A band added to the festivities. Fireworks in the evening concluded the celebration.

The Alumni Association did not persist with the radical demands set forth in the address of 1878. On 24 June 1880 the association presented the board with another address, signed by most of those who had endorsed the first; but this time no unusual elements appeared. The address paid homage to Packer and appealed to his intentions: "... We feel that the memory of Judge Packer will always be most closely identified with the schools that were established during his life-time, ..." The association requested professorships in mining and mechanical engineering.

Coppée, in one of his last pronouncements as acting president, added requests for a series of lectures in physiology, someone to continue Leavitt's course in psychology, more laboratory space and equipment, a gymnasium, the purchase of Roepper's collection of minerals, and additions to all of the university's museum collections. Coppée especially wanted instructor Severin Ringer to be given a professorship.

In sum, as voices demanding new directions for Lehigh became silent, the university appeared to be what its faculty and students had made it — a small polytechnic university emphasizing a scientific approach to engineering education with additional courses of study in general science and the classics. Lehigh aimed to prepare students for careers in engineering and engineering-related businesses and to become, with further study or training, doctors, dentists, lawyers, ministers of the Gospel, journalists, or other professionals.

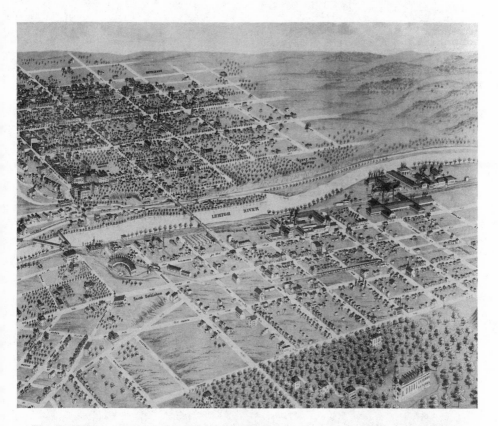

The Bethlehems, looking north from South Mountain. Although this print is dated 1878, the Lehigh campus appears, *lower right*, as it was in 1867, before the erection of the Sayre Observatory and Saucon Hall. Other landmarks include shops of the Lehigh Valley Railroad (semicircular building) and the Episcopal Church of the Nativity (immediately south of the shops). The home of R. H. Sayre, Jr., was located across the road from the Church of the Nativity.

Asa Packer.

Right Reverend William Bacon Stevens.

Packer Hall, showing the original tower and landscaping.

Professor William H. Chandler.

President Henry Coppée.

Chemical Laboratory.

President John M. Leavitt.

Lucy Packer Linderman Library. Photo by William C. Carnell, '94.

Physical education class in the new Gymnasium.

President Robert A. Lamberton.

Gymnasium. Photo by Henry Kemmerling, '91.

Packer Memorial Church, looking north toward the Bethlehems and the Lehigh River. Photo by George W. Engel, '92.

Governor Daniel H. Hastings plants a tree with President Drown, Arbor Day 1898, commemorating aid from the Commonwealth of Pennsylvania.

Professor Benjamin W. Frazier.

Professor Severin Ringer.

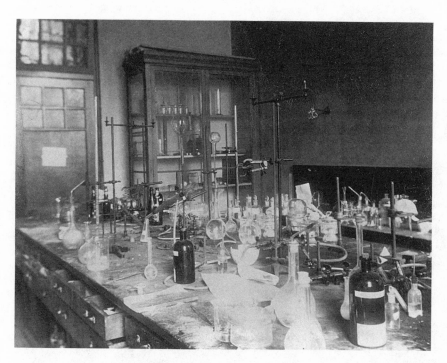

Laboratory. Photo by E. N. Wigfall, '95.

Studying. Photo by M. Brayton Graff, '94.

Staff of the 1889 *Epitome*. From l. to r: *seated on the floor*, C. H. Deans, Archibald Johnston; *seated on chairs*, W. E. Howe, A. T. Throop, W. D. Farwell (editor), J. Lockett; *standing*, C. Walker, H. M. Carson, W. Butterworth; *kneeling, far right, rear*, L. A. Round. Archibald Johnston, '89, later became general manager and a director of the Bethlehem Steel Company and the first mayor of the united Bethlehems.

President Thomas M. Drown.

Joseph W. Richards as a graduate student, 1886. Richards was later professor of metallurgy.

New Street entrance to the campus before the paving of Packer Avenue. Photo by Alban Eavenson, '91.

Baseball team, 1899. *L. to r.*, Frederick C. Wettlaufer, (manager), G. C. White, N. A. Spiers, W. H. Rodney (*back row*), J. H. Pomeroy, F. B. Gearhart, Eugene G. Grace (*center*, captain), John Wesley Grace, L. W. Bailey (*back row*), F. J. Carman, A. D. Hollingsworth, H. R. James, J. B. Reddig (manager), P. L. Reed.

Physical Laboratory burning, 6 April 1900.

President Henry S. Drinker.

Drown Hall.

John Fritz.

Fritz Laboratory about 1910.

Playing fields, 24 November 1903, showing a game of football in progress. Taylor Field was later built on the same site.

3
The Railroad Years: 1880–1900

For upward of twenty years the memory of Asa Packer was almost as potent within the Lehigh Valley and Lehigh University as his presence had been.

By his last will and testament, Packer devised all of his properties to a trust, known as the Asa Packer Estate. The trust paid legacies to parties named in the will and controlled his enterprises. It could buy and sell Lehigh Valley stock and other property, lend and borrow money, and do almost anything Packer could have done, subject to the provisions made for legatees, except abolish the estate, which could not end before the expiration of twenty-one years following the death of the last survivor of Asa and Sarah's three living children, Robert, Harry, and Mary.

The welfare of the Lehigh Valley road was the main concern of the estate, and the prosperity enjoyed by most Americans during the 1880s was favorable to it. Within the next thirteen years the trackage increased from approximately 658 to 2,425 miles. Income during the same period almost quadrupled. The Lehigh Valley route made connections with railroads leading to all inhabited parts of North America.

In the process, the railroad encouraged industrial expansion within the Lehigh Valley. The principal industries of Easton, Bethlehem, and Allentown and their satellite communities of South Easton, South Bethlehem, and East Allentown, focused on nearby natural resources of coal, limestone, ores of iron and zinc, and cement rock. Pennsylvania-Germans came from nearby farms to work in shops and factories and were there joined by immigrants from Ireland, Germany, and other countries of western and central Europe.

In South Bethlehem, the Bethlehem Iron Company, which in 1873 had begun making steel, steadily expanded. The Lehigh Zinc Company continued using local ores until the mines became too deep to be profitably operated. Then the company sold its assets to New Jersey Zinc, which operated the works in South Bethlehem until 1907, when they were closed.

Five trustees managed the Asa Packer Estate. These were men whom Packer had trained to carry on his work. In his last will and testament he named the first five: his sons Robert and Harry, Elisha P. Wilbur, Robert H. Sayre, Jr., and the president of the railroad, who then happened to be Charles Hartshorne. These adhered to the objectives Packer had set forth. During the first few years some disagreements between Sayre and

71

Packer's sons marred a unity of direction. However, Robert and Harry died within five years of their father's death. Robert A. Lamberton and James I. Blakslee took their places as trustees. Thereafter, disagreements among members of the railroad leadership were too trivial to excite public comment.

Among members of the leadership, Wilbur and Sayre retained the eminence gained during Packer's lifetime. Sayre was chairman of the board of the estate. In the disputes with Packer's sons he resigned as superintendent of the railroad but in 1885 took over the superintendency of the Bethlehem Iron Company, in which the railroad men had among them a controlling interest. Wilbur was the secretary of the estate and in 1884 became president of the railroad.

Wilbur, Sayre, and their associates controlled not only the railroad but also the enterprises that had been recipients of Packer's philanthropy, notably Lehigh University, St. Luke's Hospital—founded in 1871 on a site in Fountain Hill that in 1865 some people had thought might become the location of Packer's projected university—the Bishopthorpe School for Girls, situated near the hospital, and the Episcopal Church of the Nativity.

The men of the Lehigh Valley Railroad also had commanding financial and civic positions in South Bethlehem. They were largely responsible for the development of public utilities. The E. P. Wilbur Trust Company became the principal bank of the borough. From 1869 to 1874 E. P. Wilbur served as burgess, the equivalent of mayor, of South Bethlehem and was succeeded in the position by H. Stanley Goodwin, also a Lehigh Valley Railroad man, who remained as burgess until 1890.

The financial dependence of Lehigh University on the Lehigh Valley Railroad was obvious to all. "It is one of our boasts that this institution is a railroad university," declared Lewis T. Wolle (C.E. '77), in a commencement address. "What is good news to the Lehigh Valley Railroad is good news to the University," wrote a student.[1]

The railroad men's control of the Lehigh University board was not as immune to criticism as Asa Packer's had been. Packer, supported by the board, had in 1871 exceeded the legal number of ten trustees in the attempt to obtain help with finances. He had continued nominating trustees until by 1877 the number had stood at twenty-eight, not including the alumni trustees who joined in that year. Many of Packer's nominees were friends and associates not employed by the Lehigh Valley Railroad. Three years after his death the Lehigh board reorganized so as to conform to the provisions of the charter. The original ten, with Bishop Howe, Eckley B. Coxe, and Wilbur replacing Bishop Stevens, Joseph Harrison, and Asa Packer, were designated as charter trustees and had voting power. Those whom Packer had added in 1871 and later, plus the new alumni trustees, were nonvoting honorary members. The reorganization resulted in a board in which six of the ten voting members were railroad men. Until after the final sale of the railroad in 1899, the Lehigh Valley Railroad always had a majority on the board of Lehigh University.

Robert H. Sayre and Elisha P. Wilbur dominated the Lehigh University board as they did the Asa Packer Estate but did not imitate their former chief's cavalier treatment of the other members. From the time of Asa Packer's death, the board became a governing body for the university in fact as well as name.

Alive, Asa Packer had been generous to Lehigh University, having single-handedly paid its bills. In death he continued this generosity. Under the terms of Packer's will, Lehigh was to have the income from Lehigh Valley stock valued at $1,500,000. The will separately allowed the library to enjoy the income from $500,000 worth of stock. In a codicil, Packer directed that this amount should be reduced by the sum spent for the library building and its furnishings. The trustees of the Asa Packer Estate voted not to reduce the legacy to the library by the $110,213.58 that Packer had already spent on it but instead to treat the sum as a loan, secured by a mortgage in the same amount, thus permitting the library to remain as the beneficial owner of the full $500,000 worth of stock.

The trustees of the Asa Packer Estate did more than allow the university and the library the full earnings from their legacies; they also permitted borrowing from the estate for capital improvements. As a result, the university received annually sums from two to five times those given by Packer in the 1870s. Income for the library at times almost equaled the sums previously given to the entire university.

In short, the trustees of the estate outdid Packer in generosity. At the annual meeting of the Lehigh board in June 1880, the alumni had requested professorships in mining and mechanical engineering, and Coppée had asked for Ringer's promotion, the purchase of Roepper's collection of minerals, the addition of someone to continue Leavitt's course in psychology, a gymnasium, and more laboratory space. Within four years of this date the Lehigh board filled all of these requests.

The trustees in 1881 gave the new professorships in mining and mechanical engineering to, respectively, Edward Higginson Williams, Jr., and Joseph F. Klein.

Williams was the son of a partner in the firm of Burnham, Perry and Williams, which became the Baldwin Locomotive Works, the country's leading manufacturer of railroad engines. Williams had attended Andover and Yale, receiving a B.A. from Yale in 1872. After a period of employment by the Pennsylvania Railroad he had enrolled at Lehigh, which had awarded him degrees of A.C. (analytical chemistry) in 1875 and E.M. (engineer of mines) in 1876. Williams was the first Lehigh alumnus to join the faculty. Upon Williams's appointment to a chair of mining engineering and geology, Frazier's title was changed to that of professor of mineralogy and metallurgy.

Klein, too, had studied at Yale, having entered the Sheffield Scientific

School in 1868, from which four years later he received the degree of D.E. (dynamic engineering, a term then sometimes used to denote mechanical engineering). The appointment of Klein involved a definitive separation of mechanical from civil engineering. Henceforth, Klein would be in charge of the mechanicals and Professor Mansfield Merriman, the civils.

In response to Coppée's requests, the board purchased Roepper's collection of minerals, in 1880 promoted Severin Ringer to be professor of modern languages and literatures,[2] in 1881 filled the void in psychology by securing the services of the Reverend Frederick W. Bird as chaplain and professor of psychology, Christian Evidences, rhetoric, and declamation, and provided for two new buildings, a Gymnasium, and a Chemical Laboratory.

The Gymnasium (the present Coppee Hall) was opened in March 1883. It was modeled after the Hemenway Gymnasium at Harvard, which was supposedly the most advanced in the country, and provided room for gymnastics using Indian clubs, dumbells, rings, bars, and similar equipment. The Gymnasium also had billiard tables and space for boxing and wrestling.

The Chemical Laboratory (known to later generations as the Chandler-Ullman Building) was opened in September 1884. It consisted of a central structure with wings branching off to the east, west, and south and had approximately one hundred more square feet of floor space than did Packer Hall. It housed chemistry, mineralogy, and metallurgy. Among its more modern features were a system of speaking tubes for communication, centralized stock rooms, a large lecture hall arranged for maximum visibility, and a photographic laboratory. The building almost immediately became known among chemists as the finest in the country. It had cost an immense sum — more than two hundred thousand dollars.

The trustees did much more. In an attempt to improve the teaching of the classics they created a new position. William A. Lamberton, who had been teaching both Latin and Greek, was to continue with Greek. A new man would instruct in Latin. The person secured for this position was Henry C. Johnson, who had received baccalaureates from Cornell and Hobart. In response to a recommendation from Coppée for a series of lectures in physiology, the trustees obtained the services first of Dr. Traill Green of Easton (1882–83) and then of Dr. William Lawrence Estes, the young new superintendent of St. Luke's Hospital.

In 1879 the board had a brick house built for Janitor James Myers (the present Philosophy Building) and provided Myers with the means for beautifying the grounds. Myers thinned the woods of unnecessary brush and trees, leveled land in front of the principal buildings into terraces, and planted lawns and flower beds, the danger from ravages by livestock being past.

The trustees did not neglect the library. They created a special committee consisting of Professor Chandler (chairman), President Lamberton, and trustees Dr. G. B. Linderman, Bishop Howe, and Wilbur to supervise its activities. In 1881 the library had 21,395 bound and 2,677 unbound volumes and a staff consisting of a director (Chandler), a clerk, and a janitor. The committee began a program of adding books, manuscripts, and literary memorabilia to the collections.

People began referring to the campus as the University Park. The road coming into the park and some of the walkways were paved. A person entering from New Street passed the janitor's house on the left and faced an uphill slope containing a semicircle of stone buildings, widely spaced and interspersed with lawns and trees. Christmas and Saucon halls, in their downhill location, were decently screened off by trees and shrubs.

The trustees did not finance all projects with money from the Asa Packer Estate. With the exception of the Gymnasium, they provided nothing for athletics, other student activities, and student living. The dining service in Christmas Hall was contracted out. Rents paid for the living quarters in Saucon. E. P. Wilbur personally gave money for modernizing the heating system. A boiler house bearing his name provided steam heat through tunnels leading to Packer Hall, the Lucy Packer Linderman Library, the Gymnasium, Saucon Hall, and the Chemical Laboratory. Asa Packer's daughter Mary built a church, thereby releasing the space in Packer Hall formerly occupied by a chapel for use by the museum.

The trustees might have provided for a church if Mary had not done so, inasmuch as both students and faculty were requesting one. Mary, who had married a man named Cummings, and her brother Harry originally planned the church as a memorial to their mother, Sarah, who died in 1882. After Harry's death in 1884, Mary carried through the project by herself and extended the memorial to include all deceased members of the family. She and the Building Committee of the board selected a site near the New Street entrance to the University Park; she arranged for the construction. The official ceremonies of laying the cornerstone occurred on a drizzly 8 October 1885 and included the Masonic rite followed by an Episcopal service. The completed structure was consecrated on Founder's Day, 13 October 1887.[3]

Sayre, Wilbur, and the other trustees who lived in the Bethlehems were personally active in matters concerning the University Park and its buildings and frequented the campus in order to observe what went on there. At the same time, they respected a right of the faculty to control the educational side. Asa Packer had set precedents which the faculty and the trustees followed. Sometimes individual trustees made suggestions for improving teaching and courses of study, but nothing more. By and large, the actions of the board on educational matters were endorsements of decisions made by the faculty acting collectively in weekly meetings or individually through the departments.

Several of the educational decisions made between 1880 and 1882 rationalized the courses of instruction. At first these had been organized to provide students with a common core for their first two years and specialization within one of five schools for the remainder of their education. The schools that had been originally projected and eventually established were named General Literature, Analytical Chemistry, Civil Engineering, Mechanical Engineering, and Mining. Over the years the faculty had whittled away the common core until at the close of President Leavitt's tenure nothing of it remained; and within the School of General Literature they had added a Course in General Science. These happenings prepared the way for a reorganization. The faculty, backed by the trustees, now grouped the courses of instruction into two blocs, called respectively Schools of Technology and General Literature. The School of Technology had Couses in Analytical Chemistry and Civil, Mechanical, and Mining Engineering. The School of General Literature had the Course in Classics and two others, Latin Scientific and Science and Letters. The Classical emphasized Greek and Latin and lead to a degree of Bachelor of Arts. The Latin Scientific resembled the Classical, except that Greek was replaced by modern foreign languages and somewhat more philosophy, and the degree awarded upon completion was Bachelor of Philosophy (changed in 1883 to Bachelor of Science). The Course in Science and Letters was a new name for the former Course in General Science. Here, Latin and Greek were optional. The degree obtained upon completing the course was Bachelor of Science.

The Schools of Technology and General Literature were not administrative units. They had no deans or other personnel or organization to distinguish them. No one in the 1880s would have thought of asking to which school Professor Doolittle, in charge of mathematics, or Professor Harding of the Department of Physics, or Professor Frazier in metallurgy "belonged"; for the professors did not form part of any school. Students, on the other hand, could be identified as belonging to one or the other of the schools, except perhaps for a few specials whose individualized rosters cut across the lines separating the regular courses of instruction. A division of the student body into "technicals" and "men of general literature" or "classicals" could and did appear. But this had no counterpart among the faculty, for whom the departments were the meaningful subdivisions of the university.

With these changes the formal designation of students as first or second classmen and junior or senior schoolmen disappeared. The more usual terms of freshman, sophomore, junior, and senior — words already used in popular discourse — became official.

A rise in enrollments accompanied the additions to facilities and the changes in courses of instruction. From a low of 66 in September 1878, the number steadily grew until it reached 112 in the fall of 1880, 249 by the autumn of 1883, and 321 two years later. President Lamberton wrote in 1885 to the trustees that Lehigh was becoming better known: "Wisely and broadly have our foundations been laid. Upon them have been built two great schools, the one of General Literature, the other of Technology. Each is susceptible of infinite development and expansion."[4]

The increase in numbers of students was not uniform for the two schools. General Literature in the fall of 1883 had a high of 18 percent of the students, who were fairly evenly divided among the three courses of instruction. Thereafter, as enrollments in the university rose, the proportion in General Literature steadily declined, sinking to 8 percent by 1890.

The reasons for the discrepancy in enrollments between the two schools were essentially the same as they had been earlier. A national need for trained scientists and engineers was resulting in an increase in the number of young men studying these subjects. The number of institutions of higher education offering engineering increased from seventy in 1870 to eighty-five in 1880 and to 110 by 1896.[5] More professional societies appeared, moved by desires to raise the pay and prestige of engineers. In the 1880s the two most important of these were the American Society of Mechanical Engineers (ASME, 1880) and the American Institute of Electrical Engineers (AIEE, 1884).

Lehigh's School of General Literature also felt the influence of the growing importance of scientific and engineering education. All three of its courses, and especially those in Latin Scientific and Science and Letters, had strong sequences in mathematics, chemistry, and physics. Indeed, before 1890 the degree of Bachelor of Science was available only to graduates of the Latin Scientific and Science and Letters courses. It is reasonable to suspect that one reason for adding them to General Literature was a desire to increase the strength and attractiveness of the school. Possibly unanticipated consequences were an improvement in the humanistic education of students in technology and a potential for providing a broad general education for men who might later become teachers or practitioners in mathematics, science, or engineering.

Faculty and trustees overlooked the possibility of strengthening the School of General Literature by adding a course in business education. The Philadelphia industrialist Joseph Wharton, a personal friend of Coppée and Doolittle and a business associate of Sayre, Wilbur, and others on the boards of the iron company and the Lehigh Valley Railroad, in 1881 founded at the University of Pennsylvania a pilot project for educating youths interested in careers in commercial, financial, and civic fields. The Wharton School of Finance and Economy—the original name—was compatible with the objectives established by Asa Packer for Lehigh. Yet no one at Lehigh seems to have seriously studied it. The reason for this probably lies in ways in which decisions were made. Trustees who might have recognized the value of the Wharton experiment were reluctant to put pressure on the faculty to adopt new educational programs. President Lamberton was not an educator and provided no leadership in educational matters. Members of the faculty were indifferent toward projects unrelated to their special concerns. And so the School of General Literature leaned heavily to science and until a graduate of the Wharton School joined the faculty remained closed to education in business.

In 1883 the faculty returned to the subject of postgraduate work. They adopted a graduate program more modest but also more realistic than the one that had been devised during the Leavitt years. The program provided for independent study under supervision leading to the degrees of M.A., M.S., and Ph.D.

Like the earlier program this one was limited to students who had received a baccalaureate from Lehigh. Accordingly, it attracted few students, eight in 1883, increasing to a high of thirty-one in 1891.

The adoption of the graduate program is most notable as an indication of the leaning of various faculty toward the humanities and the sciences. In these fields advanced degrees had long been established in universities. This was not true for engineering. The lack of the word *bachelor* in the names of the degrees offered for work completed in the School of Technology indicates the position. The baccalaureate degrees of C.E., M.E., and E.M. were considered to be the highest degrees necessary for formal training in civil, mechanical, and mining engineering. A student who received a degree of this sort and wanted additional instruction satisfied his desire by taking other courses and, perhaps, earning a baccalaureate in another technological field, as Professor Williams had done, receiving an E.M. for work completed in the year following receipt of the A.C. degree. At Lehigh most of those who elected graduate work came from the Course in Analytical Chemistry or the School of General Literature, in which they had studied science. In fact, no M.S. degrees were awarded until 1891, when Joseph W. Richards (A.C. '86), received an M.S. in metallurgy en route to the Ph.D.

The faculty sought to enhance the quality of the university by improving the requirements for admission. They had good reason to be concerned, inasmuch as in the attempts to increase enrollments they were admitting a large proportion of students on condition. In 1881 31 of the 54 freshmen were conditionals. In 1884 conditionals numbered about half of the 123 freshmen.

From 1881 through 1888 the faculty yearly examined the entrance requirements for some or all of the courses of study. Professor Doolittle was especially assiduous in this regard. In 1881, for example, he studied admission in the technical departments of Harvard, Columbia, RPI, MIT, Princeton, Yale, Lafayette, Dartmouth, Cornell, Stevens, Johns Hopkins, and the universities of Cincinnati, Michigan, and Pennsylvania.

Improvements in the requirements for admission helped the School of Technology. In the early years of the 1880s some of the conditionals opted for the Latin Scientific and Science and Letters courses as being compatible with their poor preparation. When enrollments began reaching a level considered by faculty and trustees to be optimum, the faculty raised the entrance requirements for the Latin Scientific and the Science and Letters courses, and the number of applicants for these declined. In 1883 almost two-thirds of the students in General Literature had chosen these courses. By 1892 the comparable figure was one-third.

These tendencies helped to polarize the student body into classicals and technicals. The polarization can easily be exaggerated, however. The subjects studied by all of the students added up to from one-third to one-half of their respective totals. The educational bonds uniting the student body were stronger than any differing points of view stemming from membership in General Literature or Technology.

The students worked hard. The faculty, still officially blind to extracurricular activities, scheduled assignments and other academic exercises so as to take up all the time and leave the students wondering how they might "put a quart measure of work into a pint measure of time," as one student expressed the matter.[6] The faculty, while sympathetic, encouraging, and at times merciful, was also strict. Sometimes the students complained, but in general they accepted the discipline and even gloried in it.

Student opinion appeared in a magazine called the *Burr*, which began in 1881 as a monthly. As the *Burr* gained subscribers the issues appeared more frequently. Subscriptions financed it; the students wholly controlled it. The contents included news items, essays, editorials, poetry, short stories, and miscellaneous bits of information. Occasionally drawings appeared, and in later issues there were a few photographs. Almost all contributions were unsigned. Most of the factual material concerned matters at the university, although every issue also had brief items of happenings on other campuses. Shortly after the publication of the first issue the editors added a column of news of the alumni.

The pages of the *Burr* are studded with editorial comments collectively showing the pride of students in the educational aims of the university and in the reputation for hard work. Although some editorials criticized the technicals, others praised the commitment to occupational education and the mission of turning out educated engineers and businessmen in contrast to the old-style pseudoeducation of "Tom Browns." An editorial applauded Charles Francis Adams, Jr., for his desire to substitute the study of French and German for Greek and Latin. Others approved of the addition of physics as a requirement for admission to the university in the Latin Scientific and Classical courses; criticized the university for abolishing the preparatory department on the grounds that the move encouraged the admission of poorly prepared students; approved of the granting of a reading room to members of the student Society of Mechanical Engineering; ridiculed the teaching of Christian Evidences, not because of any fault of the professor, but because of the scant time given to it and the lack of student preparation in historical method; asked for elective courses; complained of the lack of instructors in Professor Ringer's department; and in various editorials asked that engineers be given a course in the common law and praised newly established offerings in hydraulics, electrical engineering, and photography. Criticism of the library for its lack of availability to students was common, as was criticism of a lack of edifying lectures by eminent people.

Students and faculty jointly participated in the Chemical Society, the Mining Club, and the Engineering Society—the parents of all course societies in the several branches of engineering. The Chemical and Engineering societies were the resurrected forms of the Chemical and Natural History Society and the Engineering Society that had disappeared in the depression years of the 1870s when enrollments were low. Both associations held meetings at which students read papers. The Chemical Society, unlike its predecessor, had no off-campus members. The Mining Club was an honorary open to juniors studying mining, metallurgy, and geology. Professor Williams had organized it in 1883 as a means of promoting interest in scholarship.

In June 1885 the Engineering Society began publishing a quarterly, the *Journal of the Engineering Society*, edited by the students. It contained papers by undergraduates on a variety of subjects, mostly in the fields of civil and mechanical engineering, and occasionally articles by the professors. Each issue contained alumni notes and reports of the proceedings of the society. Like all such ventures, the university expected the journal to be self-supporting. When in 1890 it did not pay its debts, the faculty ordered that it cease publication.

The living arrangements to which the students were subjected contributed little to unity. The trustees adhered to Packer's policy of "no dormitories." Until 1886 a few students lived in Saucon Hall, and when Saucon was put to instructional use, all had to find lodgings in hotels or with private families. The students, with much justice, complained of being overcharged. A writer for the *Burr* for September 1883 put the matter this way: "The greed of the average Bethlehemite who takes boarders is proverbial. He rents a little house for eight dollars a month, fills it with children and the odor of cabbage, and then wishes to rent his front room to the impecunious student for ten dollars a month."

Fraternities were not originally living organizations but, in view of the housing situation, soon became so. During the 1880s eleven fraternities appeared: Alpha Tau Omega (1882); Delta Phi, Psi Upsilon, and Theta Delta Chi (1884); Delta Upsilon (1885); Sigma Nu and Phi Gamma Delta (1886); Sigma Phi, Phi Delta Theta, and Sigma Chi (1887); and Delta Tau Delta (1888). In each fraternity as soon as the brothers were sufficiently numerous they rented or purchased a chapter house; and when financial conditions permitted, they hired a cook. Long before dormitories existed, about half of the student body was living in fraternities located off campus in the Bethlehems or Fountain Hill.

Eating arrangements also presented difficulties for most students. Those who lived in Saucon Hall were required to use the dining service in Christmas and complained of the quality. Many students formed eating clubs. The central figure of an eating club was usually a middle-aged or elderly woman who was willing to cook meals in her home. These clubs often took names, for example, the Cannibals, the Regulators, the Hefty Dining Club, and Skin and Bones for the one organized by students living at the Eagle Hotel. Some of the clubs fielded football and baseball teams.

Student complaints concerning board and room were unheeded except by a few alumni who as undergraduates had shared the experience. A detailed survey of the housing situation, made by the Alumni Association in 1888, ended with a recommendation that the university establish dormitories and a dining service. The recommendation went unheeded.

In spite of the official indifference to extracurricular activities, these were powerful for developing a collegial spirit. As yet no student government existed. Classes met informally and elected spokesmen. When they met together, the spokesman for the seniors presided. Most activities had little formal organization. Clubs seeming to have a continuous existence, such as the Glee Club and the dramatic society—known as Mustard and Cheese —were in actuality reorganized afresh every year.

Athletics attracted the most students. In the early 1880s, team sports at the collegiate level were still novelties. Some people treated them as fads and expected their popularity to disappear. Instead, student interest produced lasting loyalties and commitments. Instructors, professors, and alumni individually helped in coaching, refereeing, and managing. Most of the trustees became avid sports fans. The Lehigh Valley Railroad was always available for the free transportation of teams to away games.

The grading of the athletic fields in the autumn of 1882 provided a boost for interest in organized sports. Intercollegiate competition in football appeared the following year. The first game was with the University of Pennsylvania and was played on the Lehigh field with the visitors winning, 16 to 10. In the next year Lafayette hosted a contest with Lehigh and beat the Brown and White 52 to 0. Lawn tennis also appeared in 1883. Baseball and track and field, which had their origins at Lehigh in earlier years, increased in popularity as spring sports. In 1884 a Lehigh Lacrosse Club was founded. "No game has come up so quickly," wrote a contributor to the *Burr* of 20 February 1888.

The rising interest in organized sports resulted in the spring of 1884 in a reorganization of the Athletic Association. Membership was open to alumni in addition to students. The association was self-supporting on the basis of the members' small monthly dues. The students were firmly in control, having eight representatives on the thirteen-member Executive Committee. The association controlled the use and maintenance of the athelic grounds, the selection of captains and members of teams, and scheduling, although in practice most of the selection of team members was done by the captains, and the scheduling was controlled by the individual teams and the managers. In the fall of 1885 the constitution of the Athletic Association was revised, but in the essentials it remained as it had been drafted the year before.

During the 1880s four students were especially prominent in promoting the *Burr*, athletics, and other activities. One was Mark Anthony DeWolfe Howe (B.A. '86),[7] son of the president of the Lehigh board. In later life Howe was a prolific writer of poetry, histories, and biographies and an editor of the *Atlantic Monthly*. He wrote an autobiography, *A Venture in Remembrance*, which is refreshingly informative concerning student life of the times. The second student was Kenneth Frazier (B.A. '87), son of Professor Frazier. After being graduated from Lehigh, Kenneth studied art in Paris and London and became a portrait painter in New York City. The other two students were brothers, nephews of Professor Harding, Richard Harding and Charles Belmont Davis. Both were specials in General Literature. Richard remained for two years only, leaving in 1885 to finish his studies at Johns Hopkins. In later years he became a popular writer of adventure stories and a famous war correspondent. His brother Charles ('89) became an author of fiction and a dramatic critic. Charles wrote a biography of Richard, *Adventures and Letters of Richard Harding Davis*.

Howe, Frazier, and the Davis brothers formed a unique quartet. All participated in sports and were the principal stars of the Lawn Tennis Club. Frazier was the foremost illustrator for the *Burr* and the *Epitome*. His drawings, according to Howe, were "unblushingly in the manner of Du Maurier, which gave the first public intimation of Frazier's place among American artists." George Du Maurier was a writer and illustrator for *Puck* and author of the novels *Trilby* and *Peter Ibbetson*. Short stories by Richard Harding Davis appeared unsigned in the *Burr*. Richard was sometimes credited with having organized the first football team at Lehigh, although he correctly attributed the accomplishment to a fellow student, Jacob S. Robeson. Howe was principally responsible for organizing the Glee Club, of which J. Fred Wolle, the young organist of the Packer Memorial Church, was the conductor. Howe gave Richard Harding Davis credit for forming the dramatic Club, Mustard and Cheese, although Richard himself and Robeson claimed that Charles Belmont Davis was the principal organizer. The first dramatic production took place on the night of 10 April 1885, in the hall of the Sun Hotel. The plays were *Love and Money* by H. S. Haines, in which Richard Harding Davis played the lead, and *Sir Dagobert and the Dragon*, by F. C. Burnand, with Charles Davis in the part of the dragon. "The Davis brothers were certainly the stars of the evening," wrote a reviewer in the *Bethlehem Daily Times* for 11 April.

In effect, a wide range of activities claimed the attention of whoever was interested. Each year the students held several dances or hops, as they were called, using whatever facilities they could obtain permission for, for example, the drawing room in Packer Hall and the main floor of the Gymnasium. Faculty and trustees and their wives served as patrons and patronesses for the more important of these, which were duly reported in the *Bethlehem Daily Times* as though they were major social events. Students working in the photography laboratory in the chemistry building devoted much time to the art. Class dinners, the cane rush, and calculus cremation continued. In 1887 a ten-piece band made an appearance, followed several years later (1890) by a nine-piece orchestra. Other new societies included a Banjo Club (1885), a literary society called the Athanaeum (1886), an Episcopal Student Church Guild (1885), and a local chapter of the YMCA known as the Lehigh University Christian Association (LUCA) (1890).

LUCA took as a project the issuance of a handbook for incoming freshmen. The first appeared in 1890, a thin volume approximately two inches by four inches in size and containing a map of the campus as well as some general information about fraternities, athletics, and other subjects of interest to freshmen. The handbook retained this form for many years.

In classroom, laboratory, shop, and field, students and faculty worked together on terms of familiarity, made possible by their small numbers and their respect for the rights and duties associated with the status of each. Outside of the classroom the students adopted colloquial names for members of the teaching staff — "Dutchy" Ringer, "Snotty" Lambert — and reproduced these on the pages of the *Epitome* together with comments on classroom performance. The faculty took no official notice of such trivial offenses to dignity.

Although considerable turnover occurred among assistants and instructors in the decade following the death of Asa Packer, the faculty registered few changes. Among the professors of technical subjects, the only change was the resignation of James P. Kimball, who left in 1886 to become director of the mints in Washington, D.C. The trustees then terminated his position. On the nontechnical side, both of the professors in classics left in 1888 for teaching positions elsewhere. William A. Lamberton was replaced as professor of Greek by William A. Robinson, a graduate of Princeton. In the chair of Latin Languages and Literatures, Edward Morris Hyde (Trinity '73, and Ph.D., Yale '80) succeeded Henry C. Johnson.

The chaplaincy, which involved the teaching of Christian Evidences. philosophy, and psychology, exhibited the greatest turnover. By prearrangement, the Reverend Bird resigned upon completion of the Packer Memorial Church. At that time a convention of Episcopal Diocese of Central Pennsylvania placed the University on the same footing as a parish. The Right Reverend Nelson J. Rulison, assistant bishop to Howe, took charge of the university with assistance from the Reverend Albert W. Snyder, who assumed the teaching duties. The arrangement proved to be unsatisfactory. In 1889 Snyder resigned. The Reverend J. W. Kaye of Philadelphia became temporary chaplain. In the fall of 1890 the Reverend Elwood Worcester, who had studied at Columbia and in Germany, took the position.

The professional work of members of the faculty varied considerably. President Lamberton, technically a member of the faculty, was respected as a counselor and a disciplinarian but did little, if any, teaching. Severin

Ringer and the professors in classics taught much. Their outside activities, whatever these might have been, did not include significant scholarly publication. On the other hand, Coppée wrote and published on a variety of topics. Much of his work was scholarly. His title — professor of English literature, international and constitutional law, and the philosophy of history — indicates the breadth of his interests. He had become the grand old man of Lehigh, admired, respected, and sought after as a speaker on subjects ranging from art through literature and engineering.

The professors in technology were exceptionally busy with research, testing, and counseling. With the exception of Harding, they wrote and published much by way of articles, monographs, textbooks, translations of foreign works, and books representing original scholarship. A pamphlet, "Publications of the Professors, Instructors, and Alumni of Lehigh University, 1866–1893," prepared as a means of advertising Lehigh at the World Columbian Exposition in Chicago, contains the impressive record.

Much of the research and publication of the faculty in technology reflected the changing character of education in science and engineering. Whereas the Classical Course was relatively stable, the courses in science and engineering were in constant flux. Few studies remained definitive for long. No course in technology remained the same for more than a few years. In some the evolution was rapid.

Mansfield Merriman, in charge of civil engineering, provides an example of one who combined teaching with research, field work, and a broad concern for engineering education. In the 1880s he published three seminal books, *Method of Least Squares* (1884), *Mechanics of Materials* (1885), and *Treatise on Hydraulics* (1889). All three went through many editions. Merriman passed the summers from 1880 to 1885 as director of triangulation work in Pennsylvania for the U.S. Coast and Geodetic Survey. In the 1890s he was associate editor for Johnson's *Universal Encyclopedia* and for many years was joint editor with R. S. Woodward of *Mathematical Monographs* (21 Vols., 1896–1921). Merriman was in 1895 the fourth president of the Society for the Promotion for Engineering Education (SPEE), founded 1893, the original name of the American Society of Engineering Education (ASEE).

Merriman introduced the study of hydraulic and sanitary engineering to Lehigh. In the autumn of 1886 he moved an old red barn to a spot beside the stream on the eastern side of the campus on or near the site of the present Williams Hall. Chemistry had used the barn but, with the completion of the Chemical Laboratory, no longer needed it. Merriman converted it into a hydraulics laboratory, said to be the first in the United States.

A second course of study for which Merriman may have been responsible was that of Architecture. Students were asking for it. The Department of Civil Engineering already offered most of the studies considered necessary. The trustees approved the course in 1888; it was opened to students in the fall of 1889 under the direction of Ralph M. Wilcox, instructor in civil engineering.

Edward H. Williams, Jr., provides an example of a professor whose activities touched almost every part of university life. He was president of the Alumni Association from 1884 to 1886 and later served as archivist, in which capacity he originated the archives in the Linderman Library. He also held office as president of the Chemical and Natural History Society and the Engineering Society and in 1884 organized the Mining Club, a sort of prelude to his formation of Tau Beta Pi and Phi Beta Kappa. In 1886 he published the first history of Lehigh University, the *20-Year Book*.[8]

Williams probably came as close as anyone could to expressing the spirit pervading the university. He championed athletics and student publications, especially the *Burr*, while never forgetting that they were strictly extracurricular and must not be allowed to interfere with studies; and with reservations he upheld the fraternity as an appropriate social organization, he being a member of Psi Upsilon.

Like Merriman, Williams was interested in broad issues of education. On two occasions he addressed the Engineering Society on the subject and, in both, stressed the potential of engineering for contributing to liberal studies. His work in founding chapters of Tau Beta Pi and Phi Beta Kappa expresses as well as anything a faith in the liberating possibilities of engineering education. He had first organized the Mining Club and, finding its scope limited to a small group of technicals, turned to the formation of an association with broader membership. Williams was apparently influenced in the form he gave Tau Beta Pi by his perception of Phi Beta Kappa, which had in 1883 been organized nationally as the United Chapters. Williams worked alone in organizing Tau Beta Pi in 1885. Membership was open to all technical students who during their first three years had maintained standing in the top quarter of their class and were otherwise qualified.

Tau Beta Pi soon became a national honorary. In 1892 a second chapter was formed, this by a former Lehigh instructor, Professor Lester Breckenridge at Michigan State University. By 1906 the honorary had fourteen chapters and began publishing a magazine, the *Bent*, which from 1906 to 1908 went out to members from Bethlehem. (In 1930, three years before Williams died, Tau Beta Pi had 58 chapters. In 1985 it had 172.)

Williams worked with others in obtaining a charter for Phi Beta Kappa. The petition from Lehigh went forward to the United Chapters in 1884, the year before Williams organized Tau Beta Pi. Williams was not then a member of Phi Beta Kappa. Bishop Howe belonged, having been inducted into the Alpha of Rhode Island (Brown University), as did Professor Johnson, a member of the Cornell chapter who had originally been initiated at Hobart. As Williams later explained the sequence of events, Johnson suggested that Williams become a member and arranged for him to join the chapter at Hobart. When this had been done, Johnson sent in the application signed by himself, Bishop Howe, Williams, and two instructors. On 1 September 1886, the Council of the United Chapters accepted the application. Williams later wrote of the event: "I very well remember the feeling of pleasure when it was decided that a Phi Beta Kappa chapter was to be granted to Lehigh. Before that event, and the missionary work a few of us did to induce the granting of the chapter, Lehigh was looked upon as an abode of 'greasy mechanics' — pardon the simile, — and was also looked upon, askance, by the colleges given entirely to humane letters, such as were persons 'in trade' by the ancient aristocracy."[9]

Membership in the PBK chapter at Lehigh was open to any junior of high academic standing who showed himself "eminent in *literae humaniores*," irrespective of his course of study. In 1900 the maximum number of technicals who could be admitted in any one year was limited to four.

Professor Harding had the task of introducing the study of electrical engineering into Lehigh. He was a physicist at a time when engineers looked upon physics as a service discipline and a culture study, incapable of forming the basis of any career but teaching. A minute passed by the faculty on the occasion of Harding's retirement expessed the sentiment: "It was his duty to teach the subject of physics in such a way as to impart at once the broadening influence of a 'culture study,' and the thorough mastery of the principles of physical science needed by future engineers and chemists."[10] Harding did this well. By all accounts he was a great teacher.

In the early 1880s most of the nation's leading centers of engineering education had established an electrical course or were planning to do so. In 1884 Harding began a one-year Sequence in Electrical Engineering designed for specials. The course was immediately successful. Thirteen students signed for it. By 1887 the total enrollment had risen to twenty-three. On 16 October 1886 the trustees agreed to a four-year sequence in "Physical Engineering," as they first called it.

In the history of Lehigh three newly introduced undergraduate courses of study have been almost immediately successful. One was Electrical Engineering (the other two were Business Administration and Industrial Engineering). In the second year of its existence as a four-year sequence, Electrical Engineering enrolled 75 students and was second in numbers to Civil Engineering, which had 123 students.

No one was prepared for the sudden popularity. Harding improvised while the trustees hastened to provide the necessary facilities and equipment. They renovated Saucon Hall as a physical laboratory and when in a few years it proved inadequate, began seeking funds for a new building. Eventually they borrowed the money from the Asa Packer Estate. By 1895 the campus had an imposing new structure, located across the stream east of the Chemical Laboratory and slightly down the slope from it.

Mining was probably the field in which Lehigh helped the most to fill a national need. The coal fields wanted mining engineers. By 1892 Lehigh was fourth in the nation in terms of numbers of graduates in the field. Lehigh had by then turned out forty-eight E.M.s. The University of California, a supplier for the mines of the far west, was in third place with fifty-five (first and second places respectively went to the Columbia School of Mines with 402 and M.I.T. with 126).[11]

Lehigh's Course in Mining and Metalluragy had a late start. It began with the arrival in 1871 of Benjamin Frazier, a skilled mathematician with a large interest in metallurgy. Instruction in civil and mechanical engineering was basic to mining, and most of Frazier's pupils had previously earned a degree in one of these fields. Following the appointment of Williams as professor of mining and geology in 1882, mining and metallurgy became a five-year course.

The course contained the seeds of future growth, particularly in the direction of metallurgy and geology. The first development was in metallurgy. In 1890 Frazier brought about the formation of a four-year Course in Metallurgy leading to the degree of B.S. (in metallurgy) as an adjunct to the Course in Mining and Metallurgy; and the following year a similar option was approved for Mining. This essentially reduced Mining to a four-year course, although another four years elapsed before the degree of E.M. was given for completing a four-year sequence.

The alumni as a group were relatively inactive during the 1880s and 1890s. Most of them were busy making their careers. Four served as nonvoting members of the Board of Trustees. Following the death of Harry Packer, none was a charter trustee until the election of Henry S. Drinker (E.M.'71) in 1893. One (Williams) was a member of the faculty. The Alumni Association had as yet no paid executive secretary or staff. Turnouts for reunions during commencement week were small. Twenty-nine attended the annual meeting in 1884, and thirty-nine attended two years later.

During the 1880s the Alumni Association continued the practice of advising faculty and trustees on educational matters. Believing that the graduates, especially the technicals, were being held back in their careers by lack of experience in public speaking, the Alumni Association established in 1884 an oratorical contest for juniors as part of an annual celebration of the birthday of George Washington. Faculty were enthusiastic, the students less so. The caliber of the performances, according to the *Burr*, left much to be desired. Still, for several decades the contest remained a fixture of the junior year.

In 1884 the association submitted to the trustees a report complaining of the low salaries of professors and instructors, the small number of instructors, and the lack of fixed standards of scholarship. The trustees sent the report to the faculty, which took no action. In 1885 the association planned for the four alumni trustees to form a sort of visiting committee that would annually draft "a report upon the condition of the university as regards the efficiency of its operations and its response to fulfilling institutional goals."[12] The first report drafted by the alumni trustees appeared in 1886 and consisted of twenty-eight printed pages ending with a list of thirty-three recommendations. Again the trustees shifted the report over to the faculty, which delayed consideration but finally rejected outright thirteen of the recommendations, found eight to be already in force, declared three more to be ideally good but probably impractical, and accepted two as good and practicable. The remainder were ignored.

In February 1888, the faculty received from the alumni trustees a polite request for guidance in how best to act "in furthering the advancement of the institution." The faculty responded that the best ways would be to hire Lehigh graduates, promote publicity for the university, and assist in admission.

And yet, the Alumni Association persisted in giving advice. Another report, drafted in 1888, used the term *suggestions* in place of *recommendations*. The report emphasized a need for improving education in existing fields and questioned the advisability of continuing the School of General Literature. This weak gesture of hostility toward General Literature provoked an immediate outcry from the students. After some discussion, the report was tabled.

A wave of optimism accompanied Lehigh's entrance into the decade of the 1890s. Enrollment attained a high of 414 in the fall of 1890 and set a new record of 527 in 1891.

The trustees agreed that enrollment was high enough and voted to re-establish tuition at one hundred dollars per year for the technicals and sixty dollars for students in the School of General Literature, effective 1 January, 1892. In the fall of that year the enrollment set a record of 569. That was six and one-half times what it had been thirteen years earlier.

Performance in intercollegiate sports was improved. Beginning in 1888 the Lehigh Eleven had a succession of winning seasons and in the next two years took brief southern tours. Victories over Lafayette became almost monotonous. In 1890 the lacrosse team won the intercollegiate championship, and spectators at Lehigh began using a grandstand, built with money donated by Robert P. Linderman (Ph.B. '83) and the Alumni Association.

In 1889 the Borough of South Bethehem annexed the land south of Packer Avenue in order to control the runoff from the many streams. During the next few years, Packer Avenue, which had been little more than a country lane, was paved. The trustees bought about ninety-seven acres up the mountain, thereby gaining control of the sources of water that supplied the older buildings. They also built a small addition to Packer Hall to meet the needs of President Lamberton. The addition contained three rooms adjacent to the second story on the south side of the building and was supported by arches over the roadway.

Membership in the Alumni Association was increasing. In 1890 alumni clubs appeared in Philadelphia, New York, and Chicago; these were soon followed by clubs in Pittsburgh, Washington, and Northeastern Pennsylvania (Scranton). The association financed a scholarship and in 1893 gave one thousand dollars to reduce the debt of the Athletic Association.

A new face appeared in the presidency of the Board of Trustees. Bishop

Howe retired in 1891. The Right Reverend Nelson S. Rulison took charge of the diocese and became president of the Lehigh board.

The optimism that ushered in the decade was fortunate, as it helped the trustees and the faculty to meet some trials. The first began with the threat of a major economic depression. The railroads were in trouble. Bad management and rising costs were making profits disappear. By 1891 several large roads defected on loans, and the banks that had financed them failed.

The depression became a reality. The fortunes of the Lehigh Valley Railroad followed those of many other railroads. Although earnings had soared, costs per ton-mile had also increased. A lengthy strike in 1893 cut into revenues. In 1894 the company was forced to the first of a series of decisions to pay no dividends on its stock. In 1894 and 1895 the Asa Packer Estate was able to give the university small sums by selling some shares of stock; but when the prices of railroad securities plunged, this could not be continued. After 1895 the estate paid the university nothing.

At the time, Lehigh University was heavily in debt. The most recent loan had been made to finance the Physical Laboratory. In 1894 the trustees consolidated all debts with the estate. The sum then owed by the university stood at $428,112.42 at 5 percent per annum, secured by a first mortgage.

As the financial crisis developed, on 1 September, 1893 President Lamberton died of an apoplectic stroke. Coppée became acting president for the last time; and when on 21 March, 1895 he died, Professor Chandler took the position.

President Lamberton's death aggravated the financial problem. New presidents are expensive, not only for salary but also because of the opportunities that they must have for putting their ideas into practice. The trustees had to find a president when they could least afford the expense.

The trustees took steps to reduce expenses. They urged the faculty to consider reducing the number of instructors and in 1893 voted to curtail the care taken of the University Park. This meant abandoning the flower beds, that for over a decade had beautified the campus. A writer for the *Burr* lamented the decision. "There has always been one bed that has gone by the name of the graduating class of that year. Could not this at least be kept?"[13] It could not, and succeeding generations of Lehigh students had a campus of lawns, trees, and shrubs but no flowers. Repairs were postponed. The museum was allowed to decline, and in succeeding yars its collections were dispersed to the departments.

The graduate program became a casualty of the move to reduce expenses. The program had been slowly gaining momentum. In 1891 the university had awarded its first M.S. degree to Joseph W. Richards, and in 1894 it awarded a second M.S., this time in chemistry, to Herman E. Kiefer. Both students were continuing work for the doctorate. In 1894 the faculty declared a moratorium on other candidates for the Ph.D. Richards and Kiefer received their doctorates in 1895 and 1896 respectively, but there were no more. Although several other students received an M.S. or an M.A., the number of graduate students declined until a low of nine was reached in the fall of 1899. All told, from 1894 to 1900, Lehigh awarded only five M.S. and two M.A. degrees.

E. P. Wilbur was still president of the Lehigh Valley Railroad. Robert H. Sayre, Jr., superintended the works of the Bethlehem Iron Company. Together the men provided leadership for the Asa Packer Estate and the Lehigh Board of Trustees.

Their first concern was for protecting the estate, on which everything depended. Although pinched for money, its position was not hopeless. For one thing, the finances of the Lehigh Valley Railroad were in better shape than those of many other railroads. The Lehigh Valley did not become bankrupt. Also, the estate was able to benefit from the prosperity of the Bethlehem Iron Company. In 1887 the iron company had won bids for supplying the U.S. Navy with armor plate and guns, heavy forgings requiring a much different plant and equipment from that used for turning out rails. The national government was modernizing the navy and was willing to pay unusually high prices in order to encourage domestic steel companies to make the necessary technological changes. At the start of this transition, when prices were low, the Asa Packer Estate had acquired large amounts of Bethlehem Iron stock. When from 1894 to 1897 the railroad paid no dividends, Bethlehem Iron paid respectively 12, 6, 6, and 8 percent. In 1897, when Lehigh Valley stock (par $50) was lucky to be trading at $25, Bethlehem Iron stock (also par $50) traded in a few private sales at $150. Because of this appreciation, the estate possessed a reserve that could, in case of need, be transformed into cash.

These prospects probably helped Wilbur, Sayre, and the other trustees at Lehigh in securing a replacement for Lamberton. They appointed a committee consisting of William H. Sayre, Henry S. Drinker, and Eckley B. Coxe to conduct a search. The committee at first apparently looked for an efficient administrator, someone with qualities resembling those of the late President Lamberton.[14] In the end they secured an applied chemist who was both an administrator and an educator. The success came largely through the efforts of Coxe, whose industry, research, and large views on education had led some people to suggest him as a possibility. The man chosen was Thomas Messinger Drown, then teaching and administering chemistry and chemical engineering at MIT.

Drown had done postgradute study at Yale, Harvard, Freiburg, and Heidelberg and had worked in a private chemical laboratory in Philadelphia. In 1874 he became professor of chemistry at Lafayette College. There, he quickly developed a reputation as an excellent teacher and a builder of the curricula in applied science and engineering. His strength and drive to expand engineering and the sciences at Lafayette made him enemies. David B.

Skillman in his history of Lafayette College calls Drown "one of the strongest men ever connected with Lafayette" and describes the cause of his frustration as "the conflict between the old education and the new, between the classical and the scientific, then raging in many institutions."[15] In 1881 Drown resigned and returned to private practice. Two years later the Lehigh Alumni Association invited him to give an address at commencement time. He was then ending ten years of service as secretary of the AIME and editor of its principal publication, the *Transactions*. The address, "Technical Training," was later printed. In 1885 he moved to MIT.

Drown began his tenure as president of Lehigh with the fall semester 1895. On Founder's Day of that year he delivered what might be called an inaugural address, "The Educational Value of Engineering Studies." Twelve years had gone by since he had last addressed the members of the university on the same topic. Then he had expressed a fear that industrialists would back off from hiring college-trained engineers. Now, that fear was gone. He was ready to go beyond the topic of the utility of the educated engineer to industry and assert his usefulness to society at large. "My object is to show, if I can, that a course of engineering study liberally planned and faithfully carried out is capable of making not only a broadly educated man but one whose enthusiasm for truth and truth-seeking has been kindled to a living flame."

Engineering subjects, properly taught, Drown continued, would be "morally as well as intellectually elevating. To all minds this will not be the case, but to some the consciousness that the hidden laws of nature reveal themselves to him who seeks with patient thought and work, brings with it a sense of oneness with nature, and fellowship with the great minds to whom she tells her secrets." He noted that scientists and engineers so trained were amply competent to take the lead in public as well as professional affairs. Properly organized, engineering education was as liberating as anything taught on the classical side. "When the educational value of an engineering education is fully appreciated, we may have students seeking these schools for the training they afford without regard to the practice of any of the engineering professions."[16]

Drown was careful to describe the conditions under which the ideal could be obtained. One was good teaching, especially in engineering subjects. Another was exposing the students to the "broadening and humanizing influence of culture studies." Here, Drown, in company with all engineering educational reformers, had to deal with the reality of courses being too tightly sequenced with scientific, service, and engineering studies to allow much room for cultural broadening. To get around this difficulty he proposed three avenues for acquiring cultural breadth. The first was promotion of interaction between the technicals and the classicals. "The intimate association of students of engineering and of the students of the classics and literature ought to be of great advantage to both." The second avenue was that of promoting educationally related activities such as the course societies and establishing lecture series with required attendance by the students. The third avenue was extending the period of undergraduate education from four to five or six years in order to allow college-level study of cultural subjects to precede and overlap the course in engineering.

Drown's ideas on education involved a clear indication of priorities for Lehigh. He would improve the School of Technology, the main thrust; and he would support the School of General Literature as necessary to engineering education, making sure that it first served its own best interests in making preprofessional education available for would-be lawyers, ministers, physicians, businessmen, and others. Then and only then could its students, teachers, and courses help to produce the intelligent, well-rounded, and responsible engineers who were natural leaders for an industrializing America. If each school regarded first its own welfare, together they would solve the continuing problem of serving the best interests of the university and its clientele in the valley, the commonwealth, and the nation.

At the end of his first year as president, Drown reported to the trustees, "The engineering equipment of the University is very much behind the colleges of the same rank as Lehigh, and we cannot long compete with these colleges without more complete engineering laboratories and apparatus." The quality of instruction, he wrote, was very high.[17]

Undoubtedly the trustees stirred uneasily in their chairs.

The money was not there. Income from tuition covered only a small part of current expenses. A rumor that the university might have to close was hurting enrollments, which fell from the high of 569 in 1892 to 415 by September 1895 and to 365 a year later.

Nothing much was to be expected from the Alumni Association, whose members were young and had developed no tradition of giving. The trustees did what they could. They received loans of sixty thousand dollars from the E. P. Wilbur Trust Company and thirty thousand dollars each from Wilbur and Sayre. Initially these loans were unsecured. Over the next several years various persons gave money, including Drinker, Mary Packer Cummings, John Fritz, and Mrs. Eckley Coxe. Wilbur and Sayre occasionally begged money from suppliers of the railroad and the iron company.

The library was the one place in which substantial savings could be obtained. It had not been included in the mortgage given to secure the loan made by the estate to the university, being already separately mortgaged. Also, the library had in the past used part of its income to buy other securities. These continued to provide it with money after the railroad passed its dividends and were available for such disposition as the trustees of the university might want to make. In short, the library was ripe for plucking. In 1898 J. D. Brodhead, the university's counsel, arranged for transferring the first mortgage on the library to Wilbur and Sayre as security for their loans. As Brodhead pointed out, this put Sayre and Wilbur effectively in possession of the library. Sayre and Wilbur then arranged for it and its assets to be transferred to the university and for the remaining securities, such as were not needed to secure loans, to be sold. Thereafter, the library received appropriations from the university the same as the other departments, and for the next few years, those appropriations were slim. The purchase of books temporarily came to an end; the library was closed during the summer months; and the Library Committee of the board was disbanded. Duplicate copies of books were ordered to be sold—but not the collection of rare books and manuscripts.

Borrowing from Sayre and Wilbur was primarily responsible for keeping the university afloat from 1895 to 1897. And after that? The trustees cherished a hope of receiving money from the Commonwealth of Pennsylvania. Drown, Drinker, Wilbur, and Sayre went to Harrisburg on 13 January, 1897 and saw Governor Daniel H. Hastings and the attorney general, who were sympathetic but pointed out that the state could not legally aid a sectarian institution.

The university men returned to South Bethlehem. Ten days later the trustees formally dropped the connection with the Episcopal Diocese of Central Pennsylvania and passed a resolution affirming that Lehigh was not and never had been under the control of the church. This was technically true; Lehigh had been affiliated with the church but the church had not actually controlled it. The trustees then formally requested two hundred thousand dollars of the commonwealth. They received seventy-five thousand for each of the next two years, enough to keep the university operating.

Still, the university was in danger as long as the Asa Packer Estate remained insecure, for the estate held the university's mortgage. Shortly after money was received from the commonwealth, the trustees of the estate negotiated with the Drexel Company of Philadelphia for a loan. The Drexel Company was the Philadelphia arm of J. Pierpont Morgan. The Drexel Company granted the loan under the condition that the estate put up most of its Lehigh Valley Railroad stock and a large amount of iron company stock as security. This also meant ceding control over the railroad to the Drexel-Morgan interests. Wilbur retired as president of the railroad and was replaced by Alfred Walker, a representative of the Drexel-Morgan people. Lehigh University lost its privileges in using the railroad. But the estate was saved.

In 1897 Bishop Rulison died. Sayre became president of the Lehigh board, the first layman to hold the position.

On the campus President Drown took command, but with respect for the rights of the faculty in educational matters. The optimism that had received a shock upon the death of Lamberton returned. Soon members of the faculty were referring to Drown as "chief."

Even before Drown gave his Founder's Day address, faculty action was producing changes agreeable with his ideas. One of these was the addition of summer sessions for the technicals. The summer sessions had the double object of augmenting the students' acquaintance with engineering practice and making more room during the academic year for scientific studies. The pilot session began in 1893 and was a surveying course held near Coxe's mines at Freeland for civil engineering students. Other summer sessions were held beginning in 1896. Most of the summer schools were at first optional but soon were made compulsory. By 1904 they were required of all the technicals except students in Chemistry for at least two of their three summers as undergraduates.

Also, the faculty had done much before the arrival of Drown to promote lectures by outsiders as a means of expanding the scope of general education. In the country at large, lectures, sermons, and orations were popular. In the northeastern section of the United States much of the activity centered on the Chautauqua movement. In the area dominated by Philadelphia, an organization known as the American Society for the Extension of University Teaching became active. It sponsored extension lectures in a number of communities, including the Bethlehems, for about five years, beginning in 1892. Several Lehigh professors gave series of lectures. The faculty wanted more. They could not control the scheduling of extension lectures or effectively require students to attend. They were at work on a better system when Drown arrived. Out of their efforts came the University Lecture Series, an institution that was maintained with some stops and starts until 1928. Most of the lecturers were experts from off the campus. Four lectures were given during the first year, 1895−96. By 1900−1901 there were twelve annual lectures. All were open to the public. Jim Myers took attendance slips from Lehigh students at the door.

While planning for improvements in the Schools of General Literature and Technology, Drown fully cooperated with the trustees in attempts to save money. He closed out the Course in Architecture, which had few students. He and the faculty put forth a special effort to publicize the university. Bulletins appeared advertising the several courses of study. The Alumni Association undertook publication of a forty-six-page booklet by Professor Hyde, *Lehigh University, Historical Sketch*, originally written for a class book sponsored by the class of '96. Drown did not insist on capital improvements, however necessary these appeared. The Physical Laboratory was the last building to be constructed until after the financial crisis ended.

The trustees did not insist on saving money by replacing professors with instructors. In 1895 Professor Doolittle left to take charge of the Flower Observatory at the University of Pennsylvania. Drown and the trustees immediately replaced him with a mathematician of experience, Charles L. Thornburg, who had a Ph.D. from Vanderbilt. Upon the death of Coppée, the university hired as a professor William C. Thayer, who had studied at Columbia, Göttingen, and Johns Hopkins. When Lehigh attempted to "make do" with an instructor in electrical engineering, trouble arrived.

Harding, the professor of physics, was in charge of electrical engineering.

Harding had no experience in the field and was moreover aging and half deaf. In 1894 the junior electricals sent a protest to the trustees, alleging "that the course of instruction in the E.E. course was not in touch with the present advanced state of electrical science and invention, and that it was not such as to give them the best attainable preparation for the profession of Electrical Engineer." The faculty recommended that the corrective should be separate departments for physics and electrical engineering. The trustees demurred, recognizing that separate departments would involve a new professorial slot, which they could ill afford. They authorized Harding "to so organize his corps of assistants, that his staff shall embrace in the coming year one competent instructor in physics, and two instructors competent to take charge of instruction in Electricity and Electrical Engineering."[18] Harding thereupon arranged for an instructor in electrical engineering while he remained head of physics.

Still the arrangement was unsatisfactory. Enrollments were down. The following year Harding improved the situation somewhat by bringing in an internationally famous English mathematician, Dr. Alexander Macfarlane, who had been at the University of Texas. Macfarlane became a lecturer at Lehigh in charge of the electricals. The solution was temporary, for he was unavailable for a full-time appointment.

President Drown inherited the problem. Shortly after taking office, he persuaded Harding to become a professor emeritus, the first with the title in the history of the university. The trustees in 1897 approved for him an annual retirement salary of twelve hundred dollars. Drown then brought in William S. Franklin to take charge of physics and electrical engineering. Franklin had studied at the University of Kansas, Berlin, Harvard, and Cornell, where he was working for a Ph.D. degree (which he received in 1901.) Brilliant, personable, active in professional societies, and popular as a teacher, Franklin published, in coauthorship with Edward L. Nichols of Cornell, a three-volume series of texts entitled *The Elements of Physics*.[19] Franklin continued to write and publish, usually in collaboration with others. For the time being, the problem with physics and electrical engineering was solved.

In 1897 Drown asked the faculty for advice on a proposal to create junior faculty ranks of assistant and associate professor, which would make possible an increase in the number of experienced teachers without initially causing more expenditure. The faculty were well pleased with the rank of assistant professor, and the trustees made the addition. The following year the faculty agreed to allow assistant professors to vote in faculty meetings.

Possibly the faculty had some misgivings concerning the associate professorship. The minutes of the faculty and the trustees are silent on the subject. In the sequel, the trustees may have approved both ranks, although no one was made an associate professor until 1910, when several of the assistant professors were promoted.

No more important change than this was ever made in the composition of the faculty. Until 1897 the faculty consisted only of full professors, all of whom, with the exception of Williams, had been educated and had made their reputations elsewhere. Lehigh alumni who wanted a career in college teaching might begin at Lehigh as assistants or instructors but would soon have to leave for jobs at other institutions, being unable to qualify for a full professorship at their alma mater. Now some of these might remain and receive promotion to the rank of assistant professor and from that level expect to reach the top.

Action concerning assistant professorships was immediate. A few days after the rank was established, Drown recommended three Lehigh alumni for promotion, Joseph W. Richards, Arthur E. Meaker (C.E. '75), and Preston A. Lambert (B.A. '83, M.A., '91). By 1904 two Lehigh alumni had passed through the ranks of instructor and assistant professor to full professor—Richards, who became professor of metallurgy, and Howard Eckfeldt (B.S. [Met.] '95, E.M. '96), who took charge of the miners following Williams's retirement.

In spite of the uncertain financial situation, Drown assumed the role of a builder. With the faculty behind him, in 1896 he presented the Executive Committee of the board with a convincing case for strengthening general literature: "The classical course is in a most unsatisfactory condition. . . . I think it highly desirable that an earnest effort be made to secure students in this department, feeling convinced that if we can get the classical tide turned in our direction it will continue to flow with increasing volume. In order to do this we must convince the public and the preparatory schools that we are prepared to give as good a course leading to the degree of Bachelor of Arts as other colleges our size."[20]

Drown asked the Executive Committee for a professorship in history and political science and suggested free tuition scholarships for students in General Literature.

In June 1897, the Executive Committee approved a chair in history and economics. Drown secured the services of John L. Stewart, a graduate of the Wharton School at the University of Pennsylvania, to give university lectures on these subjects for the coming academic year. Stewart proved to be an excellent lecturer. In the spring of 1898 the trustees appointed him as professor at a top salary.

The trustees were also agreeable to scholarships as a means of increasing enrollments in the School of General Literature. The few scholarships that had existed during the period of no tuition had the character of being prizes or loans. The oldest and most prestigious of these was the Wilbur Scholarship, an annual award of two hundred dollars to the member of the sophomore class with the best record. Several other scholarships were provided by the Alumni Association, the trustees, and a few benefactors. Until 1898 all but a few of these went to students in technology. Drown did not necessarily object to this but wanted to use scholarships to build up the School of

General Literature. Special incentives were needed to tempt students in the humanities to enter a predominately technical university. In 1898 he recommended and the trustees approved two other sorts of scholarships. One was called "postponement of tuition." The recipient put off paying tuition until after graduation, when he was employed (this form of scholarship was continued for many years and benefited a great many Lehigh students). The other sort was called an "honorary scholarship." The trustees authorized Drown to allocate four-year scholarships to secondary schools of exceptionally high standing and ask their principals to award them to the better students. Honorary scholarships were first given in 1899, forty-two being allocated among twenty-five secondary schools.[21] In that year eight out of eighteen or 44.4 percent of the freshmen entering in General Literature had an honorary scholarship, whereas only 22.3 percent of the entering technicals had one.

Several replacements helped to sustain the School of General Literature. One was a chaplain, the Reverend Langdon C. Stewardson. The chaplaincy had been vacant for a year. The Reverend Elwood Worcester had married one of Bishop Rulison's daughters, received a leave of absence to study in Germany, and then accepted a pastorate in Philadelphia. His replacement for a year had been the Reverend Dr. Tolafiero F. Caskey, director of the American church in Dresden, Germany. Stewardson arrived in 1897 as acting chaplain, becoming chaplain the following year.

Few professors have had as great an impact on Lehigh in as short a time as did Stewardson. A graduate of Kenyon College and the Episcopal Seminary in Philadelphia, he had studied philosophy and higher education at Tübingen and Berlin and had gained a measure of renown for both preaching and scholarship. The trustees accorded him the honor of delivering the Founder's Day address in 1898, the second year of his tenure. His sermons were popular with the townspeople and his lectures pleased the students, who dedicated the 1903 *Epitome* to him. He inspired a reorganization of the LUCA with a permanent secretary to hold it together and gave a completely secular tone to his teaching of philosophy and psychology. He left in 1903 to become president of Hobart.

Replacements occurred in 1899 for both of the professorships in the classics. Charles J. Goodwin, who had studied in Berlin and had a doctorate from Johns Hopkins, succeeded William A. Robinson as professor of Greek. Robert W. Blake, who had studied at Erlangen and Princeton, took over the professorship in Latin from Hyde, who left to become dean of the college at Ursinus.

As soon as Drown took office he began work on a program combining engineering and cultural studies. On 16 December, 1895, the faculty approved a program permitting students in the literary courses to substitute technical subjects for required work in the junior and senior years, receive an appropriate baccalaureate degree, and then take the remaining technical subjects for a degree in engineering. The general literature Course of Science and

Letters was then closed out. Drown in 1896 informed the trustees that the program of "combined courses ... has attracted much attention among educators, and is believed to be the first formal scheme of this character that has been proposed by any college."[22] Few students elected the program, though. The *Register* for 1899–1900 was the first to contain reference to the "Arts-Engineering" program under the heading, "Combination of Literary and Technical Studies."

No new programs for the School of Technology appeared until the financial situation eased and enrollments rose, both of which were coincidental with a national increase of economic prosperity and the final stages of the war with Spain. The total number of students, which reached a low of 325 in the fall of 1898, bounced back in 1899 to 415, the same number as for the fall of 1895. Within the next several years the faculty added five new programs to the School of Technology.

Two of the new courses of instruction had a brief existence. One was Geology, the special field of Professor Williams, which attracted several students and was closed out shortly before Williams's retirement in 1906. The other was Marine Engineering, which was probably influenced by a flurry of naval activity during the war. There is no record of any students enrolling in the course.

Metallurgy and Electrometallurgy were two other new courses of instruction. Metallurgy had begun as a separation from mining in 1891, when the faculty had approved a four-year course leading to the degree of B.S. (Met.). In 1898 the faculty accepted the awarding of a Met. E. degree. Professor Allison Butts wrote in *Ninety-Seven Years of Metallurgy at Lehigh University*, "Lehigh was among the very first schools to adopt this cleavage between mining and metallurgy. Others began to follow, but it was a slow development."

Electrometallurgy grew out of metallurgy largely as a result of work done by a star pupil of Professor Frazier, Joseph W. Richards. As an undergraduate in chemistry, Richards had written a senior thesis on aluminum, which he enlarged and published a year later. Following several years of work for his father in a plant involving the recovery and classification of scrap metals, he returned to Lehigh for graduate study and, except for a year at Heidelberg (1897–98), remained at Lehigh for the rest of his life. He earned the first Ph.D. given by the university and became interested in the new fields of electrometallurgy and electrochemistry. In 1901 he helped to found the American Electrochemical Society. In that year, too, the Lehigh faculty approved a Course in Electrometallurgy leading to the degree of El. Met.

Richards became the first president of the American Electrochemical Society and, from 1904 until his death in 1921, the society's secretary and editor of its *Transactions*. In later life he was best known for a three-volume work, *Metallurgical Calculations* (1906–8). Nine years after his death the American Electrochemical Society established a series of annual lectures in his honor.

The fifth new course in technology was Chemical Engineering, a field that Drown had administered during his years at MIT. Professor Chandler proposed the course at Lehigh in 1899; the first students were registered in 1902. Professor Harry Maas Ullmann structured the course and wrote of the formation, "It was Dr. Drown's opinion that the arrangement at MIT. was in his time too strong in Mechanical Engineering and rather weak in Chemistry. As laid out here at Lehigh, 'in this course the training is essentially chemical and the graduates are primarily chemists with a good knowledge of Mechanical Engineering.'"[23]

The financial crisis barely touched student life. The teacher-student relationship was unchanged. Students were more interested in studies, activities, and the fads and fashions of everyday existence than in the organization and operation of the university. Their rights of petition and control were unaffected; and their activities, including sports, did not greatly depend on the financial condition of the university. To be sure, smaller enrollments meant fewer men available for athletic teams. This possibly accounted in part for a decline in winning seasons for all sports in the later years of the decade. In 1894 Lafayette began a winning streak in football, which held few bright spots for Lehigh until 1910.

The manufacture of heavy forgings by the Bethlehem Iron Company was bringing in immigrants from central and southern Europe and creating an almost chronic housing shortage for Lehigh students. Two new fraternities appeared in 1894, Kappa Alpha and Chi Psi. No other chapters were organized until 1900, when Kappa Sigma came in.

The decade of the nineties was a time of great political unrest in the United States, with parties of protest appearing in farming and working class areas to challenge Democratic and Republican orthodoxies. How political were the Lehigh students? The answer is, not very. Few came from sections where protest was strong. Engineering as a profession had a low political profile. Few student political organizations existed, and those that appeared, such as a nonpartisan Lehigh University Sound Money League in 1896, were short lived. A brief notice of a straw poll taken by someone during the presidential election campaign of 1892 showed that the students divided, 264 for the Republican Harrison, 178 for the Democrat Cleveland (who won nationally), and 4 for the Prohibition candidate Bidwell. A reader depending exclusively on campus publications for political news in 1896 would never have known that the hardest fought presidential election campaign since Lincoln's defeat of Douglas in 1860 was under way. Political news in the presidential campaign for 1900 was pretty much limited to a short notice that Republicans outnumbered Democrats among the student body by about two to one.[24]

One incident became a cause célèbre. An article appeared in the *Philadelphia Record* to the effect that Lehigh students formed a large part of Coxey's army when that troop of protesters arrived in the nation's capital. General Jacob S. Coxey was a Greenbacker and Populist from Ohio who received much national publicity for advocating inflationary measures to relieve unemployment during the depression years of 1893 and 1894. He organized a march of workers to Washington to advertise his ideas and protest the inactivity of the Congress. Acting President Coppée immediately and publicly denied the truth of the article. The *Burr* of 11 April, 1894 added to Coppée's denial an editorial condemning the irresponsibility of whoever had perpetrated the "practical joke" and of sensational newspapers in general.[25]

In 1891 the students, undeterred by the fate of the *Journal of the Engineering Society*, began a new journal, the *Lehigh Quarterly*, designed to publish the best of papers presented before all of the course societies. It contained articles by students, faculty, and alumni and included such gems as "The Lehigh University, Illustrated," by Arthur E. Meaker, "The Early Days of Football at Lehigh," by Richard Harding Davis, and "The Early Drama at Lehigh," by Richard's brother Charles. The quarterly was strongly oriented toward engineering.

The *Lehigh Quarterly*, like its predecessor, proved to have too few readers to survive. When a genuine student newspaper came out in 1894 the *Lehigh Quarterly* folded.

The newspaper was the *Brown and White*, whose initial issue appeared 14 January 1894. The *Brown and White* was published Tuesdays and Fridays when school was in session, except during the athletic seasons, when days of publication were Thursdays and Mondays. This allowed immediate coverage of sporting events, which were held on Wednesday and Saturday afternoons. In addition to sports coverage — and much advertising, for the paper had to be self-supporting — the editors provided lengthy summaries of university lectures and other major public addresses, calendars of campus events, brief notices of happenings on other campuses and of activities of alumni, coverage of course societies, meetings of the student body and the classes, and performances by groups such as Mustard and Cheese, the Glee Club, and the minstrels by whatever name they might be called — Banjo and Guitar Club, the Banjo Club, Banjo and Mandolin Club — and other items of interest to students, for example, obituaries of students, notices of additions to the faculty, schedules of final examinations, and every semester a listing of "allowable" absences, that is, the number of absences a student might take before being penalized, of every course and supplementary exercise such as chapel, gym, and university lectures. The editors did not attempt to compete with commercial newspapers on coverage of local, state, national, and international news.

After the *Brown and White* appeared, the *Burr* became a purely literary publication and as such met the fate of neglect and death experienced by all subsequent Lehigh literary periodicals. It suspended publication in 1898 (on several later occasions, e.g., 1904 and 1912, it reappeared as a magazine devoted mostly to humor).

Verses for an alma mater song appeared in the *Burr* for 12 October 1894, designed for an old tune that had already been used by several schools, including Cornell and Brown. According to Morris Bishop, author of the *History of Cornell*, the name of the tune was "Annie Lish." The author was later identified as being J. J. Gibson ('95), editor-in-chief of the *Burr*.

On several occasions the students in the 1890s collectively exercised self-discipline in matters of common concern. On 9 December 1892, disgusted with the prices charged for books and other supplies by the local stores, they organized a supply bureau as a cooperative. The trustees allowed the students a room in Christmas Hall as a base of operations.

In 1895, chagrined by the prevalence of cheating on examinations, the students began an honor court. The idea for this came from the faculty. Professor Doolittle took the initiative and found a student leader in Robert Laramy (B.A. '96, M.A. '99). In the spring of 1894 both the sophomore and junior classes voted favorably for an honor system. The next autumn Laramy promoted the idea at several meetings of the students. His plan was that the students would pledge not to cheat and would agree to inform on those who did; faculty would cease monitoring examinations; an honor court consisting of ten students chosen by the student body would try cases of alleged cheating, with subsequent review of the proceedings by the faculty, and with allowance of appeal to the faculty. In November the student body accepted the plan, and in December the faculty agreed to it with a proviso that any professor might maintain his class in the usual way if he saw fit. This last was probably a concession to Professor Chandler, who refused to accept the honor system.

The plan went into effect immediately. As with all such ventures, its success depended upon the cooperation of the students. For a while the system worked. Then time began to erode the reforming spirit. Soon those who had organized the court were graduated. In 1897 students reported that cheating was widespread and displayed reluctance to inform on fellow students. The Honor Court was belatedly organized in that year, worked for a time, and then suspended operations, only to start up again a few years later. And so it went on for many years.

Several other changes characterized the closing years of the nineteenth century. In 1896 the faculty equalized the length of the first and second terms, thereby allowing one-semester courses to be taught in either term. In 1897 the faculty reluctantly — because of the expense — agreed to the trustees' request to wear academic regalia for commencement exercises. Pattern rosters showing the subjects required in each semester appeared for the first time in the *Register* for 1898.

In 1899 President Drown and the trustees created the position of registrar as a means of relieving the president of some time-consuming duties and providing additional publicity for the university. The initial job description read in part, "He conducts all correspondence with prospective students and attends to all details of their entrance into the University. He visits schools, makes the personal acquaintance of the principals, addresses the pupils, and makes it his business to keep the university in touch with the secondary schools of the country."[26] Natt Morrill Emery, an instructor in English and a graduate of Dartmouth, was appointed registrar. The appointment was originally part time but in 1902 became full time.

In 1900 fire gutted the Physical Laboratory, which was immediately rebuilt with money provided by the insurance.

As the new century began, the financial crisis for Lehigh ended.

The loan made by the Drexel-Morgan interests to the Asa Packer Estate, for which the estate had given up control over the Lehigh Valley Railroad, had been for two years. In 1899 the estate wanted to renew the loan. Drexel-Morgan had no objection. The value of the railroad stock was stable; that of the iron company was rising. The trustees of Bethlehem Iron were organizing a holding company, to be known as the Bethlehem Steel Company, a move that excited speculators and drove up the price of Bethlehem Iron Company stock. In April 1899 the Asa Packer Estate took advantage of the high price and sold all of its shares of iron company stock and advised the Drexel people that the railroad was also for sale. Drexel made the purchase as of 1 June 1900. The estate paid off its debts and transferred to the university its share of the proceeds. The university used part of this to buy back the estate's equity of $110,213.58 in the library and had as a remainder $1,133,860 in cash, which it immediately invested in income-producing bonds. All that remained to the estate of the university's property was the mortgage on the note for $428,112.42, upon which the estate was not demanding payment of interest.

Before another year had passed, more good news for the university was reported. The trustees had accepted a recommendation from Drown to raise the tuition of the technicals from $100 to $125 a year, effective June 1901; and in spite of this, the entering class that fall was the largest in the history of Lehigh, 250 students as compared with 159 the preceding year.

As a result of the sale of the Lehigh Valley Railroad, Lehigh ceased to be a "railroad university." Into the vacuum caused by the loss of Packer's railroad stepped another benefactor, the Bethlehem Steel Company, a supporter of a different sort, but also one that had in early years been brought along by Asa Packer's lieutenants. The sequence of events suggests that the emergence of the steel company was related to the departure of the railroad; and in fact the two events were tied to a basic shift throughout America in the economic importance of the railroad and steel industries. The power of railroads was waning; that of the steel industry was rising. Any institution such as Lehigh, teaching chemistry, metallurgy, and civil and mechanical engineering and being geographically situated close to a major steel company, might have expected to benefit from the work going on in the shops and mills and from the business acumen of the company's executives.

Over the years Bethlehem Iron had taken top graduates from Lehigh. Some of them were emerging as executives. The railroad men who had originally dominated Bethlehem Iron were soon completely out of the picture. In 1901 Bethlehem Iron and its holding company, Bethlehem Steel, passed to Charles M. Schwab, who combined the two companies, retaining the name Bethlehem Steel. Schwab cleaned the management of the railroad crew and their relatives. Able graduates of Lehigh University survived the house cleaning. Among these were Edward M. McIlvain ('85), C. Austin Buck ('87), Archibald Johnston ('89), B. H. Jones ('95), Edward S. Knisely ('97), and Eugene G. Grace ('99).

The men of steel were in time as generous to Lehigh as the railroad men had been but did not exercise the same control. Never would a member of Bethlehem Steel have the power over Lehigh once possessed by Packer, Sayre, and Wilbur—not even Eugene G. Grace at the peak of his career. From the time of the sale of the Lehigh Valley Railroad, the days of patronage of the university by one industrial giant were over. The years of cooperation and mutual aid were beginning.

4
End of an Era: 1900–1919

The years of America's emergence as a world power were marked by rapid modernization, leaving little time for introspection. A "reckless and swaggering prosperity" set in, as Lehigh's Professor Stewart expressed it.[1] Corporate leaders with an eye to profit and the public's temper preached civic responsibility, practised philanthropy, and promoted designs for free competition. Suffragettes triumphed in the same decade that saw the formation of the National Chambers of Commerce, the imposing of a personal income tax, and a growing acceptance of streetcars, automobiles, the gramophone, and the silent screen.

Higher education responded to the changes. The teaching of applied science and the mechanic arts advanced in public esteem. Classical education, which a hundred years earlier had enjoyed a near monopoly, became tolerated as one of a number of courses of study. The change did not dull a spirit of liberal education, which moved from the classical mansion into a jerry-built complex of humanistic and social studies. As for applied science, much refinement was in order. The most important developments were an appreciation of the creative role of classroom and laboratory, a recognition and provision for greater specialization, and the virtual disappearance of generalists in science from the more progressive colleges and universities. As for engineering education in particular, these developments were coupled with a concern for the needs and pretensions of industrial employers. General vocational aims were often subordinated to specific occupational goals.

In the Bethlehems, Lehigh University was the scene of all the main developments and problems; for Lehigh belonged to a community that was closely attuned to the nerve centers of the nation. Trolleys and automobiles, telephones and civic groups united the Bethlehems as never before and helped to promote the consolidation in 1917 of the boroughs into a single city. Bethlehem Steel, with contacts all over the country, dominated local life. No other industry dislodged Bethlehem Steel from its positions of civic and economic influence. Its very presence reinforced vocational and occupational purposes for education while at the same time allowing toleration of goals of business and teacher education acceptable to civic-minded leaders.

Lehigh felt the change in the national temper as soon as the new century began. Enrollments rose yearly, attaining 720 in the fall of 1908. Almost all of the students came to study chemistry or engineering. Honorary scholarships, by means of which Drown had intended to increase enrollments in General Literature, only prevented them from diminishing; for by 1902 the students in General Literature comprised 6 percent of the student body, the same percentage as the school had in the middle years of the 1890s. In 1904 the trustees, on Drown's recommendation, ended the program of four-year honorary scholarships, and the proportion of students in General Literature fell even further as the recipients were graduated.

A secular spirit was present, although not as pronounced as it was at many another university and college. On campus after campus across America, requirements of compulsory attendance at chapel and courses in religion were disappearing. At Lehigh, compulsory chapel remained with support from a majority of the students. But Christian Evidences disappeared. Professor Stewardson replaced it with Philosophy of Religion, which was required at the discretion of the departments. The first department to make Philosophy of Religion Elective — Physics in 1900 — received such a favorable response from the students that the other departments soon did likewise. By 1905 no course of instruction was requiring any study of religion.

In the pattern rosters for engineering, a one-credit course in economics took the place formerly held by Philosophy of Religion and Christian Evidences.

For twenty-eight years following the resignation of Stewardson, the chaplain was a clergyman at the Church of the Nativity and was not listed as a member of the Lehigh faculty.

Money for capital improvements was still in short supply. Yet two new structures became possible through the generosity of private donors. One was a steam laboratory, erected in 1901 for the Department of Mechanical Engineering. It was a two-story addition to the boiler house and contained separate sections for boilers and engines. The second structure was Williams Hall. Professor Williams had in the past spent a considerable amount of his own money furnishing the geological quarters in the Chemistry Laboratory and in 1900 donated money for the establishment of prizes in oratory — the first Williams prizes. He then promised the money for a new building. The site chosen was the place where the hydraulics laboratory had stood. In the construction, the brook that had fed water to the hydraulics laboratory was channeled underground. Williams Hall was dedicated on Founder's Day 1903. It provided a home for Mechanical Engineering, Mining, and Geology. In the end Williams paid about half of the cost. Twenty-six other persons and industrial corporations made gifts of money or equipment to help with the furnishings.

The times were propitious for education such as Drown stood for, aiming at public service and emphasizing a combination of applied science, engineering technology, and culture studies. However, Drown had no chance to continue his work. He died following abdominal surgery on 16 November 1904. After a brief interregnum in which Professor Chandler served for the last time as acting president, and which was characterized by a weak move to bring in Stewardson as Drown's successor, the trustees chose Henry Sturgis Drinker as Lehigh's fifth president.[2]

Drinker, like former President Lamberton, had been legal counsel for the Lehigh Valley Railroad and had never served on any faculty. Neither man made any pretense of educational leadership. Both looked upon the faculty as the body in which educators should reside. In 1909, on the eve of a departure for Panama, Drinker repeated to the faculty a sentiment he had expressed several times before, that he was willing to "be guided by their experience, rather than by my judgement in matters in which I was not trained, and to give my best energies to those things for the benefit and advancement of the University for the promotion of which my past life has fitted me."[3]

Although he had not taught, he had served Lehigh in other ways. He had remained in touch with his alma mater since enrolling as a student in 1867. He had been the first graduate in mining engineering, had helped organize the Alumni Association, and had been both its secretary and president and one of the first four alumni trustees. He had served as a charter trustee, given money in time of need, lobbied for a grant from the commonwealth, and worked with Sayre, Wilbur, and the other trustees in raising money.

Drinker's talents had developed through these efforts and associations. He knew how to organize the alumni and educate them in fund raising; he knew how to inspire people with a sense of public service; and he knew how to satisfy student expectations for counseling and recognition. He rarely delegated authority but used a personal approach in almost everything he did.

Drinker also became a leader for the Board of Trustees. The railroad men, whom he had loyally served, were dying off. Robert H. Sayre, president of the board, wrote in his diary for 4 October 1905, "Drinker made his daily visit." Sayre died the following year, and Drinker made no more "daily visits" to any one. E. P Wilbur, the last of the Lehigh Valley Railroad men on the board, died in 1909. None of the replacements had as much experience as a trustee and member of the Alumni Association as did Drinker.

William A. Lathrop ('75), president of the Lehigh Coal and Navigation Company, succeeded Sayre as president of the board. When in 1912 Lathrop died, Dr. Henry Reese Price ('70) became president. Price, the alumnus of longest standing, was a surgeon specializing in eye and ear. He lived in Brooklyn. Other charter trustees in 1912 were Samuel Dexter Warriner ('90), who succeeded Lathrop as president of the Lehigh Coal and Navigation Company; David J. Pearsall of Mauch Chunk; the Right Reverend Ethelbert Talbot, Bishop Rulison's successor as head of the Episcopal Diocese of Central Pennsylvania; Rembrandt Peale ('83), a coal operator in New York City; Warren A. Wilbur, one of E. P.'s sons, who assumed many of his father's presidencies and chairmanships; Charles L. Taylor ('76), retired from the Carnegie Steel Company and a member of the Carnegie Corporation; A. N. Cleaver, a son-in-law of Robert Sayre; John Fritz, retired from the

Bethlehem Iron Company; and Charles M. Schwab. From 1912 until Drinker left the presidency, the only change among the charter trustees was the addition in 1913 of Eugene G. Grace to replace Fritz.

Drinker took upon himself the responsibility of being chief development officer, the only president voluntarily to do so before the advent of Martin D. Whitaker in 1946. Drinker singled out Charles L. Taylor and Warren A. Wilbur as aides. Both were members of the board's Executive Committee. Warren was the secretary and treasurer of the board and chairman of the Executive Committee.

To E. P. Wilbur, Charles L. Taylor, and President Drinker belongs much of the credit for a happy resolution of the university's financial obligation to the Asa Packer Estate. Taylor and Drinker had by 1908 become trustees on the estate's five-member board (Warren A. Wilbur became a trustee in 1910 following the death of his father).

The estate held the university's note for $428,112.42 at 5 percent on which interest had not been paid. This interest by 1904 amounted to $309,685 and was soon substantially more. Mary Packer Cummings and Harry Packer's widow, Mary Augusta, were the legatees who were entitled to receive the interest. Both were sympathetic to the university. Mary Packer Cummings had over the years given money to build and renovate the church aid students, and help with operating expenses. In 1908 she and Mary Augusta Packer, at the request of the trustees of the estate, agreed to transfer their rights to the income from the note held by the estate to Lehigh. As Drinker pointed out, this gift made Mary Packer Cummings second only to her father as a benefactor of the university. The trustees then formally absolved Lehigh from paying the interest due or to become due to the two ladies.

The notes and interest remained but were amply covered by the university's equity in the estate. This could not be realized until after the death of the ladies. For Mary Augusta Packer that unhappy event occurred 12 April 1911. Mary Packer Cummings died 29 October 1912. The trustees then computed the equity of the remaining heirs, that of Lehigh being 6578/12696ths, or about half. They did not liquidate the estate, which according to Packer's will could not be done before the expiration of another twenty-one years. But they divided most of the assets among the heirs and kept the rest for future income. Thereafter, the university received 6578/12696ths of the reduced yearly income.

By the time the assets of the Asa Packer Estate were distributed, Drinker had displayed his influence with alumni by encouraging them to raise money, help with student housing, support athletics, and become better organized.

As early as 1891 Professor Williams had suggested that the alumni could best aid their university by contributing money.[4] In 1899 President Drown had presented a three-point plan for alumni giving: insurance, with the university named as beneficiary; donations to help with current expenses; and gifts to an endowment. The trustees endorsed the plan and actively worked for it, but with limited success. The life insurance option proved unattractive. The other two brought in some money, possibly because Sayre and Wilbur announced that for every dollar contributed, they would forgive the university one dollar of the loans they had made to it. By the June meeting of 1901 the alumni had pledged $52,205 toward the cancellation of the $60,000 loaned by Sayre and Wilbur, although as yet a little more than one-third of the subscribed amount had been paid in.

Drinker built on this early experience. In one of his first acts as president, he encouraged the Alumni Association to take financial responsibility for a memorial building to Drown. The drive to have the alumni pay the bills was successful.

Drown Hall was the first structure built expressly for housing student and alumni activities. When completed, it contained study, reading, meeting, and chess rooms, an assembly hall, offices for the Alumni Association, the Lehigh University Christian Association, the Athletic Committee, student publications, dramatic and musical organizations, and the Supply Bureau. Many of these had formerly been in Christmas Hall, which for the immediate future was to house Classical and Modern Foreign Languages, Philosophy, and Psychology.

With prodding from Drinker, the Alumni Association in 1907 began an Alumni Endowment Fund. At the kickoff dinner for the fund, held during commencement week 1907, Drinker explained, "This is a question of a large fund, to go into the hands of the Trustees, to be conserved, and the income only used. Lehigh is not peculiar in this respect. Harvard recently raised between 1125 and 1225 thousand dollars towards a similar project." By 1908 subscriptions to the fund were $56,087 and by 1911, $138,214.

Much of the fund raising by alumni was related to student housing and athletics. Drinker proceeded on an assumption that the easiest way to activate energies and open pocket books was by calling attention to attractive projects.

Better student housing was a project that alumni could understand. Most of them had painful memories of uncomfortable and expensive rooms in South Bethlehem. Charles L. Taylor, now a charter trustee and a member of the Carnegie Corporation, was probably the author of the memorial of 1888 requesting dormitories; he had at the time been an alumnus trustee, one of the small number charged with making recommendations for improving the university. No strong objection appeared when Drinker and the trustees took steps de facto negating Asa Packer's policy of having students find room and board without any expectation of help from the university.

One step concerned fraternities. During Lamberton's presidency, the trustees had purchased for the university much land adjacent to the campus and higher up on South Mountain in order to control the streams from which water flowed to university buildings. The property was no longer needed for this purpose; the buildings now took their water from the South Bethlehem system. On 23 January 1908, the trustees decided that fraternities should be allowed to build chapter houses there, that the university would advance funds to aid them in this, and that the houses, when completed, would be subject to the rules of the university.

A year later, in 1909, the board established Sayre Park on the land, using one hundred thousand dollars donated by the children of Robert H. Sayre as a memorial to their father. The main roads were put in much as they still exist.

Almost immediately Delta Upsilon built a chapter house "on the hill." By 1913 tennis courts—paid for by Schwab—were established nearby; and Delta Tau Delta and Sigma Nu were planning chapter houses. "Every fraternity house built on our grounds simply means another dormitory section practically donated to us," Drinker told the trustees.[5] By 1916 six more fraternities had located in Sayre Park.

When the trustees announced an intention of helping fraternities to build on the campus, they were taking another step in relieving the housing situation. A dormitory and a food service were under construction. The dormitory had become possible when Charles L. Taylor persuaded Carnegie to grant $120,000. Carnegie stipulated that the building should be called Taylor Hall. The trustees then decided on a food service, or college commons (the present Lamberton Hall). When completed in 1908, Taylor Hall had rooms for 140 students, about one-fifth of the student body.

A year later, the trustees found additional living quarters for students. This involved a refurbishing of the main building of Rennig's Brewery, purchased in 1899. The trustees had originally thought of making the old brewery into a club house for unmarried members of the teaching staff. Now it became the second student residence hall.

And, as this second residence hall became available, a new instructional facility appeared on the campus, the Coxe Mining Laboratory, situated on a level with Drown Hall and slightly east of the Gymnasium.

The donor, Sophia G. Coxe, widow of Eckley, had long been a benefactor. She had given to the library her husband's valuable collection of books and journals, made numerous donations to the university and its students in the dark years of the 1890s, provided funds to help in furnishing the reconstructed Physical Laboratory, and donated to the fund for Drown Hall. (Drinker later found Mrs. Coxe a source of funds for other projects. According to a biographer, "At least $300,000 was given to Lehigh by Mr. & Mrs. Coxe.")[6]

In the domain of athletics, the alumni would undoubtedly have contributed much without encouragement from Drinker. Here, he needed to do little more than point out some opportunities and be sympathetic—tasks not difficult for him as he was an avid Lehigh sports fan.

He also had to uphold the faculty in its work of constraining athletics from interfering with academics. Faculty and alumni took over various parts of the management of the sports program. By 1909 the students, who originally had directed everything, had little power left.

In the early years of Drinker's tenure, controls by the faculty exceeded those exercised by the alumni. In 1894 athletics had been taken from the Athletic Association and placed under the supervision of a committee answering directly to the Board of Trustees and consisting of one professor, one instructor, the director of the Gymnasium, four alumni, and five students. That is, the faculty had the smallest representation. But their interest was great, especially in supervising scheduling and preventing what they called an overemphasis on sports. The faculty representative became the dominant member. Much of the time this was Professor Charles Thornburg. The obituary of Thornburg, which appeared in the *Alumni Bulletin* for May 1945, asserted that as the faculty member of the Athletic Committee, "He shortly became the virtual director of intercollegiate sports and was a prime mover in the improvement of the athletic field."

From about 1894 to 1909, the intercollegiate sports program was at a low ebb. With the increase of enrollments of the early 1900s, the faculty had stiffened the requirements for students to remain in good standing. Many potential athletes feared flunking out. From 1897 through 1909 football turned in four winning seasons (1902, 1903, 1907, 1908) and won only four of eighteen contests with Lafayette (in 1898, 1902, 1903, 1908). During the same period there were no championship teams in any sport.

Then some alumni began to put time and money into improving the picture, inevitably winning a control and largely displacing that exercised by Thornburg.

Eugene G. Grace was foremost. Born in Cape May County, New Jersey, Grace had attended public schools and, for a time, Pennington Preparatory School. At Lehigh he excelled in scholarship and athletics. Too slight of build to be a great success in football, he worked at being the best baseball player he knew how. He became a star short stop and captain of the team, earning the nickname 'Gator "because he inevitably snapped every ball that came near him."[7] The Boston Braves offered him a spot on their professional team, which he turned down in favor of employment with the Bethlehem Steel Company. He began at Steel as a crane operator and after Schwab took over the company, rose rapidly. By 1908 he was general manager of the works and a director, and five years later he became president of the company.

His first major contribution as an alumnus came about the time he became general manager of the steel company. He saw that the Lehigh program needed a full-time director and provided it with one. At the Pennington school he had a teammate named Howard Roland Reiter, who had later been three times an all-American football player at Princeton and was currently football coach and director of gymnastics at Wesleyan University, where he had distinguished himself by introducing the overhead spiral pass to football. "Bosey" Reiter came to Lehigh in 1910 as football coach and the next year was named professor of physical education and director of athletics.

Reiter brought with him to Lehigh a former Wesleyan student, a star quarterback name Vincent J. "Pat" Pazzetti. The next year Reiter hired Tom Keady away from Dartmouth as head football coach and also welcomed a transfer student from Dartmouth, George Hoban. Football at Lehigh was again on the rise. In 1912 Pazzetti was named quarterback on the all-American team and, following graduation, assisted Keady for a time in coaching. Hoban played football for three years and was captain of the team in 1914.

These stars attracted others. From 1910 through 1918, football had winning seasons, except 1911 and 1918 when the number of wins and losses was the same, and won six out of nine games with Lafayette (losing in 1910, 1911, 1915).

Reiter, Grace, and J. C. Gorman ('10) were principally responsible for Lehigh's entry into intercollegiate wrestling. The sport had been intermittently popular in intramurals, although the Gymnasium was too small to accommodate many spectators. The Alumni Association in 1910 voted a small sum for wrestling and in 1911 increased the level of support in response to strong appeals from Grace and Gorman. When the university opened that fall, William "Billy" Sheridan, a champion wrestler, was on hand, brought from the University of Pennsylvania by Reiter. Although Sheridan had only three winning seasons (and two ties) before 1919, when success came, it was lasting.

With the quality of the sports program improving, the existing facilities were woefully inadequate. Here, Charles L. Taylor took the lead. In 1913 he gave one hundred thousand dollars — the first of several large gifts — toward a new gymnasium, field house, and playing fields. Other alumni joined in the giving. The projects were completed in time for the opening of the football season in 1914. 17 October 1914 was proclaimed as Charley Taylor Day "for all that he has done for his Alma Mater."[8] Later in the year Taylor Gymnasium was the site of the intercollegiate wrestling championships.

As the construction of Taylor Gym neared an end, the trustees had the old Gymnasium converted into a home for the departments in the humanities.

Taylor also promoted a stadium, although Bethlehem Steel and its executives and suppliers provided most of the means in cash, material, and labor.

Bethlehem Steel's interest in athletics extended beyond Lehigh to include all of the nearby municipalities. Schwab was at the time living in nearby Fountain Hill and was modernizing and expanding the steel company and promoting a program of civic improvements. He had a "vision of the community of Bethlehem as an ideal industrial city, with homes, parks, libraries, educational, art, and musical facilities that shall be exceptional."[9] Schwab personally provided a new home for the public library and generously supported the Bach Choir. The Bethlehem Steel Company Band was the largest and best-equipped band in the valley. The Bethlehem Steel soccer team was one of the strongest in the nation. In 1915 the company established on eight acres in the northern part of Bethlehem a facility known as Steel Field, equipped for soccer, football, baseball, and tennis and having a grandstand.

The new stadium at Lehigh was completed in 1916. The trustees decreed that it should be constructed in sections as the money came in. The minutes of the board for 3 October 1913 indicate that in the initial stages Grace "allowed" the concrete force of the Bethlehem Steel Company to expedite the work. Warren A. Wilbur, Schwab, and Grace each gave money for a section. Various companies donated concrete.[10] Alumni clubs pledged some sections of the stadium, although not one of them fulfilled its pledge.[11]

As building progressed, the trustees gave names to some of the older structures. In 1913 they decided that henceforth the old Gymnasium should be known as Coppee Hall. In 1916 they formally renamed the old brewery as Price Hall in honor of the president of the board and in 1921 designated the Chemical Laboratory as the William H. Chandler Chemical Laboratory.

Sports besides football and wrestling felt the touch of Reiter, Grace, Taylor, and others. Lehigh had its first intercollegiate basketball season in 1913 and in that year won twelve of fourteen games. Pazzetti was also an excellent pitcher and, with others, raised the level of performance in baseball. In 1917 the team won sixteen of its twenty-two games and had the highest batting average among the eastern colleges. The lacrosse club was divisional champion in 1914 and 1916 and national champion in 1914. Track and field, which was the weakest of the officially recognized sports, also improved. Cross-country racing and swimming had beginnings in 1919. About the same time, knowing how to swim was made a requirement for graduation. Soccer, too, made a debut in the prewar era.

The alumni used money to attract good players. Sums were given in the form of scholarships, as pay for jobs, and possibly as outright gifts. The record provides no evidence that the alumni "bought" athletes, a practise reaching scandalous proportions on some campuses. Still, the faculty recognized the potential and on several occasions asked for an investigation. Drinker gave them small comfort. In 1913 he proposed to the trustees that the university offer athletic scholarships based on the criteria applied by the Rhodes Foundation, which he described as being six-tenths for scholarship and four-tenths for physical fitness; and in a controversy over the subsidizing of student athletes, he took the stand that the means by which students were financially supported was none of the university's business.[12]

The Alumni Association grew as the number of graduates increased. The membership in 1900 stood at 1,220 and within twenty years more than doubled. In 1912–13 the leadership consisted primarily of Drinker, Franklin Baker, Jr. ('95), Professor Preston A. Lambert of mathematics, secretary and treasurer, and Professor Howard Eckfeldt, head of Mining Engineering, the archivist. These decided that the time had come for a periodical similar to those being put out by alumni groups on other campuses; and so, the *Alumni Bulletin* was born. Raymond Walters ('07), who was doing double duty as registrar and as instructor in journalism, became the first editor.

For the first four years the *Bulletin* appeared quarterly, was small in size, had few pages and no illustrations, and provided news of the university and the alumni. Drinker freely used the *Bulletin* as a vehicle through which to address the alumni.

The *Bulletin* prepared the way for incorporation and a reorganization. In 1916 a Board of Directors replaced the Executive Committee. A paid secretary was provided for. Lambert resigned as secretary and treasurer and took the position of archivist, recently vacated by Eckfeldt. Walters retired as editor of the *Bulletin*.

The board hired Walter R. Okeson ('95, pronounced Ō´-kĕ-son) as the new editor and executive secretary. Okeson, or "Okey," as some alumni affectionately called him, had played football at Lehigh and had continued his activity in the game by coaching and refereeing. He imparted a personal touch to the *Bulletin*, which delighted the readers. The magazine soon became a major university publication. Page size and the number of pages were increased, and illustrations appeared. The proceedings of the Alumni Association, which had previously been separately published, were incorporated into the revised format. Advertising, another new feature, defrayed part of the expense. In 1920 the *Bulletin* became a monthly (nine, later ten, issues a year).

Okeson, Drinker, and the alumni supporting athletics had been educated to the practice of management as an art, not a science. For them, person-to-person relationships were the essential part of every task of planning and administering. While this individualistic approach remained dominant, it inhibited the appearance of administration based on rules impersonally made and enforced.

During Drinker's tenure administrative tasks accumulated and were handled in a haphazard manner. There was no system. New duties seem to have been given to whoever appeared available and was either unwilling or unable to refuse them.

Drinker had inherited a registrar, Natt M. Emery; and in 1907 the trustees, upon Drinker's recommendation, coined the title of assistant to the president and gave that to Emery. Three years later they changed the title of assistant to the president to vice president. In 1912 they gave Emery help by taking the post of registrar away from him and bestowing it on Raymond Walters as a part-time job. In 1908 Drinker put Frederick R. Ashbaugh, formerly secretary to the president, into the newly formed position of bursar. When in 1913 Jim Myers died, Drinker made J. Clarence Cranmer, who had been brought in to be university forester, superintendent of buildings and grounds. Professor Stewart took on the work of director of the library upon the death of Chandler, although Stewart had little time to give the position. T. Edgar Shields succeeded to the position of organist of the Packer Memorial Church when in 1905 J. Fred Wolle left for the University of California.

In 1907 Drinker and the trustees gave Professor Joseph F. Klein the title of dean, apparently expecting him to be a spokesman for the faculty. They did not define the duties of a dean. Klein might have asked himself, what is a dean supposed to do? The year before, he had been charged with oversight of the campus water supply and heating plant, and the board had named him superintendent of heat and light. He could understand work of this sort. But a dean? More importantly, he was head of Mechanical Engineering, with authority on a par with the other heads of departments. In giving students the news of Klein's appointment at the beginning of the academic year, Drinker seemed to be saying that Klein was to be dean because he was the oldest member of the faculty in point of service. When in 1918 Klein suddenly died, the deanship was left vacant.

In actuality, next to Drinker, Professor Charles L. Thornburg became in many respects the most important figure in administration. When Thornburg arrived as Doolittle's replacement in mathematics, he had also taken over Doolittle's position on the Committee on Standing of Students, which the faculty had created to relieve it of some work connected with the students' academic progress. At that time, Professor William A. Robinson held the post of secretary of the faculty, which had already become a catchall for incidental administrative tasks. In 1899 Robinson left the university, and Thornburg succeeded to the position of secretary of the faculty. Soon Thornburg's duties included "recording the activities of the faculty, seeing that rules were maintained, preparing rosters for examinations, keeping student records, checking on probationers and honor students, keeping up discipline and supervising buildings and grounds." Thornburg's style was characteristically individualistic and, because of his personality, autocratic. Morton Sultzer ('12) wrote of the reception given him on presenting Thornburg with a request: "'NO ... get out! GET OUT!!' came rolling out of Thornburg's office, past Dr. Drinker's open door, through Natt Emery's outer office and down the long flight of stairs that led from the administrative offices located in Packer Hall before the advent of the Memorial Building."[13]

Drinker and the heads of the departments were the principal counselors of students. Drinker had four sons of his own and possessed a knack of understanding college men. His daughter, the biographer Catherine Drinker Bowen, wrote that he organized life in the president's house so as to receive students at almost any time, and that they came.[14] Drinker was his own dean of students.

They did not wear out his patience. Professor E. H. Williams once told a meeting of the SPEE that at Lehigh, "Students have probably greater freedom outside of the classroom than in most institutions."[15] The students used their freedom. They, too, were individualistic. Although they had lost most of the control over athletics, they substantially retained it for other extracurricular activities and in daily living.

The character of the student body changed little in the prewar years. Although the number of students increased by about 50 percent, from 610 in the fall of 1904 to 901 in September 1918, the growth was within a range whereby the quantitative change did not make a qualitative difference. As before, most of the students came to study applied science and engineering and arrived roughly from the same geographic areas as earlier. The flannel-shirt crowd still predominated.

Academic responsibilities overshadowed everything else. "We have no room for the butterflies of fair weather college life," Drinker told the entering freshmen in 1906.[16] Students daily faced a specter of unfinished assignments and impossibly difficult tasks. Notices in the *Brown and White* of a student resigning an office in a campus organization "because of the pressure of work" were fairly common.

A quality of sameness and respectability pervaded many activities. The *Brown and White* contained nothing resembling yellow journalism, which was soiling the pages of many of the country's commercial newspapers. The basic format of the *Epitome* was unchanged. Mustard and Cheese gave most of its time to staging one "spectacular" or several less ambitious dramatizations per year. In 1904 a marching band was organized. Its financing by the students can be guessed at from the surviving pictures — of a small group of players inexpensively dressed in white ducks, brown sweaters, and sailor's caps. Political activity remained low. Although the cane rush was gone, class suppers, the junior oratorical contest, calculus cremation, and other traditions endured, albeit at times appearing rather shopworn. An alumnus of the 1890s returning on the eve of the war for the first time since graduation would have had no difficulty in recognizing the Lehigh of his undergraduate years.

In 1908 the students asked the university to take control of the Supply Bureau, as they could not afford the salary of a manager. The trustees complied and noted that the profits would be devoted "to the maintenance and operation and general interests of Drown Hall."[17]

The Honor Court was revived in 1904 and, with some changes, continued its work. The faculty was remarkably consistent in supporting the institution. A serious confrontation between students and faculty on the subject of an honor system occurred only once. In 1913 the faculty considered the penalty given by the court to two students convicted of cheating as being too light and demanded dismissal. The members of the court resigned in a body in protest. But the faculty still supported the court, and it was shortly reconstituted.

All-campus student government took a weak step forward when in 1914 a group known as Arcadia took over the duties of the Honor Court. Arcadia had originated in the early 1880s as a social club, one of several such, but Arcadia remained where the others disappeared. By the turn of the century it was a consultative group representing the major interests within the student body. The *Brown and White* of 24 October 1905 declared that its purpose was "to formulate and carry out plans for the advancement of the social and student life of the University and to look after the best interests of the undergraduate body." The nature of membership was changed from time to time. In 1914 it consisted of heads of campus organizations and fifteen members elected at large by the students. In the spring of 1917 the representation was altered to reflect the interests of the living groups.

Some new activities showed a growing spirit of public service. Students applied in their own ways an idea of bettering the community through private initiative, such as was being promoted by Schwab and Bethlehem Steel. Drinker gave them much encouragement.

The students opened a Free Evening School for the immigrants who were coming from central, southern, and eastern Europe to work in the steel mills. The students worked through LUCA, or, as it was now more frequently called, the Lehigh University YMCA. Some faculty participated in the school. Begun in 1907, it aimed at providing an elementary education for mechanics and steelworkers, which would be useful to them in adjusting to American customs or in becoming employable. In 1916, 285 people were reported as attending the classes.

With the worsening of relations between the United States and Germany, the YMCA expanded the evening school to include Americanization classes. "More than 1400 employees of the Bethlehem Steel Company are being taught in the English and naturalization classes of the Lehigh Y.M.C.A. Free Evening School" was an item in the February 1917 issue of the *Alumni Bulletin*. Forty-two students were serving as instructors.

Other programs of lesser scope and shorter duration accompanied the work of undergraduates and the faculty in conducting an evening school. In 1915 J. Mark Fry, general secretary of the Lehigh YMCA, began a "big brother" movement for helping less fortunate youths of the Bethlehems.

In 1909 Drinker inspired the organization of Chinese students into the Chinese Club of Lehigh University for literary purposes and the mutual profit of its members, and of Spanish-American students into a similar organization.

Drinker's support of community work by students was based on a strongly held principle of public service, which he repeated many times. For example, he told the Engineer's Club of Northeastern Pennsylvania that "the duties of our institutions of higher learning, of our universities and colleges, — should not be restricted to what is taught to students within their walls, but they should be leaders in thought, and particularly in the teaching of things that pertain to the well-being and betterment of man."[18]

Drinker's position was a local manifestation of a national movement known as the Wisconsin Idea, advanced especially by presidents Edmund J. James of the University of Illinois and Charles R. Van Hise of Wisconsin. The Wisconsin Idea was associated with the coming of age of the mechanic arts colleges and universities and their preference for vocational education and the spreading demand of many occupational groups, including engineers, for recognition as professionals. The idea of a public service function transcended a narrow argument that tax-supported institutions have obligations to taxpayers, and it applied to privately endowed as well as publicly financed institutions. In sum, as Drinker saw it, Lehigh had as much of a duty to educate citizens as did Wisconsin, Illinois, Penn State, Cincinnati, and other state and municipal universities.

Drinker carried out the ideal of public service by supporting conservation and national military preparedness.

Conservation is a broad subject. Many Americans of the era of Theodore Roosevelt were interested in some aspect of it. At Lehigh, before the presidency of Drinker, Eckley Coxe among the trustees and E. H. Williams of the faculty had been vocal in asking for better methods of mining coal in order that the nation's supply might be more intelligently obtained and used. Their interest in conservation, as well as that of some other members of the Lehigh faculty, trustees, and alumni, lay primarily with mineral resources below the surface of the earth. By contrast, the principal interest of Roosevelt, Drinker, and many others was with wealth lying on the surface in such forms as water, soils, and forests. With the exception of some work being done in civil engineering, conservation of surface resources lay outside the main interests of Lehigh's educational endeavors.

Drinker's position on conservation was almost exactly that of Theodore Roosevelt. It involved a rationally planned use of national forest reserves and waters. Drinker was not a preservationist after the manner of John Muir and others who wanted to keep forests free from commercial use of any sort; and he expressed the engineer's preference for private business over government in using them. Drinker's ideal of forest conservation in no way clashed with his general utilitarian outlook, which emphasized progress through engineering. He demanded only that engineering be responsible, meaning subordinate to a plan for conserving the raw materials it had to have in order to survive. He stressed these points in a speech to incoming students in September 1910. "The need today is not so much to withdraw and set aside our undeveloped natural resources for the use of future generations, as to be sure that they are not wasted in their use by the present generation. We don't need or want in free America too much paternal, or in other words political oversight of these matters. Let our natural resources be developed following the natural laws of supply and demand with due regard to the essential factor that private capital will never venture into the proper, broad, economical development of these resources without the assurance of a sufficiently permanent tenure to ensure an adequate return."[19]

Drinker spent a great deal of time promoting the conservation of forest resources, as his extensive correspondence shows. In 1914 he became president of the American Forestry Association, served in that capacity for three years, and also was elected president of the Pennsylvania Forestry Association. He chaired and attended conferences and congresses, worked as a member of committees, and wrote and spoke much on the subject of scientific forest management. In all of this he did not hesitate to use the facilities and prerogatives belonging to him as president of Lehigh.

Robert W. Hall, the university's first biologist, was the faculty member most sympathetic to Drinker's views. When Hall first arrived on the campus (1902), Merriman asked him to give a course in forestry to the civil engineers. "As a result I gave a one hour course to his freshmen, beginning with the year 1903–1094," wrote Hall.[20]

Drinker privately suggested to Hall that the university should have a school of forestry. Hall related the circumstance and his reply: "Dr. Drinker said he wanted to have a talk with me and as he was going to Philadelphia suggested that I get on the train and go partway. I found he was quite excited over the notion of adding a forestry school to the university. By the time we were almost at the last station this side of Philadelphia I had persuaded him that the east had enough schools of forestry and that, unless we could design a *better* one than any already existing, we would actually be doing education a disservice."[21]

The closest that Drinker came to having forestry students at Lehigh was a grant of tuition scholarships to graduates of the Pennsylvania State Forest Academy at Mont Alto who wished to enroll for subjects collateral to that of forestry, for example, road building.

The establishment of an arboretum coincided with these attempts to introduce the teaching of conservation. Hall claimed credit for originating the idea of an arboretum, although Drinker, through his contacts with foresters at the state and national levels, gave substance to the idea. The land above the campus was a natural location. Drinker brought in Cranmer as university forester and put him in charge of the project. Several years later Drinker worked with the Pennsylvania Forestry Association on a plan to lay out a plantation adjacent to the arboretum. Cranmer described the reason for the plantation: "At the time of the inception of this plantation no one in Pennsylvania had attempted a forest demonstration plot on such soils and under such conditions as were sure to be met in any program of reforestation as applied to rough, rugged, cold, rocky, barren or waste and cut over lands which were in need of reforestation in Pennsylvania. It was to meet this need and to supply such a place that would be available to any forestry students in Pennsylvania that the Forest Plantation at Lehigh University was conceived, financed, and begun." The plantation used six acres of very poor soil. Cranmer further reported that when the plantation was started, a small nursery was established on a corner of the arboretum "for growing trees for general university purposes."[22]

America's entry into the European conflict in 1917 deflected the nation's attention away from conservation. For Drinker that meant only a lull in the activity, but for Lehigh it marked the end of a development. The arboretum and the plantation remained, but the teaching of forestry died, and instruction in measures of conservation was absorbed into other courses.

By 1917 national preparedness was easily outdistancing conservation in popularity. National preparedness was as broad a subject as conservation, and in both, Drinker limited his work to a single aspect. His interest in national preparedness centered on the training of college youths.

Shortly before 1914, Drinker's urge to do something for national preparedness had a chance to come alive. Major General Leonard Wood, Chief of Staff, laid before college presidents a plan of summer training camps. Drinker publicized the plan on the campus and got eight students to attend the first camp, held in 1913 at Gettysburg. He visited the camp and returned more enthusiastic than ever. He noted that of the fifty-nine colleges and universities represented there, Lehigh had the largest contingent. He wrote an article for the *New York Times*, "The Students' Military Camp at Gettysburg," which was reprinted and circulated as a pamphlet.

Lehigh students attended the camps from then on. Twelve went to the Students' Military Instructors Camp at Plattsburg, New York, in 1915. The following summer, with talk of war with Germany running high, approximately fifty Lehigh students attended. The faculty agreed to allow one hour of academic credit for students satisfactorily completing summer camp, stipulating that the credit could not be substituted for required or elective work.

A week before Congress declared war on Germany, the faculty at Lehigh formally recommended that the U.S. government adopt universal compulsory military training. The faculty was at the time primed to accept an ROTC unit if one should become available.

Drinker left the staffing of faculty to the heads of the departments. He may have relied on Professor Robert W. Blake of the Department of Latin for oversight of some part-time positions in the arts and sciences, for during these years Blake emerged as an unofficial spokesman of faculty in the nontechnological fields.

The department heads, for their part, took full advantage of the newly authorized assistant and associate professorships. They augmented their staffs by appointments at low levels, frequently preferring graduates of Lehigh. During Drinker's tenure relatively few full professors were brought in from the outside.

As a result, the character of the faculty greatly changed. When the position of assistant professor had been approved, the faculty had numbered fourteen, all of whom had been full professors. By 1920 the faculty consisted of twenty-eight professors, eleven associate professors, and twenty-eight assistant professors. In both years the teaching staff was much larger, as it consisted of both the faculty and the instructors, assistants, and lecturers. Moreover, the faculty of the later Drinker years had an "in-house" look. Catherine Drinker Bowen wrote in 1922 that "Forty-nine out of a total of ninety-seven members of the teaching staff are Lehigh graduates."[23]

The changes were greatest among the faculty in engineering, chemistry, and physics. By 1907, with the exception of Klein in mechanical engineering, the "old guard" in these fields was gone. They had been scholars broadly educated in science, doing research and publishing much, who had learned most of their engineering through practice, respected studies in the arts and humanities, and tended to idealize education in German universities, which some of them had attended. By contrast, the newer faculty in technology had little knowledge of German universities (which after about 1912 were effectively closed to Americans), had learned proportionately more of their engineering through formal study heavily larded with science, but had little knowledge in depth of recent advances in physics, chemistry, and related sciences and were disinclined to do much research.

Outside of engineering, physics, and chemistry, many faculty old guard remained. Nine of the full professors in the arts and sciences in 1919 had joined the faculty in or before 1899; and five of them—Thornburg in mathematics, Thayer in English, Stewart in economics, Blake in Latin, and Goodwin in Greek—led all other faculty in seniority. Furthermore, only three of the arts and sciences faculty were Lehigh alumni—Meaker and Lambert in mathematics and Myron J. Luch ('02) in English. Several had studied in German or other European universities; and seven had an earned Ph.D. degree. This high level of continuity and education was not paralleled among the instructors and assistant professors in the arts and sciences, many of whom were Lehigh alumni, few of whom held the doctorate, and among whom there was much turnover.

Departments continued as before to be the principal administrative units. The schools were never such. In 1906 the faculty recommended that the word *course* be used instead of *school*, and that *General Literature* be dropped in favor of the term *Arts and Sciences*. Requirements in general literature for study in mathematics and the sciences had always been heavy, even in the classical course. The offerings in science were increasing. Accordingly, said the faculty, the new, better designations should be "Courses in Technology" and "Courses in Arts and Sciences." In 1909 the trustees agreed to the change.

In subsequent years, until America's entry into the First World War, the Courses in Technology remained as they had been at the beginning of Drinker's presidency. The Courses in Arts and Sciences had no similar stability.

Across the country, educational reform was "in the air," to put it mildly. Two points of emphasis by reformers were a vocational education using scientific method—as opposed to the old-style teaching of the classics—and education of the public as a service. The Wisconsin Idea had expressed the latter, as did a promotion of extension courses by William Rainey Harper, president of the University of Chicago. In addition, colleges and universities came under attack by political progressives and others for a presumed inefficiency, snobbishness, moral laxity, laziness of students, and other shortcomings. The attack led to a period of self-examination of aims and methods lasting roughly from 1908 to 1910.

Lehigh seems not to have been a target of criticism; nor did its faculty in engineering and applied science conduct any self-examination. But the faculty in Arts and Sciences was caught up in the spirit of self-study and reform. The years from 1908 to 1910 saw many changes in the courses of instruction, some of which were of lasting importance.

Two changes, begun much earlier, were a general summer school and teacher education. Although conceived separately, almost from the beginning they became joined at Lehigh. Their usefulness to Lehigh undergraduates appears to have been a byproduct and not the main reason for starting and, in the early years, continuing them.

In 1898 President Drown asked the heads of departments to consider the "feasibility and advisability of establishing courses in various subjects, elementary or otherwise, open to nonstudents, in connection with the Summer School."[24] The heads of departments went to work. Extension courses and the Summer School brought older people from the Bethlehems and surrounding areas onto the campus. Many came seeking instruction in order to improve performance in their jobs. Among these were school teachers, who soon were the largest occupational group taking advantage of the new opportunities.

The first professor on the Lehigh faculty to have heeded the interest of elementary and secondary school teachers appears to have been Stewart, who in 1902 was authorized by the faculty and the trustees to offer a summer course for teachers on Methods of Teaching History and Civics.

Drinker supported the community-oriented projects begun under Drown, and he found in Percy Hughes a person to supervise them. Hughes came in 1907 as an assistant professor to fill the position in philosophy vacated several years earlier by Stewardson. Hughes had received a Ph.D. from Columbia and was a follower and friend of John Dewey, then in the process of revolutionizing educational methods.

Hughes immediately developed a core of courses for teacher education. The faculty agreed that his department should be known as the Department of Philosophy, Psychology, and Education. The department soon contained an undergraduate concentration permitting students, upon receiving the B.A. degree, to become teachers in the elementary and secondary schools. Hughes also took over the extension and summer school work by which school teachers might gain extra training. He made provision for qualified students doing extra work in the extension courses to receive graduate credit. This was, in effect, the beginning of a graduate program in education.

In 1918, when many young men were in military service and the nation's schools needed women as teachers, Hughes persuaded the faculty and the trustees to allow women to study for M.A. and M.S. degrees. The motion accepted by the faculty read in part, "And provided that, as at present, classes in which women are students should largely be limited to the late afternoon, and to Saturdays, so that the general character of campus life shall not be affected by this innovation."[25]

The introspection of the faculty in Arts and Sciences from 1908 to 1910 produced not only large support for the Summer School and teacher education but also a broadening of undergraduate opportunities for vocational preparation. The broadening proceeded along two lines—more studies in science, and education for business.

Increasing the emphasis on science involved two steps. The first, taken in 1908, was the merging of the Classical and the Latin Scientific courses into a single course leading to the degree of Bachelor of Arts. The second step occurred a year later. The faculty added to the a forementioned new B.A. course four other courses in Arts and Sciences which would, however, lead to a Bachelor of Science degree. In the first, biology and chemistry predominated; in the second, geological science; in the third, physics and mathematics; and in the fourth, business administration.

The first three were closely related. The explanation that Blake used in faculty meetings to justify them, and which later appeared in the *Register*, was that they were designed for boys planning to be doctors, lawyers, geologists on government service, or teachers of science.

A different, almost apologetic, rationale accompanied the Course in Business Administration. The wording in the *Register* for 1909 was, "It is intended for those who have no inclination for the engineering courses but who are desirous of obtaining a knowledge of the bases of mining, metal, and transportation industries." The rationale betrays an intention to keep the Course in Business Administration closely aligned to those in technology.

The list of requirements for the Course in Business Administration was fairly long and contained, in addition to the same English, foreign languages, economics, chemistry, and physics found in other courses, such subjects as history of commerce, industrial history, freehand and mechancial drawing, accounting, commerical geography, physiography, public finance, business law, and public law.

Professor Stewart, a graduate of the Wharton School, probably structured the course. The trustees gave him charge over it and promised him one or two instructors if it attracted enough students. And it did. The Course in Business was offered for the first time in 1910—11, and the following year, sixteen new students enrolled, mostly freshmen, as compared with fifteen new students in all other Arts and Sciences courses. Within the next two years the trustees made good on their promise.

During the succeeding few years Professor Stewart and the faculty considerably strengthened the teaching of business administration. Among new professional courses was a two-credit offering in industrial management, also intended for seniors studying mechanical engineering.

The actual number of students attracted to business administration can only be estimated very roughly, as separate figures for enrollments in the four new B.S. courses in the arts and sciences were not published. However, the Registers show a dramatic increase of registrations in Arts and Sciences, from 95 in 1910 to 246 six years later. Most of the increase probably came from interest in business administration. In 1919, when separate figures appeared, 141 students were listed for Business ad 148 for Arts and Science.

Long before this, the apologetic rationale for studies in business had disappeared. The *Register* for 1916 advertised Business Administration as "a 'technical' course. It takes into account the fact that there is a Science of Business, with Economics as the underlying basis. ... The Course stands in the same relation to the life and calling of the manufacturer, the merchant, and other men of business as do the law and medical schools of the universities to lawyers and physicians. ... The Course is not only designed to prepare young men to enter business life, but it also offers preliminary training for the study of law, accountancy, public service and teaching."

The stability of Courses in Technology can be interpreted as a sign of orthodoxy resistant to change.

Charles R. Mann, writing in 1916 for the first major study ever made of engineering education, criticized schools for forcing students to select "from aeronautical, agricultural, architectural, automobile, bridge, cement, ceramic, chemical, civil, construction, electrical, heating, highway, hydraulic, industrial, lighting, marine, mechanical, metallurgical, mill, mining, railway, sanitary, steam, textile, telephone, topographical engineering, and engineering administration."[26]

Lehigh's offerings avoided this proliferation and conformed to the standard fields for which large and influential professional societies existed—civil, mechanical, mining, and electrical. Lehigh's additions to these fields, metallurgy, electrometallurgy, and chemical engineering, were arguably justifiable because they, too, could prepare students for employment in industries of many sorts. Chemical engineering, indeed, attracted a few more students than analytical chemistry.

Mining engineering, for which Lehigh had earlier received national recognition, remained a growing field through 1908. In 1904 Lehigh was rated ninth among mining schools in terms of numbers of graduates.[27] After 1908 the miners at Lehigh declined year by year until by 1918 they were half as numerous as they had been ten years earlier—77 in the fall of 1918, 115 in 1908.

Attempts to sustain Courses in Geology and Physics within the School of Technology failed. After Professor Williams retired, Drinker brought in Professor Benjamin L. Miller, who had a Ph.D. from Johns Hopkins and who showed little interest in geology as a technology. Physics was the brainchild of Professor Franklin. In 1900 he proposed the course, which the faculty delayed several years before approving. One student selected Physics, and the faculty terminated the course in 1905. No attempts were made to begin courses of instruction in mathematics, biology, and the more theoretical aspects of chemistry. All of these fields had an insurmountable difficulty for the Lehigh faculty: With the exception of geology and biology, for which a few governmental positions were available, none had occupational equivalents except in teaching. The faculty did not accept teaching as a sufficient occupational goal for a course in technology. Moreover, students did not enter the courses in technology in order to become teachers. Students were, by and large, aiming at industrial employment.

Consequently, when mathematics, theoretical chemistry, physics, biology, and geology appeared in courses of study, it was under the heading of General Literature or Arts and Sciences. Here, the faculty accepted teaching as a legitimate occupational goal.

This alignment with industry had long roots in the faculty's reliance on it for aid in instruction. The shops, mines, and mills of Lehigh Valley industries served as workshops for students. Foremen, supervisors, and top executives were sympathetic to requests from the heads of engineering departments for equipment. The nation's elementary and secondary schools had nothing that the engineering professors could use in the classroom. The same was true for all but a very few of the agencies of government.

John Fritz built a laboratory for civil engineering. He was eighty-seven years of age in 1909 when he announced the project. Many years earlier he had been president of both the AIME and the ASME. He had come to symbolize the highest professional standards in engineering. The five principal engineering societies had created the Fritz Gold Medal in his honor, one of the most prestigious favors a practising engineer could receive. Fritz personally supervised the building and equipping of the laboratory, which contained a central section given over to testing large specimens and smaller sections for studying problems in hydraulics and cement and concrete.

Later in the Drinker years, the trustees found the money for a wing on the west side of the Chandler Chemical Laboratory. The wing contained an assaying room, organic and quantitative analysis laboratories, a combustion room, a library, and offices.

The affinity for industry, plus a satisfaction with existing courses of study in technology, go far toward positioning Lehigh's offerings in engineering and applied science during the Drinker years.

Satisfaction with exsting courses did not imply complacency. The work of revising courses went on continuously and took into account recent developments in science and industry. Satisfaction or conservatism applies not to the content of scientific and industrial practise but to the methods and scope of teaching engineering. The faculty acted as though basic problems in teaching had been solved.

Several happenings during the period illustrate this. One was the granting of an honorary degree to Rossiter W. Raymond, longtime secretary of the AIME. Lehigh was relatively late among universities in beginning the practice of awarding honorary degrees. When the question of granting them was first raised in 1877, the faculty replied that degrees were only conferred by the university for work actually performed in the departments. For the next twenty-nine years, the opposition to honorary degrees continued. In 1906 someone — possibly Drinker — reopened the question, and the faculty finally agreed and immediately voted an honorary LL.D. to Raymond, who was by this time opposing reformers who wanted more democracy within the AIME. According to Edwin T. Layton, Jr., Raymond also opposed professional topics "such as unity and social responsibility" and charged with "hysteria" members insisting on a stricter code of ethics.[28]

Another manifestation of conservative conduct concerns the degree of Analytical Chemistry. At the time of Lehigh's founding, it had been popular among technical departments, but in later years it had given way to the more general designation of B.S. in Chemistry. Of eighty-two schools surveyed in 1904 by the SPEE, Lehigh was the only one using the term "Analytical Chemistry."[29] The faculty then voted to change the name of the degree (retroactively) to that of B.S. in Chemistry.

Also with respect to degrees, the faculty refused to act favorably on several recommendations of the SPEE. In 1910 the SPEE passed these resolutions among others:

1. A four-year engineering course should normally lead to the degree Bachelor of Science (B.S.), to which should be added a specifying phrase, as for example, Bachelor of Science in Civil Engineering. ...

6. The professional engineering degrees, C.E., M.E., etc., should be given only to graduates who present satisfactory evidence of professional work of superior quality extending over not less than three years, and who submit a satisfactory thesis.[30]

Many schools fell into line with these recommendations, but Lehigh continued its practice of awarding degrees of C.E., M.E., and so forth, to students completing the four-year course. The Lehigh faculty did not change the name of its undergraduate degrees in engineering until 1925–26, at which time it also voted to award professional degrees much as had been recommended by the SPEE.

These are minor manifestation of a reluctance to change from previous practise. Of more importance is the attitude of the faculty toward certain major trends. William E. Wickenden, reporting in 1926 on a study made by the SPEE, identified three great movements in engineering education since 1900: the cooperative plan of Herman Schneider of the University of Cincinnati; the greatly increased emphasis on economic and management phases, pioneered by Frederick W. Taylor; and the large growth of engineering research and postgraduate study.[31] All three set parameters to developments in engineering education. Lehigh's reluctance to accept any of them helps to define the conservative position of its faculty in technology.

The cooperative plan of Schneider. Schneider's plan addressed itself to the old problem of establishing a proper balance between school and shop. According to Schneider, the university need not maintain shops for practical instruction but should extensively use those in nearby plants under cooperative agreements. As the plan was administered at the University of Cincinnati, groups of students took turns shuttling back and forth every few weeks between industrial plants and the university, which provided the supervision and continuity in relating theory to practice. In the words of Schneider, "We are the only engineering school in the country where there in nothing taught, in the school, except theory."[32]

The attitude of the Lehigh engineering faculty toward the cooperative plan is all the more pertinent because Schneider was an alumnus, having received a degree of C.E. in 1894. Following a period of industrial experience he had returned in 1899 to Lehigh as an instructor under Merriman. There is reason to believe that in his four years as an instructor he developed the main ideas of the cooperative plan, presented it to the faculty, and failed to impress them with its superiority over existing methods of instruction. The University of Cincinnati hired him as an assistant professor in 1903. Three years later he instituted the cooperative plan there, and it soon became a landmark in engineering education.

The greatly increased emphasis on economic and management phases, pioneered by Frederick W. Taylor. Actually, the "scientific management" of Taylor is only one trend in the growing emphasis on education in economics and management and should be distinguished from at least one other, dubbed "commercial engineering" by A. Michal McMahon, a historian of the electrical engineering industry. Both dealt with management and can be considered as feeders to a gestating curriculum in industrial engineering. However, by the time of America's entry into the war, they had radically different attitudes toward management.

Taylor's scientific management — or, to use a term preferred by Monte Calvert, historian of mechanical engineering, *Taylorism* — was, in its inception, closely identified with mechanical engineering and the steel industry but later became generalized for virtually all disciplines and productive enterprises.[33] Taylor had begun developing his system at Midvale Steel and, after attempting to apply his principles at several other places, came in 1898 to the Bethlehem Iron (later Steel) Company, whose directors were troubled with a bottleneck in machining heavy forgings for armor plate and large guns. Taylor's original aim had been to answer the labor question by means of a piecework system, encouraging workers to greater productivity and adequately rewarding them for their effort; but the system that he developed and attempted to apply at Bethlehem necessitated a complete reorganization of shop practices according to mathematically determined rules — a reorganization that offended both workers and foremen, who cherished accustomed ways, and top management, which saw its control threatened by a new breed of "scientific" managers. Even as Taylor was demanding that the officers at Bethlehem abide by the principles laid down by himself and his henchmen, he was fired. He then set down his theories in writing, publicized them, and gained disciples. In 1906 he was elected president of the ASME and sought to apply his principles to its reorganization.

It is not surprising that Taylor failed to impress the professors "next door" when he worked for Bethlehem Iron, as at that time his reforms were in process; they had as yet produced few positive results; they were not visible to outsiders; they had not been given the dramatic literary form he later clothed them with; and they were privately much criticized by Sayre and others. Still, he attracted attention. One who was drawn to him was a young Lehigh alumnus name Morris Llewellyn Cooke (M.E. '95). While attending Lehigh, Cooke had helped to support himself by working as a reporter and editor for newspapers.[34] After graduation he entered the printing business and became impressed by Taylor's methods. He came to the notice of Taylor, who, upon becoming president of the ASME, hired Cooke to help systematize the association's publication policies.

Cooke quickly displayed a talent for politics and public relations. In 1910 he wrote a report for the Carnegie Foundation for the Advancement of Teaching, "Academic and Industrial Efficiency" (Bulletin #5), in which he emphasized the importance of research to both the teaching of engineers and efficient production. He put his talents in politics and journalism to work in attempting to reduce corruption in municipal government. He became director of public works for the city of Philadelphia in the reform administration of Mayor Rudolph Blankenberg and, in the fight to get rid of corruption, took on first the public utilities and later the railroads.

His successes received wide publicity and praise; but in the course of his fights he showed himself to be more of a traditional reformer than a disciple of Taylor. In fact, he departed rather far from Taylorism. On one point especially he went a long step away from his mentor. Taylor had demonstrated a failure of traditional managerial practices to solve the labor problem but believed the situation could be corrected. Cooke's experience with the utilities convinced him that management was incapable of exercising any real social responsibility. As a consequence, he maintained that the professional engineer, in order to meet an ideal of social responsibility, had to set himself apart from the directors of corporate business and industry. In sum, for Cooke there was no natural bond between engineering and industrial management, and engineering educators should not pretend that there was. He became one of the leaders of the rebels against the traditional practices of engineering professional societies.[35]

In the immediate prewar years, Cooke was much in the news and was mentioned several times with a touch of pride in the Lehigh *Alumni Bulletin*. Nevertheless, his attitude toward management, government, and private business sharply diverged from the bulk of opinion among Lehigh faculty and alumni, as far as this can be determined. Lehigh faculty were unwilling to accept the inference of Taylorism that corporate directors, presidents, superintendents, and the like should be subject to a higher level of scientific control, and much less willing to believe that all corporate management should be held suspect.

The idea of commerical engineering was much more acceptable, as it envisaged the enlightenment of traditional managers according to principles derived from the machine. The movement for commercial engineering is said to have originated within the AIEE, largely as a result of work done by Samuel Insull.

> Though the growth of the phenomenon was contemporary with the rise of "scientific management," its origins lay in the dilution of the idea of engineering itself. Scientific Management applied the engineering method specifically to productive process; commercial engineering, however, came out of the front office, appearing in guises as various as public relations managers and salesmen. Engineers had earlier argued that the engineer should be a businessman, now many insisted that managing a business was really engineering work.[36]

Commercial engineering agreed with the desire of Lehigh's engineering faculty to cultivate good relations with top management in business and industry. It seems to have underlaid support for requiring more economics for engineering students and adding to the university a study in business administration. But the Lehigh faculty were not yet ready to give the theory of commercial engineering an application in the form of a separate and equal course in industrial engineering. Only a few schools were pioneering in this direction.

The large growth of engineering research and postgraduate study. The word *large* must be understood in the context of what had gone before. Compared with research and postgraduate studies of the present time, the amount of these in the prewar years was very small. Most schools and departments in engineering believed, as did Lehigh, that engineering education should be basically undergraduate. A change in this point of view occurred only when industry began demanding engineers with more education in science than the standard four-year courses were providing. That demand was beginning to be heard, particularly in the electical and chemical industries.

Lehigh in these years, like most of the nation's technical schools, gave little time to graduate work. From 1899 to 1919 Lehigh awarded no doctorates and only twenty-six M.A.'s and fifty-six M.S.'s.

The indifference of the Lehigh faculty to graduate work in engineering can be attributed not only to the dominant opinion among engineers but also to the success of existing practises. The graduates of four-year programs found jobs, some of which provided advancement into management. Successful alumni supported the status quo as being best for the university. No leadership favoring graduate studies in engineering developed. And, if it had appeared, it would have been frustrated because of an inability to have professors with advanced degrees who might be willing to build graduate programs. Certainly these did not exist at Lehigh. The department heads ruled; and with the exception of Richards, they personally had little experience with graduate work. The M.S. was the top degree of William Esty (Electrical Engineering). The other three heads — Eckfeldt of Mining, Ralph J. Fogg of Civil, and Fred V. Larkin of Mechanical Engineering — possessed only the baccalaureate.

Successful graduate work in engineering at the doctoral level demanded investigation into new, specialized areas of science, obtainable only with the cooperation of a capable scientific faculty interested in research. At Lehigh the few who might have helped to supply this expertise did not remain. In 1915 Franklin of physics left for MIT following a dispute with Professor Esty. Two years later the top producing scholar in chemistry, Samuel A. Salisbury, also went to MIT, there to take over Drown's former position as director of the teaching in chemical engineering.

Still, at the time of America's entry into the First World War, Lehigh did not feel any adverse effects from a failure to promote graduate education and research. Nor did the war produce any feelings of insufficiency.

The First World War has been called *a chemists' war* to distinguish its place in the scientific and technological revolution from the *physicists' war* of the 1940s.[37] The terms are intended to indicate a growing importance of science in military operations and the mobilization of science by the government.

This mobilizing was far more crucial to victory in the second war than in the first. The First World War might as justly be styled "a civilian engineers' war"; for the national government, finding the traditional engineering resources of army and navy to be insufficient, gave work to engineers from all walks of life. A good case can be made for the proposition that in the First World War the nation's engineering talents were at least as important as its scientific know-how in tipping the scales in favor of the Allied powers. The value of engineering has possibly been hidden because, unlike the scientists, the engineers did little research, kept a low profile, and did not produce anything as visible as the scientists' National Research Council.

Engineers served as consultants, planners, supervisors, expediters, builders, teachers, trouble-shooters, and suppliers. Some worked for the army or the navy. Others held governmental posts of other sorts or helped war production in the private sector.

Everywhere, the wartime activities of engineers satisfied a growing thirst to prove their public service capacity. It was not by chance that Herbert Hoover emerged from the war as a model for engineers of what their profession could do for the good of the country.

Students, faculty, and trustees at Lehigh did almost nothing in scientific research toward winning the war. They did not expect to be asked for this sort of service. When the United States entered the conflict, the trustees and faculty formally put the university and its laboratories "at the disposal of the Government" as a sign of being willing to do whatever the government had in mind for them.[38] Fritz Laboratory did much testing for the military, other governmental agencies, and private industries engaged in war production. Some of the staff took leaves of absence for war-related work or engaged in part-time service. No comprehensive listing has ever been attempted. The indications are that at one time or another most of the teaching staff in science and technology did some sort of war work using their professional skills.

The involvement of the faculty in war-related work was looked upon as a personal matter. For the university as a whole, everyone associated with it expected the principal contributions to take forms of manpower and the training of troops in engineering-related skills. This expectation was fulfilled, with manpower coming first.

When on 3 February 1917 the United States severed diplomatic relations with Germany, many students began preparing for military duty. According to the *Brown and White*, about a hundred immediately volunteered for various branches of service. The faculty granted seniors the privilege of taking early final examinations. Some students resorted to voluntary drill sessions on the upper athletic field. In June, the faculty shortened commencement week upon discovering that few seniors planned to attend.

The summer of 1917 and the succeeding academic year passed with much unrest, especially among students who would soon be subject to conscription. Faculty and students had hoped that the university would be awarded a unit of ROTC, which had been designed to fill a need for officers. Given the sharp distinction in status between officers and enlisted men, many students facing the draft would sooner volunteer for an officer training program than enjoy a few extra weeks of freedom and become privates. Lehigh students were no different from others. But the government had more requests for an ROTC contingent than it could satisfy, and Lehigh, with many other schools, was forced to do without.

Summer training camps provided a possibility for some to become officers. In 1918 Lehigh was permitted to send seventy-one students to the camp at Plattsburg, New York. Students in technical fields who wished to keep on schedule had to attend the specialized summer sessions. Most Lehigh students waited out the time until they were called up.

The faculty revised the calendar to compress four years of education into three. They did this not by eliminating the summer sessions but by lengthening the academic working day, abolishing examination periods, and doing away with some holiday vacations and shortening the time of others. The faculty determined that the three-year sequence should go into effect 12 September 1918, about a week earlier than the usual start of the school year.

The university waited for more than a year after the declaration of war before being called upon to assist in training troops. The call, when it came, produced encampments of two sorts.

The first was called Camp Coppee. The army brought inductees to the campus for training by the faculty in technology. The army was using this sort of program at Lehigh and other universities in order to obtain skilled mechanics and technicians of other sorts. Army personnel controlled the troops, which were billeted wherever space for them could be found. Camp Coppee was formally opened 6 May 1918 "by the unfurling of a beautiful flag, a gift of Mrs. Henry Coppée."[39]

Three packages of troops arrived for Camp Coppee. The first, which came on 6 May, consisted of about 300 "rookies," mostly from Virginia and West Virginia, whose fitness for formal instruction was questionable. The second session opened 25 July for about 580 soldiers, most of whom were Pennsylvanians and somewhat more suitable subjects for education. The third session began 19 September for about 250 draftees.

The third session at Camp Coppee overlapped with the second sort of encampment at Lehigh, dubbed the Students' Army Training Corps, or SATC. This was designed for all able-bodied students of the age of eighteen and over. They would be subject to military discipline, administered by officers brought in for the purpose, while remaining full-time students on the abbreviated three-year schedule. The SATC, like the program that produced Camp Coppee, had counterparts at colleges and universities across the country. At Lehigh a single commanding officer was to be in charge of both the SATC and Camp Coppee. Captain A. G. VanAtta was given the post.

Thus, when the school year began in the autumn of 1918, the campus was home to three sorts of students: inductees brought in for Camp Coppee; Lehigh students belonging to the SATC; and Lehigh students who because of age, disability, or foreign nationality were excused from the SATC. By now, too, the Navy was recruiting students.

Confusion followed. Captain VanAtta was late in arriving to organize the SATC. Orders came from Washington to shorten all engineering courses to two years. Housing and food services were inadequate. Uniforms had not arrived so that it was impossible to tell the status of one student from another.

Before most of the difficulties could be attended to, an epidemic of Spanish Influenza reached the Bethlehems. St. Luke's could only take a few Lehigh students, being crowded with cases among townspeople. The university had to rely on its own resources, supplemented by whatever the army could supply, mainly doctors and medicines. Okeson wrote of the experience, "On Wednesday, October 9th, the epidemic having gained headway, a military quarantine was established and every man was required to domicile himself on the campus. ... On Thursday, Drown Hall was taken over by the army doctors and turned into a hospital. ... Some of the boys had already been sent to St. Luke's and three of them succumbed to pneumonia. Eleven other deaths followed at Drown Hall out of the cases treated. ... Every professor must have a pass."[40]

The quarantine was lifted early in November, and less than a week later the armistice ending the war was signed. Camp Coppee and the SATC quickly disappeared. By 11 December, all troops were gone, students were back in their usual living quarters, the four-year sequence had been resumed, and life in general was "back to normal."

Former students who had been in service returned. The veterans were not numerous and caused no great problems. Enrollments had dropped in 1917 but in the fall of 1918 attained a new high of 901, principally because of the existence of the SATC and a large freshman class. In the autumn of 1919 enrollment was again up, now reaching 1136. Faculty who had been in military or other war-related service were back. The war had occasioned very few replacements among the faculty. A wartime Course in Naval Engineering, similar to the Course in Marine Engineering that had been adopted during the Spanish-American conflict, was languishing for want of students and was closed out a few years later.

Lehigh began a program of compulsory ROTC. The faculty voted in favor of it on 2 December 1918. The trustees agreed, but asked that enrollment be voluntary for a year in order to be able to evaluate the response of students. The infantry unit that began in September 1919 attracted more than 300 students, of whom 266 stayed out the year. In 1920 the trustees agreed that ROTC should be compulsory for all students for two years, at the end of which time they would be free to decide whether or not to continue for the additional two years needed for a commission.

Compulsory ROTC had small but important influences on the men studying at Lehigh. For most it was, like brushing one's teeth, a necessary chore; but it also meant several additional ceremonies during the year, including a commissioning ceremony at commencement time, the availability of another career choice, and another avenue for the release of energy.

In addition to adopting ROTC, the faculty, without fanfare, made a change of greater import. In 1918 reorganized and altered the names of the courses of study. In the future the Courses in Technology would be known as the "College of Engineering." The B.A. Course in Arts and Sciences and the three B.S. science courses would be combined into a single sequence leading to a Bachelor of Arts degree and be known as "College of Arts and Science." The Course in Business Administration would remain as it was and henceforth be called "College of Business Administration."

As with earlier changes of nomenclature, these appear to have been made with no intention of forming administrative units. No deans or other staff immediately appeared, although Blake was still regarded as a spokesman for faculty in Arts and Science and Stewart was obviously in command of Business Administration.

Quite possibly, in 1918 no one suspected what these groupings might become.

Part Two
The New Lehigh

5
Launching the New Lehigh: 1919–1935

Many of the changes that came to America in the immediate postwar years were hostile to education. Yet education flourished.

This was true for Lehigh, situated in a city that seemed to have forgotten its heritage of culture and good order. Schwab's dream of making Bethlehem an ideal place in which to live died. Bethlehem Steel gave up its sports program and disbanded its band. Steel company executives communicated more among themselves, apart from the rest of the community. The Saucon Valley Country Club, founded in 1920, became the center of their social life. They looked on while life on the south side of the Lehigh River became disorderly and vicious. No more large foreign-born groups arrived. Second-generation immigrants were in their teens and shedding parental customs and controls. Gangs of youths organized along ethnic lines and waged war among themselves. Unscrupulous operators moved in, defying Prohibition and catering to lust.

The conditions of life in Bethlehem were, to say the least, unattractive to Lehigh students, who had never found the Bethlehems especially inspiring. Although a few student writers deplored the situation,[1] the great majority ignored it.

The faculty, too, by and large ignored the disorder. The newer members felt little loyalty to Bethlehem. Many chose to live outside the city limits and commute by trolley or automobile.

Lehigh University, like Bethlehem, was in a metamorphic state. Lehigh was, moreover, bound to Bethlehem by ties that both the city and the university sought to strengthen. A collaboration with Bethlehem Steel was as strong as ever, perhaps stronger. School teachers and others attended the Summer School and night classes. However, the emerging Lehigh had nothing of the wastrel character of Bethlehem. The new Lehigh was bound up with national developments in education. Its leadership came from outside the city, the valley, and the commonwealth.

The old Lehigh can be said to have passed into history with the resignation of President Drinker at the end of 1920 and the deaths the following year of Robert W. Blake and Joseph W. Richards. Drinker had left educational matters to the faculty, thereby permitting parochial interests to take precedence over broader visions. Blake had symbolized the centrality of the classics within the arts and sciences. Richards had represented an alliance of teaching and research at a time when Ph.D.s in science were less specialized.

The new Lehigh can be said to have fairly begun as replacements for Drinker, Blake, and Richards appeared. Charles Russ Richards, progressive dean of engineering and director of the Engineering Experiment Station at the University of Illinois, became president. Philip Mason Palmer, a native of Maine who in 1905 had replaced Severin Ringer as head of the Department of Modern Foreign Languages and who, since then, had passed many summers studying in Germany, took over the direction of a Curriculum in Arts and Science. Bradley Stoughton, former reforming secretary of the AIME — which during his tenure was reorganized as the AIMME, or American Institute of Mining and Metallurgical Engineers — succeeded Richards as head of Metallurgy and also sometimes served as a spokesman for all of the engineering departments. To these must be added the name of Neil Carothers, former Rhodes Scholar and the recipient of a Ph.D. in economics from Princeton. Carothers became head of the College of Business Administration.

Richards, Palmer, Stoughton, and Carothers did not form a team. They had been reared in an age of individualism and did not think along team lines. Each had his own supporters. But their ideas and operations meshed. Richards gave a general direction to the university. Stoughton supported him from a wide experience in professional engineering. Palmer for Arts and Science and Carothers for Business Administration worked in their respective domains to achieve the objectives defined by Richards.

All were conversant with controversies over the ends and means of higher education that had been going on by fits and starts in various parts of the country since the turn of the century. A utilitarian purpose was being widely accepted as necessary for educating the persons needed for orderly progress in an industrializing and urbanizing society. An infatuation with science and democracy carried with it an insistence that progress in higher education be based on merit, and that the meritorious should enjoy a freedom of choice. Accompanying this idea of a democratic meritocracy was a realization that greater specialization in occupations and disciplines and rapid advances in knowledge made higher education for specific jobs in the main impracticable. The general vocational purpose of higher education had to be separated from narrow occupational goals. Students should be vocationally educated, to be sure, but so as to be prepared for diversity and change.

Among engineering educators the preference for vocational as opposed to occupational aims took a special form, that of a goal of education for leadership. Engineers had emerged from their wartime experiences impressed with the country's need for organization and their own potential for providing it. What can be called the Hoover Syndrome was in the making, an ideal personalized in the life of Herbert Hoover, the engineer who as head of the Food Administration had projected an image of a wise and efficient humanitarian, the sort of leader an industrializing country ought to have.

Both radicals and conservatives among engineers became infected with the syndrome. It gained support from proponents of Taylorism, corporate engineering, and many other educators and industrialists, including Eugene G. Grace, who was quoted as hailing the great engineer as a benefactor of mankind who knew both how to build and what should be built. For a time the ideal appeared as a possible bond for strengthening a newly organized Federation of American Engineering Societies (FAES), of which Hoover was chosen as the first president.

Morris L. Cooke ('95) was among the organizers of the FAES and one of the most articulate spokesmen of the Hoover Syndrome. Okeson reproduced in the April 1921 issue of the *Alumni Bulletin* a speech that Cooke had given before the Philadelphia Engineer's Club and several other groups, "The Inspiring Outlook before American Engineering." Cooke had said,

> Every day sees us ready to broaden our definition of engineering. To the fields of design and construction we are adding operation with ever increasing emphasis. In fact there is every reason to believe that our work in the field of the management of men — the engineering of men as contrasted with the engineering of materials — is the one thing which is elevating our profession, placing it on a plane with the other professions which have dealings with men as distinguished from dealing with things. May we not look forward to a favored position among the professions in view of our dealings with both materials and men.

In 1922 the SPEE formally entered the controversy over purpose by proposing a study involving the cooperation of faculties in all of the country's leading institutions of engineering education. The study was carried out under the direction of William E. Wickenden, an industrialist and an educator formerly with MIT, and produced a series of reports, the most publicized being a preliminary report by Wickenden in 1926. This document was punctuated with expressions of leadership through engineering. "The engineer of tomorrow will not rise to leadership by abandoning his distinctive role or by permitting it to become ill-defined. He will do so by remaining essentially an engineer, by becoming a more competent engineer, by extending the reach of engineering methods and ideals to larger realms of life, and withal, by making himself a team-mate eagerly desired by other types of men." Wickenden paid homage to the FAES. "For the sanction of a definition, we may turn to the walls of the library of the United Engineering Societies, where we find inscribed in letters of gold the words, 'Engineering — the art of organizing and directing men and of controlling the forces and materials of nature for the benefit of the human race.'"

Wickenden indicated some parameters that further helped to define an engineering approach to leadership. Engineering was a problem-solving activity "concerned with tangible, measurable and contemporary achievement." These features helped to distinguish engineering leadership from political leadership, which the country had in the past, and also from the teaching of engineering. "Teaching is an altruistic investment in the engineers of tomorrow and by its nature largely incapable of objective measurement and contemporary reward."[2]

The emergence of the Hoover Syndrome, with its message of leadership through engineering, took place at a time when a great many of the nation's colleges and universities, including technical institutes, were revising practices and updating courses of study. At Lehigh the process involved nearly everybody. Beginning in 1919 and continuing for several years, the departments examined courses, the faculty reorganized its system of committees, and the Alumni Association, by means of a blue-ribbon committee, began a comprehensive study for improving almost all aspects of university operations.

Also, almost everybody began a search for Drinker's replacement. Trustees, faculty, and alumni compiled lists of possibilities. William C. Dickerman ('96), an alumnus trustee, gave the clue to the sort of president who would be ideal: "The basic thought was that there was no reason why a university could not be developed in the same way that a manufacturing proposition is developed; that many of the factors were the same, the plant, personnel and working capital all entered into it."[3] No one among the trustees, faculty, and alumni seems to have disagreed with this. On all lists the name of Charles Russ Richards appeared as a man who would bring a businesslike and engineering point of view to the development of Lehigh University.

Richards took office in 1922, following a brief period in which Vice President Emery was in charge. Faculty, alumni, and trustees quickly discovered Richards was indeed an "educational Hoover." In his inaugural address on Founder's Day 1922, and in a talk before the New York Alumni Club on 18 October 1922, he indicated acceptance of an engineering approach to management. Engineering had recently been defined, he said, "as 'the art of organizing and directing man and controlling the forces and materials of nature for the benefit of the human race.' This definition recognizes the changing status of the work of the engineer and the constantly increasing need for men who are capable of working with other men as well as with materials and processes."

In both speeches Richards explained the meaning of leadership through engineering for Lehigh. He indicated that the needs of engineering education should come first, with the understanding that those included scientific research as well as instruction. The primary function of education in business and the humanities was serving the students in engineering. He told the New York alumni, "Unlike many of the larger universities, her [Lehigh's] College of Engineering is now, and probably always will be, of chief importance. In consequence, the work of the other two colleges ... must be coordinated with that of the College of Engineering. It would seem, therefore, that the presentation of the work of these other colleges will more likely be designed to fit the requirements of engineers than is the case in a majority of institutions."

One implication was clear. Former President Drown's idea that the welfare of Lehigh depended on an equal treatment of all courses of study was to experience an eclipse. As long as Richards was in command, the Colleges of Business Administration and Arts and Science would exist principally for purposes of improving the education of engineering undergraduates, especially those capable of becoming tomorrow's leaders in business and industry.

Several other implications stemmed from Richards's engineering approach to management. As president he would be concerned with safety and economy in recognizing and dealing with problems tangible and measurable. He would exercise a centralized control over the allocation and use of resources both inanimate and human. At the same time, he would leave intangibles of teaching and counselling to others. His leadership in education would consequently respect most faculty prerogatives. The departments in engineering would continue to control their courses of study. The Colleges of Business and Arts and Science would serve the needs of engineering education but be free in other respects to establish and pursue their own objectives.

As far as can be determined, faculty, alumni, and trustees understood and accepted these implications. Trustees rejoiced in having found a man who would govern Lehigh from a business point of view. Faculty recognized in Richards a superior intelligence, experience, and drive in promoting much-needed reforms, a man whose broad views concerning engineering education meant a strengthening of subjects taught in all of the colleges.

The Alumni Association discontinued efforts at educational reform. A thirty-seven page report prepared by its committee was quietly shelved.

The momentum of support for Richards never diminished, not even when in the 1930s economic depression commanded a slowdown and retrenchment.

One of Richard's first tasks as president was that of modernizing the administration to improve services at the least possible expense. By the fall of 1924 he, the trustees, the faculty, and the Alumni Association had made a number of changes.

One was reorganizing the Board of Trustees in such a way as to give undisputable control to the alumni members. The new board numbered sixteen persons, including the ten charter trustees, now called corporate trustees, chosen for life, and six members elected by the Alumni Association, instead of four as formerly, one chosen each year for a term of six years. The alumni members were no longer called honorary trustees and could vote with the corporate trustees. There were to be four standing committees — Executive, Finance, Endowment, and Buildings and Grounds.

A second major change involved the formation of a business office headed by a comptroller and reporting to the president. The Department of Buildings and Grounds was attached to the office. Also involved were revisions of procedure for accounting and auditing and the beginning of annual budgeting.

A third change was the reorganization of the office of the dean, who was to take over the duties formerly performed by the registrar and the secretary of the faculty and in addition was to advise students in scholastic and personal affairs and to counsel the president on educational matters. This change was made easier by an automobile accident that rendered Professor Thornburg incapable of performing his former tasks as secretary of the faculty. His position was downgraded and renamed "recording secretary," with tasks largely confined to taking minutes and assisting the president in drafting an agenda for faculty meetings.

From the moment Richards had appeared on the scene, he had treated the colleges as administrative units. With the consent of the faculty, each college was to have an advisory council consisting of a few senior men elected by the faculty of the college. In addition, the Colleges of Business and Arts and Science were to have heads of curriculum who would be equal in status with the heads of curricula in the College of Engineering—which was not to have a single administrative head. In 1925 heads of curricula were redesignated as directors of curricula.

The university was to have a legal counsel and a health service organized under a medical doctor who would maintain an infirmary in Saucon Hall, give physical examinations and vaccinations to incoming freshmen, and be responsible for sanitary conditions in dormitories and dining areas.

For the first time the faculty was to elect the members of its committees, although the selection of chairmen was still left to the president. Under urging from Richards, the Committee on Educational Policy collected and revised all procedures, rules, and regulations (PRR). At a meeting on 12 September 1923, this committee reported the new PRR to the faculty, which adopted the document with provisos that the word *curriculum* be substituted for the word *course* and that all rules and regulations not contained in the new code be declared null and void.

A standardization of procedures accompanied the other changes and extended over a period of years. Standardization was not imposed as a policy but came about piecemeal and was limited to affairs shown by experience to need some sort of uniform treatment.

Many changes of lesser import followed the establishing of an administrative structure. As the tasks to be performed became more numerous and specialized, additions and alterations were made. In 1924 the position of a director of the library became full time, and in 1926 the Office of the Registrar was separated from that of the dean and was also made full time. In 1929 the college councils were enlarged from a few elected members to include all who were entitled to vote in university faculty meetings.

Richards filled the administrative positions as soon as they were created. Vice president Emery took the additional title of comptroller and thereby became head of the new Business Office. Okeson, the secretary of the Alumni Association and editor of its *Bulletin*, added to these duties those of treasurer and secretary of the Board of Trustees.

Richards brought in persons from outside for most of the other positions, thereby beginning to reduce the inbreeding begun under Drinker. Chief among these appointees was Charles Maxwell McConn, a personal friend of Richards who had been registrar and assistant to the president at the University of Illinois. McConn had much experience with admission, the keeping of student records, and the advising of students and was among the far-sighted few who were sensitive to the changes in higher education and the need for institutionalizing means of assistance and controls. Before coming to Lehigh he had published on this and other subjects in the *New Republic, Nation, Survey Graphic*, and the *Weekly Review*.

Other administrative appointments, which Richards made early in his tenure as president, included Dr. Raymond C. Bull as director of the health service and Robert S. Taylor ('95) as legal counsel.

The position of registrar had been vacant since 1921, when Raymond W. Walters had resigned to become dean of Swarthmore College. In the reorganization of 1923, the duties of a registrar were given to McConn; but in 1926 the position was separated from that of the dean and given to George B. Curtis, who had been teaching economics.

Howard S. Leach, who had been reference librarian at Princeton, replaced Professor Stewart as librarian. Stewart had been granted a leave of absence in 1924 in order to accept an appointment from Pennsylvania's Governor Gifford Pinchot to a vacancy on the Public Service Commission.

Stewart's departure also left the direction of Business Administration vacant. It was then that Richards brought in the brilliant, imaginative, and somewhat irascible Neil Carothers — who was also an excellent player and coach of tennis. Richards had by this time already elevated Philip M. Palmer to the position of director of the Curriculum of Arts and Science and brought in Bradley Stoughton to be head of the department and director of the Curriculum of Metallurgical Engineering — which now also included electro-metallurgy, the two courses of study having been joined following the death of Professor Joseph W. Richards. Stoughton arrived fresh from the work of codrafting with Horace Drury a report advocating an end to the twelve-hour working day, for which Herbert Hoover had written an introduction and which U.S. President Warren G. Harding had signed and sent to the FAES.

Subsequently, Richards had opportunities to replace three other key heads of curricula with notables brought in from other universities. One was Charles Clarence Bidwell, a physicist who had been teaching at Cornell, from which he possessed a Ph.D., to replace Harry MacNutt as director of a recently developed Curriculum in Engineering Physics. Another was Joseph W. Barker, a professor at MIT, to take the direction of Electrical Engineering from William Esty, who had died. The third was Hale Sutherland, also from MIT, appointed in 1930 to head Civil Engineering in place of Ralph J. Fogg.

Richards also filled several influential academic headships that were unaccompanied by directorships of curricula. All of these were in the College of Arts and Science. One of the appointees was Lawrence Henry Gipson, a prize-winning historian and, like Carothers, a former Rhodes Scholar. Gipson had a doctorate from Yale and was to head a newly organized Department of History and Government. Another appointee was Robert Metcalf Smith, a Shakespearean scholar with a doctorate from Columbia, to take charge of English in place of William C. Thayer, who was retiring. A third was Alfred Arnold Bennett, to succeed Preston A. Lambert, who had been acting head of Mathematics since the disability of Thornburg; and when in 1927 Bennett departed to become a professor as Brown University, Richards replaced him with Tomlinson Fort, who was dedicated to the idea that mathematicians should do research mathematics.

On the academic side, the directors of curriculum were heirs to the power possessed in the old Lehigh by heads of departments. In 1928 there were nine directors of curriculum. Richards had appointed six of them, and five of the six were new to Lehigh, Palmer being the exception. Three directors of curriculum in engineering had been in place before Richards arrived and outlasted him — Harry M. Ullmann of Chemistry and Chemical Engineering, Howard Eckfeldt of Mining, and Fred V. Larkin of Mechanical Engineering. In addition, when after several years Barker departed, Richards gave the headship of Electrical Engineering to Stanley S. Seyfert, a long-time member of the Lehigh faculty.

The necessity of cooperating with nine academic princes who directed curricula was a situation with which Richards did not quarrel. He was not always as cooperative with the alumni, who were actively governing in fund raising, new construction, and athletics.

Richards welcomed their work in fund raising. He had laid down as a condition of accepting the presidency "that the Alumni will assume the responsibility for raising these funds and that the President will not be required to devote his time and energy to the work."[4] Richards was noncommittal respecting alumni help in supervising building projects. He actively opposed their dominance in athletics.

The alumni were active through the Board of Trustees and the Alumni Association. In 1922 the board had, in addition to the six alumni members, three alumni among the corporate trustees. H. R. Price, the president, died in 1924 and was succeeded by Grace, who carried with him the support of all alumni working for Bethlehem Steel. Under Grace the number of alumni who became corporate trustees increased.

Okeson was the executive secretary of the Alumni Association when Richards became president. In 1928 Okeson was succeeded as secretary by Andrew E. Buchanan, Jr. ('18), who had been hired in 1923 as an assistant to Okeson. Buchanan lifted his voice alongside that of his former boss as a spokesman for an important sector of the alumni.

Drinker, who had been largely responsible for bringing the alumni into the work of administration, remained active for several years after leaving the presidency. His last major service as president was obtaining money for raising faculty salaries.

Across the country the salaries of faculty had been hurt by wartime inflation. They had lagged far behind compensation for comparable work in industry and the professions. John D. Rockefeller had responded to the imbalance by making $50 million available through the Rockefeller General Education Board.

Drinker took advantage of this and obtained a pledge of $250,000 from the Rockefeller board on condition that the university find an additional $750,000. Drinker then obtained a promise of $250,000 from the Carnegie Foundation. In appreciation for these achievements he received the thanks of Lehigh's board, election to the position of honorary trustee — the first in this category since the death in 1916 of the Reverend Tolman, the last survivor of Asa Packer's many choices — and a commission from the Alumni Association to chair a committee to bring in the additional $500,000.

Then a postwar depression set in. Raising the additional $500,000 became difficult. The Rockefeller board had set a time limit, which could not be met. The issue was clouding the appointment of Richards as president and was the main reason why he insisted that the alumni should relieve the president of the burden of fund raising. To be sure, money for rising costs of operation came from increases in enrollment and tuition, but these sums could not be used to satisfy the Rockefeller board. Drinker sought and obtained an extension of the time limit to the end of 1924. The response of the trustees was to undertake in cooperation with the Alumni Association a major campaign for funds with Grace as honorary chairman of the principal committee and Dickerman as executive chairman.

The Greater Lehigh Endowment Campaign, as it came to be called, was, from a contemporary point of view, an amateur production, using up a great deal of energy for limited results. Initially Richards asked for $11,500,000. Grace and the other trustees shook their heads and set a goal of $4 million to be added to endowment within four years. Okeson, who was still executive secretary of the Alumni Association as well as being treasurer of the university, was the most active of the many alumni who engaged in the drive. A sufficient amount was paid in by the end of 1924 to secure the grant from the Rockefeller board. Eventually Okeson, Dickerman, and their coworkers raised approximately $3,300,000, thereby increasing the university's endowment from a little less than $3 million in 1923 to somewhat more than $5 million by 1927.

When the Greater Lehigh Endowment Campaign had yet about two years to run, Okeson and the Alumni Association began a plan of annual giving called the Alumni Fund. The plan grew out of their experience with alumni preferring to give for tangible items such as buildings, specific programs, and equipment rather than for a faceless endowment. The proceeds were to be used for any purpose designated by the giver within the scope of programs acceptable to the university.

The Alumni Fund brought in $11,000 in the first three months of its existence (1925). Okeson called this a success and from then on promoted the fund at every opportunity. It became a reliable and important source of income. In 1929−30 it achieved a record high of $118,609.28. This figure was not matched or exceeded until the opening years of the presidency of Martin D. Whitaker.

At the beginning of Richards's presidency, when the trustees were having difficulty in collecting the money required to secure the grant from the Rockefeller board, the alumni were also having trouble paying for a structure to commemorate the students and alumni who had served in the First World War.

A total of 1,921 Lehigh men had been in uniform, of whom 46 had lost their lives. Shortly after the armistice was signed, the Alumni Association became dedicated to the idea of a large building to honor these servicemen. The plan, as it developed, was not for any addition to instructional facilities, nor even primarily to house administrative services, although these would be allowed space in the wings, but for an architecturally unique *memorial*. The style was described as being "Scholastic Gothic" with details ranging from "tall, mounting buttresses and stately windows to unexpected grotesque and grouped mullion windows with leaded casements. . . . The central portion of the Hall, which occupies the base of the tower, rises to a height of three stories, and above the entrance is a great mullioned window which, at some future time, will glow with colored glass."[5] The president and his staff would be moved from Packer Hall to the two floors of a left wing. Alumni Association offices would occupy the second floor of a right wing. An oak-paneled assembly room for the use of faculty and alumni meetings would take up the entire first floor of the right wing.

The association broke ground on Founder's Day, 4 October 1919, then delayed beginning construction until $400,000 could be raised. This took about three years. Construction began in late spring 1922. Two years later a sum of $120,000 was still needed in order to complete the hall. When, finally, it was occupied in September 1924, a deficit of $25,000 still remained. With the expectation that the money could be raised from unpaid pledges, the Alumni Association completed payment by borrowing the remaining funds from the university.

Shortly before the hall was occupied, in April 1924, Richards found money in the Forestry Fund to plant forty-six elms on either side of the drive extending west from Taylor Gymnasium. Beneath each elm was placed a concrete block bearing a bronze plate with the name of a deceased student or alumnus. The drive was renamed Memorial Drive.

Alumni had a hand in almost every physical improvement on the campus during the Richards years. Alumnus and former professor E. H. Williams, Jr., gave money in 1924 for remodeling Williams Hall. In April 1925, the trustees bought the Smith farm, a relatively flat tract adjacent to Sayre Park near the top of South Mountain. Richards proposed that the farm be used for playgrounds to relieve the congestion on Taylor Field. The trustees demurred; and six months later, Lehigh received Steel Field from the Bethlehem Steel Company for a nominal sum of thirty thousand dollars.

Money from the alumni helped with many other projects. In the summer of 1925 Saucon Hall was remodeled and used by the Department of English and the newly established Health Service. The following year Richards had a four-story addition made to join Christmas and Saucon.

The College Commons qualified for some changes. For reasons that were never publicized, students deserted the dining service until it became a losing business. In 1926 the trustees ordered the service terminated and the building renovated for use by the Department of Military Science. A small cafeteria in Drown Hall replaced the dining service.

In 1928 a new boiler plant was built, incorporating in it the old structure. The following year alterations were made to Williams Hall, including the addition of a greenhouse and quarters for animals, as well as to the Physical Laboratory, Packer Hall, and Chandler Laboratory. In 1930 all walks and drives were rebuilt. Other changes included installation of a system of bells to announce the beginning and end of classes (1926), the building and dedication of the Memorial Gates to Sayre Park (1926), and the razing of Camp Coppee, a temporary wooden structure built in 1918 in front of the Physical Laboratory (1928).

Richards, from the time of his inauguration, had placed a high priority on a building to contain studies in mechanical and electrical engineering. Okeson asked in 1926, "Who will build it?"[6] The answer came almost immediately: James Ward Packard, '84, founder of the Packard Motor Car Company.

Packard's interest in Lehigh was at the time a mystery, as he was not among the alumni who held a top position in the association or came back for reunions. "Was he ever in Bethlehem after graduating in '84?" asked Al Brodhead. "No," replied Okeson, "June, 1884, was the last time he ever saw the campus."[7] Packard shunned publicity. He had remained in Warren, Ohio, after his factory had been moved to Detroit and had hired others to manage it. At the time of the gift to Lehigh the chief of these executives was Alvan Macauley, '92, president of the Packard Motor Car Company.

Packard had a fatal illness. With death imminent, he decided to do something for his alma mater. From the correspondence between him, Richards, and Grace came the gift of securities having a market value of a million dollars. Packard did not visit the campus, even though the Alumni Association made him an alumnus trustee. Macauley represented Packard at Lehigh whenever necessary.

The firm of Visscher and Burley (T. C. "Speed" Visscher, '99, and J. L.

"Jim" Burley, '94), which had designed the Alumni Memorial and become a consulting firm for the university, was given the assignment of designing the Packard Laboratory. Packard wanted a combination of functional utility and artistic beauty. Visscher and Burley worked with professors Larkin of Mechanical Engineering and Esty and Seyfert of Electrical Engineering and with Andrew Litzenberger, an architect loaned to the university by Bethlehem Steel. Visscher and Burley adopted a design with an estimated cost of $1,200,000. Okeson sent this news to Packard, who mailed back a check for the extra two hundred thousand dollars.

Packard died 20 March 1928, before final planning for the building was completed. In his will he gave the university twenty thousand dollars and provided that after the death of his wife, one-third of his estate should come to Lehigh. The cornerstone was laid 9 July 1928. The trustees used the twenty thousand dollars to establish a research fellowship in Packard's name. At commencement exercises in June 1929, the university granted a posthumous honorary degree of Doctor of Engineering to Packard.

A side effect of the building of Packard Laboratory was the addition to the staff of Andrew Willard Litzenberger. Cranmer, for sixteen years superintendent of buildings and grounds, died 12 February 1929. Litzenberger was already working with Visscher and Burley on Packard Laboratory and took over as head of the Department of Buildings and Grounds. In succeeding years he participated in a number of community projects. He always worked closely with Bethlehem Steel, which maintained a keen interest in campus planning.

The planning and construction of a large addition to the Lucy Packer Linderman Library overlapped that of Packard Laboratory.

President Richards had inherited a problem with the library. It had woefully decayed from the days of glory under Chandler. Professor Stewart, the director from the time of Chandler until 1924, paid less attention to the library than to the teaching of economics and the work in Business Administration. During the Drinker presidency little money was spent on the library. Periodicals went unbound. As the space available for shelving books and periodicals dwindled, they were piled in the basement and began to mildew. No one bothered to keep abreast of improvements in library practice. The index for the collection was kept on hand-written cards of different sizes. Under-graduates needed special permission to use the library and, except for seniors, could not read books on the premises. A recommendation of the American Library Association to provide reading space for at least 25 percent of the student body came during Stewart's tenure and was ignored.[8]

Leach, a professional librarian, began changing the situation as soon as he arrived. Leach obtained increased appropriations for books and journals; allocated dollar quotas to the departments for the purchase of these; appealed to the alumni for donation of standard classics in English and of biographies and books on travel; and began the herculean task of binding back issues of periodicals, rearranging the collections, updating the card catalog, and rescuing the collections from the destructive work of nature. He noted the growing practice among faculty of assigning readings in library materials, took measures to make books and periodicals more accessible to students, and conducted tours of inspection for students. Systematically he reported to the faculty concerning acquisitions and circulation. The library, he said in October 1925, now had 164,562 books and pamphlets. In 1927 he reported to the alumni that in three years' time circulation had trebled, rising from 4,301 in 1923–24 to 13,204 in 1925–26. He began the practice of interlibrary loan.

In February 1927, Richards declared enlargement of the library to have first priority after Packard Laboratory. Leach appeared before the alumni on several occasions to explain the project. The planned addition would be a massive rectangle designed to flank the original building on two sides. Visscher and Burley would design the addition. Ten of the trustees, eight of whom were alumni, agreed to give twenty-five thousand dollars each over a five-year period for the project if other alumni would contribute the remainder. With these pledges made, the Alumni Association agreed to use the Alumni Fund until the balance was paid.

The announcement of plans for the library addition produced a small flurry of interest in Packer's original idea for a consulting library. Richards asked about the possibility of reestablishing the Asa Packer library fund. Some alumni responded with gifts of books and manuscripts. One of these was Robert B. Honeyman ('20), who in September 1928 gave a page of the manuscript of Darwin's *Origin of Species* and several volumes. A little over a year later he gave sixteen valuable books, including the first English translation of Euclid's *Geometry* and five protfolios of Haebler's original leaves of incunabula. Within the next thirty years Honeyman and his wife, by their gifts, more than doubled the size of the collection originally put together by Chandler.

The addition had cost about $636,500. By 1 October 1930, alumni had given a little more than $216,000 of this and borrowed $250,000 from the university's endowment with the intention of paying this back from the Alumni Fund. The remaining $170,500 had come from current income, mostly from the Asa Packer Estate. The association had difficulty in collecting the money to repay the university's endowment and by 1935 still owed more than $86,000. "Paying off an old debt is not something to produce enthusiasm and the Alumni Fund is slowly stifling under this prolonged endeavor," wrote the author of the trustees' agenda (probably Grace or Okeson, as the university was once again without a president).[9] The trustees thereupon reduced the association's obligation to $40,000 and paid the balance from the cash surplus that year.

Using the Alumni Association as an office of development was not working well. As early as 1926 Okeson had confessed to the weakness. "A salesman who is forced to make collections gets in bad terms with his customers."[10] The trustees also recognized this and on 15 April 1925 had voted to establish "a permanent organization for raising funds as part of the regular administration of the university." The decision was not implemented. Okeson remained the chief fund raiser, if anyone could be considered as such. When in 1928 he gave up his positions in the Alumni Association, he became clearly the agent of the board. In other respects the situation was unchanged.

The alumni doggedly held on to a control over athletics in spite of setbacks. They achieved a high point of control in 1919 when the memory of prewar victories was still fresh, and almost the entire sports program depended on subsidies channeled through the Athletic Committee, which operated independently of the faculty and the president.

The system was under attack. Underlying the discontent were questionable practices in many parts of the country to the detriment of intercollegiate sports. The practices included a proselyting of players from other schools, allowing nonstudents to play, and using financial and academic favors in recruiting and keeping athletes in school. Few of the shady practices existed at Lehigh. There is no evidence of proselyting or using nonstudents; and the faculty vigilantly maintained uniform academic standards for athletes and nonathletes alike. But pecuniary favors for athletes existed. The Alumni Association offered several scholarships. A Self-Aid Bureau with a self-perpetuating membership limited to fifteen gave preference to athletes. The Self-Aid Bureau had a monopoly on some jobs, for example, selling programs at football games. People heard talk of athletes receiving gifts from individual alumni and of being put on the payroll of Bethlehem Steel. At the same time, some influential alumni kept up the pressure for winning games and producing championship teams and appeared willing to fire coaches who could not provide them.

Many alumni and students disliked these pressures and opposed the inducements used in recruiting. Many members of the Lehigh faculty wanted to put an end to all subsidies.

Student attitudes were largely responsible for a showdown. The disruptions of war had dampened the willingness of students to support constantly winning teams. In the 1920s winning seasons in football about equaled losing seasons. The team did not win a game against Lafayette from 1919 to 1929. Wrestling and tennis provided the only consistently bright horizons. The wrestling squad tied with Yale for the national championship in 1927 and won it a year later. Tennis had a revival through the coaching of Carothers.[11] Other sports gave a victory-hungry alumnus little satisfaction.

In 1923 the university, as distinct from the Athletic Committee and Alumni Association, had no scholarships expressly for athletes, although athletes were eligible with other students for the regular scholarships and might qualify for tuition loans. But in June 1923 the board created sixty-four new awards. Twenty-four were full tuition scholarships, divided six per class with half in each class being given for excellence in school work and half for excellence in athletics. Forty were tuition loans. These were ostensibly based on need and bore an interest charge of 6 percent; but as everyone knew, they could be administered so as to provide subsidies for students.

The showdown occurred in 1924. Early in the year the Board of Directors of the Alumni Association passed a resolution calling for a graduate manager to provide a more businesslike administration for athletics. Richards took the occasion of adverse faculty and alumni criticism of the resolution to ask the faculty for authority to create a committee composed of ten faculty and ten alumni to study the matter. The faculty agreed to this. Later he enlarged the membership of the committee to include ten students.

The famous — or infamous — meeting of this committee produced no decisions on the issue of a graduate manager. It lasted more than five hours with the students doing most of the talking. Okeson described it for the benefit of other alumni:

> From the start it was quite evident that the graduate manager idea was to be shown no mercy by the undergraduates. No one bothered to ask what a graduate manager did or what were the normal functions at other colleges.
>
> But the big scream was the way we poor misguided alumni got battered by the very superior young men who warned us of the dangers and evils of our presumed attitude towards college sport. Too much system, said they, tends to eliminate real sport and promote the professional spirit. ... Alumni, they regretted to state, demanded impossible schedules and wanted our teams to play Harvard, Yale, Princeton, Pennsylvania, Cornell, and Penn State. ... The great trouble with the alumni, it was asserted, is that they take athletics too seriously and attach too much importance to victories. They fail to realize that undergraduates come to Lehigh to be educated and that sport is a secondary matter.[12]

Richards brought the meeting to a close by proposing a tripartite committee of faculty, alumni, and students to draft a plan of athletic control satisfactory to all. The committee produced a compromise, which was duly ratified. It involved substituting a Board of Control for the Athletic Committee and, in Richards's opinion, presented little difference from the old system. For the time being, athletics still largely escaped direction from the president's office.

The stand taken by students in the confrontation with alumni over athletics raises a question concerning the character of the student body. Was it changed from the prewar era? If it was, did it conform to the caricature of the student in the Roaring Twenties as "Joe College," a boy wearing a coonskin coat, waving a college pennant, and hugging a flapper?

Certainly the students were more numerous than they had been before the war. The trustees, taking this as an indication of increased interest in higher education, set a figure of 1,000 as ideal for Lehigh. For several years enrollments kept close to this figure. In the autumn of 1924 they rose to

1239 with 747 in Engineering, 234 in the College of Arts and Science, and 278 in Business Administration. Richards, pressed for money, welcomed the additional tuitions. Classes were larger, but Richards was unimpressed with an argument that class size is an indication of quality of education.[13] He told the trustees that the university could take 1500 students without unduly taxing existing facilities and faculty and proposed quotas for the colleges of 900 for Engineering and 300 each for Arts and Science and Business Administration. The trustees accepted the figures. Until the early 1930s, actual enrollments approximated the quotas.

The character of student bodies was evolving across the country in response to postwar shifts in morals, manners, and the material means of living. A college education was increasingly necessary for advancement in the democratic meritocracy. Many youths who in former years might have begged their parents for money to attend college now had parents begging and even forcing them (and sometimes daughters) to attend, whether or not they were college material. Often a college degree accompanied by little if any real education would serve. And "going to college" postponed the time when a young man had to work for a living. More than three times as many students received a college degree in 1930 than had earned one twenty years earlier.

Freedom from old ideas and practices was also in the air. Even the serious student was made more comfortable — and sometimes more confused — by a multiplication of mechanical gadgets and a greater variety of cheap and attractive pastimes.

In Bethlehem, Dean McConn of Lehigh told members of the Rotary Club that his position had become necessary because education had become popular.[14] In former times, he said, boys had come to college because they wanted to study; now they came because it was expected, and only some were interested in learning. A dean was needed, he said, to eliminate the unfit at the point of admission, to counsel, discipline, and in other ways to try to save the misfits who slipped by the initial screening, and to eliminate the incorrigibles. McConn later elaborated on these remarks in a book, *College or Kindergarten?* in which he labeled the college playboy as a "superkindergartener."

In his talk before the Rotary Club, McConn did not give a fair account of his duties as dean, which had little if any concern for a superkindergarten mentality. Students at Lehigh were as serious about studies as they had been in the 1880s and 1890s. The geographic areas and the social and economic strata from which they came were essentially the same for both periods, with the possible exception that in the postwar era parents had a higher average income resulting from well-to-do alumni sending their sons to Lehigh. A vocational approach penetrated all colleges and curricula. The faculties of the colleges were sensitive to a natural tendency among students to seek paths of least resistance and took pains to prevent any course of study from becoming a "gut," attractive to the lazy and the indifferent.

Among academically related activities there were some shifts of student attention from one subject to another. The University Lecture Series with its requirement of compulsory attendance was ended in 1928. The money formerly used to support it was distributed to the course societies to bring in guest lecturers. Course societies, however, were somewhat less prestigious and vital; but honor societies sprang up for almost every field of study. Calculus cremation disappeared, the last celebration being held in 1923. Other disappearances included the Washington's birthday oratorical contest for juniors and the Honor Court, finally closed by the faculty in 1922.

In 1927 the students, with assistance from the faculty, began a serious publication, *The Lehigh Review*, the first of its kind since *The Lehigh Quarterly* of the 1890s. *The Lehigh Review* provided an outlet for talent in producing essays, fiction, poetry, photographs, cartoons, and drawings and a forum for discussing university affairs. The magazine appeared quarterly with much advertising and for twelve years published many articles by students, faculty, and alumni. Sports and campus life predominated among the nonfiction with much less space being given to political, economic, and scientific subjects. Some representative titles include "Chemical Quackery," by Harvey A. Neville (Fall 1927); "The Activities Fee," by T. L. Gunthorpe ('30, Spring 1928); "Lehigh's Football Past," by John M. Blackmar ('29, Fall 1928); "What is College For?" by Dean McConn (Fall 1928); "What the Automotive Industries Expect of the Technical Schools," by Alfred R. Glancy ('03, Spring 1933); and "Bridge for Engineers," by Jack J. Dreyfus ('34, Spring 1933).

The prevailing idea of social responsibility in engineering leadership extended from the faculty to the students and reinforced a natural youthful idealism. Students vocally repulsed the immorality they observed in Bethlehem's south side, and some took on community projects as their forebears had done. The YMCA became the students' principal agency for community work. The YMCA "is one of the biggest things in college," wrote Okeson in 1925.[15] The "Y" resumed on an expanded scale the prewar activity of providing orientation for incoming freshmen and publishing a freshman handbook. In 1926 the faculty formally approved the holding of a freshman week by the YMCA preceding the opening of the fall semester.

In 1927 Lehigh's "Y" broke away from the intercollegiate YMCA, which, according to a writer for the *Brown and White*, was showing "socialistic and pacifistic tendencies."[16] The Lehigh "Y" became formally designated as the Lehigh University Union.

Frederick Thomas Trafford, former pastor of the Moravian congregation of South Bethlehem, was secretary of the Lehigh Union and received a special assignment for his community work. A mayoralty election was held in 1929 at a time when public indignation over vice in Bethlehem reached a level of intensity sufficient to support a movement for reform. Richards became active in promoting the candidacy of Robert Pfeifle on a reform ticket. The day before the election Pfeifle appeared in faculty meeting and gave a speech. He was elected and began a period of civic reform. Pfeifle appointed Trafford superintendent of police with instructions to clean up the city.

Trafford had done some of the religious counseling of students. His departure coincided with the resignation of the Right Reverend Wilmot Gateson as chaplain and dean of the Cathedral Church of the Nativity. The resignations left a vacuum in religious leadership, and professors Palmer and Hughes requested a full-time faculty replacement. The trustees responded by creating a one-man Department of Moral and Religious Philosophy. Palmer brought in a full professor, Claude Gillette Beardslee, with degrees from Yale, the Hartford Seminary, and the University of Southern California and a Ph.D. from Brown. Beardslee was also a Congregationalist minister, the first non-Episcopalian to be chaplain at Lehigh.

At the time he arrived, two years of attendance at chapel were required of students who refused an alternative of rostering a one-hour, one-year course in either Ethics and the Philosophy of Religion, Psychology of Religion and Psychology of Conduct, or the Bible as Literature. Hughes had persuaded the faculty several years earlier to adopt the alternative courses. Beardslee accepted the situation, added several other courses to this list, and introduced education in ethics into chapel services.

Devotional services at chapel remained for students who desired them but were not insisted on for the others. In effect, compulsory, worship in chapel was gone. Ethics had become the requirement.

The student body in general supported this shift. Beardslee was popular with students, as Trafford had been.

McConn also became popular, although at first the students looked upon him as infringing on their liberties. They warmed to him as the real import of his regulations appeared. For McConn's main purpose was not quelling a superkindergarten mentality but aiding students to achieve their goals in ways with which they were disinclined to quarrel.

Students entering Lehigh after the war were from their early school days exposed to more group activity and regulations than their parents had been. Consequently, freshmen at Lehigh were already susceptible to regulations in the interests of group living and to beliefs in the value of organization as a means of increasing one's effectiveness. They were also under pressure from parents to remain in school until they obtained a degree.

McConn, with support from the faculty, put in place systems of transfer, probation, and counseling designed to remind students of their responsibilities, keep parents informed of progress, temper justice with understanding in dealing with slack performance, and orient students in the directions indicated by their interests and talents.

Most young men came to Lehigh to study engineering. If they did not succeed with the study, or lost interest in it, they no longer had to drop out, as in prewar years. They might, with parental consent, transfer to Arts and Science or Business Administration. The faculty quickly adopted provisions making transfers easy. Many students took advantage of the provisions.

The office of the Dean became a place for counseling students with problems. Morton Sultzer, who had complained of the rudeness of Thornburg, complimented McConn for treating students "in a much more businesslike way."[17] McConn established the principle that the student had a right to petition for anything and insisted on the principle being respected.

For the information of students and faculty, McConn sorted out extra-curricular activities according to the time involved in them as maximum, major, and minor.[18] He reorganized registration procedures and began establishing student-faculty committees of control. He welcomed the formation of the Interfraternity Council as a means for fraternities to solve common problems and improve communications between them and the university's governing authorities. He encouraged the Lehigh chapter of Omicron Delta Kappa, formed in 1925, a leadership honorary, as a means of bringing students and administrators together and of performing useful tasks about the campus.

McConn imparted an engineering order of regularity and efficiency to almost every aspect of student life outside the classroom and off the playing field. And he worked with students conditioned to accept his ideas. Their societies adopted constitutions and bylaws, kept financial accounts and other records, and provided for publicity and continuity. It took students little time to see that formal structure gave an activity visibility and an intimation of permanence and sometimes made it eligible for funds, preference in scheduling, or representation on other councils. Good organization, students found, could often help membership drives and open the way for cooperative efforts to conserve time and energy and save money.

The spirit of McConn, if not his personal intervention, presided at decisions affecting the progress of the Marching Band. For years it had been a small, voluntary, self-supporting group, which nevertheless had become a fixture at home football games and some all-university and alumni celebrations. A time arrived in which the players became aggrieved at subsidizing the good times of others. In the spring of 1923 Joseph Ricapito, the student leader of the Band, visited Richards and told him of the players' dissatisfaction. The immediate results were decisions to give the leader of the Band a yearly salary of three hundred dollars and free tuition, to award each player a watch charm, and to supply all with uniforms at university expense. The next year the Band was formally put under the control of T. Edgar Shields.

In 1925 the ROTC adopted the Band and made it an alternative to marching drill. Almost immediately the Band was as popular as spring semester break. The major problem now became retaining members after the two years of compulsory ROTC were ended. The administration solved this by offering junior and senior members twenty dollars a year as an inducement to continue playing. By 1934 the membership was temporarily stabilized at ninety-six.

In May 1930, Lehigh cooperated with the Carnegie Foundation in administering a comprehensive examination prepared for sophomores in Pennsylvania. Richards told the faculty the following 8 September that the average score of Lehigh engineering sophomores surpassed those of 77 percent of the sophomores in the state at large; and arts and science sophomores did better by a figure of 80 percent.

Within a ten-year period, four Lehigh students were selected as Rhodes Scholars: R. Max Goepp (Chem E. '28); Dudley Lee Harley (B.A. '30); Milton Meissner (Chem E. '34); and Nelson J. Leonard (Chem. '37).

President Richards's leadership in education focused on research and engineering. He inspired the faculty and accomplished much. Yet he failed to achieve a workable relationship between teaching and research.

Richards was a national leader among engineering educators. He was active in the SPEE and became a member of the Committee Surveying Supplementary Services and Facilities (research) for the Wickenden study. In 1924 he served as chairman of the section on engineering of the AAAS. His failure to achieve a tenable relationship between research and the teaching of engineering was a failure of the entire profession.

The difficulty came from a lag between the requirements for industrial progress and the entrenched practices of engineering educators. Industry began demanding specialists in research and looked to colleges and universities to supply them. This raised a question of how to educate a student for research in engineering. An answer came easily enough — more and better study and experimentation in science and its applications. Beyond this point confusion set in. How much science and of what sorts? Here scientists and engineers parted company. Leading chemists and physicists were clear in their own minds that postgraduate work leading to the degree of Ph.D. was essential. Most engineering educators were not so sure. An editorial appearing in 1920 in *Scientific American* suggested that undergraduate education could supply all of the scientific knowledge that was required, that the postgraduate need was for a year or two of study or work in applications in a research laboratory.[19]

And what sort of activity constituted research in engineering? How did engineering research differ, for example, from routine testing? Wickenden observed in his preliminary report of 1926, "In the majority of engineering colleges research has been regarded as an optional and incidental form of activity until quite recently, and much of the work now in progress under the name is a comparatively routine form of investigation."[20]

Some thirty years earlier, Professor Mansfield Merriman, as president of the SPEE, had provided a test for distinguishing between progressive and routine work. "In all courses in construction and design the practical limit seems to be reached when the exercises are of such a nature as to give mere information and little scientific training."[21]

Merriman was one of the educators at Lehigh who regarded engineering as applied science. His thinking invariably led from application in the shop to experimentation in the laboratory. If his ideas were followed to a logical conclusion, the research engineer of the 1920s ought to have postgraduate training in those sciences having the best potential for creative improvements in shop practise. In sum, graduate studies in science were a proper and necessary means for providing the research specialists being demanded by industry.

Engineering educators almost everywhere refused this line of thinking. They were eager to improve the scientific content of undergraduate studies but not to undertake expensive new ventures in graduate programs. They were still rejoicing in the victory of the university-trained engineer over his empirical counterpart and took the position that industries such as those in electrical and chemical fields could get the scientists they wanted from departments of chemistry and physics or by training them themselves.

Wickenden summarized the reluctance of engineering educators to accept graduate work by pointing out that in 1924 only 53 percent of all institutions engaged in engineering education offered graduate opportunities even on paper, that seven-eights of all engineering graduate students were enrolled in ten institutions, and that one-fifth of these graduate students were at MIT. He noted that in 1924–25 a total of 572 graduate engineering degrees, not including professional degrees, had been conferred and that only eight of these were doctorates.[22]

Richards had no problem with understanding the nature of engineering research. He had dealt with it as director of the Engineering Experiment Station at the University of Illinois. He made the formation of a similar body, an Institute of Research, a requirement for accepting the presidency of Lehigh. On 25 April 1924, he formally laid a plan for the institute before the trustees and, with their approval, set about establishing and advertising it.

His plan designed the institute to promote research of two sorts. One was "general research," meaning projects undertaken on the initiative of its staff and the teaching force. General research would include subjects in the social sciences, the humanities, and business administration as well as in science and engineering. The financing of this would come from a special endowment. Richards asked a minimum of two million dollars for this purpose—a sum that he reaffirmed in 1927. The second was cooperative research "with individuals, firms, corporations or associations and with municipalities and governmental organizations in the investigation of problems of a far-reaching and fundamental nature whose solution will be of value to the engineering or other professions and to the public as well as to the agency supporting the investigation." Cooperative research was intended primarily to promote the progress of science and engineering. Contracts with the cooperating parties would supply most of the funds.

Richards intended that all results be given full publicity. The institute was to publish a series of monographs for the purpose. It would also see to it that the university owned all patents resulting from the efforts of its staff, making allowance for persons or agencies responsible for the discoveries leading to the patents to share in the financial rewards. He specified that the president of the university should be the administrative head of the institute.

Richards received praise for his broad views on engineering education in establishing the Institute of Research. An editor of *Engineering News-Record* complimented him on making a "remarkable departure from precedent" by creating "a device for general research rather than merely engineering research. The institute is intended to develop a desire for new knowledge in history, in language or in economics as much as in concrete or in fatigue of metals. This is to be welcomed; whatever encourages and increases the aim for more knowledge in any one field will react also on the other fields. A broadening of research activities, therefore, can not be otherwise than helpful to those who are interested in engineering research specifically."[23]

Richards supplemented his plan for the Institute of Research with a call for establishing research fellowships and a program of faculty leaves of absence. The first research fellowship came in 1924 in the form of an endowment for a "New Jersey Zinc Company's Research Fellowship in Science and Technology." The revised PRR of 1926 contained a full section on leaves of absence.

Richards also discouraged the engineering faculty from testing and counseling having no value for research. The revised rules read that when requests for testing and counseling were received, the university would "advise the employment of consulting experts, except in cases where it is reasonably clear that it may properly or desirably undertake the work itself. The university desires to render the largest service possible to the industries of the country, when this can be done without prejudice to the regular functions of teaching and research or to its relations with independent consulting experts."

In 1925 Richards took steps to reduce the amount of routine testing being done at the Fritz Laboratory. He received approval from the trustees to appoint a research professor to take charge of the laboratory and make it into a true research facility. He did not immediately obtain the person he wished, but in 1928 he filled the position with Willis A. Slater, an engineering physicist in the Bureau of Standards at Washington, D.C., and chief of the section on masonry construction. Slater died in 1931, and the position of director of the laboratory was given to his assistant, Inge Lyse, from the Portland Cement Association.

During the early years of promoting research, Richards proposed no extention of graduate work beyond the little already being done. Research fellows might or might not be graduate students. None of the eleven research fellowships established during the first ten years of Richards's presidency included a provision for free tuition. No demand for graduate programs came from the departments in Engineering.

Richards saw a need for a more efficient organization of existing graduate work. In 1927 the faculty voted a Graduate Board to replace a former committee on graduate studies. The Graduate Board included the president, the dean, and the professors in engineering, physics, chemistry, biology, geology, economics, English, German, history, and government. The key position on the committee, that of executive secretary, was given not to an engineer, a scientist, or a mathematician but to Professor Robert P. More of the Department of German.

The Institute of Research had a slender success. Although by 1933 it had turned out eighty-eight publications, many of these were reprints of scholarly articles or monographs that the faculty had published elsewhere. The trustees were unwilling to subsidize research by the faculty in Arts and Science and Business Administration. Not a cent of the two million dollars that Richards had requested for the institute appeared. The annual appropriation for its expenses was minuscule, for example, twenty thousand dollars in 1928–29.

Research and publication by faculty in Business and Arts and Science were still considered largely a private matter although promotion was being made to depend on them. A few faculty, such as Benjamin Miller and Lawrence Gipson, published much. In general the number of articles, monographs, and books coming from all departments was on the increase.

A sign of interest in research appeared in the formation of the Cosmos Club. In May 1926, eight of the newer faculty gathered to hear a paper presented by one of their number, Professor Bennett of Mathematics. They had decided the previous month they could benefit from hearing about the research being done by their colleagues in other disciplines. The group became self-perpetuating. Eventually almost all of the research-minded members of the faculty looked back with pleasure on the period of their participation in the Cosmos Club.[24]

Very little of the research done by the faculty was of immediate use to industry. Here, sponsored research, secured by means of contracts between the university and private firms, was the key. The departments having the most sponsored research were also those with the greatest interest in advanced work in science — Chemistry and Chemical Engineering; and Metallurgy with its electrometallurgical component. In the Department of Chemistry and Chemical Engineering, most of the sponsored research concentrated on leather technology and was supported by the Hunt-Rankin Leather Company and others. Edwin Raymond Theis, with baccalaureate and doctoral degrees from the University of Cincinnati, directed the research in leather technology. In Metallurgy Professor Stoughton promoted research for welding. From 1926 to 1930 the department held annual symposia on the subject, in which some of the other engineering departments participated. Beginning in 1930 the Engineering Foundation sponsored studies in the effect of the welding process on the properties of the welded metal.

The sums involved in this early sponsored research were by modern standards very small. Direct costs for the fiscal year ending 31 August 1932 were $18,043.46.

Gradually, the need for postgraduate studies leading to the doctoral degree became apparent. The greatest interest in expanding it came from some of the faculty in the sciences, the social sciences, and the humanities. Professor More of the Graduate Board advertised the idea of advanced studies. By 1930 the Alumni Association was actively supporting the cause. In 1934 Richards reported to the Board of Trustees that a graduate school was "*the greatest educational need that confronts the institution*" and explained that research, graduate work, and obtaining the best instructional staff were interdependent. But, he added, if Lehigh were to have a graduate school offering the Ph.D. degree, it would have to have at least another three million dollars for endowment.[25]

Lack of money, though, was not the greatest obstacle. An engineering faculty had to exist having the scientific knowledge necessary for turning out Ph.D.'s in engineering. Richards, in beginning to rebuild Lehigh's faculty, had more success in procuring professors capable of teaching doctoral candidates in the arts, the sciences, and business administration than in engineering.

Rebuilding a research and graduate faculty in engineering, when the country had few professionals on which to draw, would take much more time than was available to Richards.

With respect to undergraduate education, the faculty in Engineering could not be faulted. The members anticipated what Richards wanted and wholeheartedly and promptly gave him much more.

Changes in courses of study in engineering and applied science are for technical reasons not easily made. The curricula are elaborately and tightly structured. The sequence in which topics should be studied is fixed in such a way that a change in the content of one might bring about much reshuffling among the others. Students in business and the arts can choose electives for many of the credit hours they need for graduation, but not the students in engineering. As late as 1925 the men in the College of Engineering were allowed no free electives whatsoever; and the students in the Departments of Chemistry and Engineering Physics had only a slight choice. Moreover, students in the College of Engineering had to pass a number of credit hours for graduation equal to about a semester more than those required for the degrees of Bachelor of Arts and Bachelor of Science in business administration.

In spite of the difficulty in making changes, the faculty in Engineering was constantly updating courses of study. They naturally used an engineering approach, which, in the words of Wickenden, sought "*the best ratio of utility to cost that is consistent with safety.*"[26] The final aim was a graduating senior who would be maximally employable.

Since the end of the war, the engineering departments had eliminated the senior thesis, once considered the high point of undergraduate exercises, made the study of modern foreign languages optional except for German in the chemically related fields, postponed more of the field work to the summer months, and filled in the spaces caused by these eliminations with additional work in the basic and applied sciences.

Changes made with an eye to economy in the uses of money and time often produced courses that enrolled students from some or all of the branches of engineering. This in turn promoted flexibility in answering to shifts in the popularity of the several branches and made a technical adjustment to new curricula fairly easy.

Mining engineering continued to lose students, principally to civil engineering. Enrollments in chemical engineering, which had been high during the war, fell off in postwar year but after 1922 began a steady climb. The faculty boasted that the journal *Chemical and Metallurgical Engineering* listed Lehigh in 1929 as the fourth largest of fifty-five chemical engineering colleges in the United States. Enrollments in other fields remained fairly steady.

Two new curricula appeared. One was Engineering Physics, which accepted its first few students in 1924. Engineering Physics was part of Richards's plan for strengthening an area of science necessary for all branches of engineering.

The other new curriculum was Industrial Engineering. Here Fred V. Larkin, head of Mechanical Engineering, took the initiative and became director of both curricula. A study of industrial engineering was originally basically mechanical engineering plus required courses in psychology and business administration. At a later date Associate Professor Thomas T. Holme explained the inception of industrial engineering as a belated recognition of the need for applying "scientific management" to production in an age of large corporate organization.[27] Industrial Engineering proved to be popular at Lehigh. Forty students signed for it in 1925, the first fall semester in which it was offered. Most had formerly been in Mechanical Engineering.

Applied fields were the most popular among students, as had been true in earlier times. Enrollments in Engineering Physics were small by comparison with those in Electrical Engineering, a physics-based curriculum. For example, in 1926, 7 students were enrolled in Engineering Physics and 234 in Electrical Engineering. Enrollments in Chemical Engineering were approximately from nine to eleven times those in Chemistry. For example, in 1926, 10 students were listed for Chemistry and 110 for Chemical Engineering.

Excepting the addition of two curricula, the most important changes occurred as part of the study headed by Wickenden for the SPEE. Richards personally took the lead in urging the Engineering Council to undertake a comprehensive study and revision of all offerings and degrees in engineering and applied science. He asked the engineering faculty to be active in the SPEE. In 1924 fourteen Lehigh faculty were listed as being members of the SPEE. At the beginning of the 1924–25 school year, Richards obtained faculty approval to appoint a committee to assist Wickenden, consisting of the heads of the engineering departments augmented by Palmer, Carothers, R. M. Smith (English), B. L. Miller (Geology), Frank M. Weida (Biology), V. S. Babasinian (Chemistry), and A. A. Bennett and J. B. Reynolds (Mathematics).

This committee, the Engineering Council, and the university faculty completed the revisions before the end of the 1925–26 academic year. Professor Larkin later summarized the study and its results for the benefit of the alumni. First, he wrote,

> We recommended some slight revisions in the curricula which seemed to work out satisfactorily. The following year [1925] we made more drastic revision, including the provision for one-half year of uniform courses of study for all engineering freshmen. Last fall [1926] the third revision was made, including the establishment of two full years of uniformity in all engineering courses. [They were not completely uniform at the sophomore level; some variations were allowed.] ... Under the present set-up there comes a break at the end of the sophomore year at which time each student is given a comprehensive examination covering the freshman and sophomore years, which he must pass to continue in the engineering courses. ... Beginning with the present Freshman Class, four years of undergraduate work will entitle a man to the degree of B.S. in the particular branch of engineering he has studied. Another year of post-graduate work may win him his M.S. After he has five years of practical experience he may be awarded an engineering degree. The engineering curricula now call for 136 credit hours of scholastic work. This schedule is divided as follows: pure science, 30 percent; applied science, 50 percent; non-technical subjects, 20 percent.[28]

In presenting the changes to the trustees, Richards acknowledged his approval and added, "Engineering educators have gradually come to the opinion that hereafter greater emphasis should be placed upon the fundamentals of engineering, including mathematics, physics, chemistry and theoretical and applied mechanics, and less emphasis on the highly specialized details of engineering practice. They further recognize that the engineer must know something of the social sciences, which have to do with human relations and that he needs to be familiar with the methods of business organization and administration. With it all, the time has come when the graduate of an engineering course should be a man of somewhat broader and better education."[29]

Possibly the most controversial item in the revisions was the requirement of a comprehensive examination at the end of the sophomore year as an aid in determining the fitness of a student to continue the study of engineering. The examination did not produce the desired effect, as Richards pointed out in his annual address to the alumni in 1929. Nevertheless, the engineering faculty found other reasons for administering the examination, which was not discontinued until 1950.

Richards gave no special advice on educational matters to the faculties in Arts and Science and Business Administration. An advocate of breadth in engineering education, he recognized that the other colleges had to be supplied with resources sufficient for them to keep abreast of developments in their several fields of specialization. At the same time, he regarded the other colleges as being tandem to engineering and obliged to receive advice from it. He relied on members of the faculty in Engineering to provide this guidance, and his confidence in them was not misplaced. They were especially attentive to the teaching of English composition, mathematics, and economics and kept up a running and sometimes spirited controversy concerning these subjects. With respect to other fields of study within the satellite colleges, the members of the faculty in Engineering were almost as noncommittal as Richards. Carothers, Palmer, and their respective faculties and had considerable freedom within the material means at their disposal to exercise an independent judgment on educational matters.

Under the control of Carothers, Business Administration betrayed its origin as a Course in the Arts and Sciences. The curriculum included sufficient requirements in the sciences, the social sciences, and the humanities that Phi Beta Kappa found no difficulty in accepting business students for membership on a plane of equality with students in arts and science.

Carothers brought in three teachers of economics, Elmer C. Bratt, Frederick A. Bradford, and Herbert M. Diamond, each possessing a Ph.D. and being research minded, and two teachers in accounting, a field for which the Ph.D. degree was not necessary, Carl E. Allen and Roy B. Cowin (but still, Allen had a doctorate). The curriculum was simple and unspecialized. The faculty taught large classes.

The College of Arts and Science presented a far different picture. It was complex in every way that the Business College was simple. The classics had lost their position as the educational heart. Separate small Departments of Greek and Latin were set up in 1924. Most of the students electing to concentrate on Latin or Greek were "pre-theologs" — and were few. Other disciplines had dethroned the classics, but none could supplant Latin and Greek as a focus for a coherent educational policy. The college became a catchall for disciplines that did not readily fit into the other two colleges.

Some of the faculty in Arts and Science discussed their college in terms of an ideal of liberal education, expressed in slogans such as "Know thyself," "Cultural enrichment," and "Knowledge for its own sake." The ideal was a sort of Arts College counterpart to the mystique of the Hoover Syndrome. Still, a vocational spirit pervaded student attitudes and the curriculum. Professor Palmer sometimes walked a poorly defined path between vocationalism and liberal education, for example, by explaining the purpose of the college as being "general education." "We are training quite a number of men each year to become teachers, but the large majority of boys come to us to spend four years and get out of the Arts courses what they can."[30]

In 1925 existing programs in Arts and Science were scrapped in favor of a uniform system of major sequences for study in depth and a system of limited electives, styled "distribution requirements," for study in breadth. At the end of his senior year a student had to take and pass a comprehensive examination in his major sequence in order to qualify for his degree. In 1926 the faculty of the college began an honors course for superior students, who might take up to six hours of unscheduled work in each of their junior and senior years.

In the interests of making the education of all students more "general," Palmer presided over the addition of several fields of study. The coming of Professor Gipson meant an addition of history and government. "I hear we have a new department at Lehigh—history and government. What's the idea?" asked some alumni; to which Gipson responded, "The surprising thing is not that Lehigh has created a Department of History, but that she has gone so long without one."[31] In the domain of fine arts, Palmer succeeded in exchanging a part-time position for a department. For many years a local artist, Emil Gelhaar, had been employed to provide instruction to students. In 1927 Garth A. Howland joined the faculty as a full-time teacher and immediately began developing courses and a major sequence in Fine Arts. In 1929 a one-man Department of Music was formed, centering on T. Edgar Shields, leader of the Band. In the same year Dale H. Gramley arrived as an instructor in journalism, which had been taught since the days of Raymond Walters but not especially emphasized. Gramley, a professional journalist, organized courses and established a major in the subject.

A bigger change came in 1932–33 when Professor Hughes's Department of Philosophy, Psychology, and Education was split three ways. Palmer had told the trustees that sufficient students existed for majors in all three fields. In 1931 the trustees agreed to the split and ordered that it take place in two stages, with psychology being sliced off first. Accordingly, in 1932 Adelbert Ford, an expert in applied psychology from the University of Michigan, came to head Psychology. The next year Harold Prescott Thomas, with a Ph.D. from Harvard, arrived for Education.

The formation of a Department of Education signaled a considerable advance in teacher preparation. In 1920 a summer session for teachers had been held, concentrating on special education of the subnormal and mentally gifted. "A demonstration school was conducted in one of the Bethlehem school buildings and there were numerous clinical studies of children."[32] In 1923–24 Richards had reorganized the administration of the Summer School so that it would have its own budget and accounts. The faculty had left the school unchanged as to its functions of providing graduate and undergraduate courses for elementary and secondary school teachers and offering other courses for students wishing to accelerate or make up work. Hughes had reported an enrollment in the first session of 1924 of 123 students paying tuition. The number had increased almost every year, attaining a figure of 407 in 1936. In 1925 the faculty and trustees had approved a three-year teacher training program for the Summer School. Undergraduate women had been allowed to enroll in summer sessions beginning in 1929.[33]

When Thomas took over the newly organized Department of Education in 1932, he supervised a complete restructuring of the courses in teacher education.

The depression that began in 1929 affected Lehigh slowly at first, then more severely. Enrollments, standing at 1569 in September 1929, dropped to 1555 in the fall of 1930, 1486 a year later, 1373 in the autumn of 1932, and 1327 in September 1933. Reductions in alumni giving and income from endowment accompanied losses from tuition.

The trustees showed no alarm. Most of them were alumni who had been students in engineering during the depression years of the 1890s when Lehigh's existence had been in jeopardy. Since that time they had moved from engineering into management. They brought to the governance of Lehigh a businesslike engineering view, which emphasized safety and economy. When the depression began, Lehigh had no debt; and every year during the 1920s the balance sheet had showed a profit.

Trustees, Richards, and the directors of curricula met the reductions in income by practising internal economies. From 1929 to 1934 the number of teaching positions declined from 144 to 125, which was five fewer than it had been in 1925. No large building projects or extensive repairs were undertaken. Promotions among faculty were few, and salaries remained static. In 1933 Richards received permission from the trustees to reduce salaries by up to 10 percent across the board if this should prove necessary. It was not necessary; and faculty in those years of deflation enjoyed higher real incomes than in more prosperous times.

The university met the drop in enrollments by increasing the efficiency of admission. Except for a few years in the mid-1920s, the university had never had a surplus of qualified candidates for entrance, in part because as Lehigh became more attractive to prospective students the faculty raised the requirements for entrance. Richards approved of this and, fearing that declines in enrollment might cause the faculty to lower standards, cast about for means of improving recruitment. Some colleges and universities were using specialists. Andrew Buchanan, executive secretary of the Alumni Association, proposed a specialized office of admission for Lehigh. Richards demurred, fearing that it might lead to undignified and misleading advertising and asked the Alumni Association and the alumni clubs to intensify and expand their former work of recruitment.

The result was precisely the sort of "ballyhoo" Richards had feared from a department of admission. He gave in, and in 1934 the Office of Admission was formed. Wray Hollowell Congdon, with experience in teaching and administration in China and the University of Michigan, became the first director of admission. He received as an assistant E. Kenneth Smiley, who had taught English at Lehigh from 1923 to 1926 and then had left to become dean of the Junior Division at the University of North Dakota.

The results satisfied everyone. Enrollments began to rise from the low point in 1933. Beginning in 1935, the number of qualified candidates for admission exceeded the number of places available. In 1936 the fall semester enrollment stood at 1634. By 1937 the university was receiving twice as many applications as it could accept, and all but a few of applicants who were offered entry appeared on the campus in September.

In 1931 Lehigh began to receive an unanticipated income from a gold mine. This was the London Mine located two miles high in the Colorado Rockies about seven miles east of Alma. Income from the London Mine was the result of an investment made by Harry E. Packer, who had left most of his estate to Lehigh. For many years the mine had paid nothing and work had been stopped. Then the mine was reorganized and operations resumed. The income was not large, being for example approximately $13,200 in 1933–34 and $26,400 in 1934–35, but it was about the same as the university's surplus. The income continued through 1944.

Financially, the university weathered the depression well. With the exception of 1930–31, the balance sheet every year showed a profit; and in 1930–31 the deficit was only $7,893.[34]

Placement, like admission, was a depression-born office. The Alumni Association took the initiative. Alumni had from the beginning been concerned with finding jobs for graduates. When the depression of the 1930s struck, and jobs became scarce, leaders among the alumni quickly appreciated the advantages to be gained from an organized effort. In the fall of 1932 the Alumni Association started the Placement Service under the direction of John A. Brodhead, '07. Originally designed to serve alumni at all stages of their careers, it proved to be especially useful for the graduating seniors. By 1935 about 90 percent of its work was with them. In that year the association approached the Board of Trustees with a request that the Placement Service, "having justified its existence by splendid service to the University. ... be continued on the present basis for another year"; and then the university should take it over and finance it.[35] The trustees agreed to this but also gave the service, renamed Placement Bureau, a task of finding jobs for undergraduates. This meant administering the National Youth Administration or NYA, a New Deal program for providing students with part-time employment. For several years the bureau spent much time with the NYA. Upon partial recovery in the job market, the work of the Placement Bureau progressively returned to that of helping graduating seniors to find positions.

In addition to placement and admission, one other major administrative change occurred in the early years of the depression. This was a resolution of the controversy over the control of athletics. Pressures to reduce the emphasis on intercollegiate sports were increasing. In 1929 the Carnegie Foundation for the Advancement of Teaching published a study, "American College Athletics" (Bulletin #23), in which Lehigh was praised for making "a significant and courageous change of policy respecting recruiting and subsidizing" but was not one of the twenty-six institutions named as being "pure." The reason, Okeson explained with obvious embarrassment, was because of the Self-Aid Bureau, the retention of one athletic scholarship awarded by the secretary of the Alumni Association, and possibly the subsidizing of a training table.[36]

A few years later, in March 1932, the Middle States Association of Colleges and Secondary Schools startled the academic world by passing a resolution stating that institutions that gave athletic scholarships "shall be disqualified for inclusion in the approved list of institutions of higher education." Carothers attended a meeting of the Middle States Association in New York City at which the resolution was discussed, and he reported to the faculty that the resolution contained no danger for Lehigh and "was a minor measure to correct only a minor evil but that it had very deep significance, in that it represented the first concerted effort of an academic association embracing all the colleges of a section to take jurisdiction over the athletic policies of its member colleges."[37]

Nevertheless, Richards took the occasion to ask for a reform of the athletic establishment along the lines he had hoped to obtain in 1924. This time he met with little opposition. On 6 June 1932, the trustees approved a resolution that the university take over the budgeting and administration of athletic funds and, the following 1 December, abolished the Board of Control and created a new department, a Division of Athletics and Physical Education headed by a director who was responsible to the president for finances, schedules, and general policies. A faculty committee would continue to determine the eligibility of members of intercollegiate teams and have an input with respect to schedules and other matters impinging on the academic performance of players. Students and alumni were by implication excluded from this new chain of command.

The creation of a Director of Athletics and Physical Education answerable to the president virtually guaranteed that there would be no more athletic scholarships or loans administered as gifts as long as Richards remained as president. In April an announcement was made that Nelson A. Kellogg, who had been athletic director as Purdue for seventeen years, would be Lehigh's first Director of Athletics and Physical Education.

In sum, the first six years of the depression not only provided opportunity for proving Lehigh's financial soundness but also constituted a time of progress in rationalizing the university's administrative changes and increasing services for students. During these years, too, separate Departments of Psychology and Education appeared, and a Department of Moral and Religious Philosophy was formed under Beardslee.

In 1934, upon the recommendation of the Committee on Educational Policy, the faculty approved an Arts-Engineering Program, which was a more streamilined form of the "Combination of Literary and Technical Studies" program pioneered by former president Drown.

Lehigh's most notable loss coming out of the depression lay in the realm of ideals. The Hoover Syndrome died with the failure of the Hoover administration to avert economic disaster. The syndrome had included a mystique of leadership through engineering. Educators such as Richards had acted on an assumption that with proper teaching the ideal could be realized.

In fact, it could not. Socrates, in the fifth century B.C., had maintained that virtue could not be taught because there were no teachers of virtue. For the same reason, in the twentieth century at Lehigh and elsewhere, leadership could not be taught — there were no teachers of leadership.

Richards refused to accept this platonic pessimism. In 1933, as the depression deepened, he reflected on the failure of higher education to produce leaders but still held that the goal was theoretically attainable. The minutes of the faculty meeting for 6 February 1933, read in part:

> With reference to the present industrial crisis and the part which educated men should be taking therein, the President remarked that there appears to have been less leadership in these past three years than in the period of the War. ... Assuming such a lack of real leadership, may it not, he asked, be a reflection on the colleges or on the education men in industrial leadership have received? ... The Councils of the several colleges might give thought to the question whether there is anything which we are not doing which we could do to enable our graduates to cope with the situation which they of necessity are going to be obliged to face. ... Our educational institutions ought to take appropriate measures to the end that our future leaders shall base correct and sound opinions on important social and public questions in order that effective, sound decisions may be made.

Belief in the Hoover Syndrome and what it implies for leadership through social engineering has been so long out of fashion that the mystique appears today quaint. In the context of engineering education in the mid-1930s, however, the loss of the ideal was a tragedy, compounded by the failure of any new ideal to take its place.

For the next half-dozen years, disillusion and a resistance to social realities were to haunt the discussions concerning engineering ethics and social responsibilities. Alumni and teachers of engineering at Lehigh were not immune from the influence of this professional disillusion.

6
Depression, War, and Aftermath: 1935–1950

Eighteen months after Richards gave his speech on the failure of educators to produce leaders, he suffered a heart attack and had to stop working. His resignation was announced at the faculty meeting of 3 January 1935.

The board did not do as it had done when Drinker retired, that is, ask Vice President Emery to act as president. Instead, upon the suggestion of Grace, it set up a special three-man committee headed by Grace as a final authority in place of Richards. The board also formed a search committee for a new president with Grace as chairman.

These moves confirmed an evolution of power within the Lehigh Valley of which insiders had long been aware. Mr. Grace (no one ever addressed him by his first name) of Bethlehem Steel would dominate the city and the university. He would choose and decide issues within the limits of the immense economic power possessed by the Bethlehem Steel Corporation, the second largest producer of steel in the United States.

At a meeting of the trustees on 5 September 1935, Grace reported that the search committee unanimously recommended Clement C. Williams, dean of the College of Engineering at the University of Iowa, as president. Probably few doubted that Williams was the personal choice of Grace.

Clement Clarence Williams had impressive qualifications. He had taught successively at the universities of Colorado and Kansas, where he had been professor of railway engineering, and at Illinois as head of the Department of Civil Engineering. He had worked as an engineer for several railroads and published articles and books, including a book on education, *Building an Engineering Career*.[1] The year before coming to Lehigh he had served as president of the SPEE. Trustee Aubrey Weymouth had found Williams's presidential address for the SPEE, "The New Epoch in Engineering Education," "quite the finest concept of engineering education, past, present and future, that I have ever read."[2]

The selection of Williams occurred at a time of great political ferment in the United States. The New Deal of President Roosevelt was the immediate concern. The country was taking sides for or against the New Deal, and engineers and industrialists by and large found themselves against it.

167

The dominant opinion at Lehigh opposed the New Deal. Industrial leaders among the trustees and alumni were bitter about it. They fought back as a National Labor Relations Board and other governmental agencies destroyed their personnel policies and put heavy charges on profits. Tom Girdler ('01), head of Republic Steel and an alumnus trustee from 1929 to 1935, wrote an autobiography, *Boot Strap*,[3] which for about three-fifths of its length is a description of his fight against the Steel Workers Organizing Committee. Time and again the *Alumni Bulletin* showed hostility toward the Roosevelt administration. The activites of Morris L. Cooke were barely noticed. Cooke was, in the eyes of Roosevelt haters, an apostate, having become first director of the Rural Electrification Administration. The *Alumni Bulletin* praised a talk by Nevin E. Funk ('05), vice president of the Philadelphia Electric Company, one of the companies formerly opposed by Cooke, as "a noteworthy example of the engineering approach to a controversial question." In the speech Funk had charged the public with ignorance in wanting governments to regulate the rates set by electric companies[4] (ten years later Funk became a corporate trustee).

The faculty, while not being as bitter as some industrialists among the alumni, were also mostly anti–New Deal. Vocal supporters of it, such as Professor Percy Hughes, comprised a conspicuous countercurrent. More typical was Neil Carothers. A southern Democrat, Carothers had initially rejoiced in the election of FDR to the presidency and in 1933 headed the National Recovery Administration in Bethlehem. With the repudiation of the gold standard and the devaluation of the dollar, he turned against Roosevelt. In 1936, although still nominally a Democrat, he served as a campaign adviser for the Republican vice-presidential candidate Frank Knox. Carothers skillfully debated pro–New Dealers, including several senators and the perennial Socialist candidate for the presidency, Norman Thomas. Carothers published his views in series of articles in the *New York Herald Tribune* and other periodicals of large circulation.[5] In 1937 and 1938 he was a regular speaker on a weekly national radio program sponsored by the Chase Manhattan Bank.

The students, as in former years, took little interest in political subjects. This, given the character of the times, was sufficient to align them on the side of the faculty and the alumni. A poll conducted under the auspices of the *Lehigh Review* in 1939 disclosed 72 percent as having fathers who had voted for the Republican Alfred Landon in the presidential election of 1936.[6]

Although the university was, as always, nonpartisan, the one-sided alignment of its parts produced a conservative coloration accurately characterizing campus life. The engineering ideals of economy and safety had taken on political overtones of hostility to expensive welfare programs, a defense of property, and an idealization of freedom of competition.

Incoming President Williams's style perfectly fitted this mood. He was businesslike and conservative. Like all engineering educators, he sometimes talked and wrote about social responsibility; but he did not often use the term and never used it in the sense of social welfare. The "socialization of education" which was in publicly financed institutions, he told the trustees, followed that of "socialization" of transportation, express services, and utilities. "The baleful unsoundness of this tendency should be emphasized, for it has a disintegrating effect on all social and economic organization." On one occasion he informed the faculty "that he had been devoting considerable time of late to combatting the proposition that colleges should be brought under the Social Security Act," at the same time admitting that the Association of American Colleges had gone on record as favoring extending the act to include colleges. His educational report to the trustees in 1939 contains an argument that the economic ills afflicting the country were uniquely the result of governmental interference.

Williams's objectives for Lehigh were equally conservative. "Lehigh follows a conservative policy suited to the needs peculiar to its own scope and function," he wrote in a report to the trustees delivered 14 October 1938. On another occasion he said, "I foresee Lehigh a limited University true to its tradition from the founder, seeking excellence, adjusting its curricula and procedure naturally to changing circumstances. There is no need to duplicate Harvards and Yales, even if possible, but there is now and will be indefinitely in the future, need for a Lehigh to provide instruction and research in the applicatory functions of knowledge with major emphasis on science and technology."[7]

The safety and economy inhering in the engineering way were outstanding features of Williams's approach to governing Lehigh. In finances he was at least as conservative as Okeson and the trustees and chose to run the university on a balanced budget as a matter of principle. He was sensitive to the opinions of the alumni and used the *Alumni Bulletin* as Drinker had done, that is, as a medium for circulating his own views. "The Prexy's Pen," written by Williams and accompanied by his photograph, became for five years a regular feature of the *Bulletin*. He left the responsibility for educational programs to the faculty, which meant in practice to the heads of departments and directors of curricula. In administration, too, he allowed much discretion to the registrar, the dean, and the treasurer, with a result that these positions made their holders more powerful than a citing of their duties would indicate.

Yet for all his conservatism, Williams was up-to-date and forward-looking on matters of engineering education. On 7 October 1935, he suggested to the faculty that Lehigh might again start giving doctorates. This was truly progressive. Among the country's engineering educators the idea of doctoral programs was gaining only a little headway. The SPEE reported for 1936–37 that eighty-two persons in engineering had received the doctorate — and some of these may have been applied scientists whom the professional societies would not have recognized as engineers.[8] The principal professional engineering societies were not yet accepting graduate education as a necessity, as the early history of the Engineering Council for Professional Development (ECPD) indicates.

Representatives of the ASCE, AIMME, ASME, AIEE, the American

Institute of Chemical Engineers (AICE), and the National Council of State Boards of Engineering Examiners founded the ECPD in 1932 as a means of limiting the number of engineers by establishing and enforcing high standards. Part of the work of the ECPD was to be accreditation of departments of engineering. The first comprehensive accreditation began in 1935 and took two years to complete. Lehigh was accredited for all of its technical curricula except that of Engineering Physics, which the ECPD did not yet recognize as a major branch of engineering.[9] In ensuing years the ECPD carried out a plan for continuing visits to engineering schools for purposes of accreditation. At no time during its early history did the ECPD become concerned with graduate education. The possibility of accrediting graduate programs was apparently not even considered. When later the question was raised, it was answered by saying that graduate programs could not be meaningfully evaluated because of the individual character of postgraduate work.

The SPEE, like the ECPD, gave little attention to graduate work in engineering. It did not form a committee on graduate education until 1942, after a need for more graduate engineers to promote the war effort had become apparent.

Except for some firms in the electrical and chemical industries, employers of Lehigh graduates were not yet demanding engineers with a Ph.D. degree. Christopher Jencks and David Reisman have summarized the danger to which radicalism in engineering education is subject: "No engineering school can, after all, be better than the best students attracted to engineering. It can be only a little better than the best employers of engineers want it to be. If it gets too far ahead of the pack its alumni will look like 'troublemakers,' its reputation will suffer, and the quality of its applicants will decline."[10]

Although Lehigh was more than a college of engineering, all parts of the university supported the idea that the other colleges existed to improve engineering education. Williams followed in the footsteps of Richards in proposing doctoral programs for all colleges if the faculties therein were of a mind to take the initiative and shoulder the burdens. Williams also, again like Richards, understood that for a successful effort at the doctoral level the technical departments would have to take the lead.

The faculty referred Williams's suggestion of doctoral programs to the Graduate Board. On 2 March 1936, Professor Robert P. More reported to the faculty that the Graduate Board liked the proposal. The following 1 June he announced that the Graduate Board had approved doctoral programs for the Departments of Chemistry and Chemical Engineering, Physics, Metallurgy, Civil Engineering, Mechanical Engineering, Mathematics, and History. A graduate faculty consisting of full and associate professors who offered graduate work and such others as they would admit replaced the Graduate Board.

By these actions the Graduate School was born, although as yet it had no administrative head.

The school had existed for only a few weeks when Williams made a suggestion to the trustees combining an advance in education with his political bias. In connection with the financial budget for the year beginning 1 July 1936, the minutes of the Board of trustees show that Williams proposed an advanced professional program in applied economics. He wrote:

> Lehigh has an almost unique opportunity to develop a graduate school in the technologic-economic realm that would rapidly rise to recognized eminence and leadership in that field. The traditions and background of Lehigh are conservative whereas those of most of the departments of social sciences of the country are inclined toward liberalism, if not even radicalism. A college of business administration lies naturally alongside technology rather than the humanities, and graduate study in this area such as Lehigh is naturally circumstanced to administer, is one of the most serious needs in America at present and the near future.

Neither the board nor Williams followed up on this proposal for a conservative-technologic counterweight to New Deal economic studies, and at Lehigh the idea died.

With the establishing of the Graduate School, the number of postgraduate registrants sharply increased. One hundred and thirty-three students had enrolled in the fall of 1936. The following September the number stood at 176.

On 6 October 1936, the trustees approved forty-four tuition scholarships for students in graduate study.

Several administrative changes occurred during Williams's first eighteen months as president. Vice President Emery died in the autumn of 1935. For the time being his position was left vacant. Okeson took full charge of the Business Office.

In 1936 Andrew E. Buchanan resigned as executive secretary of the Alumni Association to become director of research for the Remington Arms Company, a subsidiary of duPont, where he saw at first hand the growing demand for Ph.D.'s in chemical engineering and chemistry. William "Billy" Cornelius ('89) took over Buchanan's former jobs as executive secretary of the Alumni Association and editor of the *Bulletin*.

Buchanan had been serving for almost thirteen years as an unofficial news editor for the university. Upon resigning, he recommended that the position be given to Dale H. Gramley, the associate professor of journalism, who should be allowed an instructor to assist him. This was done with the result that for the first time the university had an official News Agency.

The most important administrative changes involved the creation of deanships for the undergraduate colleges. Palmer, Carothers, and Stoughton filled the positions.

In Business Administration the addition of a dean was accompanied by the formation of departments. Professors Herbert Diamond, Roy Cowin, and Frederick Bradford become respectively heads of Departments of Economics, Accounting, and Finance.

These steps in the articulation of undergraduate colleges were made without filling the vacant post of vice-president or appointing a provost to provide some sort of coordination. A result was that the president had to perform the task insofar as it was done at all. This left the deans of Arts and Science and Engineering without much support in contending with powerful department heads. Carothers, who had long dominated his college, did not face this situation. The tension between Dean Palmer and his department heads underlies a remark in the faculty minutes for 3 November 1941; "Dean Palmer commented not altogether facetiously that the rules committee would like to cut off the heads of departments" and that Palmer favored a "less strict departmental organization."

The academic deans immediately assumed the stance that their newly acquired dignity seemed to demand. Although their work with faculty, students, alumni, and community differed considerably, they developed a uniform image through their formal appearances before the university faculty and the public.

The new deans, by publicizing the activities of faculty and departments, were also able to give their colleges identity. Thus, Stoughton in 1937 announced the accreditation of his departments by the ECPD, and Carothers reported that application had been made for membership in the National Association of Collegiate Schools of Business. In November 1938, Palmer told the faculty of the formation of an Alumni Council of the College of Arts and Science consisting of six local alumni and nine others, with Robert E. Laramy ('96), father of the Honor Court, serving as chairman.

President Williams, with the cooperation of Visscher and Burley, published a plan for buildings, which included something for almost everyone: a fine arts center and theater for the College of Arts and Science; a new building for the College of Business Administration; a large new civil engineering laboratory adjoining Fritz Laboratory; additions to physics and chemistry; a wing on the ROTC armory (the former college commons); an athletic palaestra; a student health center; and dormitories.

The plan was a wish list, although Williams did not present it as such. The strength of pressures within the university actually determined priorities. The first new projects were a dormitory and a wing to Chandler Laboratory. Congdon told the trustees that the greatest handicap in procuring students was the lack of suitable quarters. The demand for more facilities for Chemistry corresponded to the research needs of the department, a large increase in the number of undergraduates taking chemical engineering, and the advent of a graduate program. The Alumni Association voted to raise the $100,000 originally estimated as necessary, and with this understanding, the trustees in 1936 approved the project.

These buildings were ready for occupancy by 1938. The dormitory was built above Price Hall in the draw carrying the stream that in earlier years had crossed the lower campus, a draw to which Williams gave the name

Crystal Springs Ravine. The dormitory was named Charles Russ Richards House. Williams objected to the word "hall" for dormitories, saying that halls were expected to contain large halls and rooms. The addition to Chandler Laboratory was named the Henry M. Ullmann Wing. It proved to cost more than twice as much as had been anticipated. The Alumni Association agreed to increase its contribution to $150,000 and had trouble meeting the goal.

The uncertainty connected with the work of the Alumni Association as a fund raiser at this point sparked another step toward a more suitable arrangement. In 1938 Earl F. "Coxey" (the source of the nickname remains a mystery) Johnson ('07), soon to be a vice president of General Motors, became a corporate trustee and chairman of the board's Committee on Endowments. Johnson immediately surveyed the fund-raising activities of the Alumni Association and the board and gave the trustees a highly critical report. He noted that the proportion of operating expenses coming from endowment income at Lehigh was 23 percent, the lowest of a group including Brown, Bryn Mawr, Carnegie Tech, Columbia, Dartmouth, Harvard, Haverford, Johns Hopkins, Lafayette, Princeton, Stanford, Swarthmore, Yale, and Williams, and that in the years from 1925 to 1935 there had been 635 deaths among Lehigh alumni but only twenty-four bequests, three of which had come from persons not alumni. Johnson signaled the need for a general program to educate alumni, foundations, industries, and wealthy persons not alumni into a habit of giving to Lehigh.[11]

The board responded to Johnson's report by creating a Bureau of Finance "to stimulate financial aid to the University." The bureau was to consist of the chairman of the Finance Committee of the board, the chairman of the Endowment Committee, the treasurer, and a full-time executive secretary. John Irvine Kirkpatrick ('29), a former Lehigh football captain, was chosen as the executive secretary.

In response to the general concern for income, the seniors in 1938 began a class gift program whereby a participant took out a twenty-year term insurance policy of two hundred and fifty dollars with the university named as beneficiary. In the first year of this program 94 seniors participated. By 1941 the number of participants stood at 137.

The year 1938, a year of partial economic recovery for the nation, also witnessed several administrative shifts at Lehigh. Williams provided direction for the Graduate School by appointing Tomlinson Fort as dean. Fort added the position to his post as head of the Department of Mathematics. As graduate dean, Fort had the same formal position as that of Stoughton, Palmer, and Carothers, but he lacked their power. Lehigh's graduate dean, following a practice observed by most universities, possessed no independent budget for faculty or research.

Dean McConn resigned in 1938 after fifteen years of service and took the post of dean of New York University's Washington Square College. Williams elevated Congdon from the Office of Admission to the vacant deanship and made Congdon's former assistant, Smiley, director of admission. Charles Seidle came on the staff as an assistant to Smiley. Seidle had taught English at Lingnan University in Canton, China, and later worked in admission in Teacher's College, Columbia University, from which he had a doctorate.

Some other administrative appointments in the immediate prewar years included Harvey A. Neville to replace Ullmann as Head of the Department and director of the Curricula of Chemistry and Chemical Engineering (1938); Bradford Willard as head of the Department of Geology, relieving "Benjy" Miller for research and travel (1939); Allen J. Barthold as head of the Department of Romance Languages; and Loyal V. Bewley as head of Electrical Engineering in place of Seyfert (1940).

In 1939 the trustees added the title of vice president to Okeson's other titles of treasurer and secretary of the board.

Also in 1939, Stoughton, suffering from ill health, asked to be relieved of administrative duties. The board thereupon approved Williams's nomination of Gilbert E. Doan to be head of the Department of Metallurgical Engineering and of Alfred Copeland Callen to be dean of the College of Engineering and both head of the department and director of the Curriculum in Mining Engineering. He was to take the place of Eckfeldt, who, like Stoughton, was retiring from administrative duties. Callen had his degrees from Lehigh (E.M. 1909; M.S. 1911) and had most recently been head of the Department of Mining Engineering at the University of Illinois.

In 1939 Williams presented a revised list of major building projects, this time enumerated in order or priority: (1) a sports palaestra; (2) a building for Civil Engineering; (3) a health center; and (4) another dormitory.

A story is told about the decision to build the palaestra (Grace Hall). Grace asked Williams how much it would cost, and Williams immediately replied, "Three hundred thousand dollars." "I thought it would cost more," Grace is reported to have said later, but he agreed to pay for the building. At the alumni business meeting on 10 June 1939, Williams announced that Grace would finance a building costing three hundred thousand dollars for intercollegiate athletics, military drill, dances, and large indoor functions. The assembly rose to its feet and cheered.

Few if any building projects have been more popular with the Lehigh community than Grace Hall. All stood to gain something by it. Kenneth K. Kost ('31) had written in the *Bulletin* for April 1938, "The junior prom last spring was held as follows: The Senior Ball at the Coliseum (which is now being turned into a food market), the Interfraternity Ball at Dorney Park, Allentown, and the Military Ball at the National Guard Armory on Prospect Avenue." Kost might have added that Mustard and Cheese was performing most of its plays in the gymnasium of nearby Broughal Junior High School, and that there was talk of moving commencement exercises from the Packer Memorial Church, which was not large enough, to Taylor Stadium (commencement exercises were, in fact, held in the open air at Taylor Stadium in June, 1939).

By the time Grace Hall was completed the cost was more than twice Williams's original estimate. Grace probably swallowed hard, but he paid the bills.

The trustees authorized the dormitory in the spring of 1940. It was built over the summer in Crystal Springs Ravine, near Richards House, and was named after President Emeritus Henry S. Drinker, who had died in 1937.

The two other projects on Williams's priority list, a building for Civil Engineering and a health center, were not built then. War intervened before they could be seriously considered.

Graduate education made slow progress. Within several years of the formation of the Graduate School, doctoral programs were approved for electrical engineering, biology, and English. At the commencement exercises in June 1938, Associate Professor More presented four students to receive the Ph.D. degree, the first granted since the days of Joseph W. Richards and Herman E. Kiefer. These were Earl James Serfass and Charles Leslie Weidner in chemistry and Shang-Shoa Young and Vittorio DeNora in metallurgy.

The output of graduate degrees was less impressive than the enrollments. From 1936 to June 1944, the departments having the most sponsored research, Metallurgy and Chemistry and Chemical Engineering, accounted for almost half of the masters of science degrees (94 of 193) and more than two-thirds of the Ph.D.'s (18 of 26). During the same eight-year stretch, five other doctors of philosophy came from the College of Engineering—one civil, two mechanical, and two physics. The only Ph.D.'s from outside the college during the same period were three in mathematics. The Departments of Biology, Geology, History, and English had opted for doctoral programs but as yet could present no candidates for the degree.

Within the College of Arts and Science, the faculty in education overshadowed all others in graduate work. Between 1936 and June 1944, the Department of Education produced fifty-two masters of arts, or more than 43 percent of the M.A.'s. An undertermined number of recipients of the M.A. in English, history, and modern foreign languages were preparing for careers in teaching.

The war slowed the development of graduate work. From 1944 to 1946 the Graduate School at Lehigh was almost dead. Only one doctorate was granted, in chemistry. Ninety-six enrolled for the fall semester 1943, and only nineteen of these were in engineering. Dean Fort reported that almost all of the students in chemistry, civil engineering, and mathematics were employees of Bethlehem Steel and that teachers from nearby schools accounted for most of the enrollments in education, English, and history. Many of the remainder, he said, were foreign students from China and the Latin-American countries.

During the first five years of Williams's presidency, little of note happened in the domain of student life. Attendance at chapel as an alternative to a course in ethics was ended in 1937, thereby making all instruction in religion and ethics elective. In 1938 all daily chapel services were suspended for lack of attendance. In the same year, the *Alumni Bulletin* reported that four hundred automobiles were registered with Dean Congdon. The Lehigh Union disappeared in 1939 by merging with Arcadia.

In 1939 the *Lehigh Review* suspended publication. It was followed in 1940 by short-lived attempts at two other publications, the *Lehigh Bachelor* and a periodical put out by Eta Kappa Nu, the electrical engineering honorary society, *Zero Sequence*.

The rise of Hitler, the rearmament of Germany, and the possibility of another world conflict did not appreciably excite the students. Isolationist sentiment was strong. The poll conducted by the *Lehigh Review* in 1939 turned up 84 percent as disagreeing with the proposition that America's future lay long the Rhine River.[12]

A few students were becoming interested in the prospect of military service if it involved flying. In 1939 Professor Larkin received authorization from the faculty for the Department of Mechanical Engineering to offer a course in flight theory, anticipating approval by the Civil Aeronautics Administration of a program of flight training using the faculty and facilities of the department and the Allentown-Bethlehem airport. By the end of the academic year, twelve students had completed training and had been awarded certificates as private pilots. At the alumni business meeting in June 1941, Williams mentioned that eighty-seven students had taken the preliminary flight training in the aviation course and fifty-four had taken the secondary training.

In September 1940, Congress passed the Selective Service Act calling for conscription of men twenty-one years of age and over. This affected few students immediately. Even the seniors were fairly confident that they would be allowed to complete their undergraduate education.

Two months and one week before Pearl Harbor, on the weekend of Founder's Day, 3 October 1941, Lehigh University celebrated the seventy-fifth anniversary of its founding. Symposia, speeches, dinners, a luncheon at the Saucon Valley Country Club for special guests, and services at the Packer Memorial Church marked the occasion. A special feature was the dedication of three physical improvements: the Eugene Gifford Grace Hall; renovations to Lamberton Hall, which again made it a student cafeteria; and a new trophy room in Taylor Gymnasium, provided for by S. E. Berger ('89). Raymond Walters, former registrar and editor of the *Alumni Bulletin* now president of the University of Cincinnati, was toastmaster at a dinner Friday, 2 October. Many noted educators participated in the festivities, one being William E. Wickenden, now president of the Case School of Applied Science.

President Williams delivered the keynote speech at the dedication of Grace Hall. He told an audience of students, faculty, and invited guests, "If we do not take advantage of this occasion to round off a ringing statement relative to national obligations or to international aggressions, the omission does not signify insensitivity to their importance." Williams chose to spend some time on the history of Lehigh, which he referred to as the realization of a dream by Asa Packer, a "frugal, private enterpriser and strict constructionist who deprecated any socialistic control of higher education."[13]

Even as Williams spoke, faculty in the College of Engineering were beginning a second year of short courses in machine design, mechanical drawing, metallurgy, and production engineering as part of a national program directed by the U.S. Commissioner of Education and intended to reduce the shortages of engineers, chemists, physicists, and production supervisors in areas essential to national defense.

At a banquet on the evening of 3 October, principal speaker Eugene G. Grace directly confronted the issue of war. In the words of Billy Cornelius, Grace "astounded alumni and faculty as he hurled the admonition 'Don't get swelled heads' from his place on the rostrum":

> Something has failed in America, and if any category of education is responsible it must be in the fields that touch on diplomacy and economics. ... We've got to play the biggest role in our respective histories if the world is to be saved. I don't care what you are, isolationist or interventionist, you can't run away from our present world situation. We're in it, and it's a perfect mess. ... We've got to join up to do our part, to do what this country must do if civilization is to be saved. Don't go to sleep. France did.

The Second World War followed the first by twenty-one years, scarcely the period of a generation. Some veterans of the first served in the second. Yet institutions of higher education faced in 1941 a situation vastly different from what they had encountered in 1917.

Technological warfare had reached a pitch of sophistication demanding national programs of scientific research and development of weaponry, facilities for communication and transportation, and defense. The emphasis was on physics.

The educational needs for manpower were greater in the second war. More occupational skills were demanded. Higher priority was given to persons trained in science, engineering, and other useful pursuits. Institutions such as Lehigh, which in 1917 had been considered suitable for training troops in technological skills, had moved away from occupational training toward a more general vocational approach at a higher level; they were less able than vocational high schools and two-year technical colleges to provide the sort of training given at Camp Coppee, but more than ever useful for providing officers and highly educated scientists and engineers.

And, as it turned out, the period of hostilities was much longer. In the first war it had embraced one full academic year and a few months of two others, whereas in the second war it eventually covered more than three and one-half academic years. This long disruption of regular activities had to be paid for, and the costs were high.

Lehigh's contributions to the war effort were principally in the domain of supplying and training men for the armed services.

One of the first actions of the faculty following Pearl Harbor involved designing a schedule for acceleration. The schedule was ready to go into effect for the second semester of 1941–42. Unlike the acceleration developed for the First World War, the summers were used to supply the time needed. Two eight-week sessions replaced the requirement of summer industrial employment for students in engineering. Freshmen could be admitted at the beginning of any semester. The faculty added a midyear commencement ceremony.

Acceleration proved to be popular. On 17 May 1942, 693 undergraduates registered for the first eight-week summer session. On 15 July, one hundred entering freshmen supplemented them. The first midyear commencement exercises were held 18 January 1943.

With the beginning of hostilities, the program of short courses was extended, and other special courses were added. Lehigh students were not at first allowed to register for these courses. Before Pearl Harbor, Williams had referred to them as "hot-house educational programs" which could "flood the country with pseudo-engineers."[14] After Pearl Harbor, Lehigh students were allowed to enroll in some of the special courses with the proviso that they could not, without faculty approval, apply them to the credits needed for graduation. In order to emphasize their separate nature, the faculty on 15 January 1942 created a General College Division to contain them (after the war the GCD was allowed to remain under the control of the registrar and was used from time to time to take care of small numbers of students who for various reasons had to be classified as specials).

Enrollments for all three colleges held up for the first full academic year following America's entry into the war. The university had a total of 1780 undergraduates at the beginning of the fall 1942 semester, divided as follows: 1191 in Engineering; 242 in Arts and Science; 322 in Business Administration; and 25 for the General College Division.

About two-thirds of the regular students qualified for occupational deferment under the selective service regulations because of being enrolled in scientific or engineering courses. Some were in army or naval reserve programs and had not yet been called to active duty.

The university's facilities were being heavily used. Temporary wooden buildings near Packer Hall and the Physics Laboratory answered to needs for more space for housing and instruction. For a time a hotel was also used for housing, and some special students were bunked in an unused basketball court in Taylor Gymnasium.

Then the students began to leave. In November 1942 the draft age was lowered to eighteen. General Lewis B. Hershey, head of the Selective Service

Board, emphasized that occupational deferment would not permit college students to be treated as a favored class. By December 1942 many reservists, including some of those in ROTC, were being called up.

Over the following several months the number of students having occupational deferment was severely reduced, both by eliminating certain categories of deferment and by establishing quotas for the categories that remained. No exception was made for students in accelerated programs. The able-bodied Lehigh freshman who in January 1942 thought he might be able to continue his studies until graduation, knew by January 1943 that he would be drafted, if not the next week, at least at the end of the semester or, if he was lucky and his draft board lenient, not until the end of the school year.

Some faculty left for military service. The *Alumni Bulletin* for October 1942 listed twenty faculty in the armed services. Temporary or part-time teachers replaced some of these absentees, including two women — the first to teach at Lehigh — Laura Ashbaugh, wife of the bursar, who instructed in mathematics, and Mrs. Philip Palmer, who in the fall semester of 1943 taught German. Some positions were left vacant.

The year 1943 was barely under way when the Army Specialized Training Program (ASTP) and its naval counterpart, the Naval College Training Program (NCTP), appeared on the horizon as a way for some college students to remain in school. The idea behind the ASTP and the NCTP was that of using colleges and universities to train soldiers and sailors in needed skills of the sorts that, it was supposed, those institutions could provide better than others. The War Manpower Commission would select the colleges and universities appearing to have the necessary qualifications.

The trustees at Lehigh, concerned that the campus might soon be almost empty of students, applied for both an ASTP and an NCTP. The lists of institutions selected for these were published on 6 February 1943. Lehigh was 1 of 249 awarded an ASTP. Only 51 received an NCTP; and of these, only 19 had both programs. The original Lehigh program included Curricula in Chemical, Electrical, Mechanical, Metallurgical, and Mining Engineering.

No one knew exactly when the men for ASTP would arrive. Some people feared that the programs could not begin before January 1944. Williams reported to the trustees that he had visited the ASTP offices in Washington on 15 April and found there confusion and no answer to his questions.

Before any troops came, Lehigh took cognizance of a possibility to share in training troops in some much needed foreign languages. With the entry of the United States into the war, military and civilian leaders suddenly felt a strong pressure to find people who could speak fluently European and Oriental languages. Intensive training was needed to develop fluency quickly. In 1941-42 a program for this was undertaken under the auspices of the American Council of Learned Societies, using money supplied by the Rockefeller Foundation. After Pearl Harbor, numerous civilian and military officials turned to this program for help. One of the results was the inclusion of intensive language training in the ASTP.

Wilson Leon Godshall, an army reserve colonel, had joined the Lehigh faculty in 1939 to teach diplomatic history and international relations. Godshall had a friend in the ASTP office whom he went to see with a proposal to send a contingent of area language trainees to Lehigh. The proposal was accepted.[15]

The first troops for the ASTP arrived early in July. On the fifth of that month, the colonel in charge of ROTC reported to the faculty the presence of 400 soldiers in basic engineering, 82 in advanced engineering, and 123 in the foreign area and language program, a total of 605.

While Lehigh and many other institutions of higher education were training troops, some with broader vision and better facilities were taking action on a proposition that the side with the best technology would win the war. These institutions were seeking sponsorship for research and development.

The national government had taken the lead in using universities for war-related research and development in science and engineering. In June 1940 Roosevelt had created the National Defense Research Committee with "the duty of organizing research dealing with instrumentalities, materials, and mechanisms of warfare in fields which were not adequately covered by existing organizations."[16] From 1940 to 1943, the National Defense Research Committee was the most active of all the agencies concerned with scientific research. A forerunner of the National Science Foundation, the committee was divided into four divisions, each of which was subdivided along functional lines into sections staffed by representatives from universities, engineering schools, and industry. The sections received and evaluated proposals for research projects and made recommendations to the committee, which was empowered to authorize contracts and approve the release of funds for approved projects.

In the first year of its existence, ending 30 June 1941, the National Defense Research Committee placed 269 contracts with forty-seven different universities and technical schools, and 153 contracts with thirty-nine industrial laboratories.[17]

As the war continued, the national government's programs in scientific research and development, especially those related to physics, were expanded and intensified. Complexes of governmental laboratories and shops were built at Oak Ridge, Tennessee, and Hanford, Washington, for development of an atom bomb. There were many more for other purposes. Universities and institutes having highly developed facilities for graduate study and research in the physical sciences received contracts for group research and development of special projects, for example, solid fuel rockets at Caltech, the proximity fuse at Johns Hopkins, radar at MIT, and components for the atom bomb divided among experts at the University of California (Berkeley), Columbia University, and the University of Chicago. Neither these nor other centers of special research were able to supply all of the scientists and engineers needed for the jobs to be done. The excess came from industry and from the colleges and universities not having defense research contracts.

Lehigh University did not share in this major effort of research and development. Although all of the departments in science and engineering did various sorts of war-related work, sometimes for governmental agencies and sometimes for private industry, there was no war-related project of sufficient size and importance to bring in faculty and staff from outside. There was not, indeed, enough research of any sort to keep many of Lehigh's best faculty from going elsewhere.

As far as is known, no national agency sought out Lehigh for a major research assignment. By July 1942, the university had only one government contract for research, which was a small grant from the Navy, obtained through the efforts of Professor Fort.

In the summer of 1943, with the campus lacking major war-related sponsored research, some faculty leaving, and ASTP troops arriving, an event unique in the history of Lehigh took place. The president was asked to resign and submitted his resignation.

The facts of Williams's resignation have not been put into print, although the story has been often told, and in the same way, by faculty and administrators who were on the campus at the time. Buchanan, serving as an alumnus trustee, told Grace that Williams must go, that the alumni would contribute nothing more as long as he remained. When Grace asked who would tell Williams, Buchanan is said to have replied, "You. For you hired him." Grace, in his usual blunt way, asked Williams for his resignation, which bears the date of 24 July 1943 and cites health as a reason. The resignation was to take effect a year later, on 30 June 1944.

Although Buchanan probably had support from some alumni, he did not receive it through the medium of the Alumni Association, which for the time being was concerned with providing the university with good public relations. In the spring of 1943, the association decided to cancel reunions until after the war. Cornelius had resigned as executive secretary, and the young Robert F. Herrick ('34), former managing editor of the *Bulletin*, had taken his place. Herrick was assisted by Leonard H. Schick ('37). Both were busy with other affairs.

The full reasons for Williams's resignation will probably never be known. Much later, some faculty speculated that he had been caught between proponents of two opposing views concerning the future of Lehigh, the view of Grace that Lehigh should continue as a strong undergraduate engineering school and the view of some of the research-minded professors brought in by Richards that a strong undergraduate engineering education could be maintained only by a major forward push into doctoral programs and research, and that Lehigh was losing ground because of the failure of its leadership to take advantage of war-time research opportunities.

This explanation has merit as a description of trends. Harvey A. Neville, for example, the head of Chemistry and Chemical Engineering, was actively seeking sponsored research, even defying Grace (or so it has been reported) in attempting to obtain it. But the explanation fails because of presupposing a knowledge of trends that could only later have been apparent. And the explanation cannot account for the hostility toward Williams on the part of the alumni, to the extent that this might have existed. Williams had, after all, been president during difficult times—six years of depression and two years of war. He possessed a national reputation in engineering education and had strongly supported the undergraduate program while encouraging the formation of a graduate school.

Possibly if Williams had taken the lead in fund raising, his fate would have been different. Perhaps a lack of some of the intangibles of leadership provides an explanation for his resignation, such as being too outspoken on political matters, refusing to take advice, or failing in some personal relationships for which he had no compensating charisma. Although the faculty and the students accepted him, they were not warm in his support. No demonstrations or petitions accompanied his departure.

In the year that he left, Grace resigned from the Executive Committee of the board, while retaining the presidency, and Buchanan became a corporate trustee.

The timing of Williams's resignation was unfortunate. It left the university without strong leadership when it was much needed. Williams, for the ensuing year, would be a lame duck. And then? As long as the war lasted, no possibility existed for securing the sort of person Lehigh needed. A complicating problem was the illness of Okeson, the person most likely to be appointed as acting president until a successor to Williams could be found. Okeson died 4 November 1943. The board elected Kirkpatrick to his positions as treasurer and secretary of the board; and because Kirkpatrick was in the navy, the board appointed the legal counsel, Robert S. Taylor ('95), to these positions until the end of the war.

The resignation of Williams began the most depressing two years of Lehigh's existence. Williams acted as a caretaker and allowed many duties to fall on others. Smiley became director of housing and commissary for the ASTP. A committee consisting of Smiley, the five deans, and the professor of military science and tactics took charge of that program. Godshall directed the foreign area and language program, which he administered with the help of a committee consisting of himself, Palmer, and Barthold. In March 1944, Williams announced a Budget Committee with a membership of the deans of the undergraduate colleges, Palmer being chairman. As Palmer later explained, Williams "had no wish to take the responsibility for a budget which he would not operate."[18]

The ASTP was painful, although it helped the university financially. By the end of the 1943–44 year, the surplus reserved for postwar readjustments had been increased from $100,000 to $250,000.

Perhaps ASTP aided the war effort, although the point is debatable. But it was a disaster for the temper of faculty and administrators at Lehigh. It was organized on the twelve-week quarter used by state colleges and universities rather than the sixteen-week semester employed by Lehigh and most other private schools; and the courses in engineering were structured in such a way as to make most of them useless for students in the regular curricula. The lack of synchronization of ASTP with college work put an additional burden on the faculty, who were already teaching courses for students on the regular and the accelerated schedules and had been teaching without vacations from the autumn of 1942. Many now instructed in fields having little relationship to their specialties.

The ASTP virtually transformed life on the campus for the year 1943–44 into that of a military encampment, although, unlike the experience with the SATC during the First World War, the military left control of the university in civilian hands. But the troops were in uniform and regimented by officers and non-coms, who marched them to class and to study halls and supervised study halls, mess halls, and living quarters. Every afternoon the campus was a drill ground. The troops occupied Drown Hall, transforming the first floor into a mess hall and the basement into a kitchen.

The worst was that most of the students in the ASTP were uninterested in learning. Many were ill-prepared for any college work. Few were studying subjects they enjoyed. They were only marking time until the day came when they would go overseas.

The number of students in the ASTP peaked in the fall of 1943, when 1431 were on the campus. They then outnumbered civilian students by almost three to one. For the term starting in January 1944, the university had 1326 army students. After that, the foreign area and language program was discontinued and the number of students in other programs was drastically reduced. ASTP was being closed out. Eight hundred and twenty-five men were expected for the term beginning in April 1944, but only thirteen arrived.

The trustees acted to reduce expenses. At a special session held 14 April 1944, they encouraged department heads to make temporary reductions in the teaching force. On 1 July they ordered that the faculty should receive no extra pay for summer teaching.

The faculties in science and engineering continued drifting away for war-related research. The size of the faculty fell from 158 full-time in June 1942 to 49 full-time and 23 part-time by 12 October 1944. That is to say, by the fall of 1944, the university had only 31 percent of the full-time faculty it had possessed a little more than two years earlier. Moreover, the most serious losses were in the scientific and engineering fields in which the university's needs were greatest. By 1945 the Department of Physics had but one man, Bidwell, the head, who was anticipating retirement because of age.

On 14 April 1944, with the departure of Williams a little more than eleven weeks away, the trustees created an Administrative Committee consisting of the deans of the three undergraduate colleges. The action had behind it a failure of the board to persuade Palmer to accept an acting presidency. The offer was tendered—and refused—at the 14 April meeting. The most Palmer would consent to was a committee, of which he would be chairman. The Administrative Committee was, in effect, Williams's Budget Committee in new dress.

Palmer faced the faculty in his new capacity for the first time on 10 July 1944. There had been, he said, "a change in the attitude of the trustees as shown in the July 6th meeting of the Executive Committee. . . . For the first time the Faculty will be running the University." Palmer added that he had asked the Executive Committee of the board whether it wanted the Administrative Committee "to mark time here at Lehigh or to clean things up and look forward to a better University" and had received the reply that the trustees wanted the Administrative Committee to make suggestions for improvement.

The whole affair—the vesting of presidential powers in a committee of academic deans and the assertion of Palmer that this meant government of the university by the faculty—was good strategy if not good administration. The faculty was smarting from recent decisions that lightened their pocket books and promised no relief from additional onerous duties. Now they could enjoy the pleasant fiction that the responsibility rested with them for continuing the university on a shoestring for the remainder of the war.

In practice, the Administrative Committee could perform only the role of a caretaker. Palmer, Callen, and Carothers were strong-willed men with considerably different ideas as to how the university should be run and what it should be like after the war. Designs for postwar improvement were tacitly shelved.

The 1944—45 year passed quickly. In the summer of 1944, another army program, the ASTRP (Army Specialized Training Reserve Program, begun for reservists 9 August 1943), replaced ASTP. The university was promised 250 reservists for 10 July and received none. A month later 190 arrived, of whom 35 were dropped for poor scholarship before 16 October. Although the civilian-army balance for 1944—45 was in favor of the civilian by a ratio of about two to one, all enrollments were down. Undergraduate registrations reached a wartime low of 288 in the spring 1945 semester.

In faculty meetings Professor More reported for the College of Arts and Science when Palmer presided, and Neville sometimes substituted for Callen in representing the College of Engineering. Faculty and students read of the exploits of Lehigh alumni and students in all branches of service and in both theaters of operations. Most served in the European. The *Alumni Bulletin* reported in May 1945 that 3,540 students and alumni were then in service, of whom 80 percent were officers, and that 134 had lost their lives. On the campus several buildings had been closed to save money, including Grace Hall and the Packer Memorial Church. A few veterans appeared among the undergraduates enrolling in engineering.

In January 1945, the Committee on Educational Policy took the initiative in asking the faculty to adopt several new student personnel services, among them psychological testing, vocational counseling, freshman counseling, and supervision of student housing and living.

In February, with the end of the war in Europe in sight, the trustees accepted a recommendation from the Administrative Committee to abolish the accelerated program and return to the normal teaching schedule effective 1 July 1945, with the old arrangement of two summer sessions.

The academic year 1944–45 ended with the finances of the university still in the black. The reserve fund had been increased from $250,000 to $600,000. The normal schedule of faculty teaching and salaries was restored as of 1 July 1945.

As the war drew to a close, the great unfinished business was the selection of a president. A search committee of the trustees headed by Grace was assigned the task. In the meantime, the Administrative Committee could not be continued. Palmer, on orders from his physician, resigned as chairman and was granted a vacation to recover his health. The board abolished the committee as of 25 June 1945 and gave E. Kenneth Smiley Okeson's former title of vice-president, a title he was to hold in addition to that of director of admission. Smiley presided over his first faculty meeting on 2 July 1945, exactly forty-five days before the surrender of Japan. He was destined to be administrative head of the university for the first full postwar year.

The two academic years from the fall of 1945 through the spring of 1947 were transitional for everybody. While the trustees searched for and found a president (who himself had to readjust to academic administration from the private laboratory that he had headed), the campus filled to overflowing. Members of the faculty who had waded through the sloughs of ASTP breathed sighs of relief. The relief of their fellow-traveling administrators was mingled with a concern over the shortages of everything except students. Veterans returning to complete their education with the aid of the G.I. Bill of Rights had an eager "born-again" feeling, as though the future belonged to them, as indeed it did; the present itself seemed pretty good.

The veterans swelled the ranks of the undergraduate student body to a size it had never before reached. Everyone conceded that former students had a right to be readmitted, that qualified veterans who had not yet tasted higher education had a right to do so, and that these must be absorbed without diminishing the number that would normally be admitted from the secondary schools.

In the fall of 1946, 2723 undergraduates were on the campus, of whom 65 percent were veterans. About half of the veterans had been students at Lehigh before entering the service. Not until 1949 did the proportion of veterans in the undergraduate student body fall below 50 percent.

Administrators scrambled to provide for the sudden large influx. Department heads hired additional faculty, relying where necessary on graduate assistants and tolerating overcrowding in the classrooms and laboratories. In 1947 Mrs. H. Barrett (Libby) Davis, wife of the professor of speech, became an instructor in journalism and the first woman to hold a full-time position as a regular member of the faculty. Counseling services were needed, and Everett 0. Teal joined the staff as vocational adviser with the Veterans' Advisory Service. The faculty reversed itself on the decision to abolish the accelerated program and planned on keeping it at least through the summer of 1947. Mid-year commencement exercises were also continued (the last of these before their resumption in the 1980s occurred 5 February 1950).

As for housing, three temporary dormitories were built on the old tennis courts between the Sigma Nu and Delta Upsilon fraternity houses. Twenty-eight apartment units were erected on Steel Field in northern Bethlehem. Fraternities were encouraged to increase the size of their pledge classes. The university rented some space on the south side for veterans and gave the places names such as Paul House and Maxwell House. Even with these measures, university housing could accommodate only about two-thirds of the undergraduates. The rest lived wherever they could in town and nearby communities.

In the fall of 1946, about two-thirds of the undergraduates enrolled in the College of Engineering. This was well above the ideal figure established in the 1920s of 60 percent in the ratio of 3:1:1 for the three colleges, Business Administration had almost exactly its quota of 20 percent. Enrollments in the College of Arts and Science were suffering.

The veterans were in general older and more industrious. They were good students. The attrition among the freshmen who were admitted in 1946 was, in 1951, determined to be an astonishingly low 12 percent.[19]

The qualities that made the veterans good students determined them to little innovation. Although they demanded independence from authority in the manner of living, they brought no great changes to campus life. They established no experimental living units and introduced no novel extracurricular activities. A few traditions of dress and deportment disappeared; but this was always happening. None of the truly strong traditions, activities, or organizations died. Publications, athletic contests, student government, social activities, the special rituals, which had temporarily vanished in 1943-44, quietly reappeared; and nothing of significance was added. The Packer Memorial Church was reopened with the Reverend George M. Bean as chaplain. Students experimented with a new publication, the *Goblet*, which had as little success as its prewar counterpart, the *Lehigh Bachelor*. The *Brown and White*, under the control of veterans, followed an editorial policy more closely resembling that of prewar editors than the investigative reporting of the 1950s.

Vice President Smiley, in charge of the university during the first full year of the veteran-swollen enrollments, was in a position to do little more than keep the wheels turning. Callen resigned as dean of engineering but retained his post as head of the Department of Mining Engineering. Tomlinson Fort, dean of the graduate school, left to join the faculty at the University of Georgia, his alma mater. Glenn Harmeson resigned as athletic director in the spring of 1946 to become head football coach at Wabash College. Smiley allowed all three positions to remain vacant.

Smiley made one appointment of extraordinary importance. He asked Harvey A. Neville to become director of the Institute of Research, reorganized in such a way as to be of service in putting the faculty in touch with sponsored research.

The importance of the appointment came not only from the energy and ability of Neville, but also from opportunities for research that were becoming available. The national government, far from receding from the domain of research and development as it had done at the end of the First World War, was becoming more deeply involved. The welfare state, whether under the name of Roosevelt's New Deal, President Harry S. Truman's Fair Deal, or some other label, had come to stay. In the interests of economic growth and stability, the health and general social welfare of the people, and defense of the free world, the United States government was putting money into higher education, basic and applied research, and development. Controls, except those for defense, went to civilian agencies. The new direction of national governmental activities meant for institutions such as Lehigh a possibility to obtain grants for research in the sciences and engineering both from national governmental agencies and state, local, and private sources operating programs made possible by federal action.

Lehigh's reorganized Institute of Research was based on an assumption that it would never have an endowment but must obtain operating funds from the grants that it processed. The revised institute became the university's arm for aiding faculty and departments to obtain and administer grants.

By the spring of 1946, the trustees were ready with their choice of president — Martin Dewey Whitaker, a native of North Carolina with a Ph.D. in physics from New York University. Whitaker had been director of the Clinton Laboratories at Oak Ridge, Tennessee, since 1943. Smiley introduced him to the faculty on 6 May 1946. Whitaker took office the following 1 June. Alumni first met him at the victory reunion in June.

In his first recorded remarks, Whitaker hinted that he would apply engineering concerns for safety and economy to the governing of Lehigh. He told the alumni in June, "The University is a business and must be run as such." Four months later, in a report to the trustees, he declared, "Long-term plans must be made, but they must be changed as the need arises." He commented to the effect that the present organization and concentration of the colleges and departments was correct for Lehigh and that his job would be to avoid obsolescence and to guard against the attraction of expensive new programs. He remarked that salaries would have to be raised, especially for deans and key department heads, that space was needed for athletic, instructional, and health quarters, and that eventually the Colleges of Arts and Science and Business Administration would need separate buildings. He shared the trustees' concern for a swollen undergraduate enrollment but also talked in terms of an expanded regular enrollment of two thousand.[20]

The Lehigh community soon discovered that Whitaker spoke little and that his thinking benefited from a wealth of administrative experience and a rare and lively understanding of developing relationships involving politics, business, education, and research.

Grace, who had headed the search for a president, was satisfied. On Founder's Day 1946, the day of Whitaker's inauguration, Grace announced his retirement as president of the board. The announcement apparently caught the other trustees by surprise. He was still the obvious choice for president of the board. The trustees asked him to reconsider, to remain at least until a successor could be chosen. Grace agreed to this and in fact remained as president for an additional ten years.

Whitaker dealt with a board that changed little in membership during the early years of his administration. Kirkpatrick became secretary when he returned to the university in 1946 to take up his new job as treasurer of the university. Whitaker provided the board with a leadership of the sort it appreciated.

Upon becoming president, Whitaker made few changes among top administrative personnel. Smiley continued as vice-president and took charge of many administrative details. Kirkpatrick as treasurer had the oversight of all financial matters as well as of the Supply Bureau and Buildings and Grounds. Congdon continued as dean of undergraduates and director of admission; his title was changed in 1947 to that of dean of students and director of admission. In that year, too, Congdon's staff was enlarged by the appointment of John D. Leith and Charles A. Seidle as associate deans of students and Byron C. Hayes as associate director of admission. A further shift in personnel in the Office of Admission occurred in 1950, when the office was separated from that of the dean of students. Hayes became director of admission and James M. McGeady was hired as his assistant.

Whitaker also replaced the old News Bureau with a Department of Public Relations and put Robert F. Herrick, who had been executive secretary of the Alumni Association until his departure for the army, in charge.

Whitaker gave Neville strong support. Almost as soon as Whitaker became president, he asked the trustees for permission to use $250,000 of the reserve of $600,000 for research equipment. The work of gaining sponsored research went ahead as fast as the war-weakened condition of faculty and facilities permitted.

In a "Progress Report" for the *Alumni Bulletin* of December 1946—January 1947, Neville wrote that nine departments had contracts for cooperative research, including all those in engineering and the Departments of Biology and Psychology in the College of Arts and Science. The nine had among them ten contracts from divisions of the U.S. government and thirty-six projects conducted in cooperation with industrial sponsors. All of the governmental grants, he added, came from military divisions and were located in the College of Engineering.

In Neville's own Department of Chemistry and Chemical Engineering, research in leather continued under the new title of Leather Technology Laboratory. In 1946 another laboratory was organized for cooperative research, the National Printing Ink Research Institute, brought about by a request from a number of industrial leaders in the field. Neville asked Professor Albert C. Zettlemoyer to take charge of this effort.

The reorganized Institute of Research carried out former President Richards's desire for the university to support research in all departments. Money for helping faculty whose projects were ineligible for outside support came from overhead allowances in grants administered by the institute. Gipson was one of the first in the postwar era to benefit from this position. In 1946 he retired from active teaching and administration in order to give full time to his series, The British Empire Before the American Revolution. He became research professor of history with quarters on the fourth floor of the Linderman Library. By 1948 six volumes of the series had appeared.

Athletics claimed a share of the new president's attention. During the war most of the regular staff had entered the armed services and the losses in intercollegiate games had reached new highs. Wrestling was the only intercollegiate sport to maintain its prewar strength. Here, Billy Sheridan was still in charge. Football had been a disaster. George Hoban, secured as head coach in 1942, had died after one season and had not been replaced. For the next three years, the team had been coached by a volunteer, Leo Prendergast, a public school teacher in Bethlehem who had served as line coach under Hoban. Hoban's year as coach had produced a winning season (5—2—1) and a tie with Lafayette (7—7). Prendergast's three seasons were all losing; and Lehigh did not win a single point against Lafayette from the second game in 1943 until 1948.

When the war had ended, the trustees began to take corrective measures by hiring William B. Leckonby as head football coach. Leckonby had been a star player at St. Lawrence University and had subsequently played football for the Brooklyn Dodgers's professional team and football and basketball for the navy. Harmeson had not yet been replaced as athletic director. Whitaker filled the position with Percy L. Sadler, a former instructor in ROTC at Lehigh who had returned in 1946 with the rank of brigadier general to head the army ROTC. At the same time, Whitaker enlarged the coaching staff.

Courses and curricula were as usual under the control of the teaching departments. Whitaker did nothing to disturb this division of labor. Deans, department heads, and other faculty labored much to keep courses of study current with the latest scholarship and improvements in pedagogy. In keeping with a national trend, the faculty in Engineering reviewed the undergraduate culture studies program and in 1945 adopted a two-semester sequence in History of Western Civilization as part of the Uniform Freshman Year. In April 1946, the trustees agreed to a recommendation from Palmer for the formation of a Department of International Relations. This was generally recognized as acknowledging the special talents of Professor Godshall and his success in bringing the ASTP program in foreign languages and area studies to the campus.

Faculty and students saw little of their president, for he chose to govern through a small number of administrators and shunned popular acclaim and dramatic appearances. Many students and faculty considered Whitaker aloof and cold. But deans and department heads who answered directly to him knew him as a warm and friendly man who gave encouragement, support, and freedom for them to do their business.

As long as veterans predominated among the undergraduates, student life was relatively uneventful. In 1947 Arcadia requested permission to implement a plan of student evaluation of courses and instuctors, a request that the faculty promptly approved.[21] The evaluation came more from changes in values among the younger students than from the veterans. In 1948 the students established a radio station, WLRN, an event more rightly attributed to catching up with technological progress than to discovering any new principle.

More sponsored research appeared. In the fiscal year ending 30 June 1946, total expenditures for sponsored research had been $223,885. Three years later, 30 June 1949, the comparable figure was $558,936, or $2\frac{1}{2}$ times the earlier amount. Neville reported in 1949 a total of fifty-four contracts, with twenty-seven being directed by the Department of Chemistry and Chemical Engineering, twelve in Civil Engineering, and the others falling under the supervision of Departments of Mechanical, Electrical, and Metallurgical Engineering, Physics, and Psychology.

An upturn in graduate education accompanied the increase of sponsored research. In the fall of 1947, the Graduate School had 366 students, about twice the prewar enrollment. In 1949 Whitaker named Neville dean of the Graduate School. Neville took the post while remaining as head of Chemistry and Chemical Engineering and director of the Institute of Research. He hired as an assistant in the institute Preston Parr, '43, a chemist working in Philadelphia who had recently returned from graduate study in chemical engineering at MIT.

By this time, Whitaker had two other academic deanships to fill. Both Carothers and Palmer were slated for retirement. Carothers left in 1949.

Whitaker appointed Carl E. Allen as Carother's successor. Allen had served in 1947–48 as acting director of the Curriculum in Business Administration when Carothers had been on leave. Also in 1949 Robert P. More became associate dean of Arts and Science, anticipating the retirement of Palmer. More moved into the deanship in 1950.

Whitaker continued to leave the deanship of Engineering vacant and to deal individually with the heads of departments in the College of Engineering. Several of these had to be replaced. In 1947 Sutherland retired as head of Civil Engineering and director of the Fritz Laboratory and was succeeded by William J. Eney. In the same year Bidwell relinquished his post in Physics. Whitaker brought in as his replacement Frank E. Myers, whom he had known at New York University. In 1949, upon the retirement of Larkin, the Curricula of Mechanical and Industrial Engineering were given separate departmental status with Milton C. Stuart as a stopgap head of both departments.

One other top administrative position commanded Whitaker's attention before 1950. This concerned the library. Leach died in 1948 and was replaced by James D. Mack ('38), first in an acting capacity but from 1950 as head librarian.

The two most important changes during the first five years of Whitaker's presidency occurred with little publicity or planning.

One was an increase in the size of the undergraduate student body. Although the veterans did not make any lasting revisions in the quality of campus life, they altered the university because of their numbers. Deans and department heads had hastened to add faculty to accommodate them. The size of the teaching force in the spring of 1946 was given as 144. By 1949 it had grown to include 217 faculty and 71 assistants and teaching assistants. Also, from 1946 to 1950 the trustees raised tuition three times, from $400 per year for all undergraduates to $700 per year for engineering students and $625 for those in arts and business. Neither faculty, administrators, nor trustees could contemplate with equanimity reducing the size of the teaching staff and income, which must necessarily accompany a return to the prewar figure of 1500 paying students. Moreover, academic and extracurricular currents were flowing smoothly, and applications for admission from seniors in the secondary schools were holding up. In sum, a situation once regarded as temporary and of dubious worth was being looked upon as necessary and desirable.

As veterans were graduated, the number of incoming freshmen from the secondary schools increased. By 1951, when veterans accounted for only 12 percent of the undergraduates, the total undergraduate fall enrollment stood at 2651, close to what it had been from 1947 to 1950. For the next thirteen years the number of undergraduates remained near this figure.

The second change of stellar importance was the centralization of fund raising in an Office of Development under the control of the president.

When Whitaker took office, the Alumni Association was still formally responsible for fund raising, although in practice it shared the responsibility rather ambiguously with the president, the Board of Trustees, and the Endowment Committee of the board. All were novices at the business.

The organization of a professional office of development came about in the course of a major campaign for funds, the first attempted since the Greater Lehigh Endowment Fund Campaign of the mid-1920s.

The announcement that a large fund-raising campaign was being contemplated came about in an offhand sort of way. On 6 January 1947, Whitaker told the faculty that a firm of professional fund raisers, Marts and Lundy, had been retained "to survey the general endowment picture." The report that Marts and Lundy filed with the Endowment Committee of the board in the spring of 1947 described Lehigh's greatest needs as being increases in endowment for salaries, pensions, and operating expenses, for a dormitory, and for additional athletic facilities. The report further indicated that most of the money for these would have to come from alumni, and that this presented a special problem: alumni response to the preliminary survey had been "above average for college fund raising surveys," yet alumni morale was low; little had been done in past years to stimulate alumni enthusiasm and support. One of the biggest jobs, according to the report, would be a long-range public relations effort to cultivate a body of potential contributors from alumni and friends.

At a meeting on 11 April 1947, the Endowment Committee endorsed the report of Marts and Lundy and recommended a fund-raising campaign to be conducted in two stages. The first would seek $1,500,000 for a dormitory and an addition to Taylor Gymnasium. The second stage would aim at an additional $5,500,000 for other projects. The committee's report to the board declared, "The construction of a program at Lehigh University which will bring in $7,000,000 within the next several years is, in itself, an engineering problem which requires the most careful and thorough planning. It is not a simple fund raising problem at all."

Such was the inception of the Progress Fund Campaign, as the drive came to be called. Trustee E. F. "Coxey" Johnson headed the campaign, in which Marts and Lundy assisted.

The first stage was overwhelmingly successful. By June 1949, Johnson and Marts and Lundy had, through teams organized by the alumni clubs, raised a sum of $1,977,000, almost half a million dollars more than the goal.

Paul J. Franz, Jr., appeared on the scene during this first stage of the Progress Fund Campaign. Franz was in 1947 assistant director of admission, an office in which he had been working since graduation in 1944 with a degree of bachelor of science in business administration. He was active in the Home Club of the Alumni Association and soon became president of the club. As he wrote later, "Almost from the time I started work at Lehigh in the admission office, I attended alumni club meetings. Leonard H. Schick,

'37, then alumni secretary, was indulgent and allowed me to travel to as many meetings as I wanted."[22] Shortly thereafter Franz was transferred to Kirkpatrick's office and given a job of revising the faculty pension system, for which Carothers had done preliminary work. When the Greater Progress Campaign was opened, Franz volunteered to be a solicitor, was successful in getting pledges, and discovered that he liked the work. When the first stage of the campaign was concluded, Marts and Lundy suggested to Whitaker that Franz be put in charge of development, and he soon found himself with the title of assistant to the president.

Franz at this stage of his career was not yet an expert. He learned the business over the next several years from Austin McLain, a vice-president of Marts and Lundy, who worked to complete the project of raising seven million dollars. McLain had an office in the Alumni Memorial Building and from it directed all of the firm's fund-raising campaigns in the region.

The money raised by the first stage of the campaign was rapidly spent for a dormitory, athletic facilities, and several other projects. Grace suggested the name of Dravo for the dormitory to honor Francis R. Dravo ('87) and his brother Ralph ('89), who had built up and headed the Dravo Construction Corporation, one of the largest firms of its kind in the United States, and who had actively supported Lehigh in many ways. The architect was Jens Frederick Larson of New York City, who replaced Visscher and Burley, long since dead. Ground was broken in October 1948 for an addition to Taylor Gymnasium including a new swimming pool, basketball court, and boxing room. The other projects benefiting from the first stage of the Progress Fund Campaign included a central telephone switchboard, rewiring the entire campus for electricity, and purchasing a service facility, the Lehigh Valley Cold Storage Building.

The alumni gave more than money. Along with the dollars came good will and optimism for Lehigh's future, expressed in such new institutions as an annual spring dinner and awards for service.

The awards began with the probating of the will of Ralf Ridgway Hillman, class of '91, a former employee of the Bethlehem Steel Company and later a consulting engineer. Ralf Hillman's grandfather, Herman B. Hillman, had been a partner with the young Asa Packer in shipping coal on the Lehigh Canal. Ralf's bride of 1903 was Evelyn Chandler, daughter of Professor William H. Chandler and Mary Elizabeth (Sayre) Chandler, a parentage that made Evelyn a granddaughter of Robert H. Sayre. Ralf had desired to leave part of his estate to honor each year, with a large sum of money, a member or members of the staff at Lehigh for excellence in teaching or research, or for generally advancing the interests of the university.

The first award was made as a surprise to the faculty at the annual banquet of the Alumni Association on 21 June 1946. On the agenda was the presentation to the university of a portrait of Dean Palmer painted by Frederick Roscher. Palmer was ill and could not attend. Grace accepted the portrait on behalf of the university and announced the first recipient of the R. R. and E. C. Hillman award, Dean Palmer. The following year the award was also made at the alumni dinner, Professor Gipson being the recipient.

Then Whitaker changed the scene. In April 1948, he informed the trustees that the faculty would have its own annual banquet, the principal purposes being to honor staff with twenty-five years of service and to present the Hillman award. That year Vice President Smiley received it. In 1949, at the second annual faculty dinner, Professor Neville was honored and a new award was announced, the Alfred Noble Robinson Award, established by Alfred R. Glancy, '03, a vice-president of General Motors, in honor of a grandfather who had helped raise him. According to Franz, Glancy had been present when Gipson had received the Hillman and had commented, "Isn't it too bad to give so much money to an individual who is really too old to enjoy it?" Glancy came up with the idea of a service award for a member of the faculty of age thirty-five or younger.[23] Glancy specified that the award was to be spent by the recipient in "riotous living." The first to receive the Robinson Award (1949) were John J. Karakash, a young assistant professor in the Department of Electrical Engineering, and William Schempf, who had joined the faculty in 1947 as assistant professor of music and director of the Band and the Glee Club.

As far as is known, none of the recipients of the Robinson Award, then or later, followed the advice to spend their money in riotous living.

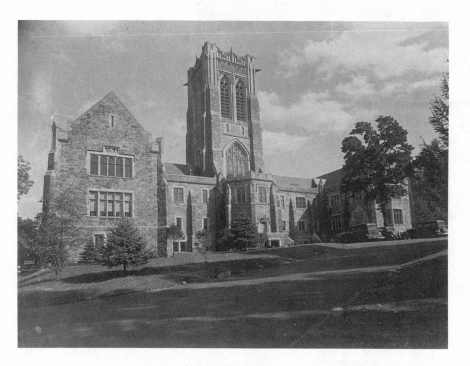

Alumni Memorial.

President Charles R. Richards.

Williams Hall about 1920.

James Ward Packard.

First Packard motor car.

Packard Laboratory.

Entrance to Taylor Gymnasium, as it was before the remodeling of the drive-in entrance in 1941 as the Berger Trophy Room.

Taylor Field following completion of the upper stands in 1953–54. Above Taylor Field and behind the gymnasium is the quarter-mile cinder track.

Philip M. Palmer, director of the curriculum, and later dean of Arts and Science.

Neil Carothers, director of the curriculum, and later dean of Business Administration.

Bradley Stoughton, director of the Curriculum in Metallurgy and first dean of the College of Engineering.

Christmas and Saucon halls as they appeared in the early 1920s.

Christmas-Saucon following the union of the two buildings in 1926.

Eugene G. Grace in 1944. Photo by Robert
Yarnall Ritchie.

President Clement C. Williams.

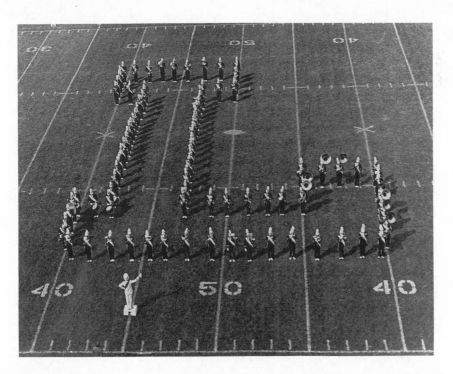

The "Marching 97": The Lehigh Band at halftime in the football game against C. W.
Post, 1970.

President Martin D. Whitaker.

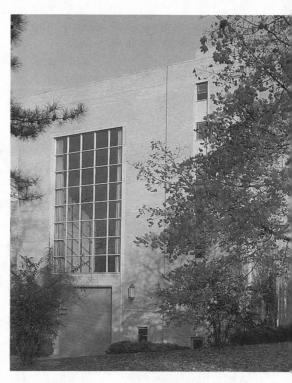

Fritz Laboratory following the renovation and enlargement completed in 1956. Photo by Ted Anderson.

Packer Hall, the University Center, following completion of renovations and additions in 1958. Photo by Joseph Ryan.

Whitaker Metallurgical and Chemical Engineering Laboratory.

Monroe J. Rathbone.

President Harvey A. Neville.

President W. Deming Lewis.

Harold S. Mohler.

Students with President Lewis during CURE demonstrations of 1968.

Maginnes Hall. Photo by Ted Anderson.

Coeducation became a reality in 1971.

Michael J. Caruso decisions Richard Beck of Cornell, 13−2. Caruso, '67, was three times undefeated at 123 pounds for both eastern and national championships.

Turkey Trot. John S. Steckbeck, director of intramural athletics, began the popular two-plus-mile November race on the slope of South Mountain. Photo by Ray Sims.

President Peter Likins.

Fairchild-Martindale Library and Computing Center. Photo by Elia Schoomer.

7

To the Centennial Celebration: 1950—1963

President Martin D. Whitaker brought much more to ideas on education at Lehigh than a bias favoring research and graduate studies. He also reintroduced the concept expressed by former President Drown calling for equality among courses of study. In doing so, he departed from the view prevailing through the Richards and Williams years that everything exists to serve engineering education.

Grace was one of the last to give voice to the old view. In 1945, when he was approaching the age of seventy, student editors had asked for his ideas concerning the future of the university. Grace had replied that Lehigh was "a technological school" and invoked the names of the "Business College and the Liberal Arts College" only to emphasize their importance to engineering education.[1]

Grace was present eight years later when the board reaffirmed Drown's position. In 1953 Whitaker put before the trustees the desirability of having a hall of liberal arts estimated to cost $2,500,000. The question was immediately raised, Would this not change the educational direction of the university? Whitaker said it would not. Grace then asked that the board express an opinion as to goals. In reply it unanimously approved a motion made by Coxey Johnson "that the Board reaffirm its now traditional [!] position that the educational programs of Lehigh University be continued as at present, i.e., that the University propose and strive to maintain a pre-eminent position in the field of engineering education and that it seek to achieve this end by maintaining three undergraduate colleges (Engineering, Arts and Science and Business Administration), each to be a service department to the other two and each to be maintained at the highest attainable degree of excellence."[2]

This contrasting of positions taken by Grace in 1945 and the board in 1953 may seem like making a distinction without a difference. Neither Whitaker nor the trustees ever denied that engineering and applied science were to form the principal thrusts of education. And from a realistic point of view, the preeminence of applied science and engineering was so deeply ingrained at Lehigh as to make talk of full equality for all courses of study absurd. Yet the affirmative attitude of the board in 1953 produced positive results. It promoted a stimulating intellectual climate, which encouraged faculty in all of the colleges to think and hope. Faculties in business and the arts dared to dream of a brighter future for their respective fields. They gave time and talents to innovative programs and, incidentally, pressured the president and the trustees for more faculty, better facilities, and greater funds for programs and professional development.

This affirmation of the equality of the colleges took place within the context of a rapidly changing world. Following the defeat of Germany and Japan, politicians, scientists, and engineers took on the job of reconstructing a war-torn world. A division of labor accompanied their efforts. Politicians—not scientists and engineers—made the key decisions in great power politics. Scientists and engineers supplied theories and techniques for concretizing the politicians' decisions.

Lehigh directly contributed to the chains of endeavor set in motion by world-shaking events. It did not produce the politicians who made the key decisions, nor even the theoretical scientists who invented new visions of time and space. Lehigh's strengths were in applied fields, especially engineering and, potentially, in the management of business. Lehigh gave to and took from governments, industries, and charitable organizations in the broad domain lying between the outpourings of theoretical science and the production of goods and services by an ever-increasing work force of highly skilled technicians.

Lehigh's very existence in the years covered by the remaining chapters of this history was closely bound up with several major trends within the broad and complex domain of applied research and development. Two of the most obvious trends were a growing need for a larger and better-educated work force and an expanding body of young people capable of supplying it. In the words of Daniel Bell, writing in the early 1970s, "Just as in the 1920s a decision was made to provide a secondary school education for every child in the country so, too, in the past two decades, the decision was made to provide a college education, or at least some years in college, for all capable youths in the country."[3] The decision was effective because the national government supplemented the aid given by the states and local governments to education as, in prewar years, the states had begun to help cities, counties, and local school boards.

These trends worked to the advantage of all institutions of higher education that aided in producing the new scientifically oriented work force. The sort of institution most hurt by the trends was the private four-year liberal arts college with little capacity for educating youths in science or science-related fields. Places such as Lehigh had only to perceive and be ready to take advantage of opportunities as they arose and to keep curricula abreast of the latest developments in their respective areas of specialization. With even a modest intention to provide an up-to-date education for science-related minds, full enrollments were possible.

Lehigh, in the years covered by this chapter, maintained a stable undergraduate enrollment while being selective and raising tuition. With the ebbing of the veterans' tide, the trustees agreed to a student body of 2,500 and were gratified for financial reasons to see a head count of approximately 2650 at the beginning of every fall semester. On several occasions the trustees increased tuition. Over a ten-year period, it was about doubled, rising from $700 for engineering students and $625 for those in arts and business in 1950 to $1400 for all undergraduates in 1961. In that year the trustees agreed to an increase of twenty-five students in the entering class for four years, until by 1965 a freshman enrollment of eight hundred would be attained. This was scheduled to bring the total undergraduate student body to about three thousand by 1968–69. The plan was carried out with the desired results; and during the period tuition went up again, to $2,000 beginning in 1968 for all undergraduates.

Quality remained at acceptable levels. The combined mathematics and verbal scores on the CEEB tests rose from a mean of 1029 in 1951 to a little over 1200 by 1958 and remained at that level. For all men entering college in the nation as a whole the combined CEEB scores for the same period were in the 900–1000 range.

The domain of admission contained some problems. One was insufficient undergraduate financial aid. National competition for the best students was keen. Scholarships were a means of attracting them. The competition was as yet relatively uncomplicated by considerations of poverty and disadvantaged minorities. Whitaker took the prevailing line of argument in basing the concern for scholarships on merit alone. He wrote, "The real justification, the basic reason for such awards, is not to improve the financial status or advancement of an individual so much as to contribute to mankind at large the service of a better-trained individual."[4]

In the early 1950s, the principal means for increasing Lehigh's supply of scholarships lay in taking advantage of judicial decisions recognizing colleges and universities as charitable institutions and a change in federal legislation granting advantages in taxation to companies for gifts to charitable bodies. The development office campaigned with private industries for endowments for scholarships. Bethlehem Fabricators, with a gift of twenty thousand dollars, became in 1951 the first corporation to respond to the call. By the end of 1957, Whitaker reported that eighty-three companies were supporting 125 students at Lehigh through scholarship aid.

Beginning with the National Defense Education Act of 1958, the national government inaugurated broad programs of financial aid for undergraduates, especially those intending to study science and engineering. The addition of these programs helped to bring many excellent students to Lehigh.

Another problem in the domain of admission came from the felt need to maintain some sort of parity among the colleges. High standards were to be observed for entrance into all three, although the specific entrance requirements might vary with differences in their several curricula. The Office of Admission, concerned with maintaining a full enrollment, took advantage of the flexibility inhering in the situation by adapting the numbers admitted into the three colleges to the numbers of applications. In the 1950s, when national attention favored science and engineering and not especially the liberal arts and business, Lehigh, with its reputation for engineering, was attracting good students for the College of Engineering, whereas enrollments in the other two colleges were suffering. This violated an ideal of parity.

From the point of view of admission, the problem was minor. Higher education recognizably had fads and fashions like almost every aspect of the fast-paced postwar life. A preference of college-bound youths for engineering might within a year or two shift to something else. Members of the faculty in Business Administration were not complaining loudly. Even though admissions were down, the Business College maintained about 20 percent of the undergraduate student body through transfers from Arts and Science and Engineering. The College of Arts and Science also received many transfer students from Engineering; but some of its faculty were complaining loudly. Therein was a factor which magnified the problem.

The complaints were heard all over the campus. Younger faculty especially insisted that if their college was truly more than a service organization for engineering, it should act like a college. Their model was the four-year liberal arts college, whether it be private like Swarthmore or Carleton or a semi-independent component of a large state university. The guiding mystique was the old one of a liberal education. Inspired faculty looked to liberal arts schools of traditional excellence for programs and techniques of teaching associated with breadth of intellectual speculation not so much in applied science and engineering as in mathematics, the theoretical aspects of the physical and natural sciences, the social sciences, the humanities, and the performing arts.

The inspired younger arts faculty got permission in 1952–53 to search. The means was a committee, called the Arts College Committee. Librarian James D. Mack made the motion for forming it. Dean More selected Professor Glenn J. Christensen as chairman. Christensen was teaching technical writing and administering a sponsored research project on a history of rockets and rocket launchers, popularly called "the bomb shelter project," and was regarded as a leader in promoting new ideas. More and Christensen selected the other members, with More giving in to Christensen's insistence on younger personnel instead of those accustomed to think of the college as being wholly a service organization. The committee was kept small and had a rotating membership. Soon, the other two colleges became interested and requested and were granted one member each on the committee.

The Arts College Committee had no budget and could draw on no other source for finances. Furthermore, it faced opposition from some arts faculty whose opinions on education were department bound. But the committee had good leadership and received broad support from the administration and large numbers of faculty in the other colleges.

Within several years the committee sucessfully brought several interdepartmental programs into being: a national venture called the Washington Semester Program, whereby selected students might study and serve as interns in the nation's capital; a Foreign Careers major; and a College Honors Program. Honors opportunities were in line with traditions at Lehigh but had previously been departmentally based. The basic plan of the College Honors Program was for qualified students to take four courses styled "Creative Concepts Seminars," one each semester respectively in the humanities and the life, social, and physical sciences, taught by outstanding teachers.

In addition to producing interdepartmental programs, the Arts College Committee materially helped to form a collegial spirit. It produced among the members a sense of pride and dignity in the College of Arts and Science, who looked forward to "changing the image of Lehigh as only an engineering school," as they sometimes phrased it, knowing that any such change could come about only over a long span of time.

Whether or not the Arts College Committee had an effect on the admission of freshmen cannot be determined.

In any event, the committee addressed itself to restricted aspects of the more general tasks facing the university. These tasks were (1) establishing a structure whereby faculty and administrators might take advantage of all opportunities as they arose, expecting most of these to be in applied science and engineering, and (2) keeping curricula up to standards demanded by granting agencies and the university's clientele, which now included not only industries and top professional schools but also good graduate schools everywhere.

The business of adjusting the structure of the university was largely in the hands of the trustees and President Whitaker.

Most of the structures were already in place and needed only some refinements to take care of increases in the work load and the specialization of functions. As always, some key personnel had to be replaced.

Until 1958 the Board of Trustees recorded no structural change. As before, the position of alumnus trustee was the door through which most of the new leadership entered. This was the route taken by Theophil H. Mueller ('18), Leonard H. Horton ('28), Monroe Jackson Rathbone ('21), Edward A. Curtis ('26), and H. Randolph Maddox ('21).

The most important events for the board began in 1956 with the retirement of Grace. Johnson, chairman of the Executive Committee, telephoned all of the other trustees and reported near unanimity on a choice of Monroe J. Rathbone as successor. Rathbone was chairman of the Standard Oil Company of New Jersey. In the course of his career he had gained much experience in labor relations and acquired a broad knowledge of national and international affairs. He had a wide acquaintance among the nation's corporate elite. Rathbone begged off from immediately accepting the presidency on the grounds of other responsibilities but indicated that he might be available in a year. The board then asked Johnson to serve temporarily as president, which he did; and in 1957 Rathbone took the position.

On the administrative side, Whitaker began the decade with Vice President Smiley in charge of many details of administration, Kirkpatrick as treasurer, Franz as an assistant in charge of the Office of Development, and Congdon as dean of students. Carl E. Allen headed the College of Business Administration. Robert P. More was dean of Arts and Science. Harvey A. Neville took charge of the Graduate School.

During the next seven years Whitaker made several changes among this small group of top executives. He gave the position of treasurer to Elmer Glick ('33) when in 1951 Kirkpatrick left for a position with the University of Chicago. In 1954 Whitaker elevated Christensen to the post of Associate dean of the College of Arts and Science and, upon the retirement of More the following year, to the deanship.

In 1953 Whitaker made Loyal V. Bewley, head of Electrical Engineering, dean of Engineering. The appointment had much of the effect of creating a new position, as for eight years the department heads in Engineering had reported directly to the president. Bewley was tough minded and within a few years made the deanship into a formidable position. In 1956 he received Charles W. Brennan from the Department of Industrial Engineering as an assistant in charge of freshmen.

In 1956, Whitaker laid before the faculty Committee on Educational Policy, the idea of having a vice president and provost. The committee was enthusiastic and recommended Neville for the position. The appointment was made. For two years Neville also held the position of Director of the Institute of Research, but he gave up the graduate deanship, which went to Frank E. Myers, who held the title while remaining in charge of Physics.

The Department of Public Relations became an important part of the Whitaker administration. It made available for public scrutiny the president's annual report, which had previously gone only to the trustees. The report was written in nontechnical language and attractively illustrated. The first appeared in 1949 and was for the academic year 1948–49. That was a year before the name "Register" was exchanged for "Catalog" for the university's principal publication. At the end of the decade the Department of Public Relations was placed under Franz. By then, too, it was putting out the *Alumni Bulletin* through a newly created subdepartment of publications.

The top administration of the Alumni Association was close to the office of the president without being formally part of the administrative structure. Exclusion of the association from the business of administering the university had come about piecemeal in response to a growing awareness on the part of everyone concerned of the need for a greater specialization of functions and clearer lines of responsibility.

In 1951 the last vestige of responsibility for raising money passed from the

Alumni Association to Franz's office. Edward A. Curtis was then president of the association. The issue in question was the solicitation of money for the Alumni Fund. Curtis wrote the trustees a letter calling to their attention the formation of the Council of Lehigh Class Agents several years earlier for the purpose of promoting annual giving, and added that the council had been acting fairly independently of the association. He recommended that the work should be centralized under control of the university administration, and the change was made: In the future the Office of Development would control the two forms of alumni giving, that is, for the Annual Fund and for capital expansion.

The results of this change were dramatic. In 1949–50 the old management had rasied $75,000. In 1950–51, annual giving was $150,000 and rose to more than $200,000 in 1952–53, more than $250,000 in 1953–54, and approximately $355,000 for 1956–57.

Although the Alumni Association was now free from active participation in running the university, close cooperation between it and the president's office remained. In 1952 Robert A. Harrier ('27) succeeded Schick as executive secretary of the association and became editor of the *Bulletin*. He delegated most of the responsibility for editing it to others.

The development office was responsible for most of the money obtained for physical improvements. As yet, governmental agencies were not funding physical developments, except for loans for student housing. But there were other sources waiting to be tapped. The development office organized a parents' committee in 1952. A bequest committee consisting of one hundred Lehigh lawyers, geographically distributed, advised alumni and friends of the university about including Lehigh in their wills. Another source was insurance. Charles K. Zug ('26), representing the Philadelphia Life Insurance Company, which had underwritten the class insurance program since 1948, told the trustees that the insurance for which the university was named as beneficiary could over a twenty-year period be as much as $1,600,000. The class insurance program, begun in 1938 and continued in every subsequent year, also benefited from specialized attention.

Sums received from corporations, foundations, parents, other friends, alumni, and by way of insurance and bequests increased almost year by year. Bethlehem Steel continued to be by far the largest corporate benefactor. In 1956–57 the Ford Foundation turned over some $930,000 to the university as part of a national distribution to aid private colleges and universities in meeting increasing expenses. In the same year almost $500,000 came from Dravo estates and trusts. In 1959–60 an additional $1,750,000 was received from the James Ward Packard trust fund.

Opportunities for increasing income exceeded expectations. The first stage of the Progress Fund Campaign had been oversubscribed by about $500,000, thereby causing fears that the larger goal of $7 million might actually be too low and that publicity for it might inhibit potential donors from giving more.

So the $7 million was raised without much publicity. An announcement of the end of the campaign appeared in the president's annual report for 1953–54. By then, much getting and spending had taken place.

The physical improvements made from 1950 to 1958 were more important in removing a backlog occasioned by depression and war than for planning for future needs. With money supplied by William P. Starkey ('00) and his sons, the Packer Memorial Church was renovated in 1951–52 and provided with a new pipe organ. In 1953–54 Bethlehem Steel financed the addition to Taylor Stadium of a press box and upper tiers of stands capable of holding 4,200 spectators.

Bethlehem Steel also provided the funds for rebuilding the Fritz Laboratory. The result was an almost entirely new building with the original one appearing as a wing. A tall central part contained one of the largest universal testing machines in the world.

Coxey Johnson, in the capacity of an anonymous donor, made a challenge grant for a health center, which was completed in 1955. After the name of the donor became known, it was called Johnson Hall.

A special campaign begun in 1954 provided money for a dormitory, the rebuilding of Packer Hall, and renovations to Drown, Lamberton, and several other buildings whose use would be changed by the rebuilt Packer. The dormitory was erected east of Taylor, where tennis courts had stood, and named McClintic-Marshall House. It was opened for occupancy in the fall of 1956. By this time the reconstruction of Packer was well under way. The interior had been almost completely gutted and large additions made to the floor space, taking care to preserve many of the lineaments of the original structure.

Before the work on Packer and McClintic-Marshall was completed, on 7 January 1956, fire caused extensive damage to Williams Hall, which housed Metallurgy, Biology, and Geology. The trustees used the insurance and other money to repair the damage and added a fourth floor, thereby gaining about ten thousand square feet of space for instruction.

The rebuilding of Packer was completed in the spring of 1958. The building included dining halls, lounges, and meeting rooms for students and faculty, a snack bar, facilities for radio station WLRN, the *Brown and White*, the *Epitome*, and other student activities, the Supply Bureau, and offices for student leaders, the chaplain, and the staff of the dean of students.

In the general shift occasioned by the completion of Packer Hall, the College of Business Administration moved from Christmas-Saucon to a modernized Drown Hall; the language departments left Coppee for rooms in the east end of Lamberton; the Department of Music took over the space in Lamberton originally used for student dining; Mathematics moved from temporary quarters south of the physics building — where Mathematics had been during the renovation of Packer — into Christmas-Saucon; and Psychology found itself in an old house at the corner of Packer and Adams, which had been the university's carpenter shop and, before that, the chapter house of Sigma Chi fraternity.

The next stage of physical improvements reflected a concern for future needs and clearly aligned Lehigh with another international trend. The stage was a planned expansion, carried forward primarily through the expertise and financial strength of the Bethlehem Steel Corporation spending profits received from supplying war-retarded economies with the steel needed for reconstruction.

The rebuilding had been going on in Europe since 1946 with aid supplied through the Marshall Plan. The work was not confined to places devastated by bombs and artillery. The United States was also "catching up" with delayed repairs and extensions in the domains of roads, bridges, and other structures. The Eisenhower administration was modernizing the nation's highways with a gigantic program of interstate routes. Almost everyone and everything in the process needed steel. "From the end of World War II into the late 1950s American steel mills could sell all they produced at almost any price. They enjoyed what economists call an oligopoly, where a few big firms control the market."[5]

Bethlehem Steel was determined to use its large profits to increase capacity and improve working and living conditions for executives and other employees. Steel executives took the lead within Bethlehem in planning for expansion and urban improvements.

The physical aspects of planning came under the jurisdiction of Frank C. Rabold ('39), head of General Services Division answering directly to the president of the Bethlehem Steel Corporation. The General Services Division controlled real estate operations, recreational facilities, security services, fleets of airplanes and limousines, and physical planning for both the corporation and the community.

The plans, as Rabold unveiled them, included new steel-making facilities along the Lehigh River, redevelopment of commercial and residential areas adjacent to the company, and the construction of a research center on the top of South Mountain. The research facility was to be built on undeveloped land adjoining that owned by the university and the city and would include a system of roads connecting it with Bethlehem on the north, the Saucon Valley on the south, and the Bethlehem-Philadelphia highway on the west.

Whitaker told the trustees of the plan for a research center at the meeting of 10 April 1957. Bethlehem Steel had decided on South Mountain for the location, he said, because of the proximity to Lehigh; the center would provide material benefits for both the corporation and the university. It would make much expensive equipment available to the university and provide customers for a computing center on the campus that would otherwise be financially unfeasible.

Other plans of Bethlehem Steel also included the university. The corporation was anticipating a massive renovation of much of the residential and commercial parts of South Bethlehem, a redrawing of major lines of transportation, and a modernizing of parts of Bethlehem bordering the old Moravian section. Governmental money for urban redevelopment was in the offing to assist with the changes. In addition, the corporation would need for the success of its plans the cooperation of governing officials and planning bodies in the state, the counties of Lehigh and Northampton, the City of Bethlehem, the university, and, indeed, the support of all influential groups that might be affected by the change.

The steel executives put their many resources to work to obtain this cooperation and by and large succeeded. Rabold's office invoked the services of Clarke and Rapuano, a large and well-known firm of architects in New York City, which had a reputation in the fields of university and urban planning. Soon Clarke and Rapuano were making comprehensive development plans for the City of Bethlehem, the Moravian College and Seminary, and Lehigh.

Rabold worked chiefly with Curtis, who in 1956 became chairman of the trustees' Committee on Planning and Development. Rabold, Curtis, Whitaker, Rathbone, and Franz were the principals in the rapidly moving sequence of events from 1956 to 1960.

In May 1958, Rabold and Curtis presented to the board the first phase of a comprehensive plan for campus development, prepared by Clarke and Rapuano. This involved property on South Mountain and in the Saucon Valley. Bethlehem Steel, the city, and the university were already buying, selling, and exchanging properties so as to give the corporation the one thousand acres it said it needed for the research center atop South Mountain. Bethlehem Steel had agreed to build the access roads at its own expense. The university's share in this involved the possibilities of obtaining about five hundred additional acres on South Mountain and much other land on gently rolling ground in the Saucon Valley, about two miles over the mountain from the main campus.

The board approved phase one of the plan at its meeting held 11 October 1958 and during the next few years appropriated close to six hundred thousand dollars to acquire the land at a cost of about one thousand dollars per acre.

Almost immediately the property on the other side of South Mountain became known as the Saucon Valley Playing Fields. The principal sporting facility built above the main campus, between the fraternities and the new Bethlehem Steel research center, was named Sayre Field.

In January 1959, Rabold informed the board concerning phase two of Clarke and Rapuano's plan for campus development. This concerned the main campus and was based in part on the idea of replacing many of the old buildings and reorganizing traffic patterns so as to put vehicular traffic on the periphery. In addition, Clarke and Rapuano contemplated taking over some residential and commercial areas of South Bethlehem, thereby extending the campus several blocks to the north. The expansion would require coordination with the city for which Bethlehem Steel was already prepared. Clarke and Rapuano's plan for the city included a civic center to be built on the north side of the Lehigh River at the end of the New Street Bridge, which would be replaced by a hill-to-hill structure overpassing the railroad tracks on the south side and terminating at Fourth Street, a block below the main entrance to the enlarged campus. The new bridge would thus tie the campus to the civic center. City center and Lehigh would figuratively look across the river at each other. It Conformed, in modern planning, to the idea conceived by E. T. Potter in 1865 and approved by Asa Packer.

Members of the board were enthusiastic. Rathbone called Clarke and Rapuano's plan "one of vision." No action was required by the board for approving phase two, inasmuch as the plan contemplated only possibilities. For many years it provided a set of guidelines for physical developing.

The board that reviewed Clarke and Rapuano's plan had an enlarged membership. Rathbone had presided in 1958 at amendments to the by-laws, which produced two new sorts of trustee, emeritus and appointed. The emeritus status was for older members who wanted to retire. The category of appointed trustee provided a means for bringing on the board men who might be of great service to the university. The revised bylaws provided for no more than six of these who, after the first set of appointees, would each serve for six years, terms being staggered.

Three persons were named as appointed trustees in 1959: Arthur B. Homer, Grace's successor as head of Bethlehem Steel; J. A. Fisher ('17), president of the Reading Company; and Hugh P. "Jim" McFadden ('25), an attorney who was chairman of the board of the Union Bank and Trust Company of Bethlehem. The following year an additional three persons were elected as appointed trustees: Robert B. Honeyman ('20); Francis M. Huffman ('22); and Edwin H. Gott ('29), a vice-president of United States Steel.

The enlargement of the board occurred at a time when a design for another major fund-raising campaign was well under way. Planning for it had been in process since 1954. Whitaker had canvased deans and department heads for ideas. Priority lists had been prepared and revised. The enlargement of the board had an appearance of forming part of the planning for fund raising.

At a meeting on 5 June 1959, the board decided that the campaign should be for twenty-two million dollars with emphasis on educational aims and objectives instead of bricks and mortar and with some flexibility as regards specific goals. The list that Whitaker presented to the alumni at the annual meeting a few days later included:

A laboratory building for Chemical and Metallurgical Engineering
An addition to the library
An addition to the chemistry building
A building to house the College of Arts and Science
A dormitory for graduate students
Twenty endowed chairs to be held as distinguished professorships
And land on South Mountain and in the Saucon Valley

Further planning for the Centennial Campaign Fund occupied most of the following year. At a meeting of the board on 22 January 1960, Rabold elaborated on plans for the Saucon Valley Playing Fields. The first phase of their development, he said, required 112 acres, all of which had been obtained. Plans for the tract included soccer, lacrosse, intramural football, baseball, and freshman baseball fields, tennis courts, parking for one thousand cars, and a building containing lockers, equipment, rooms for coaches, and related activities. Completion of the first phase would make possible the sale of Steel Field to Moravian College and release the field above Taylor Stadium, containing the old quarter-mile track, for parking. Final development of the Saucon fields would provide parking for fifteen thousand cars and provision for all spectator sports including a stadium and a large field house.

Rabold's report indicated that much of the physical expansion that might have been included in a fund-raising campaign had already been completed or was quite far advanced.

While Rabold and the trustees planned, Whitaker continued with some administrative changes. Preston Parr moved from the Institute of Research in 1956 to become associate dean of students, a post vacated by Hayes following protests by students concerning Hayes's rigorous enforcement of certain rules related to conduct. Later in the year, Whitaker announced that George Jenkins of Geology was to have Parr's former position as assistant director of the Institute of Research. Jenkins became the director in 1958, when Neville finally gave up that position. In the same year, Myers left the university, and Congdon was shifted from the post of dean of students to the deanship of the Graduate School. John D. Leith replaced Congdon as dean of students. In 1959 James W. McGeady and Samuel H. Missimer were made associate directors of admission.

Litzenberger retired as superintendent of buildings and grounds in 1959 and was succeeded by Robert W. Numbers ('50). In that year, too, Miss Edith A. Seifert became bursar, the first woman to be a member of the administration.

The Centennial Campaign was barely begun, and the physical expansion of the campus was still incomplete, when the presidency of Lehigh changed hands. On 31 August 1960, Whitaker died from cancer after a short illness. The burden of leadership passed to Neville, whom the trustees immediately named as administrative head. Although Neville was within a few years of retirement, the trustees soon elected him as president, acknowledging his request to serve only until a more permanent successor could be found.

Congdon retired in the same year, and Neville filled the position of dean of the Graduate School with Robert D. Stout (Ph.D. '44), who had been serving as head of Metallurgy. Neville in 1961 chose Christensen for the vacancy in the post of vice-president and provost and, upon the retirement of Smiley in 1962, gave Smiley's vice-presidency to Seidle. Missimer then took

Seidle's former position as director of admission. Leckonby became director of athletics and physical education in place of Sadler, who was retiring.

Leith also retired in 1962. Neville divided Leith's job three ways, moving Brennan from an associate deanship in Engineering to the position of dean of students, advancing Parr to the new position of dean of student life in charge of all activities except sports, and making Clarence B. Campbell director of residence halls.

Also in 1962 Dean Bewley returned to industrial employment. Alan Foust, who had headed Chemical Engineering, succeeded Bewley as dean of the College of Engineering.

Neville's presidency of four years' duration, including the year he served as administrative head, was a happy time for the university. The Korean war was only a memory. The entanglement with Vietnam did not produce anguishing results until after Neville's retirement. The economy prospered. Funds for research were on the increase. Faculty salaries rose even as the competition for top scholars grew. Neville, other administrators, faculty, and supporting staff enjoyed the first fruits of the work done by Whitaker. The period seemed like a golden age to those who had known the spartan life of the 1940s and 1950s.

The physical planning and development begun under Whitaker proceeded according to the schedules made earlier. Curtis remained in charge for the trustees. Rabold and his staff did much of the work. Jerome Barney ('33) was Rabold's principal assistant for university projects and was at times entirely taken up with Lehigh development. More roads and parking facilities were built on the upper campus in connection with a renewed drive to bring all fraternities into Sayre Park. In the summer of 1962, Sayre Field was completed and Steel Field was sold to Moravian College. During the ensuing year, work on the all-weather track, intramural playing fields, and a locker-office building on the Saucon Valley playing fields was finished. The Alumni Memorial Building and much of Packard Laboratory were renovated using money received for general campus development. Psychology, ousted from its home in the old carpenter shop by preparations for the chemical engineering-metallurgy building, moved into a house west of the University Center formerly occupied by Dean Palmer and took over the Sayre Observatory for a laboratory. Philosophy went into the building at the entrance to the campus formerly used as a home by Litzenberger and his predecessors in charge of buildings and grounds.

The Centennial Fund-Raising Campaign continued but was not concluded during Neville's presidency. Land for the projected new buildings was obtained through federal-state urban redevelopment procedures. For a time the campaign appeared to be dragging, and Rathbone personally assumed the chairmanship. Franz, hewing to the decision to emphasize academics rather than bricks and mortar, in the fall of 1962 held a "New Dimensions Program" in which a group of twenty-five to thirty-five friends of the university were invited to an action-filled thirty-six hours of viewing programs demonstrating advances in teaching and research being made by faculty and students. The program was successful and became the first of a number of New Dimensions productions staged during the next several years.

As soon as Neville became president, he provided the trustees with a summary of educational objectives. He wrote in his report for 1960–61, "We believe that the most appropriate and valuable contribution Lehigh can make is in the expansion and improvement of the graduate program, especially in the fields of mathematics, the sciences, and engineering. This does not mean that less emphasis will be placed upon the importance of the undergraduate colleges of the university." Neville then stated the objectives in operational terms:

> To provide more and better trained teacher-scholars for the colleges, research scientists and engineers for laboratories and industrial operations.
> To identify early, and enlist in challenging programs, those students who show capacity for advanced study and research.
> To develop continuous and accelerated programs through the undergraduate and graduate years for selected students.
> To develop new graduate programs in areas which cross or combine traditional disciplines.

His plans for achieving these objectives included: (1) teaching internships for graduate students under master teachers; (2) more graduate fellowships; (3) an extension of honors programs from the junior and senior to the freshman and sophomore years; (4) the inclusion of qualified seniors in research as apprentices under faculty supervision; (5) a program of summer scholarships for students from Lehigh and other colleges who were about to enter their last undergraduate year, in order to permit them to take advanced courses and engage in research at Lehigh or elsewhere; and (6) establishment of endowed professorships.

The objectives and plans largely ignored the humanities and the social sciences. Promoting research according to Neville's understanding had little to offer departments in nonscience-based fields, where only very small amounts of support money were available from foundations and civic groups (the national endowments for the arts and the humanities were not formed until 1965).

As for the sciences and engineering, Neville's objectives aimed at taking advantage of some fast-developing opportunities being provided by the Congress of the United States.

While preliminary discussions for the Centennial Campaign were taking place, in 1957 the USSR launched Sputnik, thereby advertising to the world Russia's leadership in space science and technology. The event occasioned only polite discussion on the Lehigh campus and had no appreciable effect on planning for the Centennial Campaign. But in Washington the launching produced a reaction from Congress by way of rapid and spectacular increases in spending for science and engineering. Lehigh and other universities quickly felt the force of the reaction.

Before Sputnik, governmental funds for research and development had increased at a fairly steady pace. Some basic patterns had emerged. Most of the support for scientific research went to universities. Industry was the principal beneficiary of funds for development; but something from the grants to industry found its way into the hands of university faculty because industries turned to them for help.

The principal governmental agencies for making grants to university personnel were formed within a few years of one another: the Atomic Energy Commission (1946); the Department of Defense (1947); the National Institutes of Health (1948); and the National Science Foundation (1950). A large part of the support for research and development reflected attitudes derived from an arms race with Russia and the Korean conflict and took the form of grants from the Department of Defense to engineering. Much of the nondefense spending was for the health sciences and came from the NIH.

After Sputnik, a rapid and intensive spending for defense and defense-related space programs became the rule for the Eisenhower and Kennedy administrations. In 1958 the National Aeronautics and Space Administration began a spectacular career in the course of which it drew many of the country's scientists and engineers into the space race. Daniel Bell reported that governmental expenditures for research and development, which were $7 billion in 1955, almost doubled by 1960 and by 1965 reached a figure of $17,700,000,000.[6] For the first time the government heavily underwrote the support for graduate education. Both the NSF and NASA inaugurated massive programs of competition for graduate fellowships. The National Defense Education Act of 1958 made grants available to the states for laboratory equipment and other aid for the teaching of science to elementary and secondary schools, guidance counseling, language programs and language instruction, the vocational training of scientific technicians, low-interest loans for students, and national defense fellowships to increase the supply of college teachers. By the mid-1960s four out of five graduate students in the natural sciences were receiving aid in the form of a fellowship or scholarship.

Defense and the "conquest of space" were not the only objects in governmental spending for education. The needs of a science-based society were far greater than could be explained by these objectives, however important they might be to national policy. For example, computers were beginning to change the nature of many occupations in fields as diverse as merchandising, banking, and library service. Management was becoming a science utilizing sophisticated mathematical and engineering knowledge. The Department of Health, Education, and Welfare, formed in 1953, in which the NIH was included, became before 1970 the principal source of governmental grants for science.

And, for reasons stemming in large part from the imperatives of competition, both economic and political, domestic and foreign, the felt need for technicians, scientists, and engineers was pressing. *More* and *faster* were the watchwords. The political part of the American democratic meritocracy responded to the demand. National programs for education began to emphasize acceleration in order to reduce the number of years needed to produce scientists and engineers.

Neville's objectives for Lehigh agreed with those established by Congress. One suspects that in elaborating his "plans" he deliberately selected those for which he knew funds were available.

Teachers for the universities as well as research workers were needed. The term *teacher-scholar*, used by Neville and many other educators, was in retrospect a convenient way of minimizing important differences between the two occupations. For Neville the concept of the teacher-scholar served as an ideal; any difficulties that might arise in pursuit of this ideal would have to be considered as they arose and were for the moment not to be allowed to divert attention from the main objective.

In his report to the trustees for 1960–61, Neville speculated that the number of graduate students at Lehigh would probably double during the next ten years. After becoming president, he transformed this into a positive goal to be attained by 1972.

The faculty possessed the educational qualifications for achieving the objectives. The work of hiring scholars with the Ph.D. degree had been going on since the time of President Richards. Long before 1960, almost all of the faculty in the humanities, social sciences, mathematics, and sciences had the doctorate. Even in engineering, where until the Second World War the doctorate had been lightly regarded, progress had been made. By 1960 55 percent of the engineering faculty had the Ph.D. (by 1970 the figure had risen to 85 percent).

Either Whitaker or Neville had appointed all of the department heads in mathematics, the sciences, and engineering. All of the departments in these fields except Industrial Engineering had doctoral programs.

The roster of heads for the relevant departments in the College of Arts and Science in 1960–61 included A. Everett Pitcher (Mathematics and Astronomy), Hugh Richard Gault (Geology), Basil W. Parker (Biology), and Josef Brozek (Psychology).

In the College of Engineering some evolution in the departments and curricula accompanied the appointment of heads.

In 1950 separate heads were prescribed for Industrial Engineering and Mechanical Engineering; and in 1952 these were Arthur F. Gould (Industrial) and J. B. Hartman (Mechanical).

Also in 1950 the Department of Chemistry and Chemical Engineering was pulled apart. In 1952 Alan S. Foust (later named dean of the college) was brought in from the University of Michigan to head Chemical Engineering. In 1959 Edward D. Amstutz took over the direction of Chemistry.

In 1956—57 the faculty and the trustees approved the formation of a separate curriculum and department for Mechanics, which for several years had been a subdivision of Civil Engineering (whose departmental name had been changed in 1950 to that of Civil Engineering and Mechanics). Ferdinand P. Beer became head of the new Department of Mechanics. The degree offered at the master's level was an M.S. in applied mechanics.

Mining Engineering, once the proudest of all departments, was closed out in 1960. There was little market for mining engineers, and few students enrolled. The last two were graduated in 1964. Robert Gallagher, the director of the Curriculum in Mining, shifted most of his teaching to the Department of Geology.

For the other engineering departments, the heads in 1960—61 were Eney (Civil), Karakash (Electrical), Joseph F. Libsch, replacing Stout in 1960 (Metallurgical), and Ray Emrich, replacing Myers in 1957 (Physics).

The desirability of having students begin studies in mathematics and science when very young was a postulate for educators. The professional engineering societies, too, had for more than seventy years studied the possibility of identifying engineering talent at the high-school level. The faculty at Lehigh did not hesitate to participate in programs whereby a boy might, with proper testing, counseling, encouragement, and courses be brought into the university already on the way to becoming a scientist or an engineer. In 1958 the Department of Mathematics, responding to the appearance of the "new math" in the nation's elementary and secondary schools, began a series of summer institutes, sponsored by the NSF, for teachers of secondary school mathematics. In February 1964, the Department of Geology began a series of Saturday seminars in oceanography for high school teachers of science. Counseling was the objective of a JESSI program, first held in 1962 by Associate Dean Brennan. JESSI, an acronym for Junior Engineers' and Scientists' Summer Institute, brought about 150 students in the tenth and eleventh grades to the campus for a two-week exposure to information and orientation with respect to a choice of a career in the fields of pure and applied science. The cosponsor was Scientists of Tomorrow, a nonprofit organization of educators and industrialists. The initial program was considered so successful that the following summer Dean Brennan hosted two JESSI groups; and in 1964 JESSI was accompanied by a similar program for the communication arts and sciences called CASSI, conducted by Professor Dale Simpson of the Department of Geology. In the summer of 1965 another program resembling JESSI, called PREVIEW, was held under the direction of Associate Professor Curtis Clump of Chemical Engineering.

When high school graduates entered Lehigh, those intending to make mathematics their major field of concentration found great freedom of choice. The Mathematics Major was within the College of Arts and Science and shared the liberal choice of free electives allowed to students in the humanities and the social sciences. Students choosing engineering found within the College of Engineering a Uniform Freshman Year, consisting of basic studies in mathematics, chemistry, physics, economics, the History of Western Civilization, and English composition. Students in science followed much the same program, although those in the College of Arts and Science had some elective choice.

All freshmen in science and engineering received special counseling. In the College of Engineering an assistant or associate dean had the freshmen as a special charge and conducted a program, with attendance required, in which each branch of engineering was explained. In the College of Arts and Science the responsibility for counseling rested with the heads of the departments.

At the sophomore level and above, science and mathematics majors in the College of Arts and Science followed departmental programs and the college program for education in breadth — the "distribution requirements." They had many free electives. In the College of Engineering the sophomores began following pattern rosters that had been drafted by the departments and approved by the faculties of the college and the university. Much discussion went into forming the content of these pattern rosters, and they were almost constantly being revised.

At the junion-senior levels, the students in engineering were under some pressure to decide between industrial employment immediately upon receiving the baccalaureate or graduate studies, which would once more involve study of the basic sciences. Dean Bewley in 1960 referred to the choices in his characteristically blunt way:

> One hears a great deal of talk nowadays about "scientific" engineering, meaning the stressing of mathematics and analytical theory in engineering education. Actually, for 19 years Lehigh has provided strong curricula in this area; and our existing curricula in Engr. Mech., Engr. Physics, and EE are as "scientific" as any in the country. It is nonsense to talk about shifting *all* of engineering education to this area, as not more than 10% of the students are capable of profiting by such training. Furthermore, the bulk of professional engineering is not of this nature.[7]

Each department in Engineering adapted its pattern roster to fit the needs of students expecting to terminate their formal study of engineering at the baccalaureate level and those wanting graduate work that might lead to a Ph.D. degree.

Students wanting to study chemistry or physics could choose between the Colleges of Engineering and Arts and Science. In general, those opting for the College of Engineering had a heavier exposure to applied science.

Almost the entire work of revising major programs in mathematics, the sciences, and engineering was done with an eye to acceleration. The faculties also used other means of speeding up the undergraduate's education. Not all of these needed outside funding. Advanced placement allowed an incoming freshman to receive credit for college-level work done in high school. Some students earned as much as a full semester's worth of advanced placement credit. The departments in mathematics, the sciences, and engineering promoted honors opportunities as means of giving able students the best possible preparation for graduate school. The Department of Mathematics in 1961 followed an example set years earlier by the Department of English and adopted honors sections of the basic sequence in calculus for the brighter and better prepared students.

Programs subsidized through governmental funds began in 1960. In that year and for several more, the NSF supplied Lehigh with money for a summer program in undergraduate research in science and engineering. The program for 1962 provided aid for twenty-seven students in the Departments of Chemical Engineering, Chemistry, Geology, and Physics. In 1964 the total number of students enjoying an NSF undergraduate fellowship for independent summer study in science and engineering reached fifty-one, for whom a residential honors house was organized. At some time during the Neville years, every department in engineering and science, except possibly those of Mechanics and Psychology, benefited from NSF money in support of gifted undergraduates.

In 1962, with funds from the NSF, the Department of Mathematics began an independent study program intended to shorten by one or two years the time needed for a student to attain the proficiency required for beginning graduate work. This program also involved summer work and was directed by Professor Albert Wilansky. It was begun with six students and had twelve enrolled by the summer of 1964.

Still another small summer program in 1964, sponsored by the NSF, was an undergraduate science participation program involving four students and directed by Associate Professor Simpson.

An unreported number of undergraduates in science and engineering worked on sponsored research projects directed by faculty.

In revising undergraduate programs, the faculties in the sciences and engineering had another concern at least as great as those of producing more engineers and scientists at faster speeds. This concern, for want of a better term, can be styled *humanizing* the engineer.

Humanizing the engineer had existed in various guises from the time engineering first became a subject of university education. The most recent phase grew out of the accomplishments of technology in and after the Second World War, which were producing fear and a sense of guilt among wide sections of the population. Nuclear fission and fusion in their military and domestic forms as bombs, power plants, and other devices supplied a potential for destroying life on earth. Noted scientists such as Albert Einstein warned of the danger. Fear of technologists and their ways accompanied a fear for the bad effects of the products of technology. For many people the engineer was no longer a hero but a threat. Books such as Kurt Vonnegut's *Player Piano* (1952) and Jacques Ellul's *The Technological Society* (1954) spelled out the possibility: If the products of engineering did not destroy life, the engineers, by imposing their techniques on social relations, would make life intolerable. Eisenhower added the authority of the president's office to help counter the danger by warning people against the growing influence of the "military-industrial" and the "scientific-administrative" complexes.

Although these fears became somewhat muted in the frenzy of support for science and technology following the launching of Sputnik, they nevertheless gained in strength. The popularity of books appearing in the years of the Kennedy administration, such as Vance Packard's *The Waste Makers* (1960) and Rachel Carson's *Silent Spring* (1962), testify to a continuing and growing concern for the effects of technology on the environment and, indeed, on the quality of life.

The tarnished image of the scientist and the engineer reinforced the interest of professional societies and college faculties in the subjects of professional ethics and its educational counterpart, culture studies. Discussion proceeded on an assumption that at least something might be done toward humanizing the technologist by exposing him at a youthful age to different aspects of culture and techniques of study. The search was on for the best aspects and techniques.

The search made by the faculty at Lehigh turned up a General Studies Program for engineering students, an interdisciplinary honors program, and a restructuring of the Arts-Engineering program and its elevation to the status of a curriculum under the control of the dean of Arts and Science. Although many motives played midwife at the birth of these programs, without the popular distrust of technology and the faculty's determination to take appropriate action, they probably would not have been born.

The General Studies Program came out of lengthy discussions in 1953–54, which established a minimum of thirty hours for nontechnical courses and reaffirmed a necessity for every student to take economics, English composition, and the History of Western Civilization. Every student had to pass one course each in the life sciences and the humanities and two from a list established by a committee headed by a director of general studies. The committee included faculty from all three colleges. The director of general studies was, by common consent, taken from the College of Arts and Science. This position was the most novel part of the program. Christensen, an active member of the American Society for Engineering Education (the new name of the old SPEE), was in 1954 made the first director of general studies. After becoming dean he allowed the position to pass to others. For many years Professor Thomas Haynes of the Department of Philosophy was director of general studies.

Interdisciplinary honors work for engineering students came about eight years later, after the College Honors Program in Arts and Science had been operating for several years. In 1962 the College of Engineering devised its own version of a college honors program. In the spring of 1963 the faculty of the university made slight adjustments to the honors opportunities of the two colleges and presented the result as a Comprehensive Honors Program, open to students in all three colleges. Professor J. Donald Ryan of Geology became the first director of the Comprehensive Honors Program.

The Arts-Engineering Curriculum was a modernized version of former President Drown's program for an integrated study of the humanities, the sciences, and engineering. Drown had hoped the program would increase the cultural content of engineering education and provide a way for the classicals and the Latin scientifics to learn more about engineering — to bridge, in other words, the "two cultures," much as these were set forth by C. P. Snow in his popular book of the same title, which appeared in 1963. For more than thirty years Drown's program had failed to attract many students. In 1934, Dean Palmer had begun to promote it. After the Second World War it appealed more and more to students tempted to try the study of engineering along with other fields or who wished to spread rigorous four-year sequences of science and engineering courses over five years.

The arrangement reached in 1953–54 was that a student during the first four years would complete the requirements of the College of Arts and Science for a B.A. degree, taking at the same time the normal first three years of an engineering sequence as his major field of concentration. For his fifth year, the student would transfer into the chosen department of engineering and, under guidance of the head or his representative, complete the normal fourth year of engineering studies to qualify for a B.S. in the appropriate field.

In 1957–58, the first year the registrar began reporting separate statistics on Arts-Engineering, the program had a fall semester enrollment of 206, representing 12 percent of all undergraduates studying engineering. For the next five years the percentage remained between 12 and 13. Many excellent students took the arts-engineering route.

Arts-Engineering, College Honors, and General Studies had potentials for negating the results anticipated from programs of acceleration: Arts-Engineering because it lengthened the undergraduate years from four to five; General Studies and College Honors because they used slots in pattern rosters that might otherwise have been filled with technical courses. Yet the prevailing testimony is that such a negation could easily be exaggerated. Arts-Engineering brought additional students into engineering. Some arts-engineers transferred to straight engineering and finished in four years. Many students intent on accelerating into graduate school avoided the College Honors Program or used its courses to satisfy general studies requirements. And the general studies figure of thirty hours was nothing really new to engineering education, being only one single-semester course more than the 20 percent established by the Lehigh faculty in the 1920s.

In the domain of graduate studies, the increasing emphasis on work leading to the Ph.D. degree in engineering had as a counterpart a declining interest in professional degrees. The trend was national. A survey of 142 engineering schools made by the ECPD in 1952 showed that sixty-two were not awarding professional degrees and that an additional thirteen were planning to abandon the practice.[8] Lehigh had awarded something more than forty degrees since the beginning in the late 1920s. On 2 May 1955, the Lehigh faculty voted to discontinue the granting of professional degrees. The final two were given in E.M. in 1960.

By the mid-1950s the nation's engineering educators were aware that doctoral studies in the applied sciences differed in some cardinal respects from those in older disciplines such as English, philosophy, the classics, and history.

For one thing, studies in the humanities culminating in a doctoral dissertation produced a specialization largely unaccompanied by cross-cultural broadening. The student, in a manner of speaking, learned "more and more about less and less." In contrast to this, engineering educators discovered that, for the applied sciences, cross-disciplinary work, especially that involving mathematics and the physical sciences, was a necessary companion to specialization.

Bewley, using physics as an example, stated the character of advanced study as well as anybody:

> The engineering student usually gains his first insight into physical principles from his general course in physics. Thereafter, as an undergraduate, he pursues matters in the engineering departments. But should he go on with graduate work, particularly at the doctoral level, he will find himself returning to the physics department. Ultimately there is very little difference between the ideas, procedures, mathematical requirements, and concepts to be found in dynamics, elasticity, heat, electricity, magnetism, light, or sound—they tend to coalesce. Actually, although it would never be recognized by the undergraduate, the theory of electricity is merely an adaptation of mechanics. In a sense, the whole of technical engineering may be thought of as filling the void between elementary and advanced physics, with tentacles deeply rooted in both these buttresses.[9]

Another major difference between doctoral work in nonscientific fields and engineering concerned the dissertation. In fields such as English, history, and philosophy, this was usually an individual project, whereas in engineering and the other applied sciences, the dissertation came out of a team effort in which the doctoral candidate assisted a project director, who was frequently his adviser. Some differences concerned with financing were related to this. The doctoral candidate in the humanities and the social sciences could expect at best only a slight support from foundations or professional societies. He was inclined to depend on a teaching assistantship for sustenance. His counterpart in the applied sciences expected and received full support as a research assistant, the money being supplied by the grant that financed the project. He was less inclined to take a teaching assistantship which would contribute nothing to his dissertation (at the same time, he had to be wary that his research project would not be terminated before the work for his dissertation was finished).

Another difference affected the recruiting practices of departments. The usual advice given prospective graduate students in the humanities and the social sciences was to go elsewhere for advanced study. A department in these fields did not expect to retain many of its own undergraduates and had to advertise widely. In the science-based fields, many students chose to remain at their undergraduate institution for graduate study. Engineering departments could count on a nucleus of students of known quality to support courses and research projects.

Excellence for graduate education in engineering depended not only on top quality students and faculty but also on strong science and mathematics departments and a selection of fields of specialization in which money for research was available. Meeting these standards presented Lehigh with many problems.

Students. In 1968 Christensen told the board that in engineering one-third to one-half of the graduate students had been undergraduates at Lehigh, whereas with the exception of mathematics, very few of the graduate students in arts and science had taken the baccalaureate at Lehigh.[10] He failed to add that many of the undergraduates who remained at Lehigh for the advanced study of engineering were well below the top of their class. Most of Lehigh's best engineering and science students took their graduate work at MIT, Johns Hopkins, Cornell, Chicago, or other schools with established and well-funded programs. For this reason, prestigious fellowships and scholarships for graduate study given by the NSF, NASA, and other organizations added almost nothing to Lehigh's graduate program. The recipients, whether undergraduates at Lehigh or at other universities, went elsewhere.

Whitaker, Neville, and the engineering faculty made the best they could of the situation and interpreted these awards as signs of respect for Lehigh's undergraduate programs. With this attitude, Neville in 1961 formed an Endowed Fellowship Committee to encourage graduating seniors to apply for prestigious fellowships in national competition. Professor Leonard A. Wenzel of Chemical Engineering was the first chairman of the committee. Many Lehigh students received the awards, but few of the holders enrolled at Lehigh.

Faculty. More were needed for research and teaching, and the supply was severely limited. Children of the "baby boom" of 1945–46 were coming of college age coincidentally with the Neville presidency and the stepped-up governmental aid to higher education. Enrollments expanded faster than the supply of qualified teachers. All fields were short; those in science and engineering were in shortest supply.

Top scholars went where salaries were highest, the material resources for research the most assured, and the opportunities for stimulation from colleagues and students the greatest. On all of these counts Lehigh had difficulty in competing for faculty with leading institutions in its class.

Strong offerings in mathematics and science. Reasonably strong in chemistry and mathematics, Lehigh was still repairing the damage done to physics

during wartime. Shortages of faculty and facilities were hampering improvement in all of these fields.

Selection of fields for research. Funds for research were essential to pay
salaries of faculty and supporting staff and stipends for graduate students.
Some of the fields at Lehigh that had been successful in producing men with
the baccalaureate for industrial employment were not among the fields for
which massive governmental aid was available. And some fields for which
aid was available had been neglected at Lehigh. As yet there were no large
governmental grants for general departmental development. There was only
the market in research projects. Any institution desiring to develop a strong
graduate program in applied science had to buy at that market. Criticism
there was of the situation, that it deprived universities of a desirable freedom;
but, for the time being, the only response was a shrugging of shoulders.

Underlying all problems was the general situation of Lehigh's small size.
Reports provided to the ASEE concerning the number of faculty in engineering at Lehigh were, for the years indicated,

1948	37
1952	37
1956	48
1959	62

It was entirely legitimate even in 1959 to ask whether a faculty of sixty-two
was sufficient for creditable performance in the graduate programs that
Lehigh was attempting. Often a field was represented by only one person.
Also, small size increased the hardships imposed by illness, resignations,
the inability to fill positions, and the pressing need to add new positions to
cover subjects that must be taught.

In 1960–61 the Committee on Educational Policy organized a subcommittee
consisting of Libsch (Metallurgy), J. Burke Severs (English), Cassius Curtis
(Physics), and Amstutz (Chemistry, chairman) to study the Graduate School
and research activities. The final document included individual reports from
all of the departments having doctoral programs except the Department of
History and Government. The reports indicate some of the specific problems that Lehigh's educators had encountered. Although the reports were
unsigned, they presumably were written by the heads of departments.[11]

Foust, then head of Chemical Engineering, reported positions unfilled for
process dynamics and kinetics and went on to comment, "We have no one in
the Department who is competent in the non-linear mathematics necessary
for advanced dynamics and controls of chemical processes; only one man of
inadequate competence in linear programming for the application of scientific
laws to management decisions, no man even acquainted with the technology
of production of semi-conductor devices, nor of the glamour metals."

Amstutz, in his report, found needs for additional staff in inorganic and analytical chemistry. Eney of Civil Engineering pointed out that more senior staff were needed to help with teaching inasmuch as faculty working on research projects had time released from teaching, amounting in some instances to 100 percent. Karakash of Electrical Engineering wrote, "The resignation of one man would cause a complete blank in the control theory area. The resignation of another will leave a complete blank in the transister circuitry area." Beer of Mechanics expressed a pressing need for staff in fluid and nonlinear mechanics. Emrich found the Department of Physics badly in need of someone to teach quantum phenomena. Pitcher stated a need for more faculty in probability and statistics.

Stout — or was it Libsch? — expressed a fear that current research projects in Metallurgy might be leading the department out of the mainstream of graduate education, that to remain within the mainstream, the department should have staff in solid state and extractive metallurgy. Karakash explained that his department had built an excellent program in power and had neglected the newer field of microwaves and computers, to which most of the money for research was going. The department, he wrote, now faced a task of coming from behind in microwaves in a wild competition for funds with more advanced departments elsewhere.

All of the department heads in engineering and science except Gould in Industrial Engineering, which as yet had no doctoral program, in one way or another admitted that their graduate programs were geared to promoting research, not teaching, and that an increase in the graduate education of Ph.D.'s in engineering and science might actually augment the shortage of good teachers. The avoidance of teaching began at the level of the graduate student. "The best graduate students will not teach," wrote Emrich in his report. Eney wrote, "We must persuade the American assistant to accept the teaching assignment, whereas his first choice is a research assistantship". Several heads mentioned the possibility of increasing the number of senior faculty to compensate for the drawing-off of graduate students from teaching. Eney pointed out that hiring instructors in an ABD (all-but-dissertation) position did not solve the problem, as these, too, were siphoned off by research projects.

Other problems involved excessive teaching loads and lack of space and equipment. Emrich for Physics and Amstutz for Chemistry were especially concerned over space and equipment, although something was being provided for them in the Centennial Campaign Drive.

Hartman of Mechanical Engineering spotted an administrative weakness. He wrote of feeling "strongly that some one should be representing Lehigh in Washington on a substantial time basis to keep the departments alert regarding available government support. This is now done on a piece-meal, catch-as-catch-can basis. We seem to be losing out in comparison with many of our sister institutions who are devoting much manpower to this function."

Solutions to problems came slowly and were, from the nature of things, never more than partial. The advances in graduate education that were made during the Whitaker-Neville years were only beginnings, yet at the time they were much appreciated and publicized.

The money received from the Centennial Campaign was spent as it came in. Construction began for the building to contain Chemical Engineering and Metallurgy. Uncommitted funds were used for renovation to the Physics Building. Although Professor Severs in English was, in 1958, the first faculty member to benefit from endowments for distinguished professorships, the next three went to Zettlemoyer in Chemistry (1960), Karakash in Electrical Engineering (1962), and Pitcher in Mathematics (1962).

In 1958 the university received several grants from the AEC for equipment to be used in a program in nuclear physics.

Attracting good students was a greater problem for engineering than for mathematics and the sciences. In the latter fields the advantages in industrial employment of having an advanced degree were evident, whereas in engineering they were still being questioned. Many of the graduate students in engineering were part-time. The college reported to the ASEE 52 full-time and 276 part-time graduate students in 1959.

The number of part-time engineering students increased in 1960, when the college began several two-year M.S. programs for employees of the Western Electric Research Center near Princeton, N.J. One program was in solid state physics and materials science and the other dealt with operations research. Instruction was held on the center's grounds.

Almost all full-time graduate students received support from research or teaching assistantships. Eventually the national government noticed the disproportionate advantage gained by a few leading universities through NSF and NASA fellowships and began giving money to other universities for the support of graduate students. In 1964 the Graduate Engineering Traineeship Program of the NSF made forty thousand dollars available to Lehigh for eight graduate traineeships. By 1966 Dean Stout was able to report a total of seventy-five fellowships funded by government money for 1966−67.[12]

Computers appeared. They had existed on the national scene since the early 1950s. Lehigh obtained its first, a Royal McBee Digital computer, model LGP-30, in 1957, using money raised by alumni giving. Within a few years faculty, students, and outsiders who rented its services were using it to capacity. In late 1962 a new and more powerful machine, the GE 225, was delivered and positioned near the older model in Packard Laboratory. The cost of the GE 225 was a quarter of a million dollars, shared by alumni giving and a grant from the NSF.

The departments, spurred by the prospect of additional faculty and support for graduate students, assisted faculty in applying for grants. Much money was available, although by no means always for research in which the departments and the faculty were interested. The dollar value and number of projects increased. In a report for the trustees on 8 April 1959, Neville gave the number of sponsored projects as "about 90" having a combined value of close to one million dollars. Sixty percent of the contract research funds, he added, came from private industry, although in the nation at large about three-fourths of all research money was coming from national and state governments. In 1960 he wrote that the number of faculty involved with sponsored research was 75 and the number of fellows and research assistants, all being candidates for degrees, was 131.

Much of the research in applied science was interdisciplinary, which meant that it did not exactly correspond to the interests of any particular department. A new sort of administrative body was needed—the research center—and it soon appeared.

The first three research centers were formed in the spring of 1962. The pilot center was in materials research and was largely the work of Libsch, who became the director. Neville explained the purpose of the Materials Research Center as being "to stimulate and encourage interaction among the science and engineering disciplines with an interest in materials, and to promote interdisciplinary research activity and interdepartmental educational opportunities."[13] The center initially involved about thirty faculty in nine departments of the Colleges of Engineering and Arts and Science as well as graduate students. Industry, government, foundations, and technical societies provided about five hundred thousand dollars in grants for supporting the work of the center in its first year.

The other two centers were Marine Science, which came about largely through the efforts of Keith E. Chave, associate professor of geology, and Information Science, the work of Robert S. Taylor, associate librarian and director of the center, and Donald J. Hillman, the newly appointed head of the Department of Philosophy.

The formation of the first three indicated how centers might arise. Departments controlled programs for teaching, but each member of the faculty was free to follow his own inclinations in choosing subjects of research. The faculty member used the services of the Institute of Research in applying for a grant and, after receiving it, in administering the project. If his project was interdisciplinary, he might work with faculty and students from other departments. A center arose when someone—an administrator or a group of faculty with interests and/or projects in the same general area—found organization and a central direction convenient and succeeded in persuading the provost, the president, and the trustees to recognize the result and establish a center having a budget and a director, which could then be used to attract additional outside support.

The appearance of centers complicated the problem of keeping research geared to undergraduate and graduate education. The personnel of centers had an interest in using support money to hire research professors who did no teaching and escaped the annoyances associated with instruction by having no departmental affiliation. A possibility existed for diverting the teaching done by departments into areas foreign to the best interests of the students. The possibility extended even to neglecting undergraduate education altogether, of making the university into what Chancellor Clark Kerr of the University of California called an "ideopolis" serving a particular industrial area.[14]

The problem demanded and received presidential action. Centers were, in Neville's time, placed under the control of the presidential office; and every faculty member belonging to a center had to have a departmental affiliation.

Thus did Neville work according to his ideal of a teacher-scholar There were to be no free-wheeling research professors, hired by center directors. Every member of the teaching force, whether or not he was hired mainly for research, would be subject to the usual departmental controls. The presumption was that the departments could thereby prevent the employment of persons who were poor teachers.

The drive for graduate education and research inevitably affected teaching departments throughout the university. By and large, the effect was positive.

Even though Neville specifically aimed the drive at promoting science and engineering, some of the plans that he proposed could be put to other purposes. Cases in point concern plans for advanced placement, honors sections for gifted students, undergraduate research, and sponsored summer study. Although Neville favored these as means of acceleration, their immediate effect was to free students from some of the usual requirements, thereby permitting them to use time thus gained for any purpose they chose. This might be cultural enrichment, satisfying a curiosity about some other field of study, or taking core courses in preparation for professional work in fields other than their majors. Many students selected alternatives such as these in preference to shortening the period of their undergraduate study.

Perhaps a more important effect of the drive for graduate education in science and engineering was the incentive given faculty in other fields to revise programs so as to prepare their own undergraduates for advanced study and to begin graduate programs themselves. The College of Business Administration provides a good example of this.

Business Administration had a small faculty, all of whom possessed the Ph.D. or other top degree in their teaching field. They relied on the other colleges for instruction in mathematics, the humanities, the social sicences — except economics — the sciences, and technical electives in fields such as industrial management. Many of the students were transfers from engineering and had a strong background in engineering and an understanding of the scientific method.

The college was in a position to develop a strong advanced program in management. It could, with proper planning, receive well-prepared students from all parts of the university and call upon the other colleges to help provide courses and equipment.

A need for advanced work in management existed. A science-based society demanded expertise in administration as well as in performance. Although the top person in a governmental agency or a corporation might be an amateur, in order to be effective, the top person had to have a corps of administrators professionally trained in the conceptual, analytical, and operational knowledge and skills of making decisions. Pilot programs to fill this need, leading to the degree of Master of Business Administration, existed in such places as Cornell, Stanford, and Columbia.

Lehigh's College of Business Administration began an M.B.A. program in 1951. The dean of the college later described the program for the benefit of faculty and administrators:

> The purpose of the MBA is for professional business management training. It does not purport to be a research type graduate degree and should not be judged as such. . . . The courses are designed to provide rigorous preparation for managerial positions. They include analytical work but do not necessarily stress research or investigative analysis. . . . The comprehensive examination is considered more appropriate to the program's purpose than a master's thesis or a general research requirement.[15]

The college awarded its first M.B.A. degree in 1953. By 1957 the M.B.A. was second only to master's degrees in education in terms of the numbers awarded.

The M.B.A. was devised not only for students who had been undergraduate business majors but also for students in other fields who had good records. The college designated a small core of courses that would permit a student to complete work for the M.B.A. in one year following receipt of the baccalaureate. The Colleges of Business and Arts and Science printed this core of courses in the *Catalog*; and the College of Arts and Science advertised an "Arts-M.B.A. Program" as one of the opportunities available to its students.

In 1968 Christensen reported that more than half of the graduate students in Business Administration, most of whom were working for the M.B.A., had been undergraduates at Lehigh. Over the years, more students entered the program from Engineering than from Arts and Science.

During the 1950s the College of Business Administration attempted no other sort of graduate program but in 1962 added two more. One was an M.S. in management science, placing emphasis on interdisciplinary study involving business administration, mathematics, and industrial engineering. The other was an M.S. in business economics for students intending to enter business or government. Neither rivaled the M.B.A. in popularity.

As for internal administration, during the Whitaker-Neville years the College of Business Administration had its difficulties. A placid life under Dean Carl Allen ended when he retired in 1960. His replacement was Carl H. Madden, formerly manager of the public information department of the Federal Reserve Bank of New York. Madden had ideas for expanding the activities of the college that met with stiff resistance from the older faculty. A stormy two years ensued. The formation of a blue-ribbon advisory committee consisting of educational and industrial leaders did not solve Madden's problems. In 1962 he took a leave of absence and did not return to the university. Herbert M. Diamond temporarily replaced him with the title of acting dean; and in February 1964, L. Reed Tripp, an expert in labor relations who possessed considerable academic experience, took the deanship.

No large amounts of money as yet came to the College of Business Administration from funding agencies. Invididual faculty sometimes obtained local sponsorship for various sorts of economic studies. In 1962–63 the Richard K. Mellon Foundation gave one hundred thousand dollars for a Frank L. Magee Professorship in Business Administration, the first chair specifically intended for the college. Dean Tripp was the initial holder of the chair. In 1962 Jack J. Dreyfus ('34), senior partner in the Wall Street firm of Dreyfus and Company, donated twenty thousand dollars to the college "to provide students with practical experience in handling investments."[16]

The College of Arts and Science was home to a variety of liberal, vocational, and occupational aims and programs. In the 1950s it contained fifteen departments: Education; Mathematics and Astronomy; three in science (Biology, Geology, Psychology); two in social science (History and Government, International Relations); and eight that might be styled arts and humanities (English, Romance Languages, German, Philosophy, Classics, Music, Religion, Fine Arts). Mathematics and English were the largest departments in the university. Religion was the smallest, having only one faculty member. The Department of English had separate Divisions of Speech and Journalism, which, except for budgetary matters, operated much like departments. All departments and divisions except Music, Religion, and Speech maintained major sequences for undergraduates.

Commitments to graduate education varied. Mathematics, Biology, Geology, History, and English had doctoral programs. Education began doctoral work in 1959. Psychology also had a doctoral program but was as yet doing little with it. These, Government, and International Relations had master's degree programs. Philosophy began an M.S. program in 1963–64. Romance languages, German, Classics, Music, Religion, and Fine Arts had no graduate programs and provided little instruction for graduate students in other departments.

In 1962–63 two more departments were added. The Arts College Committee was responsible for the drive leading to both. One was a Department of Government, formed by breaking up History and Government. The other was Social Relations. Carey B. Joynt of International Relations provided a focus for social relations in 1960 by calling for the addition of faculty in social and cultural anthropology, sociology, social psychology, and the methodology of social investigation. In 1961–62 A. Roy Eckhardt of Religion and W. Ross Yates of Government followed up on Joynt's report and on behalf of the Arts College Committee proposed a department comprising personnel in sociology, cultural anthropology, and social psychology patterned on the model supplied by Harvard's Department of Social Relations. The proposal was approved. Sociology had originally been in the Department of Economics (whose name had then been changed to Department of Economics and Sociology) in the immediate postwar years because Dean Palmer had refused to have it in Arts and Science. Members of the Faculty in Business Administration were willing to give up the position of sociologist, whose incumbent was retiring. The positions of cultural anthropology and social psychology were new to the university. A scholar in sociology, Robert C. Williamson, was retained to organize the Department of Social Relations and find teachers for the other positions.

Dean Christensen headed the college from 1955 until 1963. In his last year he was also vice-president and provost and took on W. Ross Yates as an associate dean. Yates became dean in 1963.

Enrollment in the college grew from a low of 14.2 percent of the undergraduates in the fall of 1953 to 32.2 percent ten years later. A large part of the increase could be attributed to Arts-Engineering, whose students from 1954 registered in the College of Arts and Science for their first four years, and the growing popularity of mathematics and science, whose numbers of majors within the college increased. Possibly, new programs such as those in College Honors and Foreign Careers and a younger faculty helped in attracting students into the college and keeping them there.

Whatever the specific attractions might have been, the growth and general character of the college were undeniably functions of a response to the same external stimuli as affected faculty and students in engineering and business administration. The national attention given to science and engineering was paramount. Arts-Engineering and the science departments were not the only areas in which this was evident. Even the foreign language departments benefited by obtaining funds for a language laboratory. Many members of the faculty added courses or arranged the content of courses with an eye to national and international issues and the interests of students in science and engineering.

In Philosophy the attractions of mathematics and science became the proverbial camel's nose. Ziegler, who arrived as head of Philosophy in 1950, brought in Adolf Grünbaum, a scholar in the philosophy of science, whose dynamic and logically rigorous presentations led to debates between him and a noted guest speaker, the Jesuit priest Joseph T. Clark. The usual procedure was for Clark to lecture, then ask for questions — and the debate began. Many students attended and participated in the questioning.

In 1960 Grünbaum left to take an endowed chair at the University of Pittsburgh, and in the same year, Ziegler died. But a precedent had been set for continuing the work in the mathematical aspects of philosophy. Donald J. Hillman, with a degree from Cambridge, joined the staff in 1960 and in 1962 became head of the department. Hillman and Robert S. Taylor of the library entered upon research and development in the information sciences and obtained money for their work from the NSF. One of the results of this effort was the appearance in 1963–64 of an M.S. Program in Information Science and a program leading to an M.A. degree in philosophy with emphasis on systematics, including mathematical logic, scientific methodology, epistemology, philosophy of science, and philosophical analysis. The newly orgainzed Center for Information Sciences provided a research arm for these programs.

Fears of the dangers of technology on the environment and of technocratic controls on the quality of life also had an impact. Rocco J. Tresolini in government began a constitutional law course in civil rights. The biologist Fran Trembley was speaking and writing on the dangers of technology long before the subject became popular with the general public. In 1951 he had his title changed to professor of ecology. Students flocked to his classes. In order that they might have a nearby spot in which to study ecosystems, he asked that the slope above Williams Hall be left in a wild state—a tangled bank, he called it, using a term coined by Darwin. The administration complied with the request and put up a sign, "Tangle Bank," to identify the place.

More examples could be cited. Most of the younger members of faculty in the humanities took a critical approach to science and technology. Their interests ranged far more broadly, however. Many became known across the campus for excellent teaching.

Frank S. Hook, arrived in 1952, inspired a general love for drama in addition to teaching the works of Shakespeare and other Elizabethans. Saul B. Barber, coming in 1956, gained respect from undergraduates bound for medical school for his teaching of physiology. Jonathan B. Elkus, replacing Schempf in 1957 as director of the Band, brought a Stravinsky-like freshness to musical life. He and a small group of other artists covered the campus with their productions and opened for students from all of the colleges the pleasures of performance and creativity. These other artists included Robert B. Cutler (Music, director of the Glee Club), Richard J. Redd (Fine Arts), H. Barrett Davis (speech), and Ernest N. Dilworth and John Vickrey (English, who became noted for reading poetry). David M. Greene joined the faculty in English in 1958 and soon was one of the most popular teachers in the College Honors Program for courses in the opera as drama. From the Department of International Relations came Aurie N. Dunlap, who held students and community audiences spellbound by his interpretations and delivery concerning relations between the United States and Russia. Joseph Dowling took over instruction in the History of Western Civilization, the course required of all engineering freshmen, and kept them at work and in good humor in spite of their general indifference to the subject. James R. Frakes appealed to both undergraduates and graduate students with provocative seminars on James Joyce and other notables of twentieth-century literature.

Most of what these faculty taught and did by way of cultural activities had long existed at older liberal arts colleges. A recital of such words and deeds might even annoy an alumnus or alumna who had passed four years amid such splendor. But most of the subjects and activities were new to Lehigh. They can be considered as a response to the hand of equality offered the arts and sciences by Whitaker and the trustees and held firmly forth by Neville and his associates.

Scholarship of a different but nevertheless agreeable sort occupied the time of J. Burke Severs, who in 1951 took the headship of English upon the death of Smith. Severs edited the Wells project, sponsored by the English contingent of the Modern Language Association. The Wells project had grown from a revision and extension of *A Manual of the Writings in Middle English, 1040–1500*, by John Edwin Wells, published in 1916 by the Connecticut Academy of Arts and Sciences. The scholars began the revision in 1956, giving the general editorship to Severs, who assigned the subjects for books to experts in North America and Europe. The project was of international interest and put the spotlight on Severs. The Haskins Medal of the Medieval Academy of America came to him along with other honors.

On the fourth floor of Linderman Library, Lawrence H. Gipson continued in retirement his writing of the history of the British Empire before the American Revolution, supported successively by the Institute of Research and the Rockefeller Foundation. The only extended break in his schedule occurred in 1951–52, when he journeyed to Oxford to pass the year as Harold Vyvyan Harmsworth Professor of American History. Additional awards came to him, including in 1962 the Pulitzer Prize for the tenth volume, *The Triumphant Empire: Thunder Clouds Gather in the West, 1761–1766*.

The Department of Education was in a special position, for it operated almost entirely at the graduate level; and there, its main programs were occupational, designed to produce teachers for the elementary and secondary schools. Every year the department led all others in the university in awarding master's degrees. In addition, it sponsored conferences, the most persistently popular being an annual reading conference in the spring, and workshops for guidance counselors, administrators, and teachers of various subjects. Harold Thomas, the head, encouraged elementary and secondary schools within commuting distance to regard Lehigh as a resource.

In 1959 Thomas and his faculty began programs leading to degrees of Master of Education (M.Ed.) and Doctor of Education (Ed.D.). The department awarded its first M.Ed. degrees (nineteen of them) on Founder's Day 1961. The first Ed.D. was given out at the June commencement exercises in 1963.

Excepting Education, Mathematics, Biology, and Geology, graduate work in the departments in Arts and Science gathered speed very slowly. Teaching assistantships and a few fellowships supplied by the office of the graduate dean provided some means of attracting students, but there was never enough financial support to meet the demand. As Christensen pointed out, very few Lehigh students chose their alma mater for graduate work in the humanities and the social sciences.

Every year the departments with master's programs had a few candidates for degrees. Many of these were students in education who preferred a subject-matter degree to the usual M.A. or M.S. in education. History awarded its first doctorate on Founder's Day 1954. English had its first candidate for the Ph.D. in June 1955. The first recipient of a doctorate in psychology got his diploma in June 1961, and the second, in October 1965.

In the spring 1963 the trustees decided to hold a Centennial Convocation in the fall as a means of advertising the university and its educational aims. No one seemed concerned that 1963 was two years too early to be a genuine one-hundredth aniversary.

The time for planning was short, too short for relying on the usual means of lining up panels of notables whose schedules might be fixed a year or more in advance. According to eyewitnesses, Christensen did most of the planning, including the suggestion of an appealing theme, "The exercise of man's incredible powers"; and Rathbone lined up many of the speakers, using his large acquaintance among personnel in governmental and industrial circles.

The convocation was held in October of 1963 from Thursday evening the twenty-fourth to Saturday evening the twenty-sixth. Two dinners, four symposia, and an honors convocation were planned. The public was invited to attend all of the events except the dinners. University schedules were arranged so that students and faculty might form part of the audiences.[17]

Frederick R. Kappel, the chairman of the board of AT&T, was the speaker at the opening dinner. Rathbone himself gave the principal address at a trustees centennial dinner on Friday. Twice a day a symposium was held, in subjects, respectively, of "The Problems of Peace and War" (chaired by Carey Joynt), "The Problems of Production and Human Resources" (chaired by Alan Foust), "World Communications Powers and Problems" (chaired by John Karakash), and "The Use of Man's Incredible Powers — to What End?" (chaired by Christensen). Sixteen notables participated in the symposia.

A concluding honors convocation entailed the citation of thirteen leaders from the Lehigh Valley for outstanding service and an address by the Honorable Paul Martin, secretary of state for external affairs of Canada.

The centennial convocation was the most visible part of Neville's work as the university's chief administrator. Apart from its financial importance, it gave to his presidency an appearance of academic readiness to respond to problems of national and international scope. The tone well fitted accomplishments and aspirations in teaching and research.

8

The Governance of the University:
1963–1970

In the course of about seven years, 1963–1970, the organization of education at Lehigh underwent considerable change. Some students were later inclined to say that Lehigh was "brought kicking and screaming into the twentieth century." Some other Lehigh people assessed events more moderately; but all agreed that things had changed.

Governance of the university was at the heart of the matter. Governance emerged as the main problem when some issues in solution crystallized out.

Students seeking redress of grievances were at the bottom of it all. That was, on reflection, salutary. Their education comprised the central purpose of Lehigh. Their discontent called attention to some straying from the central purpose. Their action in causing amendments to the organization of education helped to bring Lehigh back to the main road.

The principal characteristics of the student body in the Whitaker-Neville years were about what they had always been. The vast majority of undergraduates came from homes located within 150 miles of Bethlehem. In most years more than 80 percent were from Pennsylvania, New Jersey, and New York. Fewer than one-sixth had homes in other parts of the United States, although as the size of the undergraduate student body grew, the number of states of the United States that were represented increased. Very few of the undergraduates came from foreign countries.

The undergraduate student body contained few blacks or other members of what the U.S. Supreme Court once termed "insular and discrete minorities." Although data for determining the numbers of these in the early years do not exist, a few remarks are possible. There is reference to one black student in the 1880s. The reference is contained in an editorial appearing in the *Burr*, in which the writer boasted that Lehigh did not discriminate against Negroes.[1] Probably they did not apply for admission. In any event, the question of discrimination seems not to have arisen for blacks or other minorities. President Drinker, born and reared as a small boy in Hong Kong, was especially attentive to the needs of Chinese students.

The situation was different for the opening years of the new Lehigh. In the period between the two world wars many of the "best" colleges and universities actively practised discrimination. The reasons must be sought in the growing interdependence of people of different origins — reasons connected with those responsible for the appearance of collectivist policies in government. Much of the discrimination was not advertised. A search of the minutes of meetings of the faculty and the trustees at Lehigh discloses only one reference to it. In the minutes of the board for 15 April 1929, quotas are given for "alien and unassimilable races" — quotas not to be published in the *Register*: Negroes, none; Chinese, Hindus, and Japanese, ten each; Jews and Latin-Americans, fifty each. Antisemitism seems to have been behind this measure, inasmuch as the same minutes record 250 Jewish students and do not mention numbers of the other supposedly "alien and unassimilable races." Persons attending Lehigh during the 1930s have attested to the existence of some rather subdued antisemitism. Then came war, and with it, a change in attitudes. Most returning veterans and new faculty in principle did not approve of discrimination. During the early years of the Whitaker administration, the practice disappeared. Still, geographic location, high costs, high standards of admission, and the lack of interest among members of underprivileged minorities — especially blacks — combined to keep the number close to zero. By 1965 the university probably had somewhere between ten and fifteen blacks among the undergraduates.

Few precise data are available for students' religious affiliation and socioeconomic status. But here, as with the subject of racial minorities, some generalizations are possible, and all support a thesis that these features of the undergraduate student body remained fairly constant. Only a small minority was Episcopalian. The student body in the 1950s included Protestants of various denominations and many Roman Catholics and Jews. Few students called themselves nondenominational or atheist; and few were from the more fundamentalist Protestant sects. Neither great wealth nor poverty was noticeable. Most students were from middle-class families, leaning more to the upper and middle than to the lower middle-class. Their fathers worked. The parents were ambitious for their sons' success, and the sons were vocationally motivated.

The attitude toward varsity sports remained much as it had been since the appearance of competition in the 1880s, that of almost universal interest but severely restricted participation. Wrestling and football were the most constant exceptions to a qualified reluctance to compete. Gerald Leeman held to the standards maintained by Billy Sheridan and produced one strong wrestling squad after another, winning many eastern championships and usually having his squad ranked among the top ten in the country. In football, Leckonby built up the team from one of the least successful in America to one of the best among the smaller schools. The team was undefeated in 1950 and nearly so in 1957, when it won the Lambert Cup, a trophy prized among colleges and universities in Lehigh's class in the East. The Lambert Cup came to Lehigh a second time in 1961. Leckonby's record of success was not maintained by Michael T. Cooley (1961–64) or at first by Cooley's successor, Fred Dunlap (1964–76), who, together with coaches of other sports, experienced difficulties with the high academic standards and small amounts of financial aid. Behind these difficulties lay the characteristic of a student body willing to maintain a full program of intramurals yet unwilling to sacrifice the extraordinary amounts of time and attention needed to supply varsity teams with full contingents of star players.

Other activities also showed little tendency to depart from established practices. Numerous course and honor societies existed (nineteen course and thirteen honor societies in 1949–50) but contributed little to the cultural life of the campus. Band, Glee Club, dramatics, *Epitome*, WLRN, and *Brown and White* were strong, but other attempts at student publications failed. In the spring of 1962, several students in engineering, with strong support from Associate Dean Brennan and the honor societies, established a student quarterly, the *Lehigh Review*, second of that name in the history of the university, for the purpose of publishing the best in student research and creative writing. The editors put out only a few issues. There were not enough good contributions to keep the review alive. Little magazines with literary pretensions, *Quintain* (1956–57), *Endor* (1961–62), and *Paisley* (1965–66) reached small audiences.

Classes were organized and had officers but few functions. The principal associations of student government were the Residence Halls Council, the Interfraternity Council, and Arcadia. Beer drinking and weekend partying were popular. Fall and spring houseparty weekends were occasions for bringing in dates and providing housing for them. Houseparties were an almost permanent subject of criticism by faculty and administrators for breaches of socially acceptable conduct. Many faculty considered the students to be socially gauche, even rude. But the students worked hard throughout the week and were inclined to use wrestling matches, housparties, and other athletic and social gatherings as occasions for "blowing off steam" associated with a sudden release of tension.

Students sometimes discussed social, economic, and political problems, although their attendance at lectures on such subjects was slim. Few belonged to activist social or political organizations. Each year a handful of students traveled to Harrisburg to participate in a mock legislative or UN session. From 1961 to 1963 several took part in a national program known as Crossroads Africa, a sort of summer precursor of the Peace Corps. In 1958–59 Arcadia maintained a travel center to promote student study abroad, and in 1963 the Senior Class Cabinet sponsored a student for summer academic study in Europe.

During the Whitaker-Neville years, the ways in which students differed from their predecessors do not overtax one's imagination. Students of the 1950s and 1960s were more prosperous. Few had to leave school for financial reasons. The number of student-owned automobiles increased almost yearly.

Beginning early in the 1960s, students benefited from national programs of loans and scholarships.

Student living had improved. The new dining facilities in Packer Hall left no room for persistent complaints of bad food. Dormitories became officially known as residence halls and were organized in ways to evoke strong loyalties in intramurals and other competitive activities. Fraternity houses were renovated, and some were rebuilt with aid from a chapter's alumni.

Beginning in Whitaker's time, the students had specialized counseling services, which their forebears had lacked. President Whitaker made counseling a special aim. The dean of students gained an assistant and a full-time director of residence halls. Academic deans, department heads, and other faculty advised on a variety of educational matters. The Placement Office under Everett Teal increased its activity in counseling students about jobs and the requirements for obtaining them.

A freshman counseling service was organized in the residence halls in 1949 and reorganized as the Gryphon Society in 1957. In that year, too, a professional psychological counselor, Andrew J. Edmiston, was added to the staff and became the nucleus of a testing and counseling service. The Gryphons shortly added to their self-imposed duties the counseling of freshmen in the nature and difficulty of courses open to them and, with help from Tau Beta Pi, made available to freshmen the names of people, mostly upperclassmen and graduate students, willing to serve as tutors.

The chaplain became a full-time counselor in addition to having charge of the Packer Memorial Church. Chaplains from 1904 to 1931 had been divines from the Church of the Nativity. Beardslee, the chaplain from 1931–47, had taught courses and served as a one-man academic Department of Moral and Religious Philosophy. Upon his retirement the Department of Moral and Religious Philosophy was terminated and a Department of Religion established in the College of Arts and Science. Beginning at this point, the duties of the chaplain were separated from the teaching of religion as a social science. In 1947 the Reverend George M. Bean took the chaplaincy and was followed in 1953 by the Reverend Raymond A. Fuessle. In 1948 the Reverend Arthur M. Sherman became the head of the one-man Department of Religion; he was suceeded in 1951 by A. Roy Eckhardt.

The chaplain was the last member of the faculty to live on the campus, excepting the president. After several years Fuessle, too, moved into town. As a counselor he maintained an office in the University Center and was for administrative purposes under the dean of students.

In addition to enjoying considerable material prosperity, good conditions of living, and better counseling, the undergraduates had excellent educational facilities and programs, which were constantly being improved. Yet they had complaints that persisted and were heard more often as time passed.

One grievance was summed up in the slogan *in loco parentis*. According to this grievance, a society that said it wanted young men and women to be educated and was encouraging them to assume the responsibilities of adults seemed to be treating them like little children. Students entering college expected to escape a parental yoke, which they considered insufferable, and were doubly aggrieved to find it present on the campus. Lehigh students saw the trustees, administrators, and faculty as being guilty of this paternalism.

The IFC complained of exhausting and intolerable regulations concerning rushing and pledging. Beginning with the completion of Dravo House in 1949, the administration required all freshmen to live in residence halls, separated from the upperclassmen, unless they could live with their parents, and to use the university's dining services. Restrictions on parties and other social functions were especially irritating, and both the IFC and the RHC frequently complained of them.

On 13 January 1956, students demonstrated against Associate Dean Byron C. Hayes because of the regulations he imposed on a houseparty. Smiley reported to the trustees that the demonstration was not only against the regulations but more especially "against one University official whose activities over the last few years have included pressing for various improvements to the conduct of student organizations."[2] Hayes resigned.

In 1959 President Whitaker refused on technical grounds a request from Delta Omicron Theta, the student debating society, to allow socialist Norman Thomas to give a public lecture on the campus. Some faculty and student leaders arose in wrath, suspecting that the real reason lay in the known antisocialist bias of some of the trustees. The concerned faculty charged a violation of academic freedom; and the *Brown and White* took their part. Student and faculty tempers were scarcely improved when several months later the trustees tabled without action a proposal from Arcadia to change the rules so as to enlarge the freedom of faculty and student groups to have speakers of their choice.[3] Only Whitaker's death ended the affair.

In the sphere of discipline, the students complained of a lack of due process in the legal sense of a fair hearing according to established rules of law. The faculty could have changed the rules so as to require due process but did not. The dean of students and his staff were the executive and judicial arm in matters of discipline and exercised much legislative power. They dominated a faculty Committee on Discipline on which students had some representation but which lacked procedures for assuring the accused a fair hearing; and in the absence of an up-to-date disciplinary code, the dean and the committee sometimes acted arbitrarily or, as students alleged, as a father might act in chastising infants.

Students found several practices of the dean of students in academic matters to be tarred with a paternalist brush. He required reports of student progress from the faculty and sent the results to the parents, who received mid-semester "valentines" for their freshman sons and end-of-the-semester grade reports. Undergraduates desiring to transfer from one curriculum to another had to obtain parental consent.

The standard reply given by administrators to students who complained of these practices was that the parents paid the bills and had a right to know what they were getting for their money. Students easily saw the reply as question begging. The right of the parents to govern their sons' conduct was precisely what was being challenged.

The faculty were not immune from student criticism. Students believed that the faculty were enforcing some requirements whose educational value had vanished. Included among these were summer industrial employment at the end of the junior year for engineers, an Impromptu Writing Test for juniors in Arts and Science, the Senior Comprehensive Examination in Arts and Science, and some required courses in the various curricula.

the faculty was also censured for some poor teaching. The charge was not levied against senior faculty, many of whom the students applauded, but against teachers at lower levels, especially graduate assistants. Here, the difficulty lay with the push into graduate work and research. Some juniors and many seniors benefited greatly from the facilities acquired through funds for sponsored research and a stimulating exposure to professors working on the frontiers of knowledge. Freshmen and some sophomores had a different experience. They were exposed to teaching assistants whose quality might vary from excellent to inept. Following the adoption of graduate programs, a large majority of freshmen and some sophomores made contact with master teachers on the faculty only through lectures delivered once or twice a week before several hundred students. Some foreign-born teaching assistants, and even a few instructors and assistant professors, had difficulty in getting students to understand their English.

When students complained of bad instruction, they came face to face with entrenched attitudes supporting the professor's liberty within the classroom and putting a burden of proof on the student, who could never obtain proof unless it involved something measurable, such as the inability of a teacher to speak English. Student evaluations continued sporadically but were considered confidential and were given only to the teachers being evaluated. Under these circumstances, participation in end-of-the-semester evaluations was far from universal.

Undergraduate perceptions of poor teaching by graduate students did not penetrate so deeply as to link it with the growth of research and graduate education. In general, undergraduates and graduate students got on well together. Undergraduates were inclined to see the presence of teaching assistants as an absence of senior professors and part of a growing separation of students from faculty. Undergraduates complained that they saw their professors, if at all, only in the classroom.

An extreme example of this feeling of separation appeared in an account in the *Brown and White* of President Whitaker's death. "Relatively few Lehigh students ever met Dr. Martin Dewey Whitaker personally. . . . 'He welcomed our class during freshman week, and he'll speak to us again on graduation day. In the four intermediate years, I probably won't see him.' This was the average Lehigh Man's answer when questioned about the University's top officer."[4]

From time to time student groups took measures hoping to reduce the separation between them and the faculty and to improve teaching. In 1959 the senior class and Omicron Delta Kappa, the senior leadership honorary, sponsored a faculty lecture series, which was continued the following year. Arcadia, the IFC, the RHC, and the junior class in 1960–61 established a speaker's bureau of faculty to talk to living groups; and in the same year students organized a fund to reimburse faculty for entertaining students. In 1963 the IFC encouraged professors to hold courses in the fraternity houses. The following year a program of student awards for outstanding teaching was inaugurated. Several fraternities held receptions or cocktail parties expressly for faculty and distinguished guests of the university to which faculty were invited.

Measures such as these helped to improve student-faculty relations in a few restricted domains but did nothing to remove the basic causes of discontent.

Administrators and faculty also took corrective measures. The dean of students and his assistants reasoned that students should be included on committees that made and enforced the rules, that this would involve them in administration and help them to understand the reasons for the rules. Following the Hayes episode, the dean of students formed a student-faculty Committee on Student Life charged with studying the situation. The Committee on Student Life had a continuing existence and in 1960 issued a report, "The Climate of Learning," summarizing the work in improving self-government in student affairs:

> Students are equally represented on most of the standing committees which set policy in the area of student life. Moreover, student management is becoming increasingly more evident in all aspects of discipline, financial control of student activities, editorial freedom of publications, and the operation of the University Center. In addition, the student council has taken a heavier burden of responsibility, particularly in the area of social life and the regulation of parking.[5]

In 1963 Dean Parr staged what proved to be the first of a series of annual Kirby House conferences in an attempt to improve communications. The topic of the first conference was "Campus Climate — Intellectual and Social." About thirty-five undergraduate leaders, faculty, and administrators met on 9–10 September at Kirby House in the Poconos for informal discussions on the topic. The second conference, held before the opening of school the following year, dealt with the subject, "The Student and Academic Affairs."

The faculty cooperated with Dean Parr and his staff, conducted its own inquiries, and in several ways liberalized the academic side. They ruled that beginning with the fall semester 1961, ROTC should be elective for all students and that physical education, which had for years been demanded of freshmen and sophomores, should be a requirement only for freshmen. Within a few more years, even freshmen were excused. In the spring of 1963, the faculty abolished the old attendance regulations and made attendance in class a matter of individual professorial policy. The following autumn, acting on a request from Arcadia, the faculty approved *vagabonding*, or the practice of allowing a student with the consent of the instructor to sit in as an auditor for all or part of a class for which he was not formally registered. Unlike a formal audit, vagabonding did not result in any entries on the student's permanent record.

As for the use made of teaching assistants, the faculty acted in a way that did nothing to correct for their growing separation from the students. The minutes of the faculty meeting of 3 June 1963 record that when Professor Wesley J. Van Sciver (Physics) arose and said that all freshman sections "should be met by senior members of the Faculty, in all subjects," his "suggestion provoked hearty laughter from some of the faculty." The majority was strongly committed to the graduate program and took the position that poor teaching by graduate students should be corrected by attracting more and better graduate students who were motivated to teach and by providing them with proper training and supervision.

Deans and department heads were already working at this. The heads did what they could to remove misfits from the classroom and to juggle teaching assignments so as to provide an acceptable instruction for all. Some departments started training programs for teaching assistants. The Department of English began a program aimed at improving the teaching of college English both within the university and outside of it. With support from the U.S. Department of Health, Education, and Welfare, English completed plans in 1961–62 for a major expansion of its graduate program with special emphasis on the training of graduate students in techniques of teaching. Internships subsidized under the National Defense Education Act were added along with a course in the Teaching of College English.

On the issue of student participation in rule making, the faculty held firmly to their inherited rights and privileges. However much administrators might allow students to share in the regulation of student life, the faculty were determined that there was to be no counterpart to this in strictly academic matters. The faculty maintained that its knowledge and experience sufficiently prepared it for deciding on courses and curricula.

The faculty had a long history of successful student-faculty relations behind it to support this position. But values were changing. A sensitive student could see a paternalistic attitude even in faculty action to reduce requirements.

For a time, though, the students quietly accepted their exclusion from academic decision-making.

On 1 April 1963, Neville announced that he was appointing a faculty advisory committee to work with a trustees' committee to select a new president. The faculty committee came up with the name of Willard Deming

Lewis, former director of communications systems research for the Bell Telephone Laboratories. Lewis had little previous experience with college teaching, but the mind set favoring graduate work and research readily overlooked this. Lewis was a graduate in physics from Harvard, had studied at Oxford as a Rhodes Scholar, and had everything else considered necessary for the presidency. He was inducted as the tenth president of Lehigh at Founder's Day ceremonies in 1964 and was formally inaugurated a year later.

In matters of administration, Lewis shared with Neville an engineering point of view tempered by an attraction to science, which made him more partial to probabilities than to a conservative concern for safety. Lewis added to this point of view a project director's conception of teamwork in which the director takes the responsibility for decisions after carefully examining the data and consulting with those who have produced it. Charges made later by faculty activists about bad communications probably greatly perplexed him; certainly, they did not influence him in a natural preference for discussion and consultation. He met every Monday morning with the provost, the other vice-presidents, and the treasurer. The "president's cabinet," acting in an advisory capacity, became an informal part of the administrative structure.

A spirit of teamwork appeared in other of Lewis's beliefs, that is, a university such as Lehigh ought to march in step with the businesses and industries it served, pursuing goals rationally worked out between them; that Lehigh and neighboring colleges should cooperate in utilizing their diverse resources; that students, faculty, and administrators ought to continue to help with community projects; and that the university ought to take a positive attitude in seeking support from governments.

Lewis made no immediate changes of importance in administrative structures. His first two years witnessed only one shift among top administrators. Foust resigned his deanship in 1965 and took the R. L. McCann Professorship of Chemical Engineering, newly endowed by the New Jersey Zinc Company. Karakash replaced him as dean of Engineering.

Lewis was president during the final two years of the Centennial Campaign. He arrived too late to enjoy the celebration of the convocation but not too late to participate in the work of fund raising. He visited all the alumni clubs from the Atlantic to the Pacific and made such other appearances as he, Franz, or Rathbone thought advisable.

A centennial ball and an all-class reunion in the spring of 1965 celebrated completion of the first phase of the Saucon Valley Playing Fields.

Six residence houses (Centennial 1) were completed in 1965 on the upper slope behind the gymnasium and were named Leavitt, Thornburg, Emery, McConn, Smiley, and Congdon. Six more (Centennial 2) were finished during the same year behind the former cinder track, now converted into a parking lot, and designated Beardslee, Carothers, Palmer, Stevens, Stoughton, and Williams. Price Hall then ceased to be a residence and became the home of the Departments of Social Relations and, for a time, Classics.

A new library became feasible when the Bethlehem Steel Corporation gave the university $500,000. The presentation of $690,000 from Mrs. Leon Mart provided the occasion for naming the library after her deceased husband, Leon T. Mart ('23), and son Thomas L., who had died while a student at Lehigh. Grants from the United States government under the Higher Education Facilities Act furnished the remainder of the money for the Mart Library, which was completed and opened in 1969.

The most difficult project to finance was a building for the humanities and the social sciences, a Hall of Liberal Arts as the proposed structure was called. This was the only facility on the priority list designed almost exclusively for undergraduate education. Yet as the months went by, the alumni did not contribute to the project and unrestricted funds were applied to other uses. With the end of the campaign a few months away, a gift of $25,000 was the only contribution specifically listed for an arts building, and this had come from former Dean Robert P. More. The campaign ended with all projects financed except the arts building.

The trustees refused to give up on a Hall of Liberal Arts and made a special effort to raise the money. A grant of $614,000 came from the U.S. Office of Education. The development office secured a gift of $500,000 from the Surdna Foundation. The class of 1948 gave $65,000. The structure was named after Albert B. Maginnes, a former trustee of the university and of the Surdna Foundation.

Maginnes Hall was completed and occupied in November 1970. On the ground floor was the Supply Bureau, moved over from the University Center. The floors above contained the office of the dean and the Departments of English, History, Government, International Relations, Classics, and Religion, as well as classrooms. Maginnes Hall provided the university with the largest addition to classrooms since the opening of Packard Laboratory more than thirty years earlier.

On academic matters, Lewis, following in the footsteps of Whitaker and Neville, accepted the idea of parity for the three colleges but devoted most of his time to promoting applied science and engineering with emphasis on graduate programs and research.

Much was in process. The goal of doubling graduate enrollments, which Neville had set for 1972, was accomplished by 1968. The output of doctorates in the four years from October 1964 to June 1968 was about $2\frac{1}{2}$ times what it had been in the preceding four-year period, and 87 percent of the doctorates were in mathematics, science, and engineering. The increases meant that Lehigh was keeping up with the growth of graduate enrollments and doctoral awards in the nation as a whole and was doing so by an effort in agreement with the national drive for more scientists and engineers.[6]

Whitaker and Neville had built up physics and chemistry, their own special fields. Lewis, whose speciality was applied mathematics, did not alter the direction of interest. He talked to the faculty of salients, pointing out that extraordinary expenditures must at any given time be made for projects of exceptional need. In the fall of 1965 he announced as a salient the formation of a Center for the Application of Mathematics, whereby engineers, scientists, and even social scientists might be encouraged to seek imaginative uses of mathematical tools and techniques. Pitcher, who among other professional activities had in 1952–53 been one of the planners for a national Society for Industrial and Applied Mathematics, was made acting director and held that post until the arrival in 1967 of Ronald S. Rivlin, a graduate of Cambridge University in England who was internationally known for his work in applied mechanics.

Lewis encouraged everybody to apply for federal monies. A large forward step occurred when Zettlemoyer succeeded in getting a major grant from the Advanced Research Projects Agency of the Department of Defense. The agency had given the U.S. Naval Research Laboratory $3,900,000 for the support of research in corrosion of high-strength, metal alloys. Lehigh was one of four institutions selected to participate in the project. With a grant of $720,000 for three years — the largest yet received by Lehigh from a federal agency — Zettlemoyer was able to carry through a plan for a Center for Surface and Coatings Research, of which he became the director. The center was formed to promote research for understanding complex surface and coating phenomena such as might be useful to semiconductor, chemical, petroleum, metals, and ink industries. Its formation was in part an outgrowth of Zettlemoyer's work with the National Printing Ink Research Institute, which he still headed.

Following these events, on 7 February 1966, Lewis announced to the faculty that Zettlemoyer was to be assistant to the president for governmental relations and would be looking for government research money. Six months later Zettlemoyer took the newly created position of vice-president for research. His jurisdiction included the Institute of Research — soon to be renamed the Office of Research — and a staff for supplying faculty with information concerning grants, assisting them in preparing applications, and overseeing the spending of grant monies.

Almost coincidental with the announcement of the grant from the U.S. Naval Research Laboratories came news of a large bequest from Mrs. Jennie M. Sinclair for a chemistry memorial facility. Zettlemoyer raised most of the additional money needed for the facility from the Office of Education and members of the printing ink institute. By 1970, a month after Maginnes Hall was finished, a neighboring structure, the Sinclair Laboratory, was housing the Center for Surface and Coatings Research and the National Printing Ink Research Institute.

On 12 January 1968, Lewis informed the trustees that federal agencies, which had once supplied scarcely 50 percent of the university's funds for research, were now accounting for 80 percent, and that research money from business and industry was increasingly hard to get.

Lewis introduced several novelties to Lehigh in addition to the salient in the applications of mathematics and a better means of tapping government money. One novelty was the sport of squash, in which Lewis played a good game. The trustees had a squash court built near the field house in the Saucon Valley fields. Students readily came to use it. Although squash did not gain intercollegiate status at Lehigh, it was the first new sport to appear and remain since the completion of the swimming pool in Taylor Gymnasium approximately fifty years earlier.

Three other novelties threatened to impinge upon the liberties being enjoyed by faculty and departments. One was the use of committees of off-campus experts—called ad hoc committees—to advise on tenure promotions and appointments. Throughout the country the American Association of University Professors (AAUP) was taking measures to protect faculty against arbitrary treatment in hiring, dismissal, and promotion. This was occurring at a time when faculty salaries were improving, and the profession of college teaching was attracting some poorly qualified candidates. Lewis installed the use of ad hoc committees to avoid hiring the unfit while protecting the competent.

According to his plan, the academic dean was to obtain considered opinions from at least three professionally established individuals who knew the work of the person who was under consideration for a tenure promotion or appointment. These opinions, although advisory, would carry great weight and would be sent forward to the provost along with the recommendations of the dean, the department head, and—a requirement soon added—the opinions of tenured members of the candidate's department. The reform went into effect within a few months of Lewis's arrival.

A second novelty was the use of committees composed of outsiders to review and evaluate the work of departments and centers. The use of such visiting committees was not new in American higher education. The overseers at Harvard had used visiting committees since before the end of the nineteenth century. Lewis, who from 1954 had been a member of the Harvard Overseer Committee to Visit te Division of Engineering and Applied Science, was determined to make use of them for all parts of the university. According to his original plan, a visiting committee was to consist of several distinguished members each from industry, government, and academia. The committee was to assemble on the campus at least once a year and evaluate the program, department, center, set of programs, or set of departments for which it was organized with respect to goals, resources, personnel, and performance.

The trustees approved this plan of visiting committees on 4 June 1965. By June 1967, twenty-one visiting committees had been organized and made their first reports.

Faculty gave the idea of visiting committees a mixed reception. The idea had a vocational ring to it that pleased some and offended others. It conformed to the century-old desire of engineering educators for a close rapport between engineering departments and clientele industries. It aroused the suspicion of some scientists and mathematicians that their activities might be misunderstood and misrepresented to the president and the trustees. Persons holding an elevated ideal of liberal education were also inclined to question the desirability of a review by outsiders suspected of favoring a vocational approach.

In practice, such fears were groundless. Visiting committees tended to become champions of the operations they evaluated.

A third novelty was cooperation with colleges of the Lehigh Valley, which held a promise of benefits to students and some additional work for faculty and administrators.

For decades four liberal arts colleges had existed within a twelve-mile radius of Lehigh, Lafayette at Easton, Moravian in Bethlehem, and Muhlenberg and Cedar Crest in Allentown. Each had gone on through the years with its own traditions, paying almost no attention to its neighbors. In 1962 a fifth college was added within the same radius, Allentown College of St. Francis de Sales in Center Valley. Each institution contained resources in instructional materials, faculty, and courses of study not possessed by the others; and in a number of areas there was a duplication of services.

In the 1960s this academic isolationism began to break down. Early in 1962 Neville announced to the faculty that the presidents of Lehigh University and the Lehigh Valley colleges were meeting "to explore possible areas of cooperation for their common interest and their common advantage."[7] The meetings of the presidents set an example soon followed by some other administrative officers and several faculty. Within a few years the librarians developed an interlibrary loan program whereby the resources of the six libraries became available to all of their students. Other cooperative programs followed. In the spring of 1969, the Lehigh Valley Association of Independent Colleges, Inc. (LVAIC), was set up with an aim of seeking greater economy and flexibility in a variety of areas of activities including the academic program, library services, computer services, purchasing, and certain student services. On 14 December 1970, the faculty at Lehigh approved cross-listing for all LVAIC college courses for the regular academic year, at the same time preserving local faculty and departmental autonomy in educational matters by allowing them a veto over cross-listing in those fields of their special concerns.

In time the faculty accepted ad hoc and visiting committees and LVAIC as being generally beneficial. But these also called attention to the power possessed by administrators, whose numbers had been increasing in response to governmental requirements, requests for personnel services, and new societal obligations. A knowledge of the necessity for more administrators sharpened an awareness that their responsibility was only to the trustees. Many administrators seemed to have large discretionary powers and sometimes appeared to be hiding critical information from the faculty.

A separation of faculty from administration had been growing since the beginning of the new Lehigh. It had, in the eyes of Neville, Lewis, and their top advisers, reached a point of disturbing morale and hampering efforts to deal with many problems, including those involving student discontent.

At a meeting on 22 January 1960, the trustees discussed the need for greater contact with the faculty and for better means of becoming current with academic affairs. In the early fall of 1961, Neville and Christensen held a two-day conference for trustees and selected members of the administration and the faculty at Skytop Lodge in the Poconos. The conference had little effect other than that of demonstrating a need for some mechanism for bridging the gap.

At a faculty meeting on 1 June 1964, Francis Wuest, the young new head of Psychology, read a statement complaining of a lack of communication between faculty and administration, expressing dissatisfaction with a number of things, and charging that a small "in group" decided all important matters. Neville responded to this presentation in one of his last acts as president by creating a special Committee on Communication with Wuest as chairman.

The Wuest Committee, as the Committee on Communication came to be called, proceeded to attack the institution of the department head. The committee found a sympathetic audience among many of the younger faculty.

Lewis inherited the Wuest Committee. He and Christensen organized a second Skytop conference for April 1965 "to find ways to enable the department head to fill that role more effectively."[8] The discontent among the younger faculty remained. On 3 May 1965, the faculty passed a resolution requiring department heads to consult with their faculties on all important matters. The following month, in response to a recommendation of the Wuest Committee, the faculty elected an ad hoc committee to study the functional organization of the university. Professor Frank S. Hook of the Department of English became chairman of the committee.

The Hook Committee conducted the most exhaustive study made by the faculty of the university as a functioning institution since the early 1920s. The committee produced a number of changes. Two of them concerned department heads and the graduate school.

Department heads, who from time immemorial had enjoyed an indefinite tenure of office, were renamed chairmen and given three-year terms with appointment being made at the recommendation of the academic dean after consultation with the departmental faculty.

The Graduate School was reorganized. Henceforth there would be no separate graduate faculty, and the dean of the school would consult an elective Graduate Committee on all matters of policy.

These changes aimed at increasing the input of the faculty in administrative decisions. The principal opposition to them came from some faculty in the College of Engineering, who had a preference — shared by many engineering faculties across the country — for the more authoritative managerial structure prevailing in business and industry. Votes in faculty meetings on the most important changes were not unanimous.

One key recommendation of the Hook Committee was defeated. The committee, taking into account the growing size of the faculty and the reluctance of many to attend faculty meetings, proposed the formation of a representative senate. Lewis saw in the proposal a probable widening of the gap separating the faculty from the administration and took the floor to argue against it. The proposal lost, fifty-six "yes" votes to ninety-five "nay."[9]

Students were not actively involved in any of these matters. Many of the older faculty would have liked the relationship with students to remain unchanged. But student-faculty relations were sufficiently close to what the faculty wanted for themselves that structural modifications within the ranks of the faculty could not help but involve students. Faculty and student drives for a greater input into decision making ran parallel, crossed each other, and became confused. The confusion was increased by a few of the faculty activists keeping restless student leaders informed of what was going on and sometimes using student support to increase their own leverage in decision making.

President Lewis had a natural affinity for students. He never closed the door to them but listened as they talked, and he asked cogent questions. He was unfailingly polite. In unassuming ways he encouraged and rewarded scholarship and leadership.

During the first few years of Lewis's tenure, two Lehigh students won Rhodes scholarships, V. Rodger Digilio (Industrial Engineering) in 1965 and Stewart Early (Mechanics) in 1966. These were the first Rhodes scholarships won by Lehigh students since the 1930s. In 1966 Stephen F. Goldmann (Chemical Engineering) received a Marshall scholarship, the counterpart to a Rhodes, for study at Cambridge University in England, and Lewis personally began financing a scholarship for a graduating senior to undertake studies abroad.

In 1962 Jacob Blaustein ('13) made a sum of twenty-five thousand dollars available for a series of lectures by world statesmen or distinguished scholars. The Scottish historian Sir Denis Brogan began the series in 1963–64, and the next year was followed by General Maxwell D. Taylor, former chairman of the Joint Chiefs of Staff. Student representatives participated in the major receptions accompanying the Blaustein lectures.

In 1964–65 the *Brown and White* produced some lively reporting of confrontations between the commonwealth's Liquor Control Board and certain students and student groups, including the *Brown and White* itself, when agents of the LCB confiscated a film made by a student reporter. The affair added sparks to the ongoing controversy concerning students' rights and the university's control of social life.

Beginning in June 1965, commencement exercises were shortened in such a way as to provide a personal touch. The president no longer handed out most of the diplomas. Faculty distributed these following the main ceremony under circumstances allowing an informal exchange with graduating seniors and master's recipients and their families. The president continued to hand out diplomas to candidates for doctoral degrees.

The faculty kept on studying and amending academic practices and social regulations. In the second semester of 1964−65, they approved a pass-fail grading system for juniors and seniors, established a two-day review period before final examinations, approved several junior-year-abroad programs, and made the Senior Comprehensive Examination in Arts and Science optional with the departments (which killed it). In 1966−67, Wuest, now chairman of the Committee on Student Life, pursued an investigation that led to liberalizing the rules on student living, especially as concerned the presence of women in residence halls and fraternities and the use of alcohol by all living groups.

While faculty and administrators worked to eliminate discontent on the Lehigh campus, across the nation it was deepening in ways that were soon to affect events on campuses everywhere.

A movement to secure rights for blacks was underway, spurred by decisions of the U.S. Supreme Court, congressional legislation, and grass-roots action headed by civil rights leader Martin Luther King. The movement encountered the barriers of prejudice and poverty and led to violence in areas such as the Watts District of Los Angeles (1965) and Newark and Detroit (1967).

An alleged lack of social concern on the part of industrialists, publicized through publications such as Ralph Nader's *Unsafe at Any Speed* (1965), augmented fears of the effects of nuclear power and other accomplishments of science and engineering on the environment.

The ineptitude of government officials in attempts to contain the spread of communism in Cuba, Central and South America, and the Far East reduced respect for political and administrative authority.

The mass media exploited these movements and the problems keeping them active. Investigative reporting received a boost. Editors added an element of sensationalism to the real gravity of events.

Youth received the messages. Boys and girls, young men and women, were exposed to the growing furor concerning life in a science-based society. Familial and social restrictions were disappearing, social consciences were developing, and teachers and parents, in asking youth to be educated, seemed in effect to be asking them to "join the system." A natural response was, "Why? The scientist tells the engineer how to destroy the world. The engineer, financed by industry, seems intent on doing it. In the process hordes of people make money and spend it for soul-killing purposes." Following up on this line of thought, many youths took refuge in some form of emotional withdrawal. Some also physically left family, school, and place of employment. The term *alienation* appeared to describe the psychological state of disaffected youths. Communes exhibiting life styles derived in opposition to the rules of a science-based society appeared and became a new object for investigative reporting and sensational editing.

Then came the war in Vietnam, begun during the administration of President Kennedy (1961—63) and escalated under President Johnson. By the end of 1965, approximately 184,000 U.S. troops were in Vietnam, and President Johnson had ordered the bombing of North Vietnam below the twentieth parallel. The war contained intrinsically nothing to evoke a strong and universal patriotism with an accompanying self-sacrifice of liberties and life. Many people regarded the war as a fight between one giant industrial country and the satellite of another with no real meaning for them personally.

Accompanying the war was a military draft, which young men might avoid by remaining in college. There, some who would otherwise have left for a commune, stayed. Enrollments in five-year programs increased. Fear of the draft was an important part of a general reaction of youth to the Vietnamese war, which in turn was the spark for student uprisings and demonstrations on campus after campus in the late 1960s and early 1970s.

This is not the place to describe the youth movements of the sixties and seventies. The author apologizes for the preceding simplistic explanation of complex situations. Yet something has to be said in order to put the student demonstrations at Lehigh from 1968 to 1970 into context. In what follows, these demonstrations are described in abbreviated form.

Although at Lehigh the leaders of student activism showed varying degrees of alienation, as this has been defined by Kenneth Keniston,[10] they were fairly responsible and independent. They did not welcome help from off-campus rabble rousers, and the few who appeared soon left. The strongest student leadership came from the College of Engineering and was profraternity. There was no large-scale flight out of scientific and engineering curricula and relatively little slacking off in the study of these subjects.

In all of these ways the leadership at Lehigh seems to have departed from that at highly publicized liberal arts colleges and state universities, but not from the student leadership on campuses similar to Lehigh's in being dominated by engineering and applied science. At predominately technological schools, the movement was by comparison restricted to a minority of the student body, was somewhat tardy in appearing, and was restrained in tactics so as not to appeal to reporters seeking sensational material. The Lehigh campus experienced inconsequential property damage, no loss of life, and none of the travesties of unstructured learning associated with a fully alienated person's ideal of a "free university."

The somewhat pallid appearance of demonstrations at Lehigh and similar schools does not mean that students in these places idealized a safe job, a comfortable home in the suburbs, and exotic vacations in the Caribbean or that they had poorly developed social consciences. The best explanation lies in an overriding commitment to science, engineering, and the applications of these.

It is axiomatic that people who strongly believe in a central principle of life look to that principle for antidotes to any ills attributed to it. Thus, people commited to a democratic way of life look to more democracy to cure its excesses. Similarly, believers in the efficacy of science and technology might deplore the bad effects of these on conditions of living; but they also look to science and technology for correctives.

As long as students remained loyal to the study of science and engineering, they did not seriously consider exchanging the life of a student for antiacademic styles. Their demonstrations in the name of relevance were aimed at changing living and learning so as to bring these more closely into harmony with some vaguely held ideal of an improved scientific and engineering education. Vocationally oriented students in other fields, such as business administration, felt a similar attraction for the work of establishments whose ranks they intended to penetrate. Disruptive tactics, irrational arguments, and other manifestations of alienation with very few exceptions supported demands for improving, not ignoring, scuttling, or replacing, the educational inheritance.

The Vietnamese war had an effect at Lehigh as at other colleges and universities of bringing grievances to a breaking point. Even so, the considered opinion of one administrator who faced the students during those years is that without the sensations evoked by reports of uprisings on other campuses, no disruption would have occurred at Lehigh. Student leaders read the reports of happenings elsewhere, corresponded with activists from other schools, and from these gained moral support for breaking the banks of established channels to force their demands on administrators and members of the faculty.

Acts of violence in other parts of the world in the spring of 1968 made bad tempers worse. Martin Luther King was assassinated on 4 April and Robert Kennedy on 5 June. Heavy American casualties were reported in Vietnam.

On 18 and 19 April, President Lewis received in his office student representatives of a group calling itself CURE (Committee for Undergraduate Responsibility in Education). The students wanted, among other things, an explanation of university policy and proposed the formation of a goals committee of faculty, students, and administrators. Demonstrations at the flagpole and outside of Packard Laboratory followed the session of 19 April. Lewis reported to the trustees that the demonstrations were "legal and orderly, and apparently contained many students who were there just for 'kicks.'"[11]

Lewis, vice-presidents Christensen and Seidle, and trustee McFadden met with students on the evening of 22 April, explained the organization of the Board of Trustees, and answered questions. Lewis told the students he endorsed the idea of a goals committee. In his report of the meeting to the trustees, he included five recommendations: (1) "keep the restless students talking—and listening"; (2) encourage the goals committee; (3) open up to new processes of decision making; (4) put students on trustee committees *or* have a visiting committee for student affairs; and (5) prepare contingency plans for more serious disturbances.[12]

The next incident concerned the faculty. As they entered the Osbourne Room of the University Center for a regular meeting on 6 May, students handed them a five-page mimeographed document entitled "The Academic Policy Committee of Arcadia and CURE Proposals for an Improved University." The purpose of the proposals, according to a preliminary statement, was "to bring to the forefront certain grievances which pinpoint problems which contribute to the stifling atmosphere, an atmosphere which prevents the student from obtaining benefits and opportunities which are rightfully his at a quality university." Thirty-one proposals followed, in variety sufficient to make it appear as though every dissident part of the university had a hand in drafting them. Some were clearly inspired by minorities among the faculty. Among these were demands for a faculty senate (a proposal that had already been voted down), for all engineering students to take a professional ethics course, and for a history of science course. Other proposals added up to demands that the personalized education available to honor students be extended to everybody; that students have a greater voice in governing the university; that there be coeducation, scholarships for blacks, and more courses in topics such as ecology, city planning, pollution, and urban studies.

The CURE proposals called for no immediate action. The faculty was being put on notice as the president had been several weeks earlier.

Shortly thereafter the formation of the Goals Committee was announced. It consisted of representatives of the students, the faculty, and the administration.

The trustees took all of these events into account at their meeting on 31 May. Rathbone agreed with Lewis that the trustees should be conciliatory and open lines of communication with various student groups. With this in mind, he proposed the formation of a Joint Commission of University Life (JCUL) consisting of students, faculty, administrators, and trustees. When the trustees had approved this, he recommended a change in the bylaws of the board to admit an additional alumnus trustee, someone who had been graduated at least two but not more than seven years; and he recommended that the number of appointed trustees be increased from six to nine — this in order to help with a new fund-raising campaign. Shortly thereafter, Kirk P. Pendleton (B.A. '63, B.S. '64), a star wrestler in his undergraduate days and now an executive with the Pitcairn Company, became the "young alumnus" trustee.

At the final faculty meeting of the year, on 3 June, the faculty passed motions put by its Committee on Educational Policy accepting cross-listed music courses given by Moravian College and an urban studies course and revising the calendar for the ensuing year by shortening semesters from fifteen to fourteen weeks and having the instructional part of the first semester end by the beginning of the Christmas vacation.

The academic year ended quietly but with a troubling situation. Nothing had been done to remove the causes of student discontent; and two umbrella-like committees were being formed with potentially conflicting jurisdiction. Both provided for representation of students and faculty; but the University Goals Committee was heavily oriented toward students and younger faculty and contained no trustees, whereas JCUL was to have strong representation from the trustees and the administration. JCUL appeared, indeed, almost as a response of the trustees to a challenge represented by the formation of the Goals Committee.

Both committees were to be advisory. That was another source of potential trouble. They were, in short, *committees*, and student activists were rapidly becoming disenchanted with committees as a means of solving problems. Committees were appearing more and more to them as tactics used by the administration to avoid solving problems.

In 1968–69, students, faculty, and administrators made some progress in resolving issues responsible for the discontent. But on the national and world scenes, the basic conflicts were unsettled. The electricity-charged atmospheres on college campuses remained and were, if anything, intensified.

Early in the fall semester, President Lewis held a so-called "Relevance Conference" at Buck Hill Falls in the Poconos, attended by the vice presidents, academic deans, key faculty and students, and Curtis for the trustees. The students repeated demands for more seminars, courses on topics of relevance, greater attention to the needs of freshmen, and more socializing between freshmen and upperclassmen.

JCUL was constituted with President Lewis as chairman. It quickly assumed preeminence vis-à-vis the Goals Committee.

At its December meeting the faculty approved a program of "high immediate relevance" courses, which allowed departments the privilege of bypassing the regular procedure for adding courses of immediate interest to students. The faculty also abolished the Junior Impromptu Writing Test for students in Arts and Science, passed a resolution allowing departments to offer "unstructured" majors, whereby programs might be tailored to individual student interests, and established a music major using courses available at Moravian College. Later in the year the faculty approved a Program of Freshman Seminars that contained most of the advantages of the high immediate relevance courses and the Creative-Concepts Seminars of the College Honors Program.

Both students and faculty actively pursued the issue of discrimination against blacks. For students the most sensitive aspect lay in the subordination of some fraternity houses to national organizations that either demanded or countenanced discrimination. This aspect of the issue was resolved when the IFC, supported by all student and faculty groups, established local option as a policy for fraternities, thereby strengthening the position of those that had to face opposition from their national headquarters.

All groups within the university seized upon the issue of coeducation, which was dividing opinion at most of America's all-male and all-female colleges and universities. With a few exceptions, the unisex school of higher education appeared doomed. Polls showed that high school seniors overwhelmingly wanted to study on coeducational campuses.

At Lehigh, coeducation had been a feature of graduate programs since 1918. By 1964–65 the Graduate School had 252 women as full-time students. Women, both graduate and undergraduate, had been admitted into the Summer School since 1929; but students, alumni, and administrators had consistently opposed coeducation among the undergraduates during the regular academic year. A poll conducted by the *Lehigh Review* in 1939 disclosed 69 percent of the undergraduates in opposition to coeducation. When the possiblity of going coed was raised during the Second World War, with enrollments falling and an almost vacant campus in view, the alumni had resoundingly replied "No!" and the Philadelphia Alumni Club had adopted a strong resolution against the idea.[13]

Since that time, some opinions had changed. Opposition to coeducation among the undergraduates had disappeared by 1968. Many of the faculty were known to favor it. Administrators and trustees, too, were having second thoughts. Costs of attending Lehigh were mounting and reducing the size of the population from which applications for admission might be anticipated. Could Lehigh continue its high standards without going coed? Only the alumni maintained a strong opposition.

When sometime in mid-1968 the University Goals Committee began studying the issue of coeducation, Rathbone took the initiative and asked for discussions by the trustees and JCUL. In January 1969, a JCUL committee to study coeducation at Lehigh was brought into being. It became known as the Joynt Committee after the name of its chairman, Professor Carey B. Joynt of International Relations. The Joynt Committee was strongly warned to study carefully the attitudes of alumni.

About this time, faculty dissidents found another issue. In January 1969, Christensen resigned as vice-president and provost. On 3 February 1969, Lewis announced to the faculty some appointments: Zettlemoyer was to be vice-president and provost; Joseph F. Libsch was to take his former position as vice-president for research; and George P. Conard was to move into Libsch's place as chairman of the Department of Metallurgy.

Immediately Professor Van Sciver, on behalf of the campus chapter of the AAUP, expressed dissatisfaction with the failure of Lewis to consult the faculty on these appointments and moved that the elected members of the Committee on Educational Policy be considered an advisory interim committee on administrative appointments. Lewis was in an embarrassing position. He had departed from his own policy, which paralleled the view of the AAUP on the subject. He escaped from the embarrassment by indirectly admitting the error. He took the floor and spoke in favor of consultation; and the motion was passed unanimously.

When spring arrived, student demonstrations again took place. A group of students appeared at the meeting of the faculty on 7 April demanding admittance. Lewis read the rules concerning faculty meetings and asked the students to leave, which they did after depositing a prepared statement with the secretary of the faculty. Late in April, about fifty students demonstrated at Christmas-Saucon, protesting the presence of Marine Corps recruiters on the campus. In May, about six hundred gathered at the flagpole to express a desire for coeducation. On 7 May, a group of undergradute and graduate students from the Department of Social Relations conducted a brief sit-in outside the offices of the president and the provost, requesting, among other things, more faculty for their department.

By the end of the year, tempers were improving among the faculty. They were actively participating with the administrators in attempting to improve relations with the students and thereby were gaining much of what they wished by way of a greater share in governance. Also, faculty salary levels had been steadily rising. Zettlemoyer reported to the trustees "that the faculty has a feeling of participation in Univeristy problems which it had not had before, particularly in the area of long-range planning."[14]

Students, too, gained somewhat in their desire to have an increased share in the making of policies and programs. The faculty, at its final meeting of the year, passed motions allowing students to have representatives with voting privileges on the Committees of Educational Policy, Regulations and Procedures, Undergraduate Financial Aid, Undergraduate Awards, and Facilities. The faculty also created a Forum for Visiting Lectures Committee and a Library Users Committee, both having representation of students, and passed a motion prohibiting campus police from carrying firearms.

The students did not gain the privilege of attending meetings of the university faculty. A motion to this effect was held over to the following academic year.

By the fall of 1969, nothing in the situations facing the country and the world had occurred to relieve the anxieties of students. Seniors on the campus had lived with the issues of Vietnam, discrimination, and pollution for their entire college careers. The conflict in Vietnam had been intensified. The Mylai massacre and other atrocities led even moderate Americans to wonder if any good whatsoever could come of American involvement in the conflict. Inexpert attempts of officials within the Johnson administration to cover up blunders shook the faith of people in the government. Could anyone in high political office be expected to tell the truth? Reporters, columnists, and cartoonists ridiculed the Establishment. On 15 November, approximately 250,000 people marched on Washington, D.C., in an anti-Vietnam demonstration. Yet the war with its attendant problems dragged on.

At Lehigh, students did not wait for the coming of spring to express their discontent. Approximately 700 participated in the antiwar demonstration in Washington on 15 November. A little over a month later, students joined local citizens in a candlelights march to the Civic Center in Behlehem to protest the war. The *Brown and White* reprinted Herblock cartoons from the *Washington Post* and featured the highly political strip, "Gremlin Village," by student cartoonist 'Gene Mater ('71).

At the beginning of the school year, Kirby House participants adopted fifteen proposals for improving life for black students. Lewis held another relevance conference at Buck Hill Falls, attended by selected faculty and administrators and five trustees. The conference ended with the trustees acceding in part to a student demand for all meetings of the board to be held on the campus and indicated that the following January and April meetings, scheduled for New York City as was the custom for meetings at these times, would be transferred to the campus.

The Joynt Committee made a preliminary report to the Board of Trustees at its meeting on campus on 9 October. The committee had voted twelve to one in favor of coeducation, said Joynt.

On 22 October the Committee on Educational Policy formed a subcommittee to study overall university governance, chaired by Professor Lawrence H. Leder, who in 1968 had come to Lehigh as chairman of the Department of History.

Students took advantage of the novel opportunities provided by the faculty in the preceding two years. Many elected pass-fail grading. Before the year was over, twenty-three students had unstructured major programs and the faculty had offered twenty-one high immediate relevance courses. A modest Black Studies Program was in effect and included three visiting black faculty. An Urban Studies Program and an arts and science major in Environmental Science and Resource Management were in preparation.

The students also gained the objective of attending meetings of the faculty. About twenty appeared for the meeting of 8 December, anticipating a change in the faculty view of the subject. In a brief preliminary session, the faculty voted to admit them and to allow students to be observers at subsequent meetings.

By midpoint in the 1969–70 academic year, the most pressing of the students' demands for improvements in academic work had been met to an extent acceptable to the more moderate students. Even the radical leaders did not criticize the faculty for lack of good will.

Administrators and trustees, too, were conciliatory and full of good will. They opposed nothing that the bulk of the faculty clearly wanted. On 3 November 1969, the faculty established a Personnel Committee consisting of five full professors to entertain complaints brought by faculty against the administration and experienced nothing but full cooperation from the president and the trustees for this action. In meeting the extraordinary requests of students and faculty, the trustees overspent income for the first time since 1930–31. The operating deficit for 1969–70 was $274,574.[15]

As the winter passed, the attention of student leaders shifted more and more from faculty and academic programs to the administration and the trustees. JCUL was holding some closed meetings, giving as a reason that continuing campus disturbances might inhibit full and free discussions. Radical students had no difficulty in interpreting this reason as an excuse for keeping them from influencing proceedings. Then the trustees held their January meeting in New York City rather than on the campus as had been expected. All the while, the Subcommittee of Educational Policy on the Governance of the University was interviewing students and faculty and spreading the idea of a faculty-student forum to perform a large part of the governing of the university.

A new crisis was in the making. The one important issue not yet resolved was that of governance. Objectively, the issue could have been precisely formulated and rationally resolved. But rationality was hidden behind the anger and frustration of student leaders in feeling forced to plod along on a course of peaceful study when the outside world was moving in an opposite direction.

On 6 March, the *Brown and White* reported that Arcadia had declared governance of the university to be one of the most important issues facing the university. A few days later Lewis appeared before Arcadia and invited three of its members to attend the next meeting of the Board of Trustees, scheduled for the campus on 9 April. The date was not far distant, but the intervening time was not as short as were student tempers. As the date neared, student leaders decided on other means of securing action on their demands. On Sunday and Monday, 5 and 6 April, the students demonstrated. A regular faculty meeting was scheduled for Monday. The faculty assembled and agreed to cooperate with a student Ecology Action Group preparing for the celebration of Earth Day on 22 April, thereby putting a stamp of approval on the dismissal of classes on that day at the discretion of the instructor.

On Tuesday the seventh, student demonstrations were resumed. An informal meeting with the faculty on Wednesday evening, 8 April produced no visible progress. Lewis was present and made remarks that some student leaders later held against him — he had "stabbed the students in the back" they said. Later in the evening, Michael Golden, on behalf of the students, called for a strike. "Spring Lehigh!" was the slogan.

The next day there appeared on the campus a broadside bearing a large headline, "STRIKE IS ON." The accompanying story read in part:

Last night at ten, about 800 of us met in response to SPRING planting and a request from the now-defunct Arcadia. We immediately tackled the issue of university governance, which is the basis of the problems we're now facing. The large number of students, as well as the self-abolition of Arcadia and RHC, indicates that we've finally realized that the administration's claims of student involvement in decision making are just so much bullshit. ...

We unanimously decided that a University Forum (UF) composed of 50 percent faculty and 50 percent students should be the governing structure of Lehigh. ...

On Thursday the ninth, the trustees met in New York City. Lewis explained that the locale had been changed at the last moment in order to avoid a confrontation with the students. The board devoted a long session in the morning to the issue of coeducation and decided to postpone a decision on the subject.

At 4:00 P.M. the board reconvened, anticipating the arrival of three students from Arcadia. They appeared forty-five minutes late: James R. Kasser ('71), president of Arcadia at the time it disbanded; Donald F. Parsons ('70), past president of Arcadia; and Todd Tieger ('71), a member of Arcadia. The trustees listened while the former Arcadians spoke. Tieger charged the trustees with failing to understand the problems of Vietnam, the atomic bomb, pollution, overpopulation, and ecology. Kasser gave the reason why Arcadia had disbanded and suggested that five students be appointed to the Board of Trustees and that a senate with equal representation of students and faculty take over the faculty's governing functions. Parsons seconded the idea that the ongoing system of governance was unsatisfactory and invited the trustees to spend several days on the campus with the students. The meeting ended with no action having been taken.

From the trustees' point of view, the session with the students on 9 April was a step forward, inasmuch as it marked an improvement in communication. But the students who had attended returned to the campus disappointed and as angry as ever. That evening several hundred students gathered on the lawn outside Richards and Dravo, and student leaders reaffirmed the existence of a strike. A scattering of faculty and administrators looked on while other students listened and peaceably dispersed.

On Friday morning, 10 April, the faculty held an open meeting in Grace Hall, attended by about 180 faculty and from 1,500 to 1,700 students. Several trustees were in the audience. Many students and faculty talked about a student-faculty form of government. The meeting ended when the faculty passed a motion made by Professor Conard that a group of students, faculty, and administrators be chosen to make recommendations concerning a forum. That afternoon about thirty departmental meetings of students and faculty were held. The faculty convened in the evening, heard a wide range of proposals for governance, and voted to suspend classes until the following Thursday, 16 April.

Lewis immediately agreed to the "vacation" and asked for a continuance of student-faculty meetings at all levels. In addition, he asked Rathbone to convene a special meeting of the board. The meeting was held at the Saucon Valley Country Club on Sunday, 12 April, and lasted four hours. Various members of the faculty and administration analyzed the recent events. The board reviewed a draft of a forum prepared by the Leder sub-committee of educational policy, which provided for an equal number of students and faculty to control virtually all policies except personnel and those claimed by the faculty as being exclusively its own. The reaction of the trustees to the Leder plan was generally favorable. Lewis then urged a continuation of student-faculty-administration activity to produce a universally acceptable draft.

Lewis presided on Monday the thirteenth over the first of a number of sessions that considered and amended the Leder draft. At a meeting on the fifteenth, a small group, headed by Professor Wuest, was formed to go to work on a rough draft that appeared to be acceptable.

The Wuest subcommittee produced the constitution that went to the faculty on 27 April and was, with a few amendments, passed almost unani-mously. On 2 May, the trustees at a special meeting considered the consti-tution. Rathbone reviewed the events leading to its formulation, indicated that JCUL had discussed it earlier in the day, and briefly described the con-tents: A body of 125, consisting of 60 students and 60 faculty representing the several colleges and schools, and 5 members ex officio — the president, the provost, the vice president for student affairs, and two others appointed by the president — would have broad powers of legislation, recommendation, or review covering most matters falling under the control of the provost, the dean of students, and the vice-presidents for administration and devel-opment. The powers were restricted to recommendation and review with respect to personnel, courses and curricula, community relations, budgets, and academic discipline. The Board of Trustees would retain all of its tra-ditional power and authority but would be joined by two students and two faculty chosen by the Forum. Nothing in the charter of the university and very little in its body of Procedures, Rules, and Regulations needed to be changed. When the general meeting was ended, the trustees met in closed executive session and approved the constitution.

The organization of the Forum was a triumph for the Lewis administration. It satisfied the immediate demands of students and forestalled further and perhaps destructive action. The tide of student discontent was on the rise on most other campuses. Many acts of violence occurred, including the shooting on 4 May of four students at Kent State University. The *Brown and White* commented on the situation in the 5 May issue: "The invasion of Cambodia by U.S. ground forces, the resumption of heavy bombing raids over North Vietnam, Defense Secretary Laird's call for a three year extension of the draft, and yesterday's massacre at Kent State university — these issues are all involved in the hour-by-hour escalation of a nationwide student strike."

On 7 May Lewis presided over an all-university meeting called to discuss the national emergency. He declared himself in sympathy with the students, told them they had a right to make up their own minds, and asked that they keep their "consciences compatible to the faculty" if a strike were to take place. Later in the evening, about four hundred students assembled on the freshman quadrangle and called for joining the nationwide strike against the Establishment.

There were no further strikes at Lehigh. The students had won an important point with the acceptance of the Forum and had in the process spent the emotional energy needed for sustained demonstrations.

Individual faculty were finding ways for students to recover from their neglect of studies. The faculty accepted resolutions from the Committee on Educational Policy to allow exceptional uses of incompletes, absent grading, and pass-fail grading for students requesting them. A few students made liberal use of these privileges, and all turned to the task of successfully completing the school year. Seniors were as usual interested in finding jobs or entering graduate or professional schools. The registrar's statistics on grading and the overall university average show no departures from prevailing trends. A higher proportion of students than ever before received A's, the usual proportion got F's, and the all-university average rose slightly for the ninth consecutive year.

Late in May the trustees further amended the bylaws of the board to increase the number of alumni trustees from seven to eight to provide for the election of a second young alumnus. The person elected to fill the new slot was John D. Harper ('65), chairman of the Cinemette Corporation of America.

Everyone from the trustees on down was determined to make the Forum work. Elections of student and faculty members were held later in May. Early the following September, Lewis held a three-day Conference on University Life for the personnel of the Forum and other interested parties. Subsequently, a series of organizational meetings brought the Forum into existence. The members elected Professor Ferdinand Beer as chairman. James R. Kasser became vice-chairman and Professor Curtis Clump, secretary-treasurer. Representatives chosen to attend meetings of the Board of Trustees included J. Donald Ryan of Geology and Charles Vihon of Business administration for the faculty and H. J. Bell and D. W. Miles for the students.

During the next several years, college campuses across the country continued to have student demonstrations. The Peace Pact ending the U.S. involvement in Vietnam was not signed until 27 January 1973. But at Lehigh, with the organization of the Forum, students returned to the practice of expressing grievances through the established channels. RHC reappeared with essentially its former powers. A Student Activities Council replaced the old Student Activities Committee and had a general responsibility of initiating and promoting activities of interest to the entire university.

The Forum was henceforth the principal instrument of student self-government. It was unusually active during the first full academic year of operation

and after that, less so. But even when it did not operate directly, it helped
to inspire other changes. Shortly after it was organized, Lewis created an
ad hoc Committee on Discipline with Professor Ryan as chairman. As a
result of the work of this committee, on 2 April and 7 May 1973, the faculty
approved a revised "University Conduct Code" establishing due process for
all disciplinary proceedings against students.

The Forum fit the pattern that had been evolving within Lehigh since
the end of the First World War. The temptation to compare the Forum
with student government under the old Lehigh is inescapable. That earlier
government was the Honor Court, in existence for most of the time between
1895 and 1920 and operated in its last years by Arcadia. The Honor Court
was a prime (though weak) means for students to control things that mattered
to them at a time when there was no administration in a modern sense, a
time when students and faculty made a clear distinction between curricular
matters needing regulation and student life and extracurricular matters,
which were private. The only domain in which governance seemed to be
falling down was in the classroom and the examination hall. The professors
could not prevent cheating. Hence, with the approval of the authorities,
the students undertook the job themselves and formed the Honor Court,
which for many years worked sometimes well and sometimes not so well.

Eventually, changes in the composition of the student body and attitudes
toward assignments and examinations destroyed the idea that students should
patrol themselves for honest performance. Faculty and administrators assumed the task and increased the stigma of cheating. Student control of
cheating was not one of the demands leading to the organization of the Forum.
At one point the students specifically rejected the idea of an honor system.
The Forum, empirically put together as a composite answer to a number of
practical questions, was the appropriate agency of student government in
the things that students in the maturing of the new Lehigh wanted.

The Forum succeeded because trustees, president, vice-presidents, deans,
faculty, and students organized it with respect to the imperatives inhering
in the sort of education that the university was dedicated to providing.
Engineering faculty and students were prominent among the leadership in
putting the Forum together and in making it work. That does not mean an
engineering point of view governed proceedings of the Forum—far from it;
but it does mean that the Forum was organized in such a way as not to
impede an engineering and applied science point of view from dominating
the overall governance of the university.

The Forum was largely supplemental to the work of the faculty, the
administration, and the trustees. It replaced something in only a few areas.
These included matters with which students were greatly concerned, had
previously no effective influence, and were not claimed as unalterably their
own by faculty, trustees, and administrators. In all of its work, it conformed
to the traditional pragmatic approach in dealing with issues. By the time of
its formation, the university authorities were formulating more policies than

ever before, largely in sensitive areas such as the admission and hiring of minority students and faculty, tenure, leaves of absence, retirement benefits, insurance for many purposes, the students' use of alcoholic beverages, and provisions for giving students legal advice. Most of these policies were necessary in order to comply with federal and state laws or to meet the demands of an increasingly interested and litigious society.

The Forum had been planned to make or recommend policies concerning almost all issues on which the university was under pressure to take a definite stand. But altogether, these policies did not add up to any fundamental change in the usual way in which the university went about the business of defining and pursuing its educational tasks.

The Forum did not resolve the issue of coeducation. The trustees took care of this on 29 May 1970, after the constitution of the Forum had been accepted but before the Forum was organized.

On the previous 9 April President Lewis had put before the trustees a plan for admitting eight hundred women over a period of four years at a rate of one hundred each in the autumns of 1971 and 1972 and two hundred each in the following three years, without reducing the number of men. Rathbone had expressed himself as strongly favoring this plan but cautioned that additional time was needed to sound out alumni in depth and to educate them. On 29 May the trustees agreed to admit one hundred women in the fall of 1971 and another one hundred in the fall of 1972, with a review of the experience at the end of two years.

Somewhat later President Lewis requested of both the Forum and the trustees permission to admit 1,050 instead of the originally approved 900 men and 100 women, with the additional 50 being either men or women, in order to compensate for increased withdrawals among upperclassmen and a budgetary squeeze occasioned by a rising rate of inflation. In the spring of 1973, the board reviewed the experience with coeducation and voted to continue it on the basis of Lewis's original plan.

By this date figures on the attractiveness of Lehigh and its programs to women were available. The year of 1971–72 began with 169 women, well above the agreed-on maximum of 150. A year later the quota was again exceeded, with 362 instead of 250 women being present. Most of the women entered for study in the sciences and mathematics with surprisingly large minorities opting for subjects in business and engineering. The humanities and the social sciences received fewer than anticipated.

There is a postscript to the arrival of coeducation at Lehigh. In September 1981, Lewis wrote, "The advent of women has made a positive and profound difference in the quality of University life. Their presence and contributions have enriched our lives together in many ways — academic, social, cultural, and athletic." He proclaimed the year 1981 "as a time for recognition and celebration of the 10th anniversary of coeducation at Lehigh University.[16]

Many alumni, faculty, and friends of the university doubtlessly agreed with the observations of Lewis. The social and athletic effects predominated. Male and female students took advantage of relaxed controls over conduct and mingled freely in residential units. The semiannual houseparty—that old saturnalia for repressed males—died suddenly with the coming of co-education. Women invaded Taylor Gymnasium and the playing fields, fought and won through the Forum the right to join the Marching Band, ran for class office, joined in work-study programs, and, as they increased in numbers, formed sororities, the first being Alpha Phi, authorized in 1975, followed within months by Alpha Gamma Delta, Alpha Omicron Pi, Delta Gamma, and Gamma Phi Beta. The proportion of women in the undergraduate student body increased yearly and by 1980 stood at 25.9 percent.

Affirmations that coeducation had enhanced the climate of learning were more difficult to prove. After all, the professors did not employ different techniques for teaching men and women. Female and male students attended the same lectures, read the same texts, studied the same material, and were graded according to identical standards. Professors had never been hired for any special ability to teach one sex over the other.

What is incontestible is that the undergraduate student body became larger. The trustees had decided to add women to the usual number of men, not to replace men with women. The number of qualified women had been greater than anticipated so that by the end of five years, the size of the undergraduate student body had grown by almost 1,000. From the spring of 1971, when the decision to go coed had been made, to the fall of 1975, the undergraduate enrollment advanced from approximately 3,100 to 4,150, with all colleges benefiting from the increase.

The stage was set for additions to faculty and course offerings, as had happened following the influx of veterans in the late 1940s.

9

The University in Society: 1970–1980

With the issue of governance resolved, the work of the university went speedily and enthusiastically forward. In its rapid growth, Lehigh avoided the disunity and inconsistent other-worldliness attributed by Clark Kerr to the "multiversity," that conglomeration of educational communities resulting from a hasty attempt to please a rapidly changing society in an advanced stage of scientific and technological development.[1] Lehigh, while improving its plant, finances, and programs for undergraduate and graduate education, remained unified and attuned to social realities.

Unity meant for Lehigh that the university had survived the buffets of technological and social change with its personality intact. Lehigh possessed one "soul," not several, as attributed by Kerr to the multiversity. Lehigh's soul bore the stamp of applied science and engineering in a setting of the interdependence of these with the arts, the humanities, the social sciences, business and teacher education, and related intellectual and physical extra-curricular activities. Success in forming the Forum had preserved a harmonious integration at a time when administrators, faculty, and students had seemed about to walk down different roads.

Even so, organizing the Forum answered only to a crisis. What came closer than the organization of the Forum to the fundamental requirements of unity was a traditional educational discipline, obeyed in a climate of academic freedom, to which must be added the refusal of the trustees to give in to pressures for adding major new enterprises.

During the years of student unrest, the trustees had received urgent requests from off-campus sources to organize a graduate school of social work and a two-year medical college. After examining feasibility studies made for these projects, the trustees refused to begin them. On 6 October 1967, the board passed a motion to the effect that Lehigh should add professional schools "only when they are specifically relevant to Lehigh's purposes, respond to a clearly defined need with a broad geographical base, and can generate satisfactory support through tuition, grants, and gifts." On the basis of the financial standard contained within the motion, the trustees turned back a movement in 1972–73 for a law school.

Unity in promoting applied science and engineering in a humanistic setting saved Lehigh from that other fault attributed by Kerr to the multiversity, an isolation from social realities. Although in the years of unrest student activists had talked of "de-ivory-towering Lehigh," the talk had little substance. Lehigh had never had much of the ivory-tower character as this might have been understood by students; neither had it much idealism of a platonic sort, as might be called otherworldly by politicians, businessmen, and industrialists. The emphasis on vocationalism, coupled with a pragmatic outlook, kept Lehigh in touch with realities.

The later years of the Lewis presidency saw a continuation of the large and disciplined physical growth begun under Whitaker in the 1950s. Within ten years of establishing the Forum, the campus gained more than a dozen prominent structures. On the old campus appeared Rathbone Hall for student dining (1971), a new powerhouse (1974), the seven-building Trembley Park apartments west of Johnson Hall (1975), and the Sherman Fairchild Laboratory for Solid State Studies (1976). North of Packer Avenue were two new buildings for chemistry, named the Seeley G. Mudd Chemistry Building and Neville Hall (1975), and a six-story residence hall called Brodhead House (1979). Sayre Park had several new fraternity houses. By 1981 twenty-seven of the thirty-two fraternities had chapter houses on the campus pursuant to the policy announced thirty years earlier.

Across the mountain on the Saucon Valley Playing Fields were squash courts (1972), the Centennial School for the School of Education (1972), the Philip Rauch Field House (1976), and the Stabler Athletic and Convocation Center (1979).

Adjacent to the playing fields, on the south side of a trickle of water named Black River by the early settlers, were apartments for married and graduate students (SMAGS) whose several units were named for former professors Diamond, Gipson, Hartman, Severs, and More (1974). Many other buildings had been renovated and modernized, including, at the request of the Forum, the Wilbur Powerhouse, converted in 1976 into a workshop theater.

Many of the new facilities were resources for the entire Lehigh Valley as well as for faculty and students. The most obvious of these were the Saucon Valley Playing Fields, which became the scene of a wide range of activities: sports such as football, baseball, soccer, track and field, running, cross-country skiing, archery, tennis, practice golf, and lacrosse; jamborees, reunions, and expositions; and a motley lot of activities as diverse as picnicking, falconry, the training of dogs, and the flying of model airplanes. No fences barred the public from entering and using the fields. At periods of peak use—usually weekends in spring, summer, and fall—five or six hundred of the local citizenry might be found on the grounds. Less noticeable but equally important as community resources were the Centennial School, expanded facilities of libraries, computers, laboratories, classrooms, the Packer Memorial Church, the hallways of buildings in which art might be displayed, and open areas containing examples of modern sculpture.

The composition of the Board of Trustees reflected the recent changes and growth. In the space of ten years the board grew in size from about two dozen to more than forty members, not counting the representatives from the Forum. Resignations among the corporate trustees swelled the ranks of the emeriti. In 1967 the board reactivated the category of honorary trustee, a post used in the years of the old Lehigh to provide for the surplus above the charter limitation of ten and, in the new Lehigh, to retain the services of and to honor Drinker and Grace. The category of honorary trustee permitted the retention of members whose terms as appointed or alumnus trustee had expired.

Although about 90 percent of the membership consisted of alumni who had climbed to the top ranks of corporate enterprise, two trustees suggested the impression made on the board by recent events. Nancy M. Kissinger, wife of former Secretary of State Henry A. Kissinger and daughter of former trustee Albert B. Maginnes ('21), became an appointed trustee in 1978. Reginald A. Jennings ('70), partner in Pickett and Jennings, was a "young alumnus" trustee and the first black to be elected (1979).

In 1973 Rathbone retired as president of the board. Harold S. Mohler ('48), president of Hershey Foods, replaced him.

Greater than the growth of the board were the increases in numbers of faculty and the administration and staff. By 1980 the board was about $2\frac{1}{2}$ times larger than it had been in 1920. The faculty, which had numbered 96 in 1920, by 1980 numbered about 350, that is, had become $3\frac{1}{2}$ times more numerous. Administrators and members of the supporting staff, probably around thirty in 1920, had by 1980 passed the one-thousand mark, registering a growth of greater than thirty-fold.

Lewis had begun his tenure with a president's "cabinet" of four men besides himself; he ended it with seven. Franz was the only one who was with him the entire time. Libsch became vice-president for research when Zettlemoyer moved into the position of provost and vice-president. Zettlemoyer retired in 1980 and was succeeded by Arthur E. Humphrey, a chemical engineering professor and administrator from the University of Pennsylvania. Preston Parr took Seidle's vice presidency in 1970. The trustees created the position of vice president for planning in 1974; Eric V. Ottervik, who had successively been an administrative intern sponsored by the American Council on Education and an assistant to Zettlemoyer, took the post. In 1978 John W. Woltjen succeeded Glick as treasurer and vice president. The seventh member of the cabinet was Austin Gavin, a retired vice president for internal affairs from the Pennsylvania Power and Light Company, who in 1974 took a new position as executive consultant to the office of the president.

In 1974 President Lewis appointed Lora Liss as director of Affirmative Action, a name given to the policy of the national government in insisting on certain sorts of preferential treatment for women and members of minority groups, especially in employment and on-the-job benefits. Colleges and universities receiving federal funds were obliged to adhere to the principles of Affirmative Action. Lora Liss put together a program approved by the trustees on 10 May 1976, establishing goals of hiring fifty-eight women and seventy men and women from minority groups within the next six years. By this time the university had the experience of a considerale number of women among administrators and supporting staff and had some within the faculty, but was having more difficulty filling positions with blacks and members of other minorities.

In 1971 the trustees created an Office of Community Relations in response to the growing multiplication of contacts between the various parts of the university and society.

Several other positions were more obviously services for the administration itself. Among these were Offices of Physical Planning and Administrative Services. And, when in 1980 the trustees adopted a budget in excess of fifty-seven million dollars, they hired as the university's first budget director James A. Tiefenbrunn ('66, M.B.A. '72).

Library services combined a growth in numbers and the complexity of administrative functions wth those of instructional programs and research. From one small building in 1920 holding approximately 140,000 volumes, serviced by a part-time director and several clerks, the university libraries by 1980 consisted of two large buildings, Linderman and Mart, plus a storage facility. Together these held about 800,000 volumes, 8,000 serial publications, 10,000 audio-visual resources, 130,000 government documents, and special collections of rare books and manuscripts, the university archives, and congressional papers. A staff of more than sixty provided personalized assistance to faculty and students in using library resources.

A Media Center, housed in Linderman, was in 1978 providing videotaping, graphics, audio production, slide preparation, the use of audio-visual materials, film rentals, and information about commercially produced software.

In 1976 Berry G. Richards succeeded James D. Mack as director of libraries and faced the tensions associated with an accelerated rate of growth. A library, more than any other part of a university, was experiencing pressures from what was commonly called the "knowledge explosion." According to the historian of science Derek Price, the number of scientific journals doubled about every fifteen years.[2] The space being demanded by users was correspondingly great. Librarians were seeking from computers some relief from overcrowding as well as improvements in service. Computerized library services also had needs for space. Mart, not yet twelve years old, was too small.

Library services accounted for only one purpose for which the university had to have large amounts of money. Sums that would have staggered the Board of Trustees a quarter of a century earlier had to be obtained to pay for space and facilities, higher salaries and more fringe benefits, and a seemingly unending list of new services.

An inflation had accompanied the Vietnamese conflict and continued through a severe postwar recession at an average rate of better than 11 percent per year. From 1970 to 1980 the purchasing power of the dollar, considered as being worth one dollar in 1967, declined from 90.6 cents to 40.5 cents. Inflation produced both higher costs and higher incomes from which contributions might be expected. Also, it made accurate expressions of growth in monetary terms difficult. It is easy to report that from 1920 to 1980 the endowment grew from about three million the approximately seventy million dollars and that the annual budget increased from five hundred thousand dollars to nearly sixty million. It is more meaningful to measure growth in terms of numbers of students, faculty, administrators and support personnel, degrees awarded, library collections, and other purposes for which the money was spent.

Tuition rose almost yearly, as it had to in order to absorb the effects of inflation and provide for the additional charges. By 1981 it stood at $6,100 for all undergraduates.

Pressure was on to improve financial management of the endowment. In the 1960s the Ford Foundation, responding to the financial plight of colleges and universities across the country, subsidized a study of their financial management and published a booklet, *Managing Educational Endowments*, in which it charged boards of trustees with unpardonable ignorance in financial affairs and advised them to obtain professional help. In 1969 James H. Walker, chairman of the Lehigh trustees' Finance Committee, called the attention of the trustees to the study and proposed that the board confine its activity in financial matters to setting policy and leave implementation to the Finance Committee, which in turn would rely on professionals. Walker announced an intention of using the managers of the pension fund at Bethlehem Steel for daily management of the university's portfolio. In 1973 Walker proposed for the acceptance of the board a policy known as "total return concept," which he said had already been adopted by about seventy colleges and universities. The substance of the policy as defined by Walker was the use of capital gains to forestall deficits in annual expenditures. The Finance Committee, in the first year following adoption of the total return concept, sold approximately $1,600,000 worth of securities from 22 September to 31 December 1973, realizing a profit of $681,000.[3]

Alumni annual giving, which had been halted during the Centennial Campaign, was renewed in 1967–68 and in that year brought in $583,038, a sum to which 38 percent of the living alumni contributed. From this figure the fund increased almost every year and for 1980–81 brought in $2,650,000 from 52 percent of the living alumni and alumnae.

A means of recognizing the contributions of large donors accompanied this increase. On 6 October 1967, trustee Curtis reported to the board the formation of a leaderhsip club to be called the Asa Packer Society, modeled after the Tower Club at Cornell and the Benjamin Franklin Associates at the University of Pennsylvania. Membership was to be annual and open to anyone contributing one thousand dollars or more to the university. Trustee Edwin Snyder ('23) was the first chairman and presided at a kickoff dinner on 9 November 1967 in New York City. Year after year the membership increased and by the autumn of 1980 stood at 762. Lewis, in his annual report for that year, commented, "Lee A. Iacocca ('45), who has quite enough to do as chairman of Chrysler Corp., was Society chairman last year and has agreed to serve again for 1980−81."

Almost as soon as the Centennial Campaign ended, the board began preparing for another major fund-raising effort. Franz presented the board in 1968 with a ten-year capital-needs program involving expenditures of seventy-nine million dollars for buildings, equipment, and additions to endowment. Later in the year, the Planning and Development Committee of the board stressed an immediate need for more undergraduate residence halls and dining facilities and apartments for married and graduate students. Lewis pointed to pressures for sharp rises in faculty salaries.

When planning for the new campaign began, the question of university governance was not yet resolved. In 1969−70 Lewis acknowledged the interest of students in matters of planning and development by involving JCUL in discussions over priorities for a possible eighty-million-dollar ten-year effort. In the fall of 1970, the Forum and its Committee on Priorities, Planning, and Development took over the task from JCUL. The Forum disagreed with the administration over some of the priorities; but then, members of the Forum disagreed among themselves with a result that Lewis received majority and minority reports. No one disputed a pressing need for more facilities for physics and chemistry. Franz's report to the board incorporated projects found in both of the Forum's reports. The board endorsed Franz's report and planned for a ten-year development program of $66,795,000.

The New Century Campaign was organized in the autumn of 1971. Harold S. Mohler accepted the chairmanship of the national committee and announced that the Forum's representatives to the board would be included among the membership. The firm of Marts and Lundy was again hired to conduct the campaign. A first-phase goal of thirty million dollars was set, to be raised by June 1976.

The appeal had to be directed to private sources. Although 8 percent of the $25,300,000 collected by the Centennial Campaign had come from governments, by 1971 governmental programs that might provide for some of the capital improvements needed by Lehigh had ended. During the years of the Johnson and Nixon administrations, retrenchment in spending for facilities for higher education was the rule. At the same time, Libsch was yearly reporting to the faculty of increases not only in the dollar value of sponsored research but also in the proportion coming from governments. During the period of the New Century Campaign, between 80 and 90 percent of the support for research came from governments, with the national government supplying never less than 70 percent and the NSF, never less than 21 percent. In short, alumni, business, industry, and foundations were being asked to make available the capital improvements whereby government-sponsored research could be carried on.

Within two years of the opening of the New Century Campaign, President Lewis was able to announce major gifts to finance the top priority items involving chemistry and physics. The Seeley G. Mudd Foundation was providing $1,250,000 toward the $5 million needed for two chemistry buildings, one for offices and research laboratories and another for classrooms and undergraduate laboratories. The Fairchild Foundation was making a gift of $5,250,000 over the period from 1973 to 1978 for studies in solid state physics, including endowed faculty chairs in electrical engineering and physics, fellowships and scholarships, a large laboratory building, and furnishings and equipment.

Not a cent of the first $25 million raised came from governments.[4] By September 1975, the total in pledges stood at approximately $27 million.

Then other effects of economic belt-tightening began to be felt. An energy shortage accompanied by more inflation contributed to a slowdown in business. For a few months it seemed that the first phase of the New Century Campaign might have to be extended in order to reach the goal of $30 million. The postponement was unnecessary. On 4 June 1976, the board officially learned that the goal had been met, although because of inflation an additional $4,500,000 would be needed to complete all of the projects included in phase one.

The trustees delayed beginning phase two of the New Century Campaign until 1979. At a faculty meeting a year later, on 8 September 1980, Franz announced that the goal was $41,500,000 to be raised by June 1985 and that pledges of $21 million had already been obtained.

The most important new structure to be built from the funds was a library and computing center, which was to be the most costly single capital improvement ever made by the university.

By 1985 the New Century Campaign had brought in a total of $112 million. The E. W. Fairchild-Martindale Library and Computing Center was being occupied. It incorporated the gutted shell of the Mart Library and formed a new gateway to the campus. On the west stood Maginnes Hall and on the east, the Sinclair Laboratory, Neville Hall, and a garden of sculpture, most of which represented gifts from Allentown businessman Philip Berman and his wife, Muriel.

Within the College of Arts and Science, diverse points of view became more clearly defined and gave birth to many new programs.

A diversity of outlooks as much as anything distinguished the college. The only real unity was administrative and procedural. The dean maintained the budget for the departments and presided at college meetings, the one assembly providing each member of the faculty with a window through which to see what was going on in other departments. Arts and science students finalized their course preregistrations with the dean, who was also the principal adviser for arts-engineers during their first four years. The Arts College Committee still existed and from time to time suggested new ventures having a potential for increasing the college's diversity.

In 1967 G. Mark Ellis joined the college office as assistant dean. Ellis also taught English history in the Department of History. In 1972 Yates resigned the deanship and returned to teaching political philosophy. John W. Hunt, whose teaching field was English, came in from Earlham College to replace Yates. Hunt began the practice of appointing a senior member of the faculty as assistant or associate dean to perform some of the duties of the office.

The college maintained an assortment of disciplines that did not fit elsewhere but were considered desirable in themselves and for the education in breadth of all students. Hunt once called his faculty's attention to the diversity in these terms:

> The most important feature distinguishing the College of Arts and Science from the other educational units ... is the lack of a shared base among all of its departments. That is, unlike the other units, no common discipline — other than English which is common to all educational units in the University — underlies instruction in all departments and major programs. ... The faculty in our college is thus diverse in talent, temperament, and interest; faculty from different areas speak different languages in a sense; they view their educational tasks from different perspectives and define them from different assumptions.[5]

It is tempting to think of devotion to the ideal of a liberal education as a unifying objective. Palmer, More, Christensen, and Yates had believed in the value of a liberal education as expounded by Phi Beta Kappans and proponents of honors programs. Deans and members of the faculty had talked as though a liberal education consisted of a mixture of cultural appreciation and preparation for leadership and could be achieved by structuring programs so as to combine knowledge in depth and breadth with the technical skills required for scholarship.

But the deans and many other faculty also knew that a liberal education was not really an operational goal. Culture for its own sake and knowledge for leadership could not be convincingly designed because they could not be precisely defined. An ideal of liberal education was inspirational, a mystique. Even as a mystique, it was academic and aristocratic, a concept with which only a small minority of people agreed.

The vast majority of students had never subscribed to the ideal of a liberal education. Their aims expressed immediate personal goals and anxieties. Students in the sixties had wanted courses with relevance and freedom from requirements. As the counterculture, the draft, and activism passed away, the students of the seventies embraced vocational goals as their predecessors in the pre-Lewis years had done.

The principal functional use of the concept of a liberal education within the College of Arts and Science was as a rationale for opposing both a narrowly conceived vocationalism, which the arts faculty considered characteristic of the College of Engineering, and an absolute freedom of choice that might encourage students to avoid courses considered as essential to a general education, especially in mathematics, the laboratory sciences, and foreign languages.

Not even the distribution requirements of the Curricula in Arts and Science and Arts-Engineering provided a strongly unifying bond. No sooner was the crisis of student unrest faced and resolved than the faculty in the sciences showed a special concern for the rapidly growing amount of material to be learned in science and the tightening of competition for entry into the best graduate schools. Members of the faculty in science were willing to decrease the time given to distribution requirements and free electives in order to provide undergraduates with heavier doses of preprofessional courses. Many students, being strongly career oriented, accepted the science professors' point of view.

Beginning in 1971, the science faculty of the college formulated preprofessional programs resembling those in engineering as alternatives to the existing liberal arts system. The programs originally were styled as curricula to distinguish them from ordinary majors. The first were in Biology, Geological Sciences, and Environmental Sciences and Resource Management (ESRM, an interdepartmental program). Students electing the new program in place of a corresponding major in the B.A. curriculum would take considerably more required courses and technical electives; they would have to roster approximately thirty hours in the humanities and the social sciences, much as was required for students in engineering; they would in some fields need more total credits for graduation than the 120 demanded of students studying for the B.A. degree; and, upon successful completion of the program, they would be awarded a Bachelor of Science degree. On 7 June 1971, the faculty of the university approved all three programs without serious opposition and, on 10 January 1972, adopted a similar B.S. program in Psychology.

The movement toward preprofessional education did not stop at this point. In 1973 the faculty approved with some misgivings a six-year cooperative program with the Hahnemann Medical College and Hospital whereby selected students, after completing two academic years and two summer sessions at Lehigh, might be admitted to the medical school and have their first work there count toward filling the remaining requirements for a degree from Lehigh. In 1974 the university agreed to a similar six-year program with the Medical School of Pennsylvania. In 1975 the Department of Biology structured a special Major in Premedical Science for students in these programs (later, adjustments were made to permit students in both programs to remain three years at Lehigh, without having to take summer work, followed by four years at the medical school).

Other B.S. programs in the College of Arts and Science included Geophysics (1975), Information and Communication Science (1976), and Statistics (1978). In 1979 the Program in Information and Communication Science was renamed Computing and Information Science, and the administrative division that sponsored it was transferred from the Department of Philosophy to the Department of Mathematics and Astronomy (en route, as it turned out, to a resting place in Electrical Engineering). A five-year Program in Geological Engineering—a combination of civil engineering and geological sciences—was put on the books in 1978.

In 1979 the faculty approved a seven-year cooperative program with the University of Pennsylvania School of Dental Medicine similar to the program with the Medical School of Pennsylvania.

Not all of the new science programs were popular with the students. Geophysics, Geological Engineering, Statistics, the B.S. program in Psychology, and the seven-year dental program had few takers. But the medical programs and the B.S. programs in Biology, Geological Sciences, ESRM, and Computing and Information Science had respectable enrollments. In June of 1977 the college awarded sixty-six B.A.'s in the sciences and forty-six B.S.'s. In June 1980, the comparable figures were fifty-nine B.A.'s and forty-seven B.S.'s.

The increase of a vocational spirit was evident in several other ways in the years from 1970 to 1980. In 1978 a Major in Architecture reappeared after an absence of more than seventy-five years. Journalism branched out to include scientific writing. The college office and the departments began formally advising about careers available to students in the humanities and the social sciences. Intercollege committees for directing prelegal and premedical programs were formed. Several departments cooperated with local governments and private employers for giving students experience in field work as interns.

A declining interest in secondary schools concerning the study of foreign languages—a subject long considered one of the bulwarks of a liberal education—increased pressures on the faculty to drop the college's distribution requirement in foreign language. This was done in 1971. Afterward, the Departments of German and Russian and Romance Languages were united to form a single Department of Modern Foreign Languages with Anna P. Herz, the first woman at Lehigh to head an undergraduate teaching department, as chair.

In 1979 Hunt boasted to his faculty, "In virtually every area of professional activity and in all departments we are stronger, better than we were a year or a few years ago, in some areas radically so."[6]

The increase of vocational directions provides only part of the story of developments within the College of Arts and Science. Most of the rest concerns strengthening programs that had little relationship to professional preparation. The addition of women, which had raised undergraduate enrollments from about thirty-one hundred to forty-four hundred, made possible a doubling of the number of faculty in Religion, Fine Arts, Music, and Dramatics along with significant increases in International Relations, Government, Social Relations, English, and Classics. These departments, excepting English, were small, and the slight additions greatly augmented their service to students in all of the colleges.

The faculties in these subjects, along with those in History and Modern Foreign Languages, were responsible for most of the high immediate relevance courses, including those that located the special place of blacks and women in the progress of a western science-based society.

English was almost never without representation on the Phi Beta Kappa council and the staff serving the College Honors Program. The department's faculty enriched cultural life in ways as various as the humorous writings of Professor Ray L. Armstrong for the *Alumni Bulletin*, the poetry readings of John F. Vickrey, the original and inspirational teaching of Peter G. Beidler, and the publication beginning in 1971–72 by undergraduate and graduate students of a small literary arts magazine, *Amaranth*, which had a considerably longer life than any of its predecessors.

Professor David M. Greene in 1969 began putting his immense private collection of recordings of classical music on tape and giving the tapes to the university, thereby originating the Greene Collection, which he continued to develop and whose supervision fell to the library.

In 1968 Albert Hartung succeeded Severs both as chairman of the department and head of the Wells project but in 1975 relinquished the chair to Frank Hook.

Possibly the most pronounced development was a growing awareness of the place of the performing arts in the life of the university. When the word *arts* had first appeared in the Lehigh vocabulary in the context of a Course in Arts and Sciences, the word referred to the liberal arts as these were understood by existing four-year colleges, that is, studies primarily of the classics, rhetoric, mathematics, moral philosophy, and religion. At that time — the early twentieth century — Lehigh did not give academic credit for work in dramatics, music, and painting. The performing arts were considered to be activities even after lecturers or assistants were hired to provide some instruction, for example, J. Fred Wolle in music and Emil Gelhaar in painting. The performing arts became belatedly assimilated into the curricula as the faculty desired to give them continuity and respectability in response to demands for improving the humanistic content of engineering education. As late as 1970 they were, in an academic sense, underdeveloped.

The additional faculty provided means for more courses and some new programs. Music no longer had to rely on offerings at Moravian College in order to sustain a major. The Division of Speech developed a Major in

Dramatics and in 1978 was renamed as Division of Speech and Drama. The new little theater, formed from a remodeling of the Wilbur Powerhouse, provided a facility. In 1976 Jeffery R. Milet, M.F.A. Yale, took over as chairman of the division. In 1982 the division began a program called Research in Theater Technology, using a joint appointment with the Department of Electrical and Computer Engineering.

Fine Arts had augmented its staff earlier with the appointment in 1968 of Carlos J. Alvare in architecture. In 1974 Ricardo Viera became curator of the university's growing collection of art. A turning point arrived in 1978 with the coming of Nicholas Adams and his appointment as chairman. Very shortly thereafter the department was reorganized and renamed as Department of Fine Arts and Architecture. Studio Practice was recognized as a major distinct from the Major in Art History. The 1978 Course in Architecture was quite different from the one that had been closed out at the end of the nineteenth century. That course had been little more than a branch of civil engineering. The new program required no courses in civil engineering although it did demand that students take the same introductory mathematics and physics that all engineering freshmen took and required many newly established architectural courses. It also used some of the architectural courses at other area colleges through the instrumentality of LVAIC. In 1982 the department entered a consortium of colleges and universities, which provided for selected students to study during their junior year at the Institute for Architecture and Urban Studies in New York City.

Some new courses and techniques used in teaching the performing arts, the humanities, and the social sciences came as a result of a development grant of $225,000 received in 1976 from the Andrew W. Mellon Foundation. The purpose of the grant was "to increase teaching flexibility, explore the relationship between the humanities and the professions, and to encourage more effective teaching".[7]

A grant of $452,000 from the National Endowment for the Humanities in 1972 gave reality to a program known as Humanities Perspectives on Technology, or HPT. It was intended to bring a knowledge of the effects of science and technology on the quality of human life to the attention of teachers, administrators, civic and industrial leaders, and perhaps especially, students. The first director was Associate Professor Edward J. Gallagher of the Department of English. In 1976 Stephen M. Cutcliffe (M.A. '73, Ph.D. '76) joined the staff; and in 1977 Steven L. Goldman arrived as director and Andrew W. Mellon Distinguished Professor in the Humanities.

Goldman and Cutcliffe generated further support for HPT. In 1976 they received $50,000 from the NEH to encourage the formation of similar programs at other colleges. In 1979 the name of the program was changed to that of Science, Technology and Society (STS) to conform to nomenclature more usually found among historians and philosophers of science. The following year the NSF, through its program called CAUSE, granted STS

$241,000 for a program entitled "A Science and Engineering Technology Curriculum for the Improvement of a Liberal Education."

Work on a program in East Asian Studies began in 1979. Donald D. Barry of the Department of Government and Raymond Wylie of International Relations headed the organizing committee, whose efforts were rewarded in 1982 by a grant from the U.S. Department of Education.

As liberal studies gained in strength, the idea that the College of Arts and Science existed as a service department for students in engineering virtually disappeared. The service function remained; it was in fact stronger than ever; but it was also tempered by a concern for a more humanistic education for all. Even as the faculty turned more and more to a vocational outlook, they increased the opportunities for career-oriented students to broaden their understanding of the human condition.

Probably the experience of faculty and administrators with student activism in 1967–70 was largely responsible for a readiness to respond to student interests and to tolerate student ways. The faculty agreed to give formal recognition to the accomplishments of undergraduates desiring special interdisciplinary majors, more than one major program, and one or more minor programs (the June 1980 commencement program lists double majors for twenty-six and interdisciplinary majors for five of the graduating seniors in the College of Arts and Science). The program of interdisciplinary seminars for incoming freshmen, directed by Professor Thomas M. Haynes, was continued and strengthened. Reliance on independent study, seminars, study-abroad programs, and the use of undergraduate teaching internships increased. By action of the Forum, small sums were appropriated to subsidize undergraduate research projects.

The faculty in Arts and Science cooperated with those of the other colleges in liberalizing requirements. The dropping of some of the general studies requirements for students in engineering helped to remove the onus associated with required courses of a nonengineering sort. By 1980 one semester of English and one semester of economics were the only remaining absolutely required courses in General Studies. For all students within the university, the second semester of freshman English provided an elective choice.

At the level of graduate studies, the departments in the humanities and the social sciences on the whole made few gains. The Departments of Government and Psychology attempted to improve the quality of college teaching through use of programs leading to the degree of Doctor of Arts. Government became the leading department in turning out graduates with a D.A. degree. Government also began a professional Graduate Program in Public Administration, modeled after that found in many larger universities, and in 1979 awarded its first Master of Public Administration degree.

Only the doctoral programs in English and Government registered an advance in the output of degrees among the departments in Arts and Science. During the decade, English and Government were among the few departments within the university to experience a fairly steady increase in the number of doctorates granted. Still, the proportion given by English and Government was small—10.6 percent of the total for the years 1976–80.

Master's programs within the social sciences and the humanities were, as before, partly dependent upon receiving students from the School of Education, and they suffered when registrations in education declined. Modern Foreign languages had resumed graduate programs in 1971 and closed them out again in 1981, several years after they had become inoperative for lack of students. International Relations terminated its master's program in 1976 in order to concentrate all resources on undergraduate education.

In 1980, when approximately 15 percent of the undergraduate student body was majoring in a field within the social sciences and the humanities, only 5.4 percent of the graduate student body was similarly engaged.

Few if any doctoral candidates in English, History, or Government produced a dissertation through participation in a group research project. Most of them also avoided interdisciplinary subjects. Individual scholarship, applied to a narrowly defined topic, remained the preferred means of creating an acceptable thesis.

As part of this picture, no research centers or institutes appeared specifically to aid graduate students in the humanities. The point is illustrated by the Institute for Eighteenth-Century Studies, which owed its origin to Professor Gipson, who died 29 September 1971. He had several years earlier completed his fifteen-volume work on The British Empire Before the American Revolution. He left his estate to the university, which used it as an endowment to establish in 1972 the institute dedicated to his memory.

The Gipson Institute for Eighteenth Century Studies held annual or biennial conferences on subjects related to life in eighteenth-century America and made available to faculty and students small grants for research related to the eighteenth century. Most of the requests for funds came from faculty and were for the support of individual projects. The institute neither undertook research projects on its own nor helped persons interested in eighteenth-century America to obtain outside funding.

Shortly before the period of student activism, an administrative change came to the College of Arts and Science that had no immediately visible effect on goals and programs. In 1966 Education ceased to be a department within the college. It became the School of Education, and its head, John A. Stoops, became a dean.

Well before 1966, the Department of Education had ceased to be functionally dependent on the college office. Almost all undergraduate work in education had ended by 1962 When Harold Thomas, the incumbent head, retired. Shortly thereafter the little that remained was terminated. A big field was opening in graduate education. A nationwide shortage of elementary and secondary school teachers, principals, and professionals of other sorts existed. Within the Lehigh Valley a vacuum in teacher education appeared, which Lehigh could fill. Lehigh, ready with cadres and programs, became eager through the person of its provost, Glenn J. Christensen, and became doubly able through him and Stoops, Thomas's successor.

Stoops had been assistant superintendent for instruction in the Neshaminy School District, Pennsylvania, and part-time lecturer at Lehigh. From 1962 until Christensen retired as provost, the two men labored to improve instruction in the education professions. They worked on the campus, through the Middle States Association of Colleges and Secondary Schools, and with educational, civic, and political leaders at local, state, and regional levels. Never since the collaboration of Packer and Bishop Stevens in 1865 had two men at Lehigh worked together as harmoniously in as favorable circumstances to inspire growth.

They brought in new faculty, including several older men of established reputation: John S. Cartwright (1962), former superintendent of schools at Carlisle and Allentown with special responsibility for school administration; Natt B. Burbank (1964), former superintendent of schools in Colorado, specializing in secondary education and school administration; and Merle W. Tate (1965), nationally known for his work in educational research. Among the younger faculty were Norman H. Sam (1962); Robert L. Leight (1963); Alfred J. Castaldi, Estoy Reddin, and Nancy Larrick (1964); Thomas Fleck, Jr. (1965); and two who soon received Ed.D.'s from Lehigh, Alice D. Rinehart and Charles W. Guditus (both 1965), both of whom had extensive previous field experience.

The inattention given teacher education by the alumni of the colleges and the trustees was amply evident in the department's physical quarters. For years it had occupied two wood-frame barracks, the last temporary structures remaining from the era of the Second World War, situated at the southeast corner of Packer Hall. Christensen used his influence to obtain and renovate several private residences on the west side of Brodhead Avenue, downhill from the Alumni Memorial Building. The department moved into these and rented other properties in and about Bethlehem for some of its programs.

In the early years of Stoops's tenure, scarcely a month passed without the department undertaking some new activity, making an important commitment, or receiving an honor. Stoops, Cartwright, and Burbank gave effect to the Ed.D. Program, which had been authorized in 1958. Ellis Hagstrom and Norman Sam designed a fifth-year intern program for elementary and secondary school teachers, the Master of Arts in Teaching Program, patterned on a model begun at Harvard in 1952.

Norman Sam became director of the Summer School. Beginning in 1964 and every year thereafter, the number of graduate students taking summer work exceeded the number of undergraduates.

In 1965 the Pennsylvania Department of Public Instruction accepted graduates of the Master of Arts in Teaching Program for permanent certification, thereby allowing Lehigh's Department of Education to determine the standards and courses necessary for professional recognition. Accreditation by the newly formed National Council for the Accreditation of Teacher Education (NCATE) soon followed.

The department augmented its service activities, began summer workshops in children's literature, art, economics, and mathematics and inaugurated programs for training teachers and administrators for community colleges. In 1965 the department received a grant of eighty-eight thousand dollars from the U.S. Office of Education to support a program for training in educational research.

In 1966 the department formed a Lehigh Regional Consortium for Graduate Teaching Education, which within a few years included Lehigh University and Beaver, Ursinus, Allentown, Muhlenberg, Moravian, Marywood, and Wilkes colleges; and it developed a Regional School Study Council for aiding public schools in nearby areas. Also in 1966 the department began an association with Inter American, a private university with campuses located at San Juan and San German, Puerto Rico. The initial contract was for two years and was succeeded by a five-year agreement in which Lehigh augmented its assistance to Inter American through a consortium arrangement.

In February 1964, the department opened a laboratory school to take care of youth in need of special instruction. The first class met in the basement of Drown Hall. Eight children of elementary school age attended. Charles Versacci was general supervisor. Shortly thereafter Ruth B. Parr began preparing a library. During the next half dozen years, the school occupied various locations—a garage, a synagogue, churches, university structures, and abandoned public school buildings.

The energy within the department activated some special community efforts. Christensen and Cartwright worked to bring an educational television station into the Lehigh Valley. They and others inspired the formation of the Lehigh Valley Educational Television Corporation, which set about raising capital from local businesses and industries. On 8 April 1964, the trustees of Lehigh voted to lease the land needed for the station atop South Mountain for a fee of one dollar per year. WLTV began operating in 1965 with Christensen as founding president.

Another community-oriented project produced the Northampton County Area Community College. Christensen, Stoops, and other educational and civic leaders succeeded in establishing a locally chosen board with financial support coming from the area's local governments. Christensen became the first chairman of the board of the NCACC in 1966 and held the position until 1977.

The change in status for Education from a department to a school met with a general acceptance from members of the university faculty. Several faculty were added to the new school, including Lloyd W. Ashby, Raymond Bell, John A. Mierzwa, and Paul Van Reed Miller, Jr.

Within the next several years, the School of Education improved the Master of Arts in Teaching Program, gave separate professional identities to elementary and secondary school teaching and to the education service professions of Counseling, School Psychology, Administration, and Reading; and in the early 1970s it added Programs in Career Education, Social Restoration, Special Education, and Educational Measurements and Research. Candidates for the degree of Ed.D. could specialize in Administration, Reading, Educational Foundations, Counseling, or Educational Measurements and Research.

In 1967 the name of the Laboratory School was officially changed to that of Centennial School. In that year the superintendent of public instruction of the commonwealth approved it for the work being done with exceptional children. Enrollments rapidly increased as parents sought to enter children with special learning problems. Financing came from tuition, which after 1969 was supplemented by payments from the commonwealth.

In 1970 the growing number of students of secondary school age necessitated a separation from elementary school students. The elementary school was called Centennial I and the secondary school, Centennial II. A housing crisis led to negotiations for a permanent meeting place on the eastern edge of the Saucon Valley playing fields. The Forum enthusiastically supported the project. On 1 May 1972, Centennial I and Centennial II, with a combined enrollment of approximately 160 students and a children's library of upward of four thousand titles, occupied the new structure.

Until 1973 enrollments justified the expansion of programs. In that year the students in education accounted for approximately half of the total graduate student body of the university. The school in 1973–74 awarded thirty-four doctorates as compared with fifty-three given by all other parts of the university; and it gave out more than 50 percent of the master's degrees.

After 1973 enrollments declined. Rising tuition at Lehigh in the face of the national economic recession was adversely affecting all graduate enrollments. Also, the national shortage of teachers disappeared; an oversupply was forecast for an indefinite period. Other losses occurred. Hagstrom resigned; Cartwright died (1970); Burbank, Ashby, Tate, and Larrick retired. Christensen in 1969 had resigned as provost, and in 1976 Stoops gave up the deanship. Stout served as acting dean in addition to being dean of the Graduate School. In the fall of 1977, Perry A. Zirkel began a tenure as dean of education and professor of administration and supervision.

Enrollments in Education continued to drop, although they started to rise for graduate students in science and engineering. By 1979 the School of Education had only about three-fifths as many students as it had in 1973. The centennial schools fared even less well. By 1979 the enrollment was down to seventy, less than half of what it had been when the schools had occupied their new building in 1972. Income correspondingly fell.

In contrast with these buffets to enrollments and finances, members of the faculty in Education were gaining in experience and becoming more active in university affairs. They worked on university committees and in the Forum and cooperated with departments in the sciences, the social sciences, and the humanities.

In 1975 the faculty of the university voted to allow the school a representative on the Committee of Educational Policy. Paul Van R. Miller became in 1977−78 the first person from the school to serve as chairman of this committee; and after a year of energetic activity in heading it, he carried through a successful drive to revise its composition, chiefly by reducing the number of members of the administration who sat thereon.

Then on 7 December, 1979 — the anniversary of Pearl Harbor — President Lewis dropped a bomb. He met with the faculty of the school, told them that the school was not an integral part of the university in the same sense that the other three colleges were, called attention to the shakiness of its financial position, and announced that unless deficits were substantially reduced within two years, and the school was operating at approximately a break-even point by the end of five years, the trustees would close it.[8]

Members of the School of Education immediately took the matter up with the university faculty. Dean Zirkel read a statement in the Osborne Room three days later, calling the president's estimate of the school's financial condition "unrealistic and misleading," labeling the statement that the school was not an integral part of the university "capricious" and "repellant," and asking the president to withdraw a letter he had sent to the faculty on the subject "before it become self-fulfilling by destroying the school's credibility with our students, the schools, and the public."

The university faculty eagerly seized on the issue and discussed it, not so much for the merits as for the administration's failure to consult. Feelings against the administration ran high. A movement to censure the trustees and the administration was barely avoided. The faculty approved a motion declaring the failure to consult "a direct and serious affront to the entire Lehigh faculty."[9] Professor Barbara Frankel, chair of the Committee on Educational Policy, appointed a committee to investigate the matter. The outcome had nothing much in it for the School of Education but obtained from the president a promise to consult with the appropriate faculty committees in the future before announcing structural changes that substantially affected educational programs and policies.

It is unlikely that Lewis, Zettlemoyer, and the trustees wished to put an end to the School of Education. True, the trustees as a group seemed largely indifferent to it. From time to time voices among them were heard expressing fears that the growth might overshadow engineering education.[10] But they did not seriously suggest that the school be terminated. On at least one occasion Lewis expressly told the trustees that the development of the school was consistent with the purposes of the university.[11] Furthermore, the school had the faculty and the Forum behind it. A year before Lewis issued his warning, faculty had given the school a vote of confidence by accepting a highly controversial Undergraduate Education Minor. In effect, teacher education and the programs associated with it were too well entrenched within the university to be easily dislodged. A more likely explanation of Lewis's action is that he was genuinely concerned about the financial position of the school, wanted it to curtail or desist from activities that it could no longer financially support, and chose ill-advised language to convey the message.

The School of Education did some retrenching. The centennial schools gave up the building in the Saucon Valley, which became storage space for the university libraries, and rented more suitable quarters closer to the main campus. The retrenchment did not mean stalemate. The faculty in education also strengthened existing programs and developed some new ones.

The public heard no more about plans to close the school. In 1983 it was reorganized as a single department. Zirkel resigned as dean and became university professor of education. Miller took the chairmanship of the department, which shortly thereafter was restyled as College of Education with Miller remaining as dean.

The post-Neville development of the College of Business Administration contained nothing resembling the threat that shook the faculty in the School of Education. The support shown by trustees and administrators for instruction in business was part of a general respect of engineers and businessmen for each other. Moreover, the college had a wealthy and loyal body of alumni, several of whom sat on the board of trustees, whereas the alumni of the School of Education were loyal but not wealthy.

A few changes in the College of Business suggest what might be called growing pains. A general reorganization of departments followed a report of the visiting committee for the college in 1966. In 1968 the name was changed from College of Business Administration to College of Business and Economics. In 1971 Tripp retired as dean and was succeeded by Brian G. Brockway, who had taught business law. Brockway remained as dean until 1978, when he relinquished the post to Richard W. Barsness and became distinguished university professor of law.

At the undergraduate level, the college by 1968—69 was offering seven majors — Accounting, Economics, Economic Statistics, Finance, Foreign Careers, Marketing, and Management. All were broadly vocational; not one was narrowly occupational. As the notice in the *Catalog* for 1968—69 explained, "An increasing number of bachelor graduates are not going directly into business but go on to law school, to graduate study in economics, or graduate schools of business, and many of the latter go on to research and analytical studies of management or economics."

In various ways the undergraduate course was modernized and improved. The Department of Mathematics began offering a four-semester sequence in calculus, probability, and related fields especially for students in business, management, and the social sciences (BMSS), which lifted from the undergraduates in the College of Business the burden of having to take the engineering-oriented calculus sequence. A second change involved the use of facilities in the Computing Center for teaching the applications of computer technology to problems in business. A thrid was the acceptance of opportunities for undergraduates to assist in teaching and research, as promoted by the Forum. Several of the faculty in business employed undergraduates as apprentice teachers and research assistants.

Graduate teaching took up an increasingly large share of faculty time. The college offered an M.A. in economics, an M.S. in business economics, management sciences and (for a time) accountancy, the Ph.D. in economics and business and industrial economics, and in 1971 established a Doctor of Arts program that was designed for persons wishing to prepare for college teaching. By June 1980 the college had awarded 6 D.A. degrees, 27 Ph.D.'s, and 211 M.A.'s and M.S.'s.

In addition, there was the professional program leading to the degree of M.B.A., which became far and away the most popular graduate program in the university outside of the School of Education. By June 1980 the college had awarded 1,458 M.B.A. degrees. By this time, too, Lehigh as an employer had found the degree serviceable. Eight members of the administration, as distinct from the supporting staff, and three members of the teaching faculty possessed a Lehigh M.B.A. degree.

The indications were that, given enough time, the M.B.A. degree might rival engineering degrees as an emblem of the starting place for alumni to move into the front ranks of corporate management.

Outside of the classroom, the faculty in Business and Economics divided much time between professional counseling and teaching and research. In the post-Neville years, a good deal of the professional counseling and teaching was carried on through two nonresearch centers. One was the Center for Economic Education, established in 1976 as part of a nationwide network of more than 150 centers under the guidance of the Joint Council for Economic Education. In the summer the center conducted an institute for giving teachers at all levels more information concerning the content and teaching of economics. The center also sponsored workshops, seminars, and guest lectures.

The second group for professional counseling was the Small-Business Center, formed in 1977 as a means of aiding small businesses in the area while giving students practical experience as counselors, for which they received academic credit. The Small Business Center offered one-day courses for local businessmen. Representative subjects included "Designing a Budget Projection," "Business Application Using Lotus 1−2−3," and "Market Research and Organization for Export."

Much research in economics and finance resembled that in the other social sciences in taking the form of individual projects, which might or might not have outside financial support. Yet in these and related fields, a trend toward team projects existed. These, like their counterparts in engineering, could be classified as being among the applied sciences; and they naturally accepted administration through centers. In 1965 a Center for Business and Economics was organized with Professor Elmer C. Bratt as director. When in 1968 he retired, Associate Professor Warren Pillsbury took the post. The name of the center had shortly before that been changed to Center for Business Economics and Urban Studies to account for a somewhat broadened scope. In 1972 the scope was further expanded to include many other sorts of research in the social sicences, and the name was altered to that of Center for Social Research with Tripp, now retired from the deanship, acting as coordinator. Later, Professor Roy E. Herrenkohl of the Department of Social Relations in the College of Arts and Science became the director.

A special resource for both the Center for Social Research and the College of Business was a program styled the Urban Observatory, organized in the mid-seventies in Allentown. Through the observatory Allentown had access to Lehigh's research facilities for help in solving many problems. The observatory was, said Libsch, "'a laboratory' — for Lehigh research in urban technology and municipal government. In particular, the Observatory provides research opportunities related to such national problems as fiscal health of the cities, fire and police productivity, storm water, sewage and solid waste management, citizen participation and power structures in government — i.e., research involving technical, management, and social considerations."[12] Many of the projects undertaken for the Urban Observatory by the Center for Social Research and the College of Business and Economics involved undergraduates as well as graduate students and faculty.

In 1980 the Fairchild-Martindale Center for the Study of Private Enterprise was formed pursuant to the receipt of a grant of five hundred thousand dollars from Mr. and Mrs. Harry T. Martindale ('27). Professor J. Richard Aronson became director of the center, which in 1981–82 began a lecture series on themes related to the future of private enterprise, sponsored by the Scholl Foundation.

In 1973 the name of the College of Engineering was changed to College of Engineering and Applied Science in order to more accurately reflect the work going on there.

The administration of the college remained simple. Karakash retained the deanship until 1981, when he retired, relinquising the position to Donald M. Bolle of Electrical Engineering. In 1975 Professor Curtis Clump of Chemical Engineering succeeded Robert Gallagher as associate dean. A year earlier a second associate deanship had been created and filled by Arthur F. Gould, whose former position as chairman of the Department of Industrial Engineering was taken by George F. Kane.

Undergraduate enrollments fell off sharply in 1972, reflecting both a decline in the national market for engineers and the impact of the tarnished image of engineering among high-school students. After that, contrary to the national trend, applications for admission both for men and women climbed year by year to 1980, when a slight drop occurred.

The dispersal of undergraduates among the various departments contained no surprises. Most of the students were to be found in the traditional fields of civil, mechanical, electrical, chemical, metallurgical, and industrial engineering. Engineering Mechanics, which had begun a departmental existence in 1956, was joined in 1968 to Mechanical Engineering with Ferdinand Beer as chairman. Engineering Mechanics never had more than a few students.

As in former years, undergraduates preferred applied fields in preference to pure science, as can be illustrated by summaries of degrees awarded in June 1980. At that time one senior received a B.A. in Physics, six were awarded a B.S. in Engineering Physics, twelve won a B.S. in computer Engineering, and eighty-three received the B.S. in Electrical Engineering. At the same ceremonies, no one was awarded a B.A. in chemistry, nineteen budding chemists received a B.S., and seventy-three earned a B.S. in Chemical Engineering.

The rising interest in electronics was the most obvious development within the undergraduate programs in engineering.

The trend extended back into the Neville years. At the time of Whitaker's death, the Department of Electrical Engineering maintained a strong power option but did not have a comparably strong microwave program. Karakash set about making up for lost time. A major forward step occurred with the acquisition in 1964 of Walter E. Dahlke, an applied solid state physicist from Germany, with funds supplied by the NSF. Other faculty were added. Alfred K. Susskind came from MIT in 1968 to head the department. Ten years later computer engineering was separated from electrical engineering, although both remained within the department. The Program in Computer Engineering was derived partly from developments within electrical engineering and partly from work by Donald J. Hillman who directed the Program in Information Science.

In 1980 Bolle succeeded Susskind as chairman of Electrical Engineering and further strengthened the Program in Computer Science. The department was renamed that of Electrical and Computer Engineering. Three years later Bolle brought in Eric D. Thompson, who became chairman. A further reorganization included a change of name to Department of Computer Science and Electrical Engineering. The reorganized department had two divisions, Computer Science headed by Hillman and Electrical Engineering directed by D. Richard Decker.

Acquiring familiarity with microelectronic devices was the work of a relatively few years. A Computing Center had been organized in 1966 with headquarters near Electrical Engineering in Packard Laboratory. In 1968, after much discussion, the trustees agreed to add to the GE 225 a Control

Data Corporation 6400 at a cost of approximately two million dollars. The NSF was expected to pay part of the cost (which it did), and the rest was to come from the users over a six-year period.

From that time on, the use of electronic devices rapidly spread. Engineering students, at one time identifiable by slide rules hanging from their belts, now appeared indistinguishable from students in business, arts, science, and education. All students, faculty, and administrators who had to make calculations were using pocket-sized calculators. Faculty assigned problems requiring students to use computers and to devise computer programs.

The College of Engineering revised the uniform freshman year to include "Engineering 1, Introduction to Engineering Problems," described in the *Catalog* as "a three-hour course offering programming of elementary engineering problems in compiler language through lectures and preparation of problem solutions in fields represented by the college curricula." The university began dealing with a new form of plagiarism, the theft of a computer program.

In subsequent years, the center obtained other computers. These also began appearing in departments having special needs.

Scholars and journalists began talking of a "computer revolution" and "the dawn of the computer age" as though a radically new stage in the scientific and technological revolution had been reached. It is not a function of this history to investigate the truth or falsity of this claim, nor even to assess the full impact of electronics on education at Lehigh. Suffice it to say that by 1980 Lehigh seemed to be much more a consumer than an inventor of electronic devices. The university was using them to quicken the progress being made in improving administration, library facilities, classroom teaching, and the research being done in all centers and institutes.

The most immediate effects of electronic devices on Lehigh were recreational, procedural, and instructional. Electronic music was heard in Lamberton Hall and the Packer Memorial church. Graduate students began using word processors instead of typewriters to write their dissertations. Undergraduate and graduate programs in computer science appeared. In the Administrative Systems Office, Thomas J. Verbonitz computerized the university payroll system. The registrar's office came under pressure to computerize some of its operations. When the decade ended, plans were under way to house the Computing Center beside the library in what materialized as the E. W. Fairchild-Martindale Library and Computing Center.

Some of the most spectacular work in computer studies was begun in 1979 by a program entitled CAD/CAM (Computer Assisted Design/Computer Assisted Manufacturing). CAD/CAM was originally based on the Departments of Mechanical Engineering and Mechanics and Industrial Engineering. These two departments began CAD/CAM with the idea of improving the instruction of undergraduates in the application of computers to design and to manufacturing systems. A goal of $5,500,000 was set, to be reached within five years. By the end of eighteen months, $4,400,000 had been received from government and private sources, including $2 million in cash from IBM. Courses and laboratories containing the latest computers were set up in the two departments. Within several years of its beginning, the program was expanded to include laboratories in civil and electrical engineering. Graduate instruction was added, including an interdisciplinary Manufacturing System Engineering (MSE) program.

In addition to serving the on-campus population, the Computing Center gained a large off-campus clientele. The original NSF grant for establishing it provided for the center to be the focus of a regional educational computing network. Soon ten educational institutions in the Lehigh region were joined to the center by means of telecommunications facilities. Other nonuniversity users such as Behlehem Steel purchased its services. When the decade closed, the Computing Center was appearing as a nucleus for making Lehigh University a technology center for the Lehigh Valley.

All of the research centers and institutes used computers. All were also interdisciplinary. In 1980 there were nine research centers and six institutes serving science and engineering. A survey of membership lists as of March 1981 shows 65.4 percent of the faculty in Engineering and Physical Sciences and almost all of the faculty in Biology and Geology as belonging to or being associated with one or more institutes or centers. Less than 20 percent of the faculty in other parts of the university were similarly affiliated.

Fritz Laboratory was now called a center. Testing, using the machine installed in 1955, remained important as research along independent lines expanded. During the 1960s the staff of Fritz Laboratory grew from 80 to 130, the amount of research increased, and two salients appeared. One was a Tall-Buildings Program, begun by Lynn S. Beedle, the director of the laboratory. The program dealt not only with the design of tall buildings but also with their social, political, and economic environment. The other salient was called Structural Analysis. Its origin could be traced back to the mid-1950s, when the laboratory had successfully bid on an invitation issued by the National Cooperative Highway Research Program to define fatigue resistance of bridge welds. John M. Fisher (Ph.D. '64) became the dominant figure in the salient of Structural Analysis, which also included metallurgists such as Stout and, somewhat later, Alan W. Pense (Ph.D. '62).

Both salients continued their development through the 1970s. The growth of the tall-buildings project embraced the organization and operation of a Council on Tall Buildings and Urban Habitats with members from more than seventy countries and a five-volume publication, *Monograph on Planning and Design of Tall Buildings*. The work on fatigue was furthered by a Structural Stability Research Council. Both councils had their headquarters on the Lehigh campus. In 1977 the Pennsylvania Department of Transportation arranged for the Fritz Laboratory to initiate a major study of the fatigue behavior of bridges in the commonwealth. The work of the laboratory led to the Structural Stability Research Council's *Guide to Stability Design Criteria for Metal Structures*, the leading reference book in the field. In 1983 Fisher and Pense were called upon to find reasons why a section of Route I—95 in Connecticut had fallen into the Mianus River, killing four persons. Later, they investigated other disasters and defects to which considerable publicity was attached. In 1983 the work on tall buildings became the subject of an Institute for the Study of the High-Rise Habitat.

In many ways Fritz Laboratory was typical of all research centers. The faculty associated with it came from all three colleges and many departments, although one department (in this case, Civil Engineering) provided what might be called a permanent cadre. The faculty associated with Fritz Laboratory had great freedom of choice in applying for grants in support of projects compatible with the broad aims of the center and the facilities available. Sometimes private parties or public agencies made immediate and profitable use of the results of the research. Often the results were only potentially useful. They were always made available to the general public through professional literature and, if they had popular appeal, through the mass media.

Being loosely organized, the typical research center appeared as a self-adjusting mechanism to correct for changes in the factors affecting its operation. Research centers at Lehigh remained flexible through a respect for liberty of research and teaching and a sensitivity to shifts in the sources of funds as these became available in response to frictions in a rapidly changing society. A few centers, such as the Fritz Laboratory and the Computing Center, depended on certain sorts of large and expensive equipment and projected an appearance of stability although their operations were almost constantly in flux. Most centers lacked this dependency and seemed unstable. Their components might consist of institutes, laboratories, offices, task forces, or other sorts of association. These were formed, changed direction, broke apart and were reorganized, increased or decreased in size or importance, altered in membership or policies, even disappeared, often with astonishing rapidity. Yet at any given moment, the center was vibrant and concerned with the advancement of knowledge.

Energy research provides an example of a cluster of activities that in the 1970s took form as a center. Early in the decade, an energy crisis, or "crunch" as it was more picturesquely called, brought home to Americans the limited extent of the world's remaining resources of timber, coal, oil, and gas. Government, industry, foundations, and educational institutions participated in a scramble to find other sources of energy and to make a more efficient use of traditional forms. Soon the scientists studying energy had also to be concerned with economic, political, and environmental effects, which researchers in other fields were identifying. At Lehigh in 1972, a Task Force for Energy Research was organized, which by 1975 had seventeen projects involving eighteen faculty from all three colleges and was variously funded by four industrial concerns, four governmental agencies, and three professional societies. The projects, wrote Libsch in his report to the faculty on 8 September 1975, involved research pertaining to "(1) environmental control of fuel combustion products; (2) properties and handling characteristics of coal as well as fluidized bed combustion; (3) synthesis catalysts in coal processing; (4) solar and electrochemical energy storage; (5) materials behavior in nuclear and coal gasification reactors; (6) heat transfer; (7) off-shore drilling stuctures; and (8) econometric models related to electric utility systems."

For the next several years, the work of the task force represented the most rapidly expanding research activity within the university. In 1978 the task force was reorganized as the Energy Research Center. The university *Catalog* for 1979 listed thirty-three participating faculty. Professor Edward K. Levy of the Department of Mechanical Engineering and Mechanics was the director. All departments in the College of Engineering as well as the Departments of Social Relations, Economics, and Management and Marketing, were represented.

The Energy Research Center maintained close ties with industry. Among other activities it operated an Energy Liaison Program through which participating companies and government agencies had access to faculty consultants, made use of laboratory facilities and library services, and received assistance on research problems, feasibility studies, and other projects related to energy. An Energy Intern Program provided opportunities for graduate students to receive part of their training in industry. The participating student could do a research internship under the joint supervision of company research staff and a faculty adviser.

Bioengineering represented another cluster of activities that became organized within a research center. The work in bioengineering was closely associated with Laszlo K. Nyiri, who worked with Marvin Charles of the Department of Chemical Engineering. The two developed a project sponsored by NASA that was concerned with the design of a "bioreactor" for early space laboratory flights and was intended to "help determine the behavior of mammalian cells under zero-gravity conditions including their capability to produce hormones not produced under terrestrial gravity."[13] The project, together with others maintained by faculty in the Departments of Chemical Engineering, Civil Engineering, Chemistry, and Biology, served as a prelude to the formation in 1980 of the Biotechnology Research Center with Charles and the provost, Arthur E. Humphrey, as codirectors.

Other research centers for science and engineering included the Applications of Mathematics, Information and Computer Science, Marine and Environmental Studies, Health Sciences, Materials Research, and Surface and Coatings Research.

The Center for Marine and Environmental Studies was the most recent form of the Center for Marine Science, begun in 1962 by Keith Chave and in his day based largely on faculty in Geology and Biology. It had broadened its scope to include engineering and now had laboratories in Williams and Chandler-Ullmann halls, in Fritz Laboratory, and at Stone Harbor, New Jersey. James M. Parks of Geology was the director.

The Center for Health Sciences was established in 1972, "designed to coordinate the activities of the Institute of Pathobiology, Biological Chemistry and Biophysics, Visual Science, and Bioengineering."[14] The Institute of Pathobiology had been created in 1971 and had originally been attached to the Center for Marine Science. A later reorganization of the Center for Health Sciences eliminated the institute and established two divisions, dealing respectively with (1) Biological Chemistry and Biophysics and (2) Bioengineering. Ned D. Heindel, Howard S. Bunn Professor of Chemistry, became the director.

Institutes engaging in research, which were often separately identified, were usually attached to centers or departments. Among the research institutes in 1979 were those designated (1) Emulsion Polymers; (2) National Printing Ink (organized as part of the Center for Surface and Coatings Research); (3) Metal Forming (attached to the Department of Metallurgy and Materials Engineering); (4) Pathobiology; (5) Wetlands (operating with the Center for Marine and Environmental Studies); and (6) Thermo-Fluid Engineering and Science, which included staff from the Departments of Chemical Engineering, Mechanical Engineering and Mechanics, and Physics.

Occasionally one heard allegations to the effect that the dependence on sponsored research interfered with academic freedom, meaning in this context the right of a member of the faculty to pick the subject of his study. The allegations had some substance, inasmuch as support, whether private or public, usually came with strings attached.

On the other hand, as long as the university had the means for physical expansion, sponsored research helped to prevent obsolescence. When grantsmanship produced a major project, the persons needed for conducting it could be hired if they were not already present, and most of the faculty so obtained could be used by the departments for teaching. That most of the research faculty were young (sometimes coming fresh from a postdoctoral fellowship or even still working on a dissertation) goes almost without saying. As long as the university could afford to add faculty and staff in this way it could keep abreast of many technological developments in the teaching provided for the students, even when the rates of social and technological change alarmingly speeded up.

The number of faculty hired principally for research in science and engineering was growing. Some of the research faculty taught only one course, and that for graduate students. Some did not meet classes at all, although they might give occasional lectures and advise students on doctoral dissertations. Graduate enrollments in engineering had declined in the post-Vietnamese recession but, beginning in 1974, again began to rise. In the fall of 1980, the college had 447 graduate students, with about 53 percent being full time, that is, rostering at least twelve semester hours. During the same period the number of foreign-born graduate students, especially from Taiwan and mainland China, was also rising. All of this helped to keep graduate and undergraduate programs up-to-date.

While teaching programs expanded, Lehigh's position as a resource for local governments and industries within the Lehigh Valley also grew. This was true in spite of the extensive services provided to industries, governments, and civic groups by the valley's five four-year colleges and two community colleges. Largely because of an emphasis on advanced work in science, engineering, education, and business, Lehigh could supply aid not duplicated by the other educational institutions.

One source of aid came from facilities. As Libsch noted in a report to the faculty on 8 September 1980, "Research equipment continues the course of greater sophistication, shorter obsolescence, and substantially higher initial as well as maintenance costs." Local industries sometimes recorded savings by using equipment at Lehigh instead of purchasing their own, for example, buying computer time and using the testing machine in Fritz Laboratory.

A second source of aid to the community came from the teaching faculty. With the advent of community colleges, Lehigh in 1967 had closed out a small adult educational program, although some departments in engineering had continued giving short noncredit courses in subjects for which enrollments were sufficient to pay the costs. In 1978 the university established an Office of Continuing Education headed by a director who coordinated the short courses and expanded the program. The *Catalog* for 1981−83 described continuing education programs as being "self-contained educational packages, designed to meet the needs of specific adult groups. Their content, schedules, and timing are adapted to best serve the audiences for which they are developed. ... These programs carry no regular academic credit, but participants can earn continuing education units (CEU's) in appropriate offerings." Most of the courses were scheduled for two or three days on subjects included within the curricula of engineering and business, for example, "Industrial Robots for Manufacturing," taught by Professor Mikell P. Groover of Lehigh's Department of Industrial Engineering, "Project Management," offered by Ronald LaFleur of the Project Management Assistance Corporation, and "New Strategies in Foreign Exchange Risk Management," taught by Professor Carl Beidleman of Lehigh's Department of Finance.

As the Lewis administration drew to a close, Lehigh resembled a tree whose roots were flourishing because the branches were healthy and growing.

The physical campus exemplified the situation. All of the major structures of the old Lehigh — the roots — remained in constant, heavy use. They flourished because of a will to retain them and a discovery that with suitable renovations they could serve a progressive education.

Even the Packer Memorial Church, whose original religious orientation differed from the secularism of the new Lehigh, often bustled with activity. Chaplain Hubert L. Flesher, who had arrived in 1971, made the church an essential part of a policy of ecumenism. There, too, the Bethlehem Bach Choir, founded by J. Fred Wolle in 1899, held festivals on two weekends in May; and the Lehigh Glee Club performed vespers at Christmas-tide. Other concerts, services, and convocations utilized the church's facilities. Early in the 1980s, Chaplain Flesher conducted a successful campaign of renovation.

The instructional buildings of the new Lehigh—the branches—spread fanlike out from the older structures and signified an unrestricted possibility of growth commensurate with what the roots could support.

Bishop William Bacon Stevens had summarized those roots in the commencement address of 1869. Asa Packer's university, he had said, was established to serve America by providing a scientific education capable of producing alumni who would

> make their studies tell in their practical benefits in developing the resources of the land, in opening up new highways of communication, in broadening the range of human comfort, in increasing the productive power of machinery, in utilizing the agencies of the material world, and in doing those things which make the world a better place to live in, draw out of it new treasures, add to man's domestic and social comfort, and elevate him in the scale of moral beings. These are the kind of men needed in this bustling, wrestling, grasping age.

The age in 1980 was still "bustling, wrestling, grasping" and still needed the kind of men Bishop Stevens had looked to Lehigh to provide.

The bishop had continued the discourse by observing that science, to be fruitful, had to serve higher purposes. He had held these to be moral and religious. Presidents of the university, faculty, and alumni in later years had broadened the scope and replaced the bishop's focus with a more naturalistic orientation. The surviving idea was that of scientific education accompanied by cultural, humanistic, and liberal studies, that is, studies in the human condition.

According to Packer and Stevens, all studies, being practical, were to be accomplished by using resources drawn from the Lehigh Valley, the commonwealth, and the nation. Applied science was to be the foundation. This necessitated constant attention to the wishes and needs of the community, especially of its industries.

By 1980 the emphasis on applied science in the service of community remained, although the means of accomplishing it had evolved. In Packer's time, the university had looked to the valley's shops, mines, and railroads for some of the instruction given to students. Beginning with the end of the First World War, this practice was reversed. Lehigh developed as a resource for the persons and organizations on which it had previously depended. It was now supplying instruction, advice, equipment, and facilities for individuals and for industrial, commercial, social, and civic groups.

Events in the 1980s continued to cement the new relationship through expanded programs of teaching and research and additional instructional and extracurricular facilities. A new venture expressing the altered relationship was the organization in 1983 (with help from the commonwealth) of a Ben Franklin Technology Center, a consortium of private and public groups for stimulating the formation and improvement of science-based enterprises within the Lehigh Valley region. Another salient involved an extension of aid to the financially embarrassed Bethlehem Steel Corporation. Lehigh (again with help from the commonwealth) in the mid-1980s purchased most of the Homer Research Laboratories of Bethlehem Steel atop South Mountain and began using them for educational purposes.

The evolving relationship with society at large gave Lehigh a double position. As a technology resource, it was a creditor and society, a debtor; but from a pedagogical point of view, these roles were reversed. Lehigh had to pass through the communities of its clienteles in order to do its job, analogous to the progression of work in the old buildings, "passing through" work in the new structures to gain renewed vigor. Lehigh was in society's debt for understanding its needs and for the sort of student who might best be able to supply these needs. To be itself, and to know itself, it had to take essential elements of its being from the outside world to which it was giving much.

Harvard Professor Daniel Bell had pointed out that a professional and technical class was gaining ascendency in ruling the world, manifesting "the centrality of theoretical knowledge as the source of innovation and policy formulation."[15] Bell's thesis has to be modified in the light of America's democratic meritocracy. Politicians with nonscientific ways of thinking and acting are still in charge of public policy; their strength depends only in part on a meritocracy based on theoretical knowledge. This merit principle is stronger for management in business, industry, and the administrative side of governments than for leadership among social and political groups utilizing popular elections. Even so, elected leaders have to consult the possessors of theoretical knowledge. In turn, the technical elite, in order to be able to work effectively with elected officials, has to have a broad understanding of the human condition.

In the terms used by Bell, Lehigh's historic purpose has been that of supplying the country with experts primed to advance the dominance of theoretical knowledge through practical work as scientists, engineers, teachers, businessmen, and professionals having comparable scientific outlooks.

By 1980 thirty-seven thousand alumni and alumnae were spread around the globe as evidence of the extent to which the purpose was being fulfilled, living proof that education at Lehigh, being "right for the times," as President Likins had said, was yet no more than Packer's principles could bear.

Notes

Abbreviations

AIEE	American Institute of Electrical Engineers
AIME	American Institute of Mining Engineers
ASCE	American Society of Civil Engineers
ASME	American Society of Mechanical Engineers
B&W	the *Brown and White*
FM	Minutes of the faculty
JEE	*Journal of Engineering Education*
LAB	*Lehigh Alumni Bulletin*
LL	Linderman Library, Lehigh University. (Where the only repository is the Lehigh Room of the Linderman Library, the citation is Lehigh Room, LL.)
PC	Lehigh University Presidents' Correspondence, 1866–1921
SPEE	Society for the Promotion of Engineering Education
TM	Minutes of the Board of Trustees

Introduction

1. Daniel Bell, *The Coming of Post-Industrial Society: A Venture in Social Forecasting* (N.Y.: Basic Books, 1973), 14.

Chapter 1. Founding

1. A. K. McClure, *Old Time Notes of Pennsylvania* (Philadelphia: John C. Winston Co., 1905), vol. 2, 79–80, 82.

2. William Bacon Stevens, "The Lehigh University, Its Origin and Aims: Historical Discourse" pamphlet. (Philadelphia, publisher unknown, 1896), 13. Copy in Lehigh Room, LL. The discourse was delivered on the first University Day, June 24, 1869, and is still the best single source of information concerning the founding of Lehigh University.

3. The early history of engineering education was until recently combined with that of applied science, although the origins of the two were different, and applied science is a much broader subject. A nineteenth-century account of considerable value is Abram S. Hewitt, "A Century of Mining and Metallurgy in the United States," ASME *Transactions* 5 (May 1876–February 1877): 164–96. A report appearing approximately forty years later, which has supplied later scholars with useful information, is that of Charles R. Mann, *A Study of Engineering Education*, Bulletin #11 of the Carnegie Foundation for the Advancement of Teaching (N.Y.: 1918). The next important survey in point of time was that of the report of the SPEE written by William

E. Wickenden, catalogued as Society for the Promotion of Engineering Education, *Report of the Investigation of Engineering Education 1923–1929*, (Pittsburgh, Pa.: SPEE, 1930). See also William E. Wickenden, "The School of Engineering," in *Higher Education in America*, ed. Raymond A. Kent (Boston: Ginn & Co., 1930), 192–242. Several recent summaries of the early history of engineering education are Huge A. Meier, "The Ideology of Technology," in *Technology and Social Change in America*, ed. Edwin T. Layton, Jr., (New York: Harper & Row, 1973); Edwin T. Layton, Jr., *The Revolt of the Engineers* (Cleveland, Ohio: The Press of Case Western Reserve University, 1971); and Lawrence P. Grayson, "A Brief History of Engineering Education in the United States," *JEE* (December 1977): 246–64. Indispensable are the now fairly numerous histories of engineering education in specific countries and of individual engineering colleges, professional societies, disciplines, and technological achievements.

4. Grayson, "A Brief History of Engineering Education," 250.

5. Quoted in R. W. Raymond, "Biographical Notice of Eckley B. Coxe," AIME, *Transactions* 25 (1896): 470.

6. William Bacon Stevens, *Autobiography* typescript, Lehigh Room, LL.

7. The rumor—styled by the author a "tradition"—is described in David B. Skillman, *The Biography of a College: Being the History of the First Century of the Life of Lafayette College*, vol. 1 (Easton, Pa.: Lafayette College, 1932), 279.

8. This article is reproduced, pp. 5–9, in Philip M. Palmer, "History of the College of Arts and Science, Lehigh University" unfinished ms. typescript, Lehigh Room, LL.

9. Henry B. Nason, ed., *Biographical Record of the Officers and Graduates of the Rensselaer Polytechnic Institute, 1824–1886* (Troy, N.Y.: William H. Young, 1887), 566.

10. Edgar Fahs Smith, "Charles Mayer Wetherill, 1825–1871," *Journal of Chemical Education* 29 (1929): 2174.

Chapter 2. Settling In: 1866–1880

1. *The Education of Henry Adams* (first published by the Massachusetts Historical Society, 1918; reprint, N.Y.: The Heritage Press, 1942), 221, 224.

2. Probably the best of the early descriptions of Packer Hall is that of William Griffith, '76, reproduced in "Life at Lehigh in the 'Seventies,'" *LAB* 8, no. 3 (December 1920): 6. A description of the architectural features can be found in Sarah Bradford Landau, *Edward T. and William A. Potter: American High Victorian Architects* (Ph.D. diss., New York University, 1978).

3. Morris Bishop, *A History of Cornell* (Ithaca: Cornell University Press, 1962), 85–90.

4. For example, at Cornell between 1868 and 1876, tuition varied between twenty and sixty dollars a year. At Lafayette in 1866 it was forty-five dollars yearly, a sum raised to seventy-five dollars per year for the engineering course when it became fully established.

5. Henry S. Drinker, Alumni Address, 6 June 1916, *Proceedings of the Alumni Association, 1915–16*, 34–35.

6. Most material concerning the preparatory class is contained in *FM* from 1871 to 1873. See also Minutes of the trustees' Executive Committee, 1 July 1872.

7. Dropout rates are estimated by comparing the size of the first year class with that of the senior class three years later. At this early period there were almost no students transferring in from other colleges and universities or transferring within Lehigh from one school to another.

8. Joseph M. Levering, *A History of Bethlehem, Pennsylvania, 1741—1892* (Bethlehem, Pa.: Times Publishing Co., 1903), 762. On 1 September 1877 an article appeared on the front page of the *Bethlehem Daily Times* to the effect that a Mr. S. Howard-Smith, a graduate of Columbia College, was opening a private preparatory school for Lehigh in the Anthracite Building (the headquarters of the Lehigh Valley Railroad). Nothing more appears concerning this earlier attempt at a private preparatory school.

9. Right Reverend William B. Stevens, "Report of the Bishop," *Journal of the Diocese of Pennsylvania* (1872): 40—41.

10. In 1916 Professor Benjamin Miller, on a trip to Brazil, talked with one of the early alumni. "The oldest graduate met was Raymundo Floresta de Miranda, M.E. '72. Mr. de Miranda was sent to Lehigh by the Brazilian Government and most of his time since returning to Brazil has been spent in the construction and operation of the Government railroads." *LAB* 3, no. 3 (April 1916): 25.

11. Catherine Drinker Bowen, *A History of Lehigh University* (Bethlehem, Pa.: The Lehigh Alumni Bulletin, 1924), 68.

12. "The University's First Four Years," *The Lehigh Quarterly* 1, no. 1 (January 1891): 57—58.

13. Ernst Earnest, *Academic Procession: An Informal History of the American College 1636 to 1953* (Indianapolis, Ind: The Bobbs-Merrill Co., 1953).

14. Letter from an alumnus, *Burr* 3, no. 10 (June 1884): 118—19. The entire mock program for 26 June 1873 is reprinted in Griffith, "Life at Lehigh," 3.

15. "The University's First Four Years," 57—58; "In the Old Days," *LAB* 9, no. 4 (January 1921): 19.

16. E. H. Williams, *The Lehigh University, 1866—1886* (South Bethlehem, Pa., 1886), 76 (hereafter cited as Williams, *20-Year Book*).

17. Williams, *20-Year Book*, 108; "In the Old Days," 20.

18. *B&W* 28 January 1895. The thought is also expressed in Eckley B. Coxe, Annual Address of the Alumni Association of Lehigh University, 19 June 1878 (untitled) (Philadelphia, Pa., 1878).

19. *FM*, December 18 1876; 24, 29, 31 January, 2, 6, 12 February, 5 March 1877.

20. *TM*, 20 June 1878.

21. Drinker presented the "address" to the board on behalf of the Alumni Association, *TM*, 20 June 1878. The address was printed by the association. Copy in LL.

Chapter 3. The Railroad Years: 1880—1900

1. *Burr* (24 January 1894).

2. Ringer was first promoted to the rank of assistant professor and a few months later was elevated to a full professorship. This was the only assistant professorship given before the trustees formally adopted the rank in 1897.

3. The ceremony and the speeches at the laying of the cornerstone, together with a description of the church and of the contents of the cornerstone, may be found in *Exercises at the Celebration of the Founder's-Day, Thursday, October 8, 1885*. The ceremony and speeches at the consecration of the church are contained in *The Service of the Consecration of the Packer Memorial Church of the Lehigh University*. Both are published by the university. Copies in Lehigh Room, LL.

4. *TM*, 18 June 1885.

5. William E. Wickenden, "Evolutionary Trends in Engineering Curricula," in Wickenden, *Report*, 547.

6. *Burr* (December 1884).

7. The son deliberately joined "De" and "Wolfe" instead of separating the two words as his father did.

8. The *20-Year Book* was anonymously published. Only later was the authorship established as that of Williams.

9. E. H. Williams to Prof. Goodwin, 14 April 1912. This letter and all other material on the founding of Phi Beta Kappa at Lehigh are to be found in the Phi Beta Kappa record book, Lehigh Room, LL.

10. *FM*, 7 June 1897.

11. "The Growth of American Mining Schools and Their Relation to the Mining Industry," AIME *Transactions* 23 (1894): 415.

12. *Minutes of the Alumni Association*, 17 June 1885. A copy of the report of 9 August 1884 is attached to *FM*, 18 June 1884.

13. *Burr* 13, no. 8 (13 December 1893).

14. See letter, Joseph Wharton to Henry S. Drinker, 15 May 1894. Wharton Papers, Friends Historical Library, Swarthmore College.

15. Skillman, *Lafayette College*, 37, 40.

16. Drown's Founder's Day address was published by the university. Copy in Lehigh Room, LL.

17. *TM*, 17 June 1896.

18. *FM*, 9 May, 18 June 1894.

19. In the 1890s American universities produced only fifty-four Ph.D.'s in physics, and almost all of these came from Johns Hopkins, Cornell, Yale, Harvard, and Chicago. Daniel J. Kevles, *The Physicists* (N.Y.: Alfred A. Knopf, 1978), 76–80. The *Physical Review* began publishing in 1893 with a subsidy from Cornell. The American Physical Society was organized in 1899. Professor Nichols of Cornell, one of the nation's leading physicists, was one of the organizers of the society.

20. Minutes, Executive Committee, Board of Trustees, 19 December 1896. See also president's report in *TM*, 16 June 1897.

21. Following is a complete list of schools and the number of scholarships awarded each in 1899: Allentown High School (1); Bethlehem High School (2); Lehigh Preparatory School (3); Moravian Parochial School (2); South Bethlehem High School (1); Harrisburg High School (1); Kutztown State Normal School (1); Franklin and Marshall Academy (1); Mercersburg Academy (1); Perkiomen Seminary (1); Philadelphia Central High School (5); Philadelphia Central Manual Training School (2); Shady Side Academy (1); the Hill School (1); School of the Lackawanna (Scranton) (1); Harry Hillman Academy (Wilkes-Barre) (1); West Chester State Normal School (1); Williamsport High School (3); W. Leal's School (Plainfield, N.J.) (1); Trenton, N.J. State Model School (3); Elmira (N.Y.) Free Academy (1); Rome (N.Y.) Free Academy (1); Washington, D.C., Central High School (4); Washington, D.C., Eastern High School (2); Washington, D.C., Western High School (1). The Mechanical and Mining Institute of Freeland is not included because Coxe had separately provided for it.

22. President's report, minutes, Executive Committee, Board of Trustees, 19 December 1896.

23. H. M. Ullmann, "The Period 1894–1938," in Robert D. Billinger, *A History of the Department of Chemistry and Chemical Engineering of Lehigh University, Bethlehem, Pennsylvania, 1866–1941*, ed. Robert D. Billinger, mimeo, 34. Copy in Lehigh Room, LL.

24. *Burr* (11 November 1892). See also *B&W*, 25 October 1900. Bowen, *History of Lehigh*, 80–81, gives a few more examples of student political activity. Some *Epitome*s contain party preferences of seniors.

25. *B&W*, 2 April 1894. Bowen, *History of Lehigh*, 81, gives in part the text of the article in the *Philadelphia Record*.

26. Minutes, Executive Committee, Board of Trustees, 23 January 1902.

Chapter 4. End of an Era: 1900–1919

1. Response to the presentation of Sayre Park, pamphlet in LL.

2. The move to bring in Stewardson as president is briefly mentioned in Robert H. Sayre, *Diary of Robert Heysham Sayre*, 12 June 1905.

3. *FM*, 7 February 1910.

4. *Burr* 11, no. 8 (8 December 1891).

5. *TM*, 3 October 1913.

6. *LAB* 13, no. 6 (March 1926).

7. H. T. Morris, in Class of 1891, *50-Year Book*, 31. Copy in Lehigh Room, LL. And see *B&W*, 9 May 1917.

8. Drinker in *LAB* 2, no. 1 (October 1914).

9. Raymond Walters, *The Bethlehem Bach Choir* (Boston: Houghton Mifflin Co., 1918), 200.

10. *LAB* 1, no. 3 (April 1914), contains details of the number of barrels of concrete donated by each company.

11. See Okeson's comments in *LAB* 7, no. 2 (November 1919): 2.

12. Drinker, speech to faculty on 13 September 1912, in letterbook, PC, LL.

13. "In Memoriam: Charles L. Thornburg," *LAB* 32, no. 7 (May 1945): 43; Morton Sultzer, "The University Then and Now," *LAB* 25, no. 5 (February 1938).

14. Catherine D. Bowen, *Family Portrait* (Boston: Little, Brown & Co., 1970), 38–40.

15. E. H. Williams, "The Place of the Intercollegial Scientific Fraternity in an Engineering College," SPEE *Proceedings* 15 (1907): 299.

16. Drinker speech to freshmen, fall 1906, in PC, LL.

17. Executive Committee Report, *TM*, 10 June 1908.

18. Drinker, speech to Engineer's Club of Northeastern Pennsylvania, Ms., n.d., in PC, LL.

19. Drinker, speech to freshmen, 10 September 1910, Ms. in PC, LL.

20. Robert W. Hall, "History of the Lehigh Arboretum," typescript in LL, 2, 8.

21. Ibid, 2, 8.

22. J. C. Cranmer, "Development of Forestry at Lehigh," *LAB* 15, no. 4 (January 1928): 11, 14.

23. Bowen, *History of Lehigh*, 60, 49.

24. *FM*, 14 November 1898.

25. *FM*, 4 February 1918.

26. Mann, *Study of Engineering Education*, 25.

27. SPEE *Proceedings* 14 (1906): opposite p. 96.

28. Layton, *Revolt of the Engineers*, 94.

29. SPEE *Proceedings* 14 (1906): opposite p. 96.

30. Wickenden, *Report*, 357–67, discusses the issues involved at length.

31. Ibid., 822.

32. Quoted in Walter Okeson, "The Cooperative Plan," *LAB* 8, no. 5 (1921): 6.

33. Monte Calvert, *The Mechanical Engineer in America, 1830–1910* (Baltimore: The Johns Hopkins Press, 1967), 242.

34. Kenneth E. Trombley, *The Life and Times of a Happy Liberal: A Biography of Morris Llewellyn Cooke* (N.Y.: Harper & Brothers, 1954), 2–3.

35. Layton, *Revolt of the Engineers*, 155–214.

36. A. Michal McMahon, *The Making of a Profession: A Century of Electrical Engineering in America* (N.Y.: IEEE Press, 1984), 108.

37. Kevles, *The Physicists*, 137.

38. *LAB* 4, no. 2 (May 1917); and see *FM*, 27 March 1917.

39. "Camp Coppee," *LAB* 5, no. 4 (May 1918): 4–6.

40. *LAB* 6, no. 2 (November 1918): 5.

Chapter 5. Launching the New Lehigh: 1919–1935

1. See for example D. C. Hartmann, "What's Wrong with Bethlehem?" *Lehigh Review* 5, no. 2 (Winter 1932–33): 15–16.

2. Wickenden, *Report*, 53, 61, 70.

3. *LAB* 10, no. 8 (May 1923); 8 no. 9 (June 1921). See also "Lehigh's Future: Taking Account of Stock," *LAB* 10, no. 5 (February 1923).

4. *TM*, 7 February 1922.

5. Matlock Price, "The Alumni Memorial Administration Building for Lehigh University," *LAB* 10, no. 6 (March 1923): 8.

6. *LAB* 14, no. 1 (October 1926).

7. "The History of the Brodhead Bequest," *LAB* 25, no. 9 (July 1938): 18.

8. On the condition of the library, see especially *FM*, 29 September 1924.

9. *TM*, 2 October 1935.

10 *LAB* 13, no. 6 (March 1926).

11. Neil Carothers wrote an excellent short history of tennis at Lehigh, "Lehigh Writes Name in the Annals of Tennis," *LAB* 16, no. 6 (March 1929): 9–11, 16.

12. "News and Comment," *LAB* 11, no. 5 (March 1924): 1–2.

13. "President Richards wasn't convinced that considerable numbers lessened teaching effectiveness a great deal. In his day classes sometimes surpassed the 30 mark." J. B. Reynolds, *A Seventy-five Year History of the Department of Mathematics and Astronomy*, 91–92, typescript, n.d. Copy in Lehigh Room, LL.

14. The speech was reprinted in *LAB* 13, no. 6 (April 1923).

15. "News and Comment," *LAB* 13, no. 1 (October 1925).

16. *B&W*, 11 October 1927, 3.

17. *FM*, 5 December 1932.

18. *FM*, 7 April 1930, contains McConn's complete list.

19. "The University in Industry," *Scientific American*, 27 March 1920, 328.

20. Wickenden, *Report*, 236.

21. Mansfield Merriman, "Past and Present Tendencies in Engineering Education," SPEE *Proceedings* 4 (1897): 25.

22. Wickenden, *Report*, 237.

23. *Engineering News-Record* 93, no. 21 (20 November 1924): 815.

24. Early records of the Cosmos Club are in the Lehigh Room, LL.

25. *TM*, 10 June 1934.

26. Wickenden, *Report*, 199.

27. Thomas T. Holme, "Industrial Engineering at Lehigh Comes of Age," *LAB* 34, no. 6 (April 1947): 6–7, 14.

28. Larkin to the alumni at the homecoming reunion, 1927. *LAB* 14, no. 6 (March 1927): 15.

29. *TM*, 14 June 1926. See also Richards's report to the alumni, *LAB* 13, no. 9 (June 1926).

30. *LAB* 14, no. 6 (March 1927): 14.

31. "New Faces on the Campus," *LAB* 12, no. 1 (October 1924): 11.

32. *LAB* 8, no. 1 (October 1920).

33. *FM*, 6 May 1929.

34. See *FM*, 2 November 1970, in which Elmer Glick compared the deficit of 1969–70 with that of 1930–31.

35. *TM*, 2 October 1935.
36. *LAB* 17, no. 2 (November 1929): 15.
37. *FM*, 7 March, 6 June 1932.

Chapter 6. Depression, War, and Aftermath: 1935–1950

1. Clement Clarence Williams, *Building an Engineering Career*, McGraw Hill, 1934. The book had a third edition in 1957.
2. Quoted in "Clement Clarence Williams, Lehigh's New President'" *LAB* 23, no. 1 (October 1935): 5.
3. Tom Girdler's *Boot Strap* was written in collaboration with Boyden Sparkes (N.Y.: Charles Scribner's Sons, 1943).
4. N. E. Funk, "The Public Utility Football," *LAB* 22, no. 8 (May 1935): 4–5.
5. In 1934 seven of the articles by Carothers were published in book form by Farrar & Rinehart, *Experimenting with Our Money*. Several of Carothers's speeches were also published and copyrighted.
6. "The Review Student Poll," *Lehigh Review* 12, no. 2 (December 1939): 10–11.
7. Quoted in Billy Cornelius, *The Lehigh Story* (Bethlehem, Pa.: Privately published, 1946), 116.
8. SPEE *Proceedings* 27 (1936).
9. The accreditation done by the ECPD in 1935–37 was not the first one affecting departments in Lehigh's College of Engineering. The AIChE, for example, had begun earlier and had accredited the Curriculum in Chemical Engineering in 1932. Terry S. Reynolds, *75 Years of Progress: A History of the American Institute of Chemical Engineers, 1908–1983* (N.Y.: AIChE, 1983), 15, 192.
10. Christopher Jencks & David Riesman, *The Academic Revolution* (Garden City, N.Y.: Doubleday & Company, 1968), 227.
11. The report is in *TM*, agenda file 1937.
12. "The Review Student Poll," 10–11.
13. Williams's speeches and other events of the celebration of the seventy-fifth anniversary are covered in detail in Cornelius, *The Lehigh Story*, 108–20.
14. *TM*, financial budget for the year beginning 1 July 1941.
15. *TM*, 16 October 1943.
16. I. L. Kandel, *The Impact of the War upon American Education* (Chapel Hill: University of North Carolina Press, 1948), 143.
17. "Higher Education Cooperates in National Defense," *American Council on Education Studies*, ser. 1, vol. 5, no. 15 (November 1941): 23.
18. *FM*, 10 July 1944.
19. *TM*, 31 January 1951, 16 January 1952. For information on academic averages, see Congdon's report in *FM*, 10 March 1947.
20. *LAB* 33, no. 9 (July 1946): 24; *TM*, 11 October 1946.
21. *FM*, 2 June 1947.
22. "Master of the Soft Touch Leaves Legacy of Laughter," *LAB* (Spring 1988): 27.
23. Ibid., 25.

Chapter 7. To the Centennial Celebration: 1950–1963

1. "Lehigh's Future," *LAB* 33, no. 1 (October 1945): 7.
2. *TM*, 5 June 1953.
3. Bell, *Post-Industrial Society*, 216.

4. Report of the President, 1951–52, 7.

5. John Strohmeyer, *Crisis in Bethlehem* (Bethesda, Md.: Adler & Adler, 1986), 29.

6. Bell, *Post-Industrial Society*, 234.

7. *TM*, 22 January 1960.

8. ECPD, 20th Annual Report (1952), 18.

9. Loyal V. Bewley, "A New Concept of Engineering Education," *LAB* 47, no. 5 (February 1959): 8. The article originally appeared under the title, "Reorientation in Engineering Education," in *Journal of Engineering Education* 48, no. 7 (March 1958): 497–507.

10. *TM*, 12 January 1968.

11. "The Graduate School and Research Activities," a report to the Educational Policy Committee by the Subcommittee on the Graduate School and Research Activities (April 1961), typescript. Copy in Lehigh Room, LL.

12. *FM*, 7 February 1966.

13. Report of the President, 1961–62, 2. See also *FM*, 5 February 1962.

14. Clark Kerr, *The Uses of the University* (Cambridge: Harvard University Press, 1963), 90.

15. Speech at Skytop Conference, 21–23 April 1966, typescript. Copy in Lehigh Room, LL.

16. *TM*, 19 January 1962.

17. The proceedings were later extensively reported in "Lehigh University Centennial Convocation 1963." Copy in Lehigh Room, LL.

Chapter 8. The Governance of the University: 1963–1970

1. *Burr* 6, no. 2 (October 1886): 14.

2. *TM*, 18 January 1956.

3. *TM*, 6 April 1960.

4. *B&W*, 23 September 1960.

5. *FM*, 6 June 1960.

6. For national figures on graduate enrollments and the production of doctorates during these years see Bell, *Post-Industrial Society*, 220–21.

7. *FM*, 8 January 1962.

8. *TM*, 14 April 1966.

9. *FM*, 5 June 1967.

10. Kenneth Keniston, *The Uncommitted: Alienated Youth in American Society* (N.Y.: Harcourt, Brace & World, 1960), esp. 80–81.

11. Minutes of the Executive Committee of the Board of Trustees, 13 May 1968.

12. Report filed with *TM*, 31 May 1968.

13. *LAB* 31, no. 8 (June 1944): 5.

14. *FM*, 9 December 1968.

15. *FM*, 2 November 1970.

16. *FM*, 14 September 1981.

Chapter 9. The University in Society: 1970–1980

1. Kerr, *Uses of the University*, 18–19.

2. Bell, *Post-Industrial Society*, 179.

3. *TM*, 24 January 1974.

4. *TM*, 24 January 1974.

5. John Hunt, Memo to faculty in Arts and Science (mimeographed), 4 October 1978. Copy in Arts College Office.

6. *FM*, College of Arts and Science, 8 October 1979.

7. *FM*, College of Arts and Science, 20 September 1976.

8. A letter from Lewis to the faculty explaining the trustees' decision replaced the offensive statement that the School of Education was not an "integral part of the university" with the sentence, "However, the School of Education is an independent part of the University so that its problems can be faced separately from those of the other three colleges." *FM*, 10 December 1979.

9. *FM*, 4 February 1980.

10. See for example *TM*, 12 January 1968.

11. *TM*, 13 January 1967.

12. *FM*, 12 September 1977.

13. Libsch, report to the faculty, *FM*, 11 September 1978.

14. Libsch, report to the faculty, *FM*, 5 February 1973.

15. Bell, *Post-Industrial* Society, 14.

Bibliography

Information gathered from interviews has been described in the introduction to this history.

Most of the written and printed sources are located within the Lehigh Valley. An exception is the collection of *Joseph Wharton Papers*, housed in the Friends Historical Library, Swarthmore College.

Repositories visited within the valley but external to the Lehigh campus are the Canal Museum at Easton, custodian of the *Diaries of Robert Heysham Syare*; the Moravian Archives, Bethlehem, with a complete collection of the church journal, *The Moravian*, and the registers of the Sun Hotel; the Bethlehem Public Library with useful maps, city directories, and local histories; and the corporate offices of the Bethlehem Steel Corporation, possessing the minutes of the board of directors and stockholder's meetings of the Bethlehem Iron Company.

The two most important documentary sources are to be found on the Lehigh campus but outside of the Lehigh Collection. One of these is the Minutes of the Board of Trustees and of its Executive Committee, maintained in the Office of the Treasurer. The other is the Minutes of Meetings of the Faculty, in custody of the Office of the Registrar. The registrar's office also has much statistical information concerning students and a corrected set of commencement and Founder's Day programs, which are the best sources of information concerning numbers of graduates. The Office of Admission has information and statistics about applications and incoming classes.

Other sources external to the Lehigh Collection include the *Gipson Papers*, a special collection maintained by the Institute for Eighteenth Century Studies and housed in the Linderman Library; a draft of the first *Register, 1866*, in the handwriting of Henry Coppée, kept in the vault, Linderman Library; microfilms of newspapers, the *Brown and White, Daily Times* (Bethlehem), *Bethlehem Globe*, and the *Globe-Times* (Bethlehem), also in the Linderman Library; and Minutes of Meetings of the Faculty, College of Arts and Science, located in the College Office, Maginnes Hall.

The Lehigh Collection contains most of the documentary sources. Professor E. H. Williams, Jr., as archivist for the Alumni Association, originated the collection. Over the years it has become the principal repository for material pertaining to the history of Lehigh. Much of it has been used in preparing this book, including the following:

Asa Packer. One box contining clippings, letters, and reprints.

Asa Packer Estate. Complete minutes of the trustees, account books, and related papers.

Alumni Association. Early minutes and proceedings; records, 1893–98, 1908–17 (3 boxes); directories.

Cosmos Club. Early records.

Department and college histories (typescript or mimeo):
Butts, Allison. *Ninety Seven Years of Metallurgy at Lehigh University*, 1963.
Billinger, R. D., ed. *A History of the Department of Chemistry and Chemical Engineering of Lehigh University, Bethlehem, Pennsylvania, 1868–1941.*

Beaver, J. L. *A Brief History of the Electrical Engineering Department from Its Origin to the Present Time*, n.d. (ca. 1945).

A Brief Record of Mechanical Engineering and Mechanics at Lehigh University, n.d. (ca. 1970).

Foust, Alan. *The Bicentennial: Lehigh University's Contribution to Engineering Education*, January 1976.

Hall, Robert W. *A History of Biology at Lehigh*, 1945.

———. *A History of the Lehigh Arboretum*, n.d.

Reynolds, Joseph B. *A Seventy-Five Year History of the Department of Mathematics and Astronomy at Lehigh University*, n.d.

Whitcomb, Lawrence. *The Lehigh Geology Department, 1930–1945*, 1981.

Financial records of Lehigh Univeristy. Account books, receipts, memoranda, etc., mostly for the early years.

Histories of Lehigh. Those written by Williams, Hyde, Bowen, and Cornelius are listed under "General Works." In addition there is a chronology of events in typescript ending with the year 1978–79, apparently prepared by the office of the president.

Libraries. Records of acquisitions, circulations, mostly from the early years.

London Mine. Various reports and papers.

Manuscripts:

Palmer, Philip A. Draft of beginning of a history of the College of Arts and Science.

———. Notes and partial draft of an article on Severin Ringer.

Jencks, Thurston R. Plan for Lehigh University (1866).

Stevens, William Bacon. *Autobiography*.

Coppée, Henry. Drafts of speeches.

Periodicals, collections of:

The Bent

The Burr

Epitome

Journal of the Engineering Society

Lehigh Alumni Bulletin

The Lehigh Review (1927–1939)

The Lehigh Review (1962–1963)

Phi Beta Kappa. Early minutes and records.

Plans and blueprints for buildings.

Presidents' Correspondence, 1866–1921 (67 boxes).

Publications, Lehigh, Series.

Registers (1866–1949)

Catalogs (1950–present)

Handbooks for students

President's reports

Publications, Lehigh. Speeches and sermons.

Commencement.

Baccalaureate

Founder's Day.

Publications, Lehigh. Miscellaneous.

Lehigh University Centennial Convocation, 1963.

Dedication of Sayre Park.

50-Year Book (class of 1891).

Publications, faculty. An incomplete collection of books, monographs, and articles

by and about members of the faculty. Among this collection are two pamphlets concerning Asa Packer:
"Golden Wedding"
"Records of the Testimonials to the Hon. Asa Packer" (given at a dinner in Bethlehem, 23 November 1865).
Reports
"The Graduate School and Research Activities," a Report to the Educational Policy Committee by the Subcommittee on the Graduate School and Research. Planning documents.
Miscellaneous reports of conferences and committees
Scrapbooks. Many of these concern the early years at Lehigh.
Theses of engineering seniors.
Theses of graduate students.

The foregoing list does not exhaust the sources in the Lehigh Collection that were used in preparing this history, much less the resources of the collection as a whole, which contains other material pertaining to athletics, student life, finances, publications of alumni, publications of local industries, student notebooks, faculty lecture notes, Lehigh songs, pictures of graduating seniors from the nineteenth century, and articles about Lehigh.

General Works

Adams, Henry. *The Education of Henry Adams*. New York: The Heritage Press, 1942.
Aldrich, William S. "Research and Publication among Engineering Teachers." SPEE *Proceedings* 9 (1901): 249–60.
American Council on Education. *Studies, Higher Education and the War*. Report of a national conference of college and university presidents held in Baltimore 3–4 January 1942. Series 1, vol. 6, no. 16, February 1942.
———. *Studies, Higher Education Cooperates in National Defense*. Report of a conference of government representatives and college and university administrators, held in Washington, D.C., 30–31 July 1914. Series 1, vol. 5, no. 15, November 1941.
———. *Studies, Organizing Higher Education for National Defense*. Report of a conference called by the National Committee on Education and Defense held in Washington, D.C., 6 February 1941. Series 1, vol. 5, no. 13, March 1941.
———. *Studies, Engineering, Science, and Management Defense Training*. By Roy A. Seaton, dean, Division of Engineering & Architecture, Kansas State College. Series 1, vol. 6, no. 16, 1941.
American Society for Engineering Education. *Characteristics of Excellence in Engineering Technology Education*. Final report of the evaluation of technical institute education, 1962.
Andres, James G. "In Search of the Engineering Method." *JEE* 78, no. 1 (October 1987): 29–30, 55–57.
Appleton's Annual Cyclopaedia and Register of Important Events of the Year 1879. New York: D. Appleton & Co., 1884.
Archer, R. P. *The History of the Lehigh Valley Railroad*. Berkeley, Calif.: Howell-North, 1977.
Barish, Norman N. *Engineering Enrollment in the United States*. New York: New York University Press, 1957.
Bell, Daniel. *The Coming of Post-Industrial Society: A Venture in Social Forecasting*. New York: Basic Books, 1973.

_____. *The Reforming of General Education*. New York: Columbia University Press, 1966.

Berelson, Bernard. *Graduate Education in the United States*. New York: McGraw-Hill Book Co., 1960.

Bewley, Loyal V. "Reorientation in Engineering Education." *JEE* 48, no. 7 (March 1958): 497–507.

The Biographical Encyclopaedia of Pennsylvania of the Nineteenth Century. Philadelphia, Pa.: Galaxy Publishing Co., 1874.

Birmingham, Stephen. *"Our Crowd": The Great Jewish Families of New York*. New York: Harper & Row, 1967.

Bishop, Morris. *A History of Cornell*. Ithaca: Cornell University Press, 1962.

Blackman, Emily C. *History of Susquehanna County, Pennsylvania*. 1873. Reprint. Susquehanna County Historical Society & Free Library Association, 1970.

Bowen, Catherine Drinker. *A History of Lehigh University*. South Bethlehem, Pa.: *Lehigh Alumni Bulletin*, 1924.

Brenckman, Fred. *History of Carbon County, Pennsylvania*. Harrisburg, Pa.: James J. Nungesser, 1913.

Brooks, Harvey. "The Research University: Doing Good, and Doing It Better." *Issues in Science and Technology* 4, no. 2 (winter 1988): 49–55.

Browne, Charles Albert, and Mary Elvira Weeks. *A History of the American Chemical Society: Seventy-five Eventful Years*. Washington, D.C.: American Chemical Society, 1952.

Brubacher, John S., and Willis Rudy. *Higher Education in Transition: An American History, 1636–1956*. New York: Harper & Brothers, 1958.

Calhoun, Daniel H. *The American Civil Engineer: Origins and Conflict*. Cambridge: The Technology Press, MIT, 1960.

Calvert, Monte A. *The Mechanical Engineer in America, 1830–1910*. Baltimore: Johns Hopkins Press, 1967.

Carlson, W. Bernard, "Academic Entrepreneurship and Engineering Education: Dugald C. Jackson and the MIT-GE Cooperative Engineering Course, 1907–1932." *Technology and Culture* 29, no. 3 (July 1988): 536–67.

Carnegie Foundation for the Advancement of Teaching. *Thirty-sixth Annual Report, 1942–43*. New York: Carnegie Foundation.

Carothers, Neil. *Experimenting With Our Money*. New York: Farrar & Rinehart, 1934.

Cheyney, Edward P. *History of the University of Pennsylvania, 1740–1940*. Philadelphia: University of Pennsylvania Press, 1940.

Cochrane, Rexmond C. *The National Academy of Sciences: The First Hundred Years, 1863–1963*. Washington, D.C.: National Academy of Sciences, 1978.

Condit, Uzal W. *The History of Easton, Pennsylvania*. George W. West, 1885.

Cooke, Morris Llewellyn. *Academic and Industrial Efficiency*. Bulletin #5. A report to the Carnegie Foundation for the Advancement of Teaching, 1910.

Cornelius, Billy. *The Lehigh Story*. Bethlehem, Pa.: privately published, 1946.

Cullum, George W. *Biographical Register of the Officers and Graduates of the U.S. Military Academy at West Point, N.Y.* 2 vols. New York: D. Van Nostrand, 1868.

Dictionary of American Biography. 28 vols. New York: Charles Scribner's Sons, 1928–81.

Donovan, Arthur L. Engineering in an Increasingly Complex Society. In *Engineering in Society*, National Research Council, 81–129. Washington, D.C.: National Academy Press, 1985.

Drown, Thomas M., "The Study of Modern Languages in Engineering Courses." SPEE *Proceedings* 4 (1897): 250–54.

Earnest, Ernst. *Academic Procession: An Informal History of the American College, 1636 to 1953*. Indianapolis: Bobbs-Merrill Co., 1953.

ECPD. *Annual Reports*, 1933–1956.

Engineering News-Record. (Before 1917 *Engineering News* and *Engineering Record.*)

Florman, Samuel C. *The Existential Pleasures of Engineering.* New York: St. Martin's Press, 1976.

Fores, Michael. "Transformations and the Myth of 'Engineering Science': Magic in a White Coat." *Technology and Culture* 29, no. 1 (January 1988): 62–81.

Fox, Dixon R. *Union College: An Unfinished History.* Schenectady, N.Y.: Graduate Council, Union College, 194?.

Franklin, William S. "A Course in Physics for Engineering Students." SPEE *Proceedings* 15 (1907): 308–15.

———. "The Teaching of Elementary Mechanics." SPEE *Proceedings* 15 (1907): 316–34.

———. "The Teaching of Physics to Engineering Students." SPEE *Proceedings* 11 (1903): 261–68.

———. *Bill's School and Mine.* South Bethlehem, Pa.: Franklin, MacNutt and Charles, 1913.

French, John C. *A History of the University Founded by Johns Hopkins.* Baltimore: Johns Hopkins Press, 1946.

Friedel, Robert. "Engineering in the twentieth Century." *Technology and Culture* 27, no. 4 (October 1986): 669–73.

Fritz, John. *Autobiography.* New York: AIME, 1912.

Gerard, Felix R. *The Lehigh Valley Railroad, 1846–1946.* A Centenary Address. The Newcomen Society, 1946.

Girdler, Tom M., Jr. *Boot Strap.* New York: Charles Scribner's Sons, 1943.

Goldman, Steven L. *Issues in American Engineering Education: A Selective Review of the Literature.* Draft report prepared for the Office of Technology Assessment of the Congress of the United States. Typescript. Bethlehem, Pa., 1987.

Grayson, Lawrence P. "A Brief History of Engineering Education in the United States." *JEE* 68, no. 4 (December 1977): 246–63.

Hall, Newman A. "ECPD Accreditation of Graduate Study: Problems and Possibilities." *JEE* 52, no. 8 (April 1962): 534–38.

Havemann, Ernest, and Patricia Salter West. *They Went to College: The College Graduate in America Today.* New York: Harcourt, Brace & Co., 1952.

"Henry Sturgis Drinker, E.M., LL.D." Lehigh Valley Coal Company *Employe's Magazine* 1, no. 2 (October 1913): 50–51.

Hewitt, Abram S. "A Century of Mining and Metallurgy in the United States." AIME *Transactions* 5 (May 1876–February 1877): 164–96.

Hillman, Donald J. "Decision Making with Modern Information and Communications Technology: Opportunities and Constraints." In *Science, Technology, and the Issues of the Eighties: Policy Outlook*, 55–70. A report prepared for the NSF. Boulder, Colo.: Westview Press, 1982.

Hislop, Codman. *Eliphalet Nott.* Middletown, Conn.: Wesleyan University Press, 1971.

Hollis, Ernest Victor. *Philanthropic Foundations and Higher Education.* New York: Columbia Univeristy Press, 1938.

Howe, M. A. DeWolfe. *A Venture in Remembrance.* Boston: Little, Brown & Co., 1941.

Howe, Mark Anthony De Wolfe. *Memoirs of the Life and Services of the Right Reverend Alonzo Potter, D.D., LL.D.* Philadelphia, Pa.: J. B. Lippincott & Co., 1871.

Hutchinson, Charles E., and Carol B. Muller. "Educating Engineers: In Praise of Diversity." *Issues in Science and Technology* 4, no. 4 (Summer 1988): 71–74.

Hyde, Edmund M. *The Lehigh University: A Historical Sketch.* South Bethlehem, Pa.: Lehigh University, 1896.

Jencks, Christopher, and David Riesman. *The Academic Revolution.* Garden City, N.Y.: Doubleday & Co., 1968.

Johnson, Clyde S. *Fraternities in our Colleges*. New York: National Interfraternity Foundation, 1972.

Jordon, John W., Edgar M. Green, and George T. Ettinger. *Historic Homes and Institutions and Genealogical and Personal Memoirs of the Lehigh Valley, Pennsylvania*. 2 vols. New York: Lewis Publishing Co., 1905.

Journal of the Convention of the [Episcopal] *Diocese of Central Pennsylvania*, 1872.

Journal of the [Episcopal] *Diocese of Pennsylvania*, 1872.

Kandel, I. L. *The Impact of the War upon American Education*. Chapel Hill: University of North Carolina Press, 1948.

Kasson, John F. *Civilizing the Machine: Technology and Republican Values in America, 1776−1900*. New York: Grossman Publishers, 1976.

Kemper, John Dustin. *The Engineer and His Profession*. New York: Holt, Rinehart & Winston, 1967.

Keniston, Kenneth. *The Uncommitted: Alienated Youth in American Society*. New York: Harcourt, Brace & World, 1960.

Kerr, Clark. *The Uses of the University*. Cambridge: Harvard University Press, 1963.

Kevles, Daniel J. *The Physicists: The History of a Scientific Community in America*. New York: Alfred A. Knopf, 1978.

Kidder, Tracy. *The Soul of a New Machine*. Boston: Little, Brown & Co., 1981.

Knowles, Malcolm S. *The Adult Education Movement in the United States*. New York: Holt, Rinehart & Winston, 1962.

Kohlstedt, Sally Gregory. *The Formation of the American Scientific Community: The American Association for the Advancement of Science, 1848−1860*. Urbana: University of Illinois Press, 1976.

Landau, Sarah B. *Edward T. and William A. Potter: American High Victorian Architects*. Ph.D. diss., New York University, 1978.

Layton, Edwin T., Jr. *The Revolt of the Engineers*. Cleveland, Ohio: The Press of Case Western Reserve University, 1971.

────. "Science as a Form of Action: The Role of the Engineering Sciences." *Technology and Culture* 29, no. 1 (January 1988): 82−97.

────, ed. *Technology and Social Change in America*. New York: Harper & Row, 1973.

Levering, Joseph M. *A History of Bethlehem, Pennsylvania, 1741−1892*. Bethlehem, Pa.: Times Publishing Co., 1903.

Mann, Charles R. *A Study of Engineering Education*. Bulletin #11. Carnegie Foundation for the Advancement of Teaching. New York, 1918.

Mathews, Alfred, and Austin N. Hungerford. *History of the Counties of Lehigh and Carbon*. Philadelphia, Pa.: Everts & Richards, 1884.

Mayer, Alfred G., and Robert S. Woodward. *Biographical Memoir of Alfred Marshall Mayer, 1836−1897*. Washington, D.C.: National Academy of Science, 1916.

McClure, A. K. *Old Time Notes of Pennsylvania*. 2 vols. Philadelphia, Pa.: John C. Winston Co., 1905.

McConn, Max. *College or Kindergarten?* New York: New Republic, 1928.

McGrane, Reginald C. *The University of Cincinnati: A Success Story in Urban Higher Education*. New York: Harper & Row, 1963.

McMahon, A. Michal. *The Making of a Profession: A Century of Electrical Engineering in America*. New York: IEEE Press, 1984.

Mechanical Engineers in America Born Prior to 1861. A Biographical Dictionary. New York: ASME, 1980.

Meiksins, Peter. "The 'Revolt of the Engineers' Reconsidered." *Technology and Culture* 29, no. 2 (April 1988): 219−46.

Merriman, Mansfield. "Past and Present Tendencies in Engineering Education." SPEE *Proceedings* 4 (1897): 16−30.

――――. "Teachers and Text-books in Mathematics in Technical Schools." SPEE *Proceedings* 2 (1895): 95–103.

Morison, Samuel Eliot. *Three Centuries of Harvard: 1636–1936.* Cambridge: Harvard University Press, 1936.

Munroe, Henry Smith. "The School of Mines and Associated Schools." Chap. in *A History of Columbia University, 1754–1904.* New York: Columbia University Press, 1904.

Nason, Henry B., ed. *Biographical Record of the Officers and Graduates of the Rensselaer Polytechnic Institute, 1824–1886.* Troy, N.Y. William H. Young, 1887.

National Cyclopaedia of American Biography. 62 vols. New York: James T. White & Co., 1893–1984.

Noble, David E. *America by Design: Science, Technology, and the Rise of Corporate Capitalism.* New York: Alfred A. Knopf, 1977.

One Hundred Years of Nativity. Bethlehem, Pa.: Committee on the Centennial, n.d.

Park, Clyde W. "A Glance Toward Culture." SPEE *Proceedings* 27 (1937): 207–13.

Parker, Garland G. *The Enrollment Explosion.* New York: School & Society Books, 1971.

Pepin, Andrew J., and Agnes Q. Wells. *Earned Degrees Conferred 1977–78.* Washington, D.C.: National Center for Education Statistics, U.S. Department of Education, 1980.

"Philip Mason Palmer – In Memoriam." *Pennsylvania-German Folklore Society* 16 (1951): 198–201.

Portrait Gallery With Biographical Sketches of Prominent Freemasons Throughout the United States. New York: John C. Yorston & Co., 1892.

Raymond, Rossiter W., and Henry S. Drinker, "Biographical Notice of John Fritz." AIME *Transactions* 47 (1914): 4–15.

Reynolds, Terry S. *75 Years of Progress: A History of the American Institute of Chemical Engineers, 1908–1983.* New York: AIChE, 1983.

Rivlin, Alice M. *The Role of the Federal Government in Financing Higher Education.* Washington, D.C.: Brookings Institution, 1961.

Rosenberg, Nathan. *Technology and American Economic Growth.* New York: Harper & Row, 1972.

Rosengarten, J. G. "Obituary Notice of Henry Coppée, LL.D." *Proceedings, American Philosophical Society* 34, no. 149 (17 May 1895): 357–60.

Ross, Earl D. *Democracy's College: The Land-Grant Movement in the Formative Stage.* Ames: Iowa State College Press, 1942.

Ruml, Beardsley, and Sidney G. Tickton. *Teaching Salaries Then and Now: A 50-Year Comparison with Other Occupations and Industries.* Bulletin #1. New York: Fund for the Advancement of Education, 1955.

Sagendorph, Kent. *Michigan: The Story of a University.* New York: E. P. Dutton & Co., 1948.

Schrader, Michael C. *Bench and Bar.* Vol. 5 of *One Hundred Years of Life in Northampton County, Pa.* Easton, Pa.: Northampton County Bicentennial Commission, 1976.

Skillman, David B. *The Biography of a College: Being the History of the First Century of the Life of Lafayette College.* 2 vols. Easton, Pa.: Lafayette College, 1932.

Smith, Edgar Fahs. "Charles Mayer Wetherill, 1825–1871." *Journal of Chemical Education* 29 (1929): 1076–89, 1215–24, 1461–77, 1668–80, 1916–27, 2160–77.

Stark, John. *What Every Engineer Should Know About Practical CAD/CAM Applications.* New York: Marcel Dekker, 1986.

Stine, Jeffrey K., "Professionalism Vs. Special Interest: The Debate over Engineering Education in Nineteenth Century America." *Potomac Review* 26–27 (1984–85): 72–94.

Strohmeyer, John. *Crisis in Bethlehem: Big Steel's Struggle to Survive*. Bethesda, Md.: Adler & Adler, 1986.

Stuart, Milton C. *Asa Packer, 1805–1879*. A Newcomen Address, 1938.

Thornburg, Charles L. "Athletics for Engineering Students." SPEE *Proceedings* 15 (1907): 668–72.

Trombley, Kenneth E. *The Life and Times of a Happy Liberal: A Biography of Morris Lewellyn Cooke*. New York: Harper & Brothers, 1954.

Veysey, Laurence R. *The Emergence of the American University*. Chicago: University of Chicago Press, 1965.

Vonnegut, Kurt, Jr. *Player Piano*. New York: Delacourte Press, 1952.

Wadsworth, M. Edward. "The Elective System in Engineering Colleges." SPEE *Proceedings* 4 (1897): 70–85.

Walters, Raymond. *The Bethlehem Bach Choir*. Boston: Houghton Mifflin Co., 1918.

———. *University of Cincinnati: Highlights Past and Present*. New York: The Newcomen Society in North America, 1952.

Wertenbaker, Thomas J. *Princeton: 1746–1896*. Princeton: Princeton University Press, 1946.

Wickenden, William E. *Report of the Investigation of Engineering Education, 1923–1929*. 2 vols. Pittsburgh, Pa.: SPEE, 1930.

———. "The School of Engineering." In *Higher Education in America*, edited by Raymond A. Kent, 192–242. Boston: Ginn & Co., 1930.

Williams, Clement C., and Erich A. Farber, *Building an Engineering Career*. 3d ed. New York: McGraw-Hill Book Co., 1957. (1st edition by C. C. Williams, 1934).

Williams, Edward H., Jr. "The Place of the Intercollegiate Scientific Fraternity in an Engineering College." SPEE *Proceedings* 15 (1907): 295–300.

———. *The Lehigh University, 1866–1886*. South Bethlehem, Pa., 1886.

Wilson, Edmund. *The Twenties*. New York: Farrar, Straus & Giroux, 1975.

Wolle, Francis. *A Moravian Heritage*. Boulder, Colo.: Empire Reproduction & Printing Co., 1972.

Worcester, Elwood. *Life's Adventure: The Story of a Varied Career*. New York: Charles Scribner's Sons, 1932.

Yates, W. Ross, ed. *Bethlehem of Pennsylvania: The Golden Years, 1841–1920*. Bethlehem, Pa.: The Bethlehem Book Committee, 1976.

Index

Academic performance of students, 153–54, 209

Acceleration, programs for, 222–25, 227

Activities, students: changes in after Second World War, 190; general character of, 47. See also *individual activities*

Adams, Henry, 36

Adams, Nicholas, 282

Administration: academic deanships created, 171; character of and changes in, early years, 52, 76; departmental reorganization, 1960s, 254; under Drinker, 113–14, 120–21; name "college" replaces "course," 132; in 1920s, 139–42; position of vice president and provost created, 212; size in 1980, 273; under Williams, 172–74. See also *individual centers, divisions, departments, and offices*

Administrative Committee (1944–45), 183–85

Admission, Office of: created, 163–64; separated from Office of the Dean, 188

Admission: studies by faculty, 1880s, 78

Advanced placement, 224–25

Affirmative Action, 273–74

Allen, Carl E., 161, 191, 212, 235

Allentown, 21, 71, 291

Allentown College of St. Francis de Sales, 253

Alma Mater (song), 101

Alumni: and admissions, 163; and fund-raising under Richards, 142–44, 147–48; and placement, 164; number of in 1980, 300. See also *Alumni Association; Trustees, Board of*

Alumni Association: activities, 1880s and 1890s, 87, 88; Address of 1876, 55–56; Address of 1878, 57; all-class reunion of 1965, 249; and control of athletics, 149; educational study by (1919–22), 138–39; fund-raising criticized (1937), 173; incorporated, 113; membership, 112; organized, 55; recommendations of 1886 and 1888, 81, 87, 88; and Second World War, 181; supports graduate work, 158. See also *Alumni; Alumni Bulletin*; Athletics; Trustees, Board of

Alumni Bulletin, 112–13, 169, 181. See also *Alumni Association*

Alumni clubs, 88, 163

Alumni Fund, 143–44, 213, 275. See also *Alumni Association*; Finances

Alumni Memorial Building, 144, 146, 219

Alvare, Carlos J., 282

Amaranth, 281

American Association for the Advancement of Science (AAAS), 24, 25, 50, 154

American Association of University Professors (AAUP), 252, 261

American Council on Education, 273

American Council of Learned Societies, 179

American Electrochemical Society, 98

American Institute of Chemical Engineers (AIChE), 170

American Institute of Electrical Engineers (AIEE), 77, 128, 169

American Institute of Mining Engineers (AIME), 50, 91, 124, 125, 136, 169

American Institute of Mining and Metallurgical Engineers (AIMME). See American Institute of Mining Engineers (AIME)

American Philosophical Society, 24

American Society for Civil Engineers (ASCE), 25, 50, 169

American Society for Engineering Education, 230, 232. See also Society for the Promotion of Engineering Education (SPEE)

318